GREAT VOICES OF THE
REFORMATION

EDITED

WITH AN INTRODUCTION

AND COMMENTARIES

by

HARRY EMERSON FOSDICK

RANDOM HOUSE : NEW YOR

GREAT VOICES

OF THE

REFORMATION

AN ANTHOLOGY

FIRST PRINTING

Library of Congress Catalog Card Number: 52–5550
Manufactured in the United States of America
by H. Wolff, New York

ACKNOWLEDGMENTS

For permission to reprint excerpts from copyrighted works, the editor and publisher are indebted to the following:

J. M. Dent & Sons, Ltd. for an excerpt from *The Journal of George Fox*, revised by Norman Penney, Everyman's Library.

E. P. Dutton & Co., Inc., for an excerpt from *The Journal of George Fox*, revised by Norman Penney, Everyman's Library.

Hodder and Stoughton, Ltd., for *Martin Luther's Address to the Christian Nobility of the German Nation*, edited by Henry Wace and C. A. Buchheim.

Meador Publishing Company for an excerpt from *The Loci Communes*, by Philip Melanchthon, edited by Charles L. Hill.

The Mennonite Historical Society for excerpts from *The Schleitheim Confession of Faith*, translated by Dr. John C. Wenger; *The Life and Writings of Menno Simons* and *Two Kinds of Obedience*, by Harold S. Bender.

Philosophical Library for an excerpt from *John Knox's History of the Reformation in Scotland*, edited by William Croft Dickinson.

G. P. Putnam's Sons for excerpts from *Balthasar Hübmaier*, by Henry C. Vedder and *Philip Melanchthon, The Protestant Preceptor of Germany*, by James William Richard.

Henry Regnery Company for an excerpt from *The Journal of John Woolman*, edited by Janet Whitney. Copyright, 1950, by Henry Regnery Company.

Reverend George W. Richards for an excerpt from *The Latin Works of Huldreich Zwingli*, translated and edited by George W. Richards and Clarence Nevin Heller.

Charles Scribner's Sons for an excerpt from *The Church* by John Huss, in the Schaff translation.

The United Lutheran Publication House for an excerpt from *Preface to St. Paul's Epistle to the Romans*, translated by Dr. Charles E. Hay.

The Westminster Press for an excerpt from *Instruction in Faith* by John Calvin, translated and edited by Paul T. Fuhrman. Copyright, 1949, by The Westminster Press.

PREFACE

THIS ANTHOLOGY ENDEAVORS TO PRESENT, WITHIN THE LIMITS
of a single volume, the major emphases of Protestant thought
from John Wycliffe to John Wesley. The term "Protestant"
—for a brief discussion of which the reader may turn to the
Epilogue—originated long after Wycliffe, and by Wesley's
time had far outgrown its first meaning, but no other word is
now available to connote the entire movement of thought
and life which led up to and followed the dissevering of
Christendom in the sixteenth century. The negative significance of the word in present usage, however, is unfortunate,
for, as this anthology should make evident, while the Reformation certainly involved *protest* against Roman Catholicism, it was at heart an affirmation, a vigorous *protestation* of
positive principles.

My endeavor has been to make this anthology an objective
statement of historic fact, and to avoid partisan propaganda.
To be sure, the editor is a Protestant, and the major purpose
of the book is to make available to Protestants, in a condensed and accessible form, the gist of the historic documents
which reveal the convictions of the early Reformers. Nevertheless, I trust that such Roman Catholics, on the one side,
or agnostics, on the other, as may read this anthology, will

recognize my honest attempt to present a fair appraisal of the Protestant movement, of its historic background, and of its basic ideas.

To compress within one volume the essential message of the diverse personalities involved in the Reformation forces on the anthologist a very astringent selectivity. What is included here probably none would wish left out, but things left out some may well wish included. In this difficult task of selection, my ideal has been so to put myself in the place of the Reformer, and so to let him sit in judgment on my culling of material, that he would not feel misrepresented by the quotations chosen. As for the General Introduction and the Commentaries on individual Reformers, I have tried, as briefly and objectively as I could, to sketch the historic and biographical background, in order that the quoted passages might be the more intelligible.

I am, of course, unpayably indebted to many books and to the generous assistance of many libraries in furthering the research which such an anthology as this requires. In particular, I owe more than I can express to my friend, Dr. Cyril C. Richardson, Washburn Professor of Church History at the Union Theological Seminary, for his invaluable counsel.

Harry Emerson Fosdick

CONTENTS

Contents

Contents

Contents

INTRODUCTION

MARTIN LUTHER (1483–1546) RIGHTLY CLAIMS SO CENTRAL
a place in the story of the Protestant Reformation that popular thought not uncommonly pictures the Reformation as beginning when Luther nailed his theses on the church door at Wittenberg or stood his ground for conscience's sake before the Emperor at Worms. Historically decisive though these events were, however, they were the climax of a long preparation, as well as the origin of a long consequence. However great an individual may be, his total influence depends upon his focusing strong social trends and drives precedent to him and now concentrate in him. Luther launched his attack on the abuses of the Roman church by assailing papal indulgences, sold for the remission of sin's penalties in Purgatory, but in the preceding century John Wessel (1420–1489) had attacked indulgences in so similar a way that Luther himself wrote: "If I had read his books before, my enemies might have thought that Luther had borrowed everything from Wessel, so great is the agreement between our spirits."

Rebellious discontent with the abuses of the Roman curia, with the lax morals of monks and clergy, with the financial exactions of the papacy, and even with the pope's claim to sovereign authority in the church had long been rife and often vocal. Sometimes this discontent took the form of loyal self-reformation by the church within the church. Sometimes it spilled over into outspoken revolt, as in the case of Hincmar, archbishop of Rheims (805–882) who proposed to free the church in France from the pope's authority, and who, when threatened with excommunication, replied that if the Holy Father came into France to excommunicate, he would depart excommunicated. Repeatedly this dissatisfaction with the church was expressed in societies of unworldly Christians, frequently mystics, quietly withdrawing into their own fellowships for Bible study, prayer and holy living, so that, as a modern Roman Catholic puts it, each of these numerous groups "drew apart from their co-religionists, a hive ready to swarm." Sometimes, rebellious discontent voiced itself, in well-thought-out, deliberate revolts, led by intellectuals and representing downright heresy based on theological conviction. This anthology begins with John Wycliffe [c. 1320–1384] and John Huss [c. 1373–1415] because they represent so clearly the pre-Lutheran revolt against the current ecclesiasticism that Luther wrote to Spalatin in 1520, "We were all Hussites without knowing it."

When Luther protested against the sale of indulgences, he had no prevision of the consequences. No one was more surprised and at times dumbfounded than he was, as the revolt against Rome proliferated. He himself said once: "No good work comes about by our own wisdom; it begins in dire necessity. I was forced into mine; but had I known then what I know now, ten wild horses would not have drawn me into it." All unaware, he had come in the nick of time; he set a match to an explosion long preparing.

In the sixteenth century the mediaeval world was breaking up, and nothing in the new world which was emerging could be altogether as it had been before. Luther was nine years old when Columbus discovered America. On that day when he faced the Emperor at Worms, Ponce de Leon was in Florida seeking the fountain of eternal youth, and Magellan was in the antipodes on the first circumnavigation of the globe. When Luther was fourteen Vasco da Gama rounded the Cape of Good Hope, sailed up the eastern coast of Africa and, crossing the Indian Ocean to Calicut, solved the major commercial problem of the time—how to get directly to the East. The resultant possibilities of worldwide commerce changed the whole economic situation. Trading companies were created to take advantage of the opened doors; massed capital made immense profits from the new opportunities; families like the Welsers and the Fuggers grew incredibly wealthy from their ever-widening network of business interests; canny investors shared the new riches, like a "certain native of Augsburg" who, from 500 gulden entrusted to a merchant company, gained 24,500 gulden in seven years. Alongside the traditional princes of state and of the church a new princedom emerged—the wealthy merchants. The mediaeval trading cities, with their guild organizations of artisans, lost their grip, and the guild system disintegrated. As for the idea which had underlain mediaeval economic life, that land was the only basic source of wealth, that and the social relationships founded on it became an anachronism.

This revolutionary upheaval increased the discontent of the peasants. Their condition had always been one of comparative penury—John Böhm, writing when Luther was a young man said, "Their lot was hard and pitiable"—but with the break-up of the mediaeval world, the realization of their needlessly forlorn estate became acute, and for a century before Luther peasant uprisings were common. The four forest cantons of Switzerland witnessed a rebellion, the news of which resounded through Europe, when the peasants, tying their scythes to their alpenstocks, defeated with these crude pikes the old-time chivalry sent against them. A new day had come. The peasants dreamed that they could win their rights. They need not submit to laws that forbade fishing in streams which ran by their doors or hunting in forests where they had been born and reared. They need not submit to the excessive exactions of secular and ecclesiastical overlords who took a killing tithe from everything their slender gardens grew. "They look so narrowly after their profits," wrote an Englishman, "that the poor wife must be countable to them for every tenth egg, or else she getteth not her rights at Easter, and shall be taken as a heretic." When Luther was ten years old a typical insurrection broke out in Elsass—the Bundschuh revolt—whose emblem was a poor man's shoe and whose motto was, "Only what is just before God"; and while this and many another rebellion were ruthlessly suppressed the peasant unrest was angry and continuous.

Nor was this social unrest merely an affair of the peasants. It was not simply the serf against his master, the poor against the rich, the debtor against the creditor. It was a ferment which permeated the whole social order. The most abject dregs of the population were sometimes too whipped and prostrate to rebel but, in more favored areas, as privilege increased, the vision grew of more privilege still and, far from content, the spirit of revolt was intensified. It struck out against the old feudal overlords, against oppressive laws and galling fiscal exactions, against the luxury of the powerful, and especially against the priests. Wrote a Spaniard [1] of the time:

I see that we can scarcely get anything from Christ's ministers except for money; at baptism money, at bishoping money, at marriage money, for confession money—no, not extreme unction without money! They ring no bells without money, no burial in the church without money; so that it seemeth that Paradise is shut up from them that have no money. The rich is buried in the church, the poor in the churchyard. The rich man may marry with his nearest kin, but the poor not so, albeit he be ready to die for love of her. The rich may eat flesh in Lent, but the poor may not, albeit fish perhaps be much dearer. The rich man may readily get large Indulgences, but the poor none, because he wanteth money to pay for them.

[1] Juan de Valdez, brother of the secretary of Emperor Charles V.

Alongside the economic revolution profound political changes were afoot. Feudalism was disintegrating; the power of once isolated and sovereign principalities dwindled; monarchy moved up into ascendancy over the lesser nobility. Especially in three lands, France, England and Spain, strong, coherent kingdoms emerged, and if in Germany and Italy this process of unification was less evident, nevertheless within these lands powerful states under dynastic rulers were created, and the ideas of absolute monarchy and the divine right of kings subverted the old feudal system. As the might and authority of autocratic monarchs grew, conflicts with the papacy became inevitable. During mediaeval days the pope's power had been so extended that hardly any area of any country's life, civil as well as ecclesiastical, was altogether outside his domain. Papal taxes drained one land after another of colossal revenues; papal courts claimed adjudication of all sorts of cases which the king's courts jealously desired to handle; the clergy claimed exemption from prosecution under the criminal laws of the lands where they lived; the authority of Rome infringed repeatedly upon sovereign rights claimed by proud, ambitious monarchs. The stage was being set for the rebellion of kings against the supremacy of the pope.

Thus Christendom was in the throes of a momentous social revolution when Luther spoke up in Wittenberg.

Moreover, an intellectual revolution was afoot with equal, if not profounder consequences. Copernicus (1473–1543) was only ten years older than Luther, and Luther was within a decade of death before the new astronomy was widely publicized, but the awakening intellectual life that made Copernicus possible, the venturesome, audacious thinking, the unbridled curiosity and zest for fresh discovery—*that* was in full course long before. To be sure, the Protestant Reformers did not always welcome the new knowledge. Luther never believed in the Copernican astronomy. "People gave ear to an upstart astrologer," he said, "who strove to show that the earth revolves, not the heavens or the firmament, the sun and the moon. . . . This fool wishes to reverse the entire scheme of astronomy; but sacred Scripture tells us that Joshua commanded the sun to stand still, and not the earth."

Nevertheless, the intellectual revolution, which the Reformers often failed to understand, profoundly affected the Reformation. Men's minds were casting off the old scholasticism and were demanding a liberty unknown for centuries. Even when new truth was long denied—Rome denounced Galileo's astronomy as "absurd" in 1616—the new truth was still there, raising disturbing questions, casting doubt on old views, teasing men's minds out of lethargy and apathy into curiosity, wonderment and quest. So Sir Henry Wotton, English ambassador at Venice, sending a copy of Galileo's book to King James, wrote that it was "the strangest piece of news that he hath ever yet received from any part of the world."

This amazing awakening of mind and spirit is the heart of the Renaissance, the beginning of which is commonly dated in 1453, when Constantinople fell into the hands of the Turks, and when, among the other consequences, learned Greeks fled west. That was thirty years before Luther's birth. Well before that, however, the Revival of Learning had been under way; at least as early as Petrarch (1304–1374) the Humanists had been enthusiastically welcoming the discovery of the ancient literature of Greece and Rome and had inaugurated a new era of intellectual emancipation.

The discovery of classical Greek and Latin manuscripts opened up a new world to the scholars of the time. Here in the ancient authors were intellectual insight, ethical truth, spiritual grandeur and aesthetic beauty, quite outside of and antedating not only mediaeval scholasticism but the Christian church itself. The minds of men had been crying for emancipation and here it was, in a world free from the dictates of dogma and the despotism of ecclesiastical control. As John Addington Symonds says, "That rediscovery of the classic past restored the confidence in their own faculties to men striving after spiritual freedom; revealed the continuity of history and the identity of human nature in spite of diverse creeds and different customs; held up for emulation master-works of literature, philosophy and art; provoked enquiry; encouraged criticism; shattered the narrow mental barriers imposed by mediaeval orthodoxy."

The results were far-reaching and profound. Canon law came under devastating criticism, and the substitution for it of civil law, based on the codes of Justinian and Theodosius, was one of the most radical changes in that changeful era; it went a long way toward causing the church to be regarded in time as administratively a department of the state. In literature, architecture, painting and sculpture, ancient manuscripts and works of art were objects of reverence like that given to relics of the saints, and archeological expeditions were holy crusades on which men went, crying, like Cyriac of Ancona, "I go to awake the dead." With passionate devotion the Humanists turned to the study of ancient philosophy. For men like Pico della Mirandola, Platonism and Christianity were fused into an esoteric religion for the educated, while popular superstitions were left to the common herd, and one of the Humanists burned two candles in his home, one before the Virgin Mary and the other before a bust of Plato.

All this, at first, was not associated with any conscious disloyalty to the Christian church. Popes like Nicholas V (1447–1455) and Julius II (1503–1513) were sponsors of the new learning and its enthusiastic devotees. Nonetheless, the new movement was a radical revolution. Absorption with post-mortem salvation in a world to come, while not by any means renounced, was balanced and sometimes displaced by frank delight in this present world—the beauties of nature, art, literature, the zest of fresh discoveries and the joy of venturesome thinking.

The effect on education was momentous. Within a century

and a half seventeen new universities were founded in Germany. Gutenberg died only fifteen years before Luther was born, and printing made possible a hitherto undreamed-of availability of books for the eager students. Scholars labored tirelessly at the original Hebrew and Greek texts of Scripture, and altogether the era which preceded and encompassed the period of the Reformation was one of the most intellectually exciting in all history.

Its effect upon the attitude of its devotees toward Christianity in general and the Roman church in particular can best be seen and felt in such a man as Erasmus. He was Luther's contemporary, sympathetic with much that the Reformer taught, but remaining a faithful member of the Roman church, and before his death was offered a cardinalate. As the leading Humanist of his time, however, he illustrates the inevitable tension between current Romanism and the spirit of the Renaissance. He was sick of the old scholastic theology. "Theology itself I reverence," he wrote, "and always have reverenced. I am speaking merely of the theologastrics of our time, whose brains are the rottenest, intellects the dullest, doctrines the thorniest, manners the brutalest, life the foulest, speech the spitefulest, hearts the blackest that I have ever encountered in the world." Again and again he returns to his attack on the ignorance and obscurantism of monks, friars and priests. "It may happen," he writes, "it often does happen, that an abbot is a fool or a drunkard. He issues an order to the brotherhood in the name of holy obedience. And what will such an order be? An order to observe chastity? An order to be sober? An order to tell no lies? Not one of these things. It will be that a brother is not to learn Greek; he is not to seek to instruct himself. He may be a sot. He may go with prostitutes. He may be full of hatred and malice. He may never look inside the Scriptures. No matter. He has not broken any oath. He is an excellent member of the community. While if he disobeys such a command as this from an insolent superior there is stake or dungeon for him instantly."

As for the moral profligacy of the priests and mendicant orders, Erasmus writes repeatedly with unrestrained wrath:

Other qualifications are laid down by St. Paul as required for a bishop's office, a long list of them. But not one at present is held essential, except this one of abstinence from marriage. Homicide, parricide, incest, piracy, sodomy, sacrilege can be got over, but marriage is fatal. There are priests now in vast numbers, enormous herds of them, seculars and regulars, and it is notorious that very few of them are chaste. The great proportion fall into lust and incest, and open profligacy. It would surely be better if those who cannot contain should be allowed lawful wives of their own, and so escape this foul and miserable pollution. In the world we live in the celibates are many and the chaste are few.

This was a loyal Roman Catholic speaking who asserted that "never will I be tempted or exasperated into deserting the true communion." He illustrates the long overdue rebellion within the church against intolerable abuses. When Luther launched his protest, Erasmus at first did not think of him as disloyal. "He was attacking practices," Erasmus wrote, "which every honest man condemned, and was contending with a set of harpies, under whose tyrannies Christendom was groaning." In the end he refused to follow Luther, thought that he was going much too far, feared the consequences of a split church, and clung to the Roman communion with desperate fidelity. He longed for a reformation, however, a revival of New Testament Christianity, and with unmitigated realism he pictured the evils the sight of which left him heartsick and discouraged:

There are monasteries where there is no discipline, and which are worse than brothels. There are others where religion is nothing but ritual; and these are worse than the first, for the Spirit of God is not in them, and they are inflated with self-

righteousness. There are those again, where the brethren are so
sick of imposture that they keep it up only to deceive the vulgar.
The houses are rare indeed where the rule is seriously observed,
and even in these few, if you look to the bottom, you will find
small sincerity.

It is not surprising that the saying gained currency that
Erasmus laid the egg and Luther hatched it.

The testimony is unanimous that the church in Luther's
day desperately needed reformation. Adrian VI, elected Pope
in 1522, was a man of piety and learning; he valued the
ascetic life, was strictly virtuous himself, and saw with clear
eyes the corruption of the church. He would have cleaned
the Augean stables if he could, would have disciplined the
monastic orders and the secular clergy, and would have banished the sordid sale of indulgences, the simony, nepotism
and immorality that made Rome a scandal. He found the
task too huge. The curia could not pay its way without selling indulgences; and to cancel, as he wished to do, the whole
system of papal exactions—reservations, indults, exemptions,
expectancies—would have left stranded a host of ecclesiastical lawyers in Rome who had spent all their substance to
buy their places in the curia. He died, a defeated reformer,
the year after his induction.

When Luther was seven years old Savonarola began his
prophetic ministry in Florence. He was a mediaeval scholastic and a loyal son of Rome; the reformation for which he
toiled and died was not theological but moral. He was a
Puritan before the Puritans, and he set himself to cleanse
Florence, Italy and the church of their scandalous corruption. He faced, however, in Alexander VI, the reigning
pope, probably the most degenerate character who ever disgraced the papacy. Guicciardini (1483–1540), the famous
Italian historian who from intimate personal experience
knew the inside of the Roman curia, called Alexander after
his death, "the extinct serpent who by his immoderate ambition, pestiferous perfidy, monstrous lust, and every sort of

horrible cruelty and unexampled avarice—selling without distinction property sacred and profane—has compassed the destruction of so many by poison, and was now become its victim." It was this pope by whose order Savonarola was burned at the stake, when Luther was a lad of fifteen. "Luther himself," writes Villari, "could scarcely have been so successful in inaugurating his Reform, had not the sacrifice of Savonarola given a final proof that it was hopeless to hope in the purification of Rome."

This familiar picture, however, of a decadent church against whose corruptions the Protestant Reformers rose in wrath is far from being the full explanation of the Protestant Reformation. There was just as genuine wrath among loyal Roman Catholics themselves against these flagrant evils as there was in Luther and Calvin, Zwingli and John Knox. It was Dante (1265–1321) who freely consigned popes to hell, deploring those

> "whose avarice
> O'ercasts the world with mourning, under foot
> Treading the good, and, raising bad men up."

It was Chaucer (1340–1400), who scoffed at the traveling Pardoner with his wallet "brimful of pardons come from Rome, all hot." It was not a Protestant but an orthodox Roman Catholic bishop who closed a nunnery in England because of "the negligence and improvidence and disssolute disposition and incontinence of the religious women." It was a conscientious Catholic clergy and an increasingly able and aroused Catholic laity who attacked the plural holding of benefices, the non-residence of the clergy in their parishes, the commuting of penance for money, the false accusing of individuals in order to get blackmail from indulgences, and the papal court's immorality and arrogant abuse of power. A reformation was inevitable, and the only question was whether it would be achieved by the church itself without disruption or would cause a split, rending Christendom asunder. The Counter-Reformation, which went far toward cleansing the ancient church of its most shocking immoralities and inaugurating higher standards and stricter discipline, from pope to lowliest monk, was in process while the great Protestant Reformers were still alive. Ignatius Loyola, one of the Counter-Reformation's most influential pioneers, was only eight years younger than Luther. But the Counter-Reformation was too little and too late. A drive had started —not simply a protest against universally recognized ecclesiastical evils, but a deep and moving demand for regenerating personal faith and a genuinely vital Christian way of life— which called for more radical revolution in the church than any Counter-Reformation could produce.

Luther himself illustrates this drive. He came from a plain miner's family and was reared in a pious home. The appeal to fear, powerfully used in the church, struck terror into his youthful conscience, and he never forgot the stained-glass window in the parish church of Mansfeld where Jesus, with frowning face, seated on a rainbow with sword in hand, threatened judgment to come. How could he save his soul?— that question obsessed him. He studied at the village school, at St. George's School in Eisenach, at the University of Erfurt; he secured his degrees as Bachelor and Master, and then, prepared for a successful career in law, he suddenly entered the Erfurt Convent of the Augustinian Eremites, where later he became a monk. He himself has told us why: he did not trust himself to save his soul amid the temptations of the outer world; he saw no way to do it except by the austerities of a monastery.

He became the embodiment of monastic piety. He fasted, scourged himself, piled penance on penance, confessed and sought absolution for every slightest peccadillo he could accuse himself of, until he was ordered to stop confession until he had done something wrong enough to be worth confessing. Luther wrote later (1518) that no pen could describe his mental torture. He was struggling to achieve his soul's salvation by "good works," and he was getting nowhere. Then the light began to dawn, and one day, as he read the Epistle to the Romans in his cell, it came full flood upon him. "The just shall live by faith"—through that window the sun poured in. Salvation was a gift, a largess of God's grace, not to be bought by good works but received into a trustful and hospitable heart. Good works were not the operative cause of a transformed life but its consequence. God himself, revealed in Christ, could come into a man, forgiving his past sins, regenerating his spirit, making of him a new creature. This experience was Luther's Damascus Road and, so far as he was concerned, it was the beginning of the Reformation.

The revolutionary implications of this experience were not at first apparent, but they were nonetheless there. The elaborate apparatus of current ecclesiasticism with its pilgrimages, its adoration of saints and relics, its auricular confession to a priest, its penances and indulgences had no relevance to this experience of God's saving grace, immediately available to the believing and trustful soul. Salvation was not conferred by the church, and by the church it could not be withheld. Such implications Luther was unaware of in the first flush of his deliverance from doubt, despair and defeat. Only gradually did they come to light. But it was this experience, nonetheless, which launched the Reformation.

There is no understanding of the Reformation without insight into this spiritual hunger for a vital, inward religion and this experience of God's grace immediately available to the individual person, which Luther illustrates. From the twelfth century on a long series of fellowships, brotherhoods, sects had arisen, widely differing in endless ways, but sharing a common search for a direct, redeeming relationship between the soul and God. In one degree or another they were all in revolt against what they regarded as abuses in the contemporary church, but deeper than revolt and denial was their positive affirmation—God in Christ was immediately available to the hospitable soul. By one route or another all these groups—Albigenses, Waldenses, Paulicians, Bogomiles, Béguines, Paterini, Humiliati, Brethren of the Free Spirit, Lollards, Beghards, Picards, Fraticelli, and many more—came through to certain common consequences: the individual stood up in his own right decisively confronting God; the layman emerged as, no less than the priest, having direct access to God's grace; the priesthood of all believers displaced the old monopoly of a sacerdotal clergy; the idea of an invisible, spiritual church, made up of true believers redeemed by their personal experience of regeneration, became primary, and the visible church became secondary. The revolutionary result followed that a redeemed layman could be God's minister and could even officiate at the sacraments, while at the hands of a priest of evil life a sacrament was no sacrament at all.

Some of these brotherhoods put their major stress on a pure ethical life; as a modern Roman Catholic writes, "The Middle Ages suffered from a growing nostalgia for the Sermon on the Mount." Others were definitely mystical; joining themselves to the great tradition of Catholic mysticism, they found their God within themselves in transforming and sometimes ecstatic personal experience. Some of the sects were definitely heretical in theology, like the Albigenses infected with Manichaeanism imported from the East. Others made little of theology, centering their attention on withdrawal from worldly living, often defined in terms of moralistic legalism. Some were quietist, content with individual regeneration. Others were social reformers, sponsors and leaders of sometimes desperate revolts. Some were sober, intelligent, well-considered expressions of New Testament Christianity, seriously endeavoring to reproduce the character and spirit of the early church. Others were fanatical, going to wild, emotional extremes, until they made the very word "enthusiasm," an opprobrious term. Some, like the Albigenses, repudiated the Roman church. Others, like the Waldenses, regarded themselves as a movement of reform within the church. All of them, however, contributed to certain common results: the emancipation of the individual from ecclesiastical control, the self-assertion of the laity against the priesthood, and the conception of the true church as a fellowship of saved souls rather than an ecclesiastical establishment.

The presence and popular influence of these pre-Reformation sects are made evident by the Inquisition which from the thirteenth century on was devoted to their extirpation. "The cities," so one bishop said in 1190, "are filled with these false prophets"; and Berthold of Regensburg estimated, in the thirteenth century, that there were 150 of these heretical sects. The savage story of the Inquisition's brutality need not be rehearsed here. That whole era, in civil as well as ecclesiastical domains, was from our standpoint cruel and bloodthirsty and, when in possession of power, Protestants and Catholics alike could be barbarous. The records of the Inquisition do make clear, however, that these various sects were threateningly large in numbers and dangerous to Rome in their popular impact. They had to be put down if the Roman church's unity was to be preserved, and the motive power which sustained them was more than negative revolt—it was positive spiritual hunger for a vital personal religion, with God's grace immediately available to any man who would accept it.

Luther's experience, therefore, in the monastery at Erfurt was not untypical. He had detoured around the paraphernalia of ecclesiasticism and had been found by God directly in his own heart. It is significant that concerning *Theologia Germanica*, one of the outstanding mystical writings of the Middle Ages, Luther said that, next to the Bible and the works of St. Augustine, it had influenced him more deeply than any book he ever read.

The open break between Luther and Rome was the direct result of his personal experience. The sale of indulgences had become one of the main financial resources of the papacy. It was part of a vast apparatus—auricular confession, priestly absolution, penance—developed with the merciful intent of constructing official channels through which divine forgiveness could be brought to sinful men. Christ and the saints, so the theory ran, had accumulated a vast treasury of merit, and this treasure was at the disposal of the Holy Father for the saving of his people. He could mediate the rich store of merit, gathered by the Savior and the saints, to those who lacked merit of their own, and so could reduce the penalties of purgatory for those who else must expiate their sins by ages of torment there. All this was mercifully intended, but the next step was fatal: when the pope needed money, he could and did *sell* the indulgence which he was by theory empowered to *give*. So the sale of indulgences began and while the profits were sometimes used for benign purposes, such as building cathedrals and hospitals, it went to such lengths of organized plunder at last that it became a major scandal. As Erasmus exclaimed, "The Court of Rome clearly has lost all sense of shame; for what could be more shameless than these continued indulgences."

The crux of the matter lay in the fact that if the pope had power thus to *grant* relief from the penalties of purgatory, he could also *withhold* it. It was not simply true, as a contemporary jingle put it, that

> As in the box the money rings,
> The soul from purgatory springs.[1]

The logical conclusion was that if in the box the money did *not* ring, the soul in purgatory remained doomed. Under such pressure the sale of indulgences was pushed by every ingenuity of propaganda, and when Tetzel came to Saxony to exercise his salesmanship in Luther's bailiwick, Martin

---

[1] *So wie das Geld im Kasten klingt,*
Die Seele aus dem Fegfeuer springt.

rebelled. He had experienced God's grace "without money and without price." Whatever else might be true or untrue in the complicated apparatus of salvation by papal mediation, he knew that *this* was false and scandalous.

In this anthology we shall try to trace, in the words of the participants, the major trends of the Reformation which followed. Philip Melanchthon entered the lists, Luther's warm friend and loyal backer, to whom he said as he started for Worms, "My dear brother, if I do not come back, if my enemies put me to death, you will go on teaching and standing fast in the truth; if you live, my death will matter little." Huldreich Zwingli, only a year younger than Luther, led his Swiss canton, Zurich, in its revolt against Rome, with widespread consequences. John Calvin, twenty-five years younger than Luther, made Geneva one of the most powerful centers of the Reformation. John Knox, thirty-two years younger than Luther, decisively influenced by Calvin, became leader of the new movement in Scotland. "John Knox thundereth out of the pulpit," wrote a contemporary, "so that I fear nothing so much as that one day he will mar all. He ruleth the roost, and of him all men stand in fear." England, under Henry VIII, broke with Rome, not on the issue of theology or the sacraments, but on the issue of papal supremacy, making the king head of the church as well as of the state. "This is our doctrine," said Bishop Jewel, when Queen Elizabeth was consolidating the reformed English church, "that every soul, of what calling soever be he—be he monk, be he preacher, be he prophet, be he apostle—ought to be subject to king and magistrates."

Not alone in such outstanding personalities and revolts, however, is the meaning of the Reformation to be seen. The Luthers and Calvins and kings could have done nothing, had there not been widespread among the people both indignant rebellion against the abuses of the Roman church and zealous piety, seeking a religion of personal experience, vital power and intelligent credibility. If one forgets the Huguenots and Mennonites, the Moravians, the Socinians, the Quakers, the Baptists, the Seekers, the Wesleyans, one misses major trends in the movement of reformation. They were not uncommonly crowded underground, assailed alike by Catholics and Protestants. They were sharply at odds with one another and sometimes with the ruling powers in church and state. Some of the most important of them fairly got their heads up and had their say only when the Reformation had run its course for nearly two centuries. But they represent ideas and motives which from the beginning lay deep in the popular revolt against Rome.

No anthology, within the limits of such a book as this, can possibly do justice to these major trends in Protestantism. The historical background which binds the whole story together must be barely sketched. Let the reader turn to some such volumes as *A History of the Reformation*, by Thomas M. Lindsay, and *The Crisis of the Reformation*, by Norman Sykes, for a fuller account. Nor can justice be done to any of the early Protestant writers who are quoted. Only a taste can be given of their thought and quality. That taste, however, can be revealing, and if it leads the reader to eat more heartily, devouring the biographies of the Reformers and the books in which they took their dangerous stand, because for conscience's sake they could "not do otherwise," this anthology will be amply justified.

HARRY EMERSON FOSDICK

New York
January, 1952

JOHN
WYCLIFFE

c. 1320 - 1384

ON

JOHN WYCLIFFE

IN 1572 A PICTURE WAS PUBLISHED IN A BOHEMIAN PSALTER
representing Wycliffe striking the spark, Huss kindling the
coals, and Luther brandishing the flaming torch. In the
heyday of his power, Wycliffe was the pride of Oxford University, the foremost schoolman of his day, and the most
influential preacher in England. He could not, however, stay
in any ivory tower; he was too stirred with sympathy for common folk and with horror at the corruption of the church.
He did strike the spark of the Reformation, so that two centuries afterwards the Bishop of London, in a letter to Erasmus, said concerning Lutheranism: "It is no question of
some pernicious novelty: it is only that new arms are being
added to the great band of Wycliffite heretics."

Wycliffe's protest began against the wealth of the ecclesiastics. For generations the church's monopoly of the means
of salvation had been put to monetary use. Redemption from
purgatory and hell was worth paying for and the English
people, rich and poor, had paid well. Especially the wealthy
had poured vast bequests into churches and monasteries for
the repetition of masses for the donors' souls, until a large
part of the land and wealth of England was in ecclesiastical
hands. To this Wycliffe attributed the corruption of the

3

church. It was being ruined by Mammon, he said; it should be disendowed and stripped of its wealth for its own soul's sake. There was a strong ascetic strain in Wycliffe's thinking.

He had given up hope that the church would reform itself. The only power which could accomplish reformation lay in the hands of the nobility. Generations of lords had bequeathed to the ecclesiastics the riches which were corrupting them, and now, in view of the abuses, the lords should take back what their fathers had given. What "Piers Plowman" was saying, Wycliffe echoed: "Take their lands, ye lords!"

At the beginning, therefore, Wycliffe lined up with the nobility against the clergy. He was out to reform the church, to humble its arrogance, to strip the prelates of their luxury, to turn them out of their high offices in the state and put them to their proper spiritual ministries, to restore Christian simplicity and voluntary poverty to the monasteries, and to secure for local parishes the service of devout, disciplined, and educated priests. To achieve this end he turned to the nobility; they alone had power to accomplish his purposes. To be sure, the lords, too, were corrupt. "They destroy their poor neighbours," he said, "and make their house a den of thieves"; "Now cometh example of pride, gluttony and harlotry from lords' courts to the commons." His major aim, however, was to reform the church, and who had authority to do that except the king and the nobles? The king, therefore, should undertake the work of reformation, should seize and distribute to the lords for the sake of the people the vast endowments of churches and monasteries, should compel bishops to discipline their clergy, to remove immoral and inefficient priests, to end the evils of non-residence and see to it that local parishes were served by worthy pastors.

Far beyond Wycliffe's power to see, this appeal from the church to the state involved momentous consequences; it even helped to pave the way for the doctrine of the divine right of kings; but Wycliffe was too intelligent not to perceive some major implications of his position, and he was too courageous to shrink from facing them. Behind the worldliness, luxury and Mammon-worship which he thought were ruining the church stood the basic evil—the church's supposed monopolistic control of the means of salvation. It was this sole possession of the keys of heaven and hell, used for financial gain, which was debauching Christendom—so Wycliffe thought—and he attacked the whole system: the necessity of auricular confession to a priest, corporal penance, pilgrimages and relic worship, financial substitutes for penance, special masses for the dead, the idea of a treasury of merit in the pope's control, and the sale of indulgences.

This radical revolt against the papal system was encouraged by the lamentable estate of the papacy in Wycliffe's time. During the greater part of Wycliffe's life, the pope was throned in Avignon, France, where for seventy years the Holy Fathers were in exile from Rome. Not the pope but the king of France was supreme and during the whole period of the exile only Frenchmen were popes, and the supposed spiritual head of Christendom was little more than a court bishop of the French king. Then in 1377—seven years before Wycliffe's death—the great schism began, one pope in Avignon, the other in Rome, each with his college of cardinals, and each hurling bulls and excommunications at the other's head. This schism, which was to last for forty years, broke down the last shred of Wycliffe's confidence in the papacy. He repudiated the pope's supremacy over the church and his power to bind and loose. "Antichrist," he said, "hath cast his cast to make all men subject to the pope and lead them after that him liketh. Lord, where is freedom of Christ, when men are casten into such bondage? Christ made his servants free, but Antichrist hath made them bond again."

Schoolman that he was, Wycliffe had to have a basic theory to support his revolt and, to that end, he developed his doctrine of "Dominion," which had momentous implications. All dominion, he taught, is from God, and those on earth who hold dominion possess it only as God's henchmen. This theory of derived power had an obvious feudal background, but Wycliffe introduced into it a radical new factor—no intermediary lords could stand between each man's soul and God; every man who exercised dominion had his commission directly from on high. God's dominion, however, can reside only in those who stand in his grace, are regenerate men, willing what God wills; all others possess no true dominion, and, whether kings or popes, their sovereignty is false and may be denied and repudiated. Written in Latin, with all the recondite subtlety of scholastic argument, this theory made its stormy way into the minds of the schoolmen. Wycliffe himself was chary of its application to kings —he did not favor violent revolution—but as to the pope's spiritual dominion he applied it fearlessly, until he desired the end of the papacy, of the whole hierarchy and of the monastic establishments, and would have left parish priests as little hampered by ecclesiastical superiors as they are in Presbyterianism today. In the last year of his life he crowned his heretical career by denying Transubstantiation. He asserted the spiritual presence of Christ in the bread and wine of the sacrament, but repudiated the transformation of the substance of the elements, which the orthodox dogma affirmed.

Scholar and schoolman though he was, throughout his writings one feels his kinship with the common people. It is of them he constantly is thinking, of their spiritual destitution, their economic ills, their neglected estate in their poorly served parishes. He exalted the laymen, and among the Lollards, who carried on his work after him, laymen were the preachers. Wat Tyler's Rebellion, a furious revolt of the underprivileged which during Wycliffe's later years shook England to the very center, was blamed by his enemies on Wycliffe's teaching. In the first edition of his English translation of the Scriptures, Wycliffe said: "This Bible is translated and shall make possible Government of people, by people, for people."

The popular extension of Wycliffe's ideas in England flowed in two main channels—the translation of the Bible into English and the widespread preaching of the Wycliffite "Poor Priests." The varying fortunes of Wycliffe himself and of his ideas, and especially the persistent continuance of his aftermath, the Lollards, who survived till Luther's time, cannot be recounted here. *England in the Age of Wycliffe,* by G. M. Trevelyan, is an excellent history of the times, and *John Wycliffe,* by Lewis Sergeant, *The Life of Wyclif,* by H. B. Workman, *The People's Faith in the Time of Wyclif,* by B. L. Manning, and *Wycliffe and Movements of Reform,* by R. L. Poole, are valuable treatises. The surprising denouement, so far as Wycliffe himself is concerned, is that while he was condemned by the pope and driven from Oxford, he died a natural death in his parish at Lutterworth.

The anthologist faces grave difficulties in culling representative abstracts from his writings for the modern English reader. Many of his most important Latin works have not been translated, and his English works are couched in the archaic verbiage and style of his period. We present two brief passages from his translation of the Bible, one of the major achievements of his life. "The worthy realm of France," he wrote, "notwithstanding all lettings, both translated the Bible and the Gospels with other true sentences of doctors out of Latin into French. Why shoulden not Englishmen do so? As lords in England have the Bible in French, so it were not against reason, that they hadden the same sentence in English." In the other excerpts, which we present, the ancient English has been modernized to make it readable.

Thirty years after Wycliffe's death, the Council of Constance, which sent John Huss to the stake, condemned Wycliffe also and ordered that his bones be exhumed and burnt.

This was done and the ashes were cast into the River Avon. His enemies, who thought they had now finished him, did not foresee history's verdict:

> "The Avon to the Severn runs,
> And Severn to the sea;
> And Wycliffe's dust shall spread abroad
> Wide as the waters be."

LUKE XV: 11-32

AND HE SEIDE, A MAN HADDE TWEI SONES; AND THE YONGER
of hem seide to the fadir, Fadir, gyue me the porcioun of
catel, that fallith to me. And he departide to hem the catel.
And not aftir many daies, whanne alle thingis weren gederid
togider, the yonger sone wente forth in pilgrymage in to a
fer cuntre; and there he wastide hise goodis in lyuynge lech-
erously. And aftir that he hadde endid alle thingis a strong
hungre was maad in that cuntre, and he bigan to haue nede.
And he wente and drough hym to oon of the citeseyns of that
cuntre. And he sente hym in to his toun, to fede swyn. And
he coueitide to fille his wombe of the coddis that the hoggies
eeten, and no man gaf hym. And he turnede agen to hym
silf, and seide, Hou many hirid men in my fadir hous han
plente of looues; and Y perische here thorough hungir. Y
schal rise vp, and go to my fadir, and Y schal seie to hym,
Fadir, Y haue synned in to heuene, and bifor thee; and now
Y am not worthi to be clepid thi sone, make me as oon of
thin hirid men. And he roos vp, and cam to his fadir. And
whanne he was yit afer, his fadir saigh hym, and was stirrid
bi mercy. And he ran, and fel on his necke, and kisside hym.
And the sone seide to hym, Fadir, Y haue synned in
to heuene, and bifor thee; and now Y am not worthi to be

clepid thi sone. And the father seide to his seruauntis, Swithe
brynge ye forth the firste stoole, and clothe ye hym, and
gyue ye a ryng in his hoond, and schoon on hise feet; and
brynge ye a fat calf, and sle ye, and ete we, and make we
feeste. For this my sone was deed, and hath lyued agen; he
perischid, and is foundun. And alle men bigunnen to ete.
But his eldere sone was in the feeld; and whanne he cam,
and neighede to the hous, he herde a symfonye and a croude.
And he clepide oon of the seruauntis, and axide, what these
thingis weren. And he seide to hym, Thi brother is comun,
and thi fadir slewe a fat calf, for he resseyuede hym saaf.
And he was wrooth, and wolde not come in. Therfor his
fadir wente out, and bigan to preye hym. And he answerde to
his fadir, and seide, Lo! so many yeeris Y serue thee, and Y
neuer brak thi comaundement; and thou neuer gaf to me a
kidde, that Y with my freendis schulde haue ete. But aftir
that this thi sone, that hath deuourid his substaunce with
horis, cam, thou hast slayn to hym a fat calf. And he seide
to hym, Sone, thou art euer more with me, and alle my
thingis ben thine. But it bihofte for to make feeste, and to
haue ioye; for this thi brother was deed, and lyuede agen;
he perischide, and is founden.

I CORINTHIANS XIII (MODERNIZED)

If I speak with tongues of men and of angels, and I have not
charity, I am made as brass sounding, or a cymbal tinkling.
And if I have prophecy, and know all mysteries and all cunning, and if I have all faith, so that I move hills from their
place, and I have not charity, I am naught. And if I depart
all my goods in to the meats of poor men, and if I betake my
body, so that I burn, and if I have not charity, it profiteth to
me no thing. Charity is patient, it is benign; charity envieth
not, it doeth not wickedly, it is not upblown, it is not covetous, it seekest not the things that be its own, it is not stirred
to wrath, it thinketh not evil, it enjoyeth not on wickedness,
but it joyeth together to truth; it suffereth all things, it be-

lieveth all things, it hopeth all things; it sustaineth all things. Charity falleth never down, whether prophecies shall be void, or languages shall cease, or science shall be destroyed. For a part we know, and a part we prophesy; but when that shall come that is perfect, that thing that is of part shall be avoided. When I was a little child, I spake as a little child, I understood as a little child; but when I was made a man, I avoided the things that were of a little child. And we see now by a mirror in darkness, but then face to face; now I know of part, but then I shall know, as I am known. And now dwell faith, hope, and charity, these three; but the most of these is charity.

Library of the World's Best Literature, Vol. XXXIX
Charles Dudley Warner, Editor
New York, J. A. Hill & Company.

From

HOW THE OFFICE OF

CURATES IS ORDAINED

OF GOD

THE OFFICE OF CURATE* IS ORDAINED OF GOD; FEW DO IT WELL
and many full evil, therefore test we their defaults, with
God's help.

I. They are more busy about worldly goods than virtues
and good keeping of men's souls. For he that can best get
riches of this world together, and have a great household, and
worldly array, is held to be a worthy man of holy church,
though he know not the best point of the gospel. Such a
one is praised and borne up by the bishops and their offices.
But the curate that gives himself to study holy writ and teach
his parishioners to save their souls, and live in meekness,
penance, and busy labour about spiritual things, and cares
not about worldly respect and riches, is held to be a fool, and
destroyer of holy church. He is despised and persecuted by
high priests and prelates and their offices, and is hated by
other curates. This makes many to be negligent in their spiritual cures, and to give themselves to occupations and business
about worldly goods. These negligent curates think but little,
how dearly Christ bought man's soul with his precious blood
and death, and how hard a reckoning he shall make at
doomsday for those souls. They would seem to be out of

* By curate was meant any minister who has the care of souls.

12

Christian faith—for they make not themselves ready to come thither, and to answer how they came into their benefices, and how they lived and taught, and spent poor men's goods. For if they had such a faith in their minds, they would begin a better life, and continue therein.

II. The second default is, that they run fast, by land and by water, in great peril of body and soul, to get rich benefices; but they will not knowingly go a mile to preach the gospel, though christened men are running to hell for want of knowing and keeping of God's law; and certainly here they show, indeed, that they are foully blind with covetousness, and worship false gods, as St. Paul saith.

Since they so much love worldly riches, and labour for them night and day, in thought and deed, and labour so little for God's worship and the saving of Christian souls, who can excuse these covetous clerks from simony and heresy? Neither God's law, nor man's law, nor reason, nor good conscience. And let the king and his council inquire how much gold goes out of our land, for purchase of benefices, into aliens' hands, and how much is given privately to men in the land. They shall find many thousand pounds.

III. The third default of evil curates is, that they are angels of Satan to lead men to hell; for, instead of truly teaching Christ's gospel, they are dumb, or else tell men's traditions. Instead of example of good life, they hurt their parishioners in many ways—by example of pride, envy, covetousness, and unreasonable vengeance—cruelly cursing for tithes, and evil customs. And for example of holy devotion, devout prayer, and works of mercy, they teach idleness, gluttony, drunkenness, and lechery, and maintaining of these sins, and many more. For since priests are called angels (messengers) in holy writ, and these curates bring not the message of God, but of the fiend, as their wicked life showeth, they are not angels of God, but of the fiend. St. Peter was called Satan by Christ, as the gospel telleth, because he

was contrary to God's will, and savoured not of heavenly
things; well then are these evil curates so called, since they
are more contrary to God's will, and savour less of spiritual
things, and the saving of Christian souls.

IV. The fourth error is, that they think more of statutes of
sinful men than the most reasonable law of Almighty God.
For they dread the pope's law, and statutes made by bishops,
and other officers, more than the noble law of the gospel.
Therefore they have many great and costly books of man's
law, and study them much, but few curates have the Bible
and expositions of the gospel, they study them but little and
do them less. But would to God that every parish church in
this land had a good Bible and good expositions on the
gospel, and that the priests studied them well, and taught
truly the gospel and God's commands to the people! Then
should good life prevail, and rest, and peace, and charity;
sin and falseness should be put back—God bring this end to
his people!

V. The fifth default is, that they practise strife and plea
(law) and gather envy and hate from laymen for tythes.
They leave preaching of the gospel, and cry fast after tythes,
and summon men to account, and by force take their goods,
or else curse them seven foot above the earth, and seven foot
under the earth, and seven foot on each side, and afterwards
draw men to prison as though they were kings and emperors
of men's bodies and goods; forgetting wholly the meekness
and patience of Christ and his apostles, how they cursed not
when men would neither give them meat, nor drink, nor
harbour; but Christ blamed his apostles when they would
have asked such vengeance, as the gospel of St. Luke teaches.
And St. Peter biddeth to bless other men, even enemies, and
not to have will to curse. Paul also teacheth that we should
not do evil for evil, but overcome an evil deed by good doing.

VI. The sixth default is, that they teach their parishioners, by their deeds and life, which are as a book to them, to

love and seek worldly glory, and to be careless of heavenly things. For they make themselves busy, night and day, to get worldly advancement, and their own worship and dignity in this world, by pleading and striving therefore, considering it great righteousness to hold forth and maintain points of worldly privilege, and dignity; but about spiritual dignity, and high degree of heavenly bliss, they will not strive against spiritual enemies; for they strive not who shall be most meek and willingly poor, and most busy in open preaching and private counselling how men shall obtain heaven, as Christ and his apostles did. But they, like moles, remain rooting after worldly worship, and earthly goods, as though there were no life but only in this wretched world.

VII. The seventh error is, that they teach sinful men to buy hell full dear, and not to come to heaven which is proffered them for little cost. For they teach Christian men to suffer much cold, hunger, and thirst, and much waking, and despising, to get worldly honour; and a little dirt by false warring, out of charity; if they bring them much gold they absolve them lightly and to think themselves secure by their prayers, and grant them a blessing. But they teach not how their parishioners should dispose themselves to receive gifts of the Holy Ghost, and keep conditions of charity, doing truth and good conscience to each man, both poor and rich. And if they are poor by the chances of the world, or willingly, by dread of sin, they set them at nought, and say they are cursed, because they have not much muck; and if they have much worldly goods, got with false oaths, false weights, and other deceits, they praise them, and bless them, and say that God is with them and blesseth them.

VIII. The eighth default. They shut the kingdom of heaven before men, and neither go in themselves, nor suffer other men to enter, for they shut up holy writ—as the gospel, and commandments, and conditions of charity, which are called the kingdom of heaven—by false new laws, and evil glossing, and evil teaching. For they will neither learn themselves, nor teach holy writ, nor suffer other man to do it, lest their own sin and hypocrisy be known, and their pleasurable life withdrawn. Thus they close Christ's life and his apostles' from the common people, by the keys of antichrist's judgment and censures; and they make them not so hardy as to say a truth of holy writ against their accursed life, for that shall be held to be detraction and envy, and against charity! Therefore they make the people follow their teaching, their statutes, and their customs, and to leave God's teaching; and thereby lead them blindly to hell, and thus close the kingdom of heaven from them.

IX. The ninth error is, that they waste poor men's goods on rich furs and costly clothes, and wordly array, feasts of rich men, and in gluttony, drunkenness, and lechery. For they sometimes pass great men in their gay furs and precious clothes—they have fat horses with gay saddles and bridles. St. Bernard crieth, Whatever curates hold of the altar more than a simple livelihood and clothing, is not theirs, but other men's.

X. The tenth default is, that they haunt lords' courts, and are occupied in worldly offices, and do not take care of their parishes, although they take more worldly goods from them than Christ and his apostles. Certainly it is great treachery; for what man durst undertake to keep men who are besieged in a feeble castle by many strong enemies, and then flee into a swineherd's office, and let enemies take the castle and destroy it? Were not this open treason? and would not this keeper be guilty of the loss of the castle, and all men therein? So it is of the curates and Christian souls of which they take care, who are besieged by fiends, when they leave them unkept, and busy themselves in worldly offices and lords' courts. Are not these lords, who thus hold curates in their courts and worldly offices, traitors to God Almighty, since they draw away his chief knights from their spiritual battle, when and where they were most needful for this service?

XI. The eleventh error is, that they attend more to wrongful commandments of sinful men, than to the most rightful commandments of God. For if the pope or bishop send a letter to receive a pardoner to deceive the people, by grants of many thousand years of pardon, he shall be despatched; although if there come a true man, to preach the gospel freely and truly, he shall be hindered for wrongful command of a sinful man. And thus they put God's commandment and his rightful will behind, and put sinful man's will and wrong commandments before; and thus for their own worldly profit and bodily ease they stop their parishioners from hearing of God's law, which is food for the soul, and lead them blindly to hell. These are evil fathers who thus cruelly starve their subjects' souls, and drive them to damnation, for love of worldly muck, or bodily ease, or for dread of wretched antichrists, who are traitors to God and his people. . . .

Ye curates, see these heresies and blasphemies, and many more, which follow from your wicked life and wayward teachings. Forsake them for dread of hell, and turn to good life and true teaching of the gospel and ordinances of God, as Christ and his apostles did, for reward of heavenly bliss. And in confessions, and in other speeches, reprove more the breaking of God's commands, than the breaking of commands of new pilgrimages and offerings; and teach Christian men to turn such vows already made, into better alms, as Christ teaches in the gospel.

O Almighty God, bring curates into holy life, and true teaching after Christ and his apostles. Amen.

Writings of the Reverend and Learned John Wycliff, D.D.
Philadelphia: Presbyterian Board of Publication, 1842.

From

ANTICHRIST'S LABOUR
TO DESTROY HOLY WRIT

AS OUR LORD JESUS CHRIST ORDAINED BY THE WRITING OF
the four evangelists, to make his gospel surely known, and
maintained against heretics, and men out of the faith; so
the devil, even Satan, devises by antichrist and his worldly
false clerks, to destroy holy writ and Christian men's belief,
by four accursed ways or false reasons. 1. The church is of
more authority, and more to be believed than any gospel.
2. That Augustine said he would not believe the gospel if
the church had not taught him so. 3. That no man alive
knows which is the gospel, but by the approving of the
church. 4. If men say that they believe this is the gospel of
Matthew or John, they ask, Why believest thou that this is
the gospel? as though they would say, There is no cause
but that the church confirmeth and teacheth it.

These four evidences, and many more, the fiend makes, to
blind men in their belief, that they should not know what is
sin, or what is virtue; which is truth, which is falsehood;
which is good, which is evil; which are God's commands,
and which are the fiend's lies; thus to bring all men blindly
to hell and their new religion. And principally friars preach
these evidences, and sow them among ignorant men in the
country, to stop poor priests and ignorant men, that they be
not hardy to speak of the gospel, holy writ, God's commandments, joys of heaven, of sins, and of the pains of hell, lest

they stir men to rise out of their sins for dread of pains, and to live in virtuous life, to have the bliss of heaven. . . .

Let us now see this bringing in the first accursed ground, that the church is of more authority and credence than the gospel. They say that Nicodemus, and many more, wrote the gospels of Christ's life and his teaching, but the church put them away, and approved the four gospels of Matthew, Mark, Luke, and John—then the church might as well have put out the four, and approved the other gospels; since it was in full power of the church to reprove and condemn which they would, and to approve and to accept which they liked, and therefore men, say they, should believe the church more than any gospel.

First, These crafty heretics understand by the church, the pope of Rome and his cardinals, and the multitude of worldly clerks assenting to his simony, and worldly lord-ship, above all kings and emperors of this world. For else it were not to their purpose to magnify the church as they now do. True men say that the clergy who first were wise, and holy of life, were stirred up by the Holy Ghost to take these four gospels, and they charge not Christian people with more, since these are enough and profitable at the full, and are figured in many prophecies of God's law. And these four witnesses were accepted of the Holy Ghost, to write these things for man's instruction, which we may not stay to tell now. But certainly the church might not have put away the gospels, and have accepted the others; for then it had done against the will of God, and against the truth of Jesus Christ, and against the charity of the Holy Ghost, to put away these witnesses that knew more of God's purity, and were holier of life, and to take witnesses not so skilled in God's will, nor so holy of life, nor so meek, nor so stable in faith and love of Jesus Christ. . . .

See now the second wheel in this devil's wain [wagon]. They bear upon Augustine that he saith thus; That he would not believe the gospel unless the church said it. True men, being answered thus, suppose that Augustine said this word. But he said to this intent, That unless Christ, head of holy church and saints in heaven, and the apostles of Christ that are holy church, said and approved this gospel, he would not believe thereto. And this understanding is full true, and reasonable, and according to the words of Augustine; but they understand them, that unless the multitude of accursed worldly clerks approve this for the gospel, Augustine would not believe the gospel of Jesus Christ; and since Augustine was, and is, so great a doctor of holy church, no man should believe the gospel, unless the church of these prelates confirm that this is the gospel of Christ; and unless the multitude of antichrist's clerks approve the gospel or truth of holy writ, no man should hold the gospel, or any command of God, or maintain any truth against antichrist, and his worldly prelates. But what heresy might sooner destroy Christian man's belief? and God forbid that Augustine were in perilous heresy, or any Christian man, therefore it is leasing [falsehood] to slander St. Augustine with this accursed error, to colour their own false understanding and heresy by this holy doctor.

For by this accursed wheel, antichrist's clerks condemn Christian men's faith, the commands of God, and points of charity, and bring in their own crooked laws, to hold up their pride and covetousness, and to curse men for doing works of charity. Men must upon pain of damnation receive their wicked deeds as belief, and forsake the gospel of Christ, and take fiends' leasings instead of God's lore! And more cursedness to destroy Christian men's faith, than will ensue from this understanding, no man or fiend can imagine till the day of doom. Therefore, Christians should stand to the death for maintaining Christ's gospel and true understanding thereof, gotten by holy life and great study, and not set their faith or trust in sinful prelates and their clerks, nor in their understanding of holy writ. . . .

See now the third wheel of Satan's car; these deceitful clerks and religious of Lucifer say, that no man knows which is the gospel, but by the approving and confirming of the church; but true men say that to their understanding this is full of falsehood. For Christian men are certain of belief by the gracious gift of Jesus Christ, and that this truth, taught by Christ and his apostles, is the gospel, though all antichrist's clerks cry ever so fast the contrary, upon pain of curse, imprisonment, and burning. And this belief is not grounded on the pope and his cardinals, for then it must fail and be undone, as they fail and sometime are destroyed; but it is grounded on Jesus Christ, God and man, and on the Holy Trinity. So it may never fail but in default of him that should love God and serve him, and faileth on these two points. For almighty God, and his truths, are the foundation of Christian men's faith. And as Paul saith, other foundation may no man set besides that which is set, that is, Jesus Christ. Therefore, though antichrist and all his worldly clerks are buried deep in hell, for their simony, pride, and covetousness, and other sins, yet Christian faith faileth not, for they are not grounded thereon. But Jesus Christ is the ground thereof, for he is our God and our best Master, ever ready to teach true men all things that are profitable, and needful to their souls, and this teaching may not fail, but for inability of him that should receive this blessing.

The fourth wheel of Belial's cart is this; when Christian men say they know by belief that this is Christ's gospel, these malicious heretics ask, Why they believe that this is gospel? But true men ask of them again, Why they believe that God is God? And if they tell a good sufficient cause, we tell the same cause why we believe that this is Christ's gospel. But these heretics would have this cause to be, that it is for that their prelates teach that theirs is Christ's gospel; and they would have all their false purposes as of this cause; that whatever the prelates teach openly, and maintain steadfastly, were of as great authority or more than Christ's gospel. And so they would destroy holy writ and Christian faith, and maintain that whatever they do were no sin! But Christian men take their faith of God, by his gracious gift, when he giveth it to them; knowing and understanding truths needful to save men's souls, by grace to assent in their hearts to such truths. This men call faith, and of this faith Christian men are more certain than any man is of worldly things, by any bodily knowledge. . . .

Hereby, and by many more deceits, Christian men should know how the new religionists are false prophets, and accursed sects, of which Christ and his apostles prophesied before, and taught men to know them by their works, which are hypocrisy, covetousness, and maintaining of sin, by false preaching, flattering false counselling and slandering of true men; and making men secure of spiritual help by false letters of fraternity, and many other novelties brought up by hypocrisy and covetousness. . . . And may God Almighty strengthen his little flock against these four wheels of Satan's car, against antichrist's clerks and helpers, and make them strong in rightful faith, hope, and charity, to seek truly the worship of Jesus Christ, and the saving of men's souls, to despise antichrist's boast and feigned power, and willingly and joyfully to suffer pain and reproof in the world, for the name of Jesus and his gospel, to give firm example to others, to follow and attain the high bliss of heaven by glorious martyrdom as other saints did before. May Jesus of his endless might, endless wisdom, endless goodness, and charity, grant to us sinful wretches this boon! Amen.

Writings of the Reverend and Learned John Wycliff, D.D.
Philadelphia: Presbyterian Board of Publication, 1842.

From

THE TRIALOGUS

ON INDULGENCES

ALITHIA. We have here touched on the subject of indulgences; and as the granting of these appears to me quite in
accordance with this blasphemous presumption of the friars,
I could wish that you would say something on this topic.

PHRONESIS. As the pride of those who hate God ever
tends upward, so although the fountain head of heresy
and sin takes its rise in the very beginning of darkness, the
rivulet of the friars strives unnaturally to raise itself above
its source. I confess that the indulgences of the pope, if they
are what they are said to be, are a manifest blasphemy, inasmuch as he claims a power to save men almost without
limit, and not only to mitigate the penalties of those who
have sinned, by granting them the aid of absolution and indulgences, that they may never come to purgatory, but to
give command to the holy angels, that when the soul is separated from the body, they may carry it without delay to its
everlasting rest.

The friars give a colour to this blasphemy, by saying that
Christ is omnipotent, and excels all his good angels, and that
the pope is his plenary vicar on earth, and so possesses in
every thing the same power as Christ in his humanity. It is

23

here that lawyers, in common with the friars, cry as wolves, and, contradicting themselves, say, that when they consider the power of this God upon earth they cannot lift up their face to heaven. Whence, to declare the power of the pope, the false brethren, according to the secrets of their faith, proceed as follows:

They suppose, in the first place, that there is an infinite number of supererogatory merits, belonging to the saints, laid up in heaven, and above all, the merit of our Lord Jesus Christ, which would be sufficient to save an infinite number of other worlds, and that, over all this treasure, Christ hath set the pope. Secondly, that it is his pleasure to distribute it, and, accordingly, he may distribute therefrom to an infinite extent, since the remainder will still be infinite. Against this rude blasphemy I have elsewhere inveighed. Neither the pope, nor the Lord Jesus Christ, can grant dispensations, or give indulgences to any man, except as the Deity has eternally determined by his just counsel. But we are not taught to believe that the pope, or any other man, can have any colour of justice to adduce for so doing; therefore, we are not taught that the pope has any such power. . . .

This doctrine is a manifold blasphemy against Christ, inasmuch as the pope is extolled above his humanity and deity, and so above all that is called God—pretensions which, according to the declarations of the apostle, agree with the character of Antichrist; for he possesses Caesarean power above Christ, who had not where to lay his head. In regard to spiritual power, so far as the humanity of Christ is concerned, it would seem that the pope is superior to our Lord Jesus Christ; for it behoved Christ to suffer the most bitter passion for the salvation of man; and we believe, that on the ground of the Divine justice, men attain to whatever happiness may be theirs, by virtue of Christ's passion. But this renegade says, that it is allowable that he should live as luxuriously as he may choose, and that, by the bare writing of one of his scribes, he can introduce wonders, without limit,

into the church militant! Who, then, can deny his being extolled above the Lord Jesus Christ, in whose life we read not
that Christ, or any one of his apostles, granted such absolutions or indulgences? Yet, had such power been at their command, it is on many grounds probable that they would not
have been absolutely idle in the use of it, especially when
Christ condemns the slothful servant, for not trafficking with
the talent entrusted to him; and he requires at the hand of
the prelate the souls committed to his care, and lost through
his negligence, as appears from the third chapter of Ezekiel.
Which alternative, then, should we maintain—that Christ
and his apostles possessed no such power, or that they were
culpable in hoarding such treasure, in place of bringing it
forth for the good of the church? But what greater insanity
than to adopt such a conclusion!

Similar in its folly is the doctrine which teaches, that the
pope dispenses those same merits of the saints, for the service of men, to any extent, according to his pleasure. For it
behoves Christ to do more, both on his own part, to fulfil
the claims of justice; and on that of the sinner, whom it
becomes him to affect, imparting grace to him, that he may
prove worthy of the Divine assistance.

The same may be said concerning the fiction of the keys of
Antichrist, for it is not necessary that the believer should in-
sist on the foundation of this pretension, since the argument
will be found to be one without sequence. Christ, they say,
granted to Peter, the apostle in the nearest degree following
his own example, such power over the keys, and therefore
we ought, in the same manner, to concede to Antichrist,
who, in word and deed, is still more pre-eminently his opposite, as great, or even greater, power in the church! Christ
gave to Peter, and to others possessing a knowledge of the
law of God, power of judging according to the law of that
knowledge, both in binding and loosing, agreeably to the
church triumphant. But, now, this renegade will not be regulated by the mind of the church above, nor by any authority;

but, as might be expected from Antichrist, he sets forth new laws, and insists, under pain of the heaviest censure, that the whole church militant shall believe in them; so that anything determined therein, shall stand as though it were a part of the Gospel of Jesus Christ.

In such infinite blasphemies is the infatuated church involved, especially by the means of the tail of this dragon— that is, the sects of the friars—who labour in the cause of this illusion, and of other Luciferian seductions of the church. But arise, O soldiers of Christ! be wise to fling away these things, along with the other fictions of the prince of darkness, and put ye on the Lord Jesus Christ, and confide, undoubtedly, in your own weapons, and sever from the church such frauds of Antichrist, and teach the people that in Christ alone, and in his law, and in his members, they should trust; that in so doing, they may be saved through his goodness, and learn above all things honestly to detect the devices of Antichrist!

ON PENANCE

ALITHIA.   You would oblige me now by stating your views of the sacrament of penance. To define it seems difficult, for it is said that penitence hath three parts, like a harp, namely, contrition of heart, confession with the mouth, and satisfaction by deeds—and its genus, accordingly, is not easily specified, these three things being diverse in genus.

PHRONESIS.   It appears to me that penitence consists in the condition of the mind, and that these other things, which are called the parts of penitence, are its accidents, which go together to form its completeness. Contrition belongs to the mind alone, and is not an object of sense, inasmuch as the contrite confess to the Lord. And this department of penitence, though little esteemed, is yet of the greatest virtue, so that without it the rest avail nothing. Confession is made up of this feeling, and of oral utterance made to God alone. And thus the fathers under the old law, in common with those of the New Testament, were accustomed to confess. Penitence, in the sense of satisfaction by works, is made up of the two former, together with a confession made to the priest in private.

Now from a regard to gain, it is to this last view of penitence that we give most attention. But whether this third kind is necessary to salvation, or on what authority it was introduced, is with many a matter of dispute. But we must confide on this point in John, who, in his gloss on the decrees, says, after stating many opinions which he censures, that Innocent III invented it, and to confirm it, established the law "Omnis utrusque sexus," which is set forth in the fifth decretal. But in my opinion, as I have explained at length, it would be better for the church did she content herself with the first and second kinds of penitence as above mentioned. But though the third form (confession to a priest) is injurious to many, and is the cause of many evils to both parties (the priest and the confessing), nevertheless it brings many good results to the church, and since it might possibly be well conducted, it appears to me that it may be, by supposition, necessary, and so really necessary, forasmuch as many, through shame of being obliged to confess the sin, and of submitting to the penance enjoined, and from the fear of being obliged to make confession of what they have done elsewhere, are deterred from repeating their sin.

No one can believe that a man may not be saved without confession of this kind, for, otherwise, all the dead from Christ's ascension to the time of Innocent III are lost—a horrible thing to believe. Rather do we think, that a much greater number are lost under the law of that pope on this subject, than would ever have been lost for the want of it. Besides, it generally happens, that he who absolves, is not acquainted with the magnitude of the sin confessed, just as he knows not if the man who is confessing be contrite; though he is well aware that unless he be so, his sin is not removed. How, then, can he utter falsehoods in the name of Christ, and so impudently absolve sin, and enjoin a penance which he cannot know as being proportioned to the transgression? Neither is it lawful to burden the church with new traditions, especially such as are of a suspicious character, for what we have is already sufficient. And the laws about confession in the Scripture have served us well enough for more than a thousand years. On what ground, then, is it that without a law, a third kind of penitence has been introduced in a manner so unlikely? It appears to me, that this papal law is to be admitted as far as the discretion of the person who confesses may deem profitable.

ALITHIA. I see, brother, that you allow but little weight to this papal law; and it seems to me, that for the same reason, you would make light of the absolution from penalty and guilt, and the full remission of sin granted by the pope, and of that burden of sin which the prelate often aggravates by fulminating his horrible excommunications, and so the decision of the court of Rome, on such matters, would fall to the ground.

PHRONESIS. The observations you make seem to involve much truth, inasmuch as in the Scriptures, without any additions on the part of the Roman court, it is sufficiently set forth how every man should regulate his life. And if the injunctions of Scripture are attended to, it follows that the man who lives to the end the life so prescribed, will be saved. Hence all these fictitious dogmas are generally promulgated to keep the people in subjection, and to detain them in a fallacious obedience; and a blasphemous covetousness is the damnable root of the whole of them.

Let us look, then, and see what is enjoined and commanded by the Lord, in the law of perfect liberty, and observe it, and abstain from what is forbidden, and from giving attention to laws newly ordained, and this will be enough. Accordingly, what is over and above, is not only evil in its origin, but is itself evil, and blinds many. Concerning all vows, promises, and other private observances, let the believer look up to the almighty power of Jesus Christ; let him bend all the strength of his soul to living henceforth in more perfectness, so as to be serviceable to the church; let him repent of his past evil life, strengthen within him the purpose of sinning no more; and this, in my opinion, sufficeth to destroy his guilt, and to save him, whatever our superiors may say to the contrary. But in all this, let the believer beware of any insincerity toward God. With regard to the words in Matthew xvi., "Whatsoever ye bind," &c., let the believer demand from the false bishop when he alleges this saying of our Lord's, if his own life of holiness, by its resemblance to the life of Peter, is such as to make him a true vicar of Peter. If the presumptuous hypocrite shall impudently affirm that it is so, ask him to show the similarity of his life to that of Peter, more especially in the grace given him to work miracles, and in the lowliness of his poverty. Peter presumed not on the possession of such power, how then can this hypocrite claim it? And since he cannot prove himself a true vicar of Christ, or a member of the church of Christ, what is it to him that Christ promised this power to the blessed Peter, seeing he is neither Peter, nor by the lowness and holiness of his life the vicar of Peter?

Tracts and Treatises of John de Wycliffe, D. D.,
Edited by the Rev. Robert Vaughan, D. D.
London: Blackburn & Pardon, 1845.

OF PERFECT LIFE
or,
The Counsel of Christ

CHRIST, NOT COMPELLING, BUT FREELY COUNSELLING EACH
man to perfect life, saith thus, If any man will come after
me let him deny himself, and take his cross and follow me,
Luke ix. Then let us forsake ourselves, such as we have made
us in doing sin, and dwell we such as we are made by grace.
If a proud man be converted to Christ, and is made meek,
he hath forsaken himself. If a covetous man ceaseth to covet,
and giveth his own things, he hath denied himself. If an evil
liver changeth his life, he hath denied himself. The cross of
Christ is taken when despisings for the love of truth are not
forsaken, but taken; when the flesh is punished by abstinence, and when compassion and pity towards our neighbour
is truly kept; when man is crucified to the world, and the
world crucified to him, setting the joy thereof at nought. . . .

But let us not make so sure of the Lord's mercy, that we
heap sins upon sins; neither say we while youth endureth,
Let us follow our desires, and at the last, in age do penance
for our sins, for the Lord is merciful, he shall not have mind
of our sins. Lord Jesus, turn us to thee, and then we shall be
turned. Heal thou us, and we shall be truly whole. For without thy grace and help no man may be truly turned or
healed. For they are but scorners who today turn to God,

and tomorrow turn away. What is turning to God? None but turning from the world, from sin, and from the fiend. What is turning from God? None but turning to the changeable goods of this world, to pleasing likeness of creatures, to works of the fiend, and to lusts of the flesh. To be turned from the world, is to set at nought, and to put out of mind all likings, joys, and mirths thereof, and to suffer meekly all bitterness, slanders and troubles thereof, for the love of Christ; and to leave all occupations unlawful and unprofitable to the soul, so that man's will and thought be dead to seek any thing that the world seeketh and loveth.

Therefore the prophet speaketh in the person of souls perfectly turning to God, saying, Mine eyes, that is, my thought and intent shall ever be to God. For he shall draw my feet, that is my soul and my affections, out of the snare, and the net of the love of this world. He that is truly turned to God, fleeth from vices, beholdeth not the solaces or comforts of this world; but setteth his mind so steadfastly on God, that he well nigh forgetteth all outward things; he gathereth himself all within; he is reared up wholly into Christ.

Those that will turn truly to Christ must flee occasions, words, sights, and deeds, exciting to sin. For when the fiend seeth one among a hundred who withstandeth his enticings, and turneth to God, and followeth the steps of Christ, by virtues, despising the joys of this present life, and seeking to love everlasting heavenly things, he findeth a thousand frauds to beguile and trouble, and a thousand manner of temptations to cast him down from God's love to the love of the world. And he beginneth at the least, that by foul thoughts he make him to be foul towards God. He bringeth to man's mind the lusts which he hath used before, and telleth to his thought that he may not leave all his worldly and fleshly likings; and saith, It is too hard for a man to put himself from all present mirth. He stirreth up fantasies, and vain thoughts innumerable, and unprofitable affections which before were asleep.

The fiend reareth against such a soul, slanders, backbitings, persecutions, tribulations, false challenges, false accusings of divers sins, and divers manner of hates. One time he tempteth by sharp outward diseases; another time by false glosings and likings, and so forth. He calleth again to mind delight in things loved before. He enflameth the heart and the flesh with foul burnings. He beginneth by small enticings, and pursues to the greatest flame of wickedness. And he studieth thus busily to blow against us all manner of temptations and tribulations, by how much he seeth that by the mercy of God we are escaped out of his power. For he seeketh nothing so much as to separate a man from the holy and everlasting love of Jesus Christ, and to make him love failing things and uncleanness of this world.

OF TEMPTATION
or,
Of Virtuous Patience

HE THAT IS TRULY FED WITH THE BREAD THAT CAME DOWN from heaven, boweth not his love to those things to which the fiend enticeth. Temptations are overcome by patience and meek suffering. What is patience?—a glad and willing suffering of troubles. He that is patient mumurs not at adversity, but rather, at all times, praises God with the prophet.

Evil men always grudge in adversities, and flee them as much as they may. For while they are unmeasurably given to visible things, they are deprived from true hope of everlasting things. They find solace or comfort only in earthly goods, for they have lost the savour of heavenly things. There is no soul of man in this world which cleaveth not either to the Creator or the creature. If he love the creature he loseth God, and goeth to death with that which he loveth. Such love is the beginning of travail and folly, in the middle it is languor and wretchedness, and in the end it is hate and pain. He that truly loveth his Maker refuses in will and liking all things that are in the world. He hath sweetness to speak of him and with him; to think upon his Maker is refreshing to him. He closes his outer senses lest death enter in by the windows, lest he be occupied unprofitably with any vanity. Sometimes there are reared against him despisings, reproofs, scorns, and slanders. Therefore it is needful that he take the shield of patience, and be ready to forget and to forgive all wrongs, and to pray for the turning to good of them that hate him and hurt him. No man is showed to himself whether he be strong or feeble, unless he be tempted when he is at peace. Many men seem to be patient when they are not impugned, but when a light blast, I say not of injustice, but of correction, touches them, their mind presently turns into bitterness and wrath, and if they hear one word against their will, they yield two more sternly again. Into their council come not, O my soul! The darts of the enemy are to be quenched with the meekness and sweetness of the love of Christ. Give not way to temptation, be it ever so grievous. For the greater the battle the more glorious the victory, and the higher the crown. Blessed is the man that suffereth temptation, for when he is proved to be true, he shall take a crown of life. Flee as much as thou canst the praising of men. Despise favour, worship, and all vain glory, and gladly sustain or suffer enmities, hates, backbitings, or reproofs. And so by evil fame, and by good praise; by tribulations and gladnesses, cease thou not to press forward to heavenly kingdoms.

When thou art tempted or troubled, think upon the remedy that our Saviour saith in his gospel. Watch ye and pray ye, that ye enter not into temptation. He saith not, Pray ye that ye be not tempted. For it is good and profitable to good men to be tempted and troubled, as is shown by what the prophet saith, To him that is tempted and troubled, God saith, I am with him in tribulation; I shall deliver him, and shall glorify him. Let no man think himself to be holy because he is not tempted, for the holiest and highest in life have the most temptations. How much the higher a hill is, so much is the wind there greater; so, how much higher the life is, so much stronger is the temptation of the enemy. God playeth with his child when he suffereth him to be tempted, as a mother rises from her much beloved child, and hides herself, and leaves him alone, and suffers him to cry, Mother, mother, so that he looks about, cries and weeps for a time, and at last when the child is ready to be overset with troubles and weeping, she comes again, clasps him in her arms, and kisses him, and wipes away the tears. So our Lord suffereth his loved child to be tempted and troubled for a time, and withdraweth some of his solace and full protection, to see what his child will do; and when he is about to be overcome by temptations, then he defendeth him, and comforteth him with his grace. And therefore, when we are tempted, let us cry for the help of our Father, as a child cries after the comfort of its mother. For whoso prayeth devoutly, shall have help oft to pray, and profits much to establish the heart in God, and suffers it not to bow about, now into this, and now into that. The fiend is overcome by busy and devout prayer, and becomes as feeble and without strength to them that are strong and persevering in devout prayers. Devout prayer of a holy soul is as sweet incense which driveth away all evil savours, and enters up by odour of sweetness into the presence of God.

Writings of the Reverend and Learned John Wycliff, D. D.
Philadelphia: Presbyterian Board of Publishers, 1842.

JOHN HUSS

c. 1373 – 1415

JOHN HUSS

AT HIS LIFE'S CLOSE JOHN WYCLIFFE, DESPITE THE SEEMING
defeat of his cause, stood his ground saying, "I believe that
in the end truth will conquer." But the next act in the drama
which he started he could not have guessed. About five years
after Wycliffe's death, John Huss, a Czech, entered the University of Prague in Bohemia and there, discovering Wycliffe through his books, became his lifelong disciple. The sister of King Wenzel of Bohemia had married Richard II of
England, and among the Bohemians who followed her to
her new home were students bound for Oxford. There Wycliffe's writings were the center of excited controversy, and
in returning students' hands they came to Prague. In 1411
Huss wrote that Prague had been reading Wycliffe for
twenty years.

Huss became a lecturer at the University, dean of the faculty of philosophy, and for a time the University's rector,
but it was mainly his popularity as a preacher which made
him, even as a young man, the most conspicuous and influential figure in Bohemia's religious life. He was a devout
priest; his personal character was above reproach; and his
sensitive conscience, strongly influenced by Wycliffe's example, was soon concerned with the corruption of the

37

church. "Our bishops and priests of today," he said in one of his sermons, "and especially our cathedral canons, and lazy mass celebrators, hardly wait for the close of the service to hurry out of church, one part to the tavern and the other part hither and thither to engage in amusements unworthy of a priest. . . . Like Judas, who went away to the High Priest to sell Christ, many of our priests, profligate in their lives like beasts, run away from the table of God, the one to serve Mammon, the other wantonness, the one to the gaming table, the other to the dance or chase, all of which are forbidden to priests. And these very ones who ought to be leaders in imitating Christ are his chief enemies."

Although at first unhampered and heartily supported by the city and the university, Huss was obviously headed for trouble—the more so because he outspokenly defended Wycliffe whom Rome had denounced. In one of his sermons Huss said:

Bohemians are now declared to be heretics—that sacred Bohemian notion of which a proverb declares, "No Bohemian can be a heretic." Here within this city, they say, there are countless heretics whom they term Wycliffists. As for me, I confess before you that I have read and studied the works of Master John Wycliffe, and that I have learned from them much that is good. Truly, not everything I have read is of the same weight with me as the Gospel, for only to the Holy Scriptures will I maintain such reverent obedience; but why should we not study the books of Wycliffe in which are written thousands of sacred truths?

Formal charges were soon made against the Czech preacher; in 1410 over two hundred manuscripts of Wycliffe were burned in the court of the archbishop's palace; the campaign was on to extirpate the English Reformer's influence and to silence Huss. Preaching to a crowded audience Huss defended Wycliffe against what he called the pope's misinformation, and cried to the people: "Behold, I have appealed against the archbishop's decree and do now appeal. Will you stand by me?" And the people shouted, "We will and do stand by you." In consequence, Huss was excommunicated; his contumacy became a *cause célèbre;* but, despite excommunication, Huss continued preaching.

His anti-papal stand was encouraged by the fact that there were then three competing popes, and John XXIII, who was recognized in Bohemia, wanting money for a war against the King of Naples, opened the sale of indulgences in Prague. The character of John XXIII admits of no doubt. The same Council at Constance which sent Huss to the stake deposed John on accusations so heinous that fourteen of the seventy charges were denied public reading. He was deposed for such offenses as selling high ecclesiastical offices to children, selling the head of John the Baptist for fifty thousand ducats, for adultery with his brother's wife, for the rape of nuns and for sodomy. The emissaries of this pope came to Prague to sell indulgences, and Huss rebelled. "So far as the mandates of the Roman pontiff are . . . according to the rule of Christ," he said to the papal delegates, "so far I intend most certainly to obey them. But if I find them to be at variance, I will not obey them, even if you put before my eyes fire for the burning of my body." When, in consequence, the sentence of aggravated excommunication was pronounced against Huss, and the whole city of Prague was placed under papal interdict, Huss, at the king's request, retired from the town for two years and wrote his greatest work, *The Treatise on the Church.*

Huss' stand was not identical with Wycliffe's. He did not stress the privilege of ascetic poverty; he gave a more generous place to tradition; he distinguished more clearly a man's character from his office, and did not come so near saying that a wicked man has no rights at all. Fundamentally, however, the two agreed. The pope is not infallible; if he lives in sin he is no true pope at all; and in matters of faith and discipline he may err like other men. "To rebel against an erring pope," Huss wrote, "is to obey Christ." The power

of pope and priest to absolve from sin is limited; the absolution is void save as the recipient stands in God's grace, for
only God can absolve. The true church is not the papal ecclesiastical establishment, but—so Huss wrote—"is the number
of all the elect and the mystical body of Christ, whose head
Christ is; and the bride of Christ, whom of his great love he
redeemed with his own blood." The state has the right and
duty to supervise the church. Huss called on the kings of
Bohemia and Poland to stop the sale of clerical positions,
and thus, like Wycliffe, appealing to secular rulers to correct
ecclesiastical abuses, was guilty of what one Roman Catholic
scholar called "an error most pernicious and scandalous,
inducing laymen to perpetrate sacrilege, and subversive of
the liberty of the church."

Behind all else in Huss' teaching stood his devotion to the
Scriptures as the ultimate guide of life and thought. Here we
run decisively upon one of the major issues dividing Roman
Catholicism from the whole movement which issued in the
Protestant Reformation. According to Roman dogma one did
not believe in the church because the Scriptures say so, but
believed in the Scriptures because the church says so. When
Prierias answered Luther's Theses, he put the matter unmis-
takably: "Whoso does not rest upon the doctrine of the Roman church and the Roman pope as an infallible rule of
faith, *from which even the Holy Scriptures derive their
authority,* he is a heretic." A century before Luther, Huss
broke with that position. To him the Scriptures were primary
and authoritative. He said that, when he stood before the
judgment seat of Christ, he hoped it would be found that
he had not denied a single iota of what the Scriptures taught.
This issue was becoming crucial in Huss' time, because the
Bible was being translated into the vernacular of the people.
At first the Roman church had been apathetic concerning
this oncoming popular availability of the Scriptures, but in
1408 Archbishop Arundel struck a warning note. Calling Wycliffe "that pestilent writer of damnable memory," he pro-

nounced his "wickedness" to be that "he prepared a new translation of the Scriptures into his mother tongue." On this point, with all its implications, Huss was a Wycliffite.

So the drama of John Huss moved to its tragic ending. The Council of Constance condemned him as a heretic and he, refusing to retract, was burned at the stake. He had been long prepared for this cruel conclusion. "It is better to die well than to live ill," he wrote. "One should not flinch before the sentence of death. To finish the present life in grace is to go away from pain and misery. He who fears death loses the joy of life. Above all else truth triumphs. He conquers who dies, because no adversity can hurt the one over whom iniquity holds not sway."

The Czech word, *hus*, means goose, and one of John Huss' friends, writing about him from Constance, said that the Goose was not yet cooked. Five centuries afterwards we still use that phrase in our vernacular, having long since forgotten its origin. That friend told the truth about Huss—his goose was not cooked. Bohemia rose in fury at the news of his execution. The Hussites, despite military crusades against them and merciless persecution, were never crushed out. In Luther's day they were largely absorbed into the general body of Protestants, and later the Bohemian Brethren and the Moravians stemmed out from them.

Those who would know more fully the story of John Huss and what he stood for should read such books as *Wiclif and Hus*, by Johann Loserth, *John Huss*, by David S. Schaff, and *John Hus and the Czech Reform*, by Matthew Spinka.

From

THE TREATISE ON
THE CHURCH

IF HE WHO IS TO BE CALLED PETER'S VICAR FOLLOWS IN the paths of virtue, we believe that he is his true vicar and the chief pontiff of the church over which he rules. But, if he walks in the opposite paths, then he is the legate of antichrist at variance with Peter and Jesus Christ. Therefore, St. Bernard writes as follows: "Among these things thou walkest in the van, a shepherd overornamented with gold . . . Not in this way did Peter act, or Paul frisk about." And he adds: "Either deny to the people that thou art shepherd or show thyself such. He is Peter who is not known to go about in processions, ornamented with gems or silks, not clad in gold or carried by a white horse, or compassed about with soldiers, and surrounded by bustling servants. Without such things, Peter believed he was able to fulfil sufficiently the salutary commandment: 'If thou lovest me, feed my sheep.' In things like these thou hast followed not Peter, but Constantine." Thus far Bernard.

That holy man knew that Pope Eugenius ought to be a vicar in poverty and humility, not in pride but in feeding the sheep, following Peter. For that man is a true vicar of him whose place he fills and from whom he has lawfully received the procuratorial power. But no one can truly and acceptably to Christ rule in Christ's stead or the stead of Peter without following him in his life. . . . Thus there is required for such an office as that of vicar conformity of life and authority from the person instituting it, and to such a vicar the Saviour at the Last Supper committed the institution of the venerable sacrament. And constituting his disciples his vicars that they might so do in remembrance of him, he said: "I have given you an example that ye also should do as I have done to you," John 13 : 15. He also said: "Whosoever shall do and teach them he shall be called great in the kingdom of heaven," Matt. 5 : 19.

On this point St. Jerome says: "It is not easy to fill the place of Peter and Paul in occupying the chair of those who reign with Christ, because it was said, 'they are not the children of saints who hold the places of saints, but they who do their good works.'" St. Gregory says the same: "Neither places nor orders make us near to our Creator, but our good works bind us together or our evil works separate us." Likewise Chrysostom says: "Many priests there are, and few; many in name, and few in works. See, therefore, how ye sit in the official chair, for the chair does not make the priest, but the priest makes the chair: the place does not sanctify the man, but the man the place. Not every priest is holy; but every holy person is a priest. He who sits well in the official chair gives honor to the chair; he who sits there ill does injury to it. Therefore a bad priest gets criminality from his priesthood, not dignity.". . .

The words which Christ said to Peter, "Verily I say unto you whatsoever ye shall bind on earth shall be bound in heaven, and whatsoever ye shall loose on earth shall be loosed in heaven," because of misunderstanding, frighten many Christians so that they are filled with servile fear, while others are deceived by them and grow proud because of the fulness of their supposed power. Therefore, the following things are to be laid down: first, that it is not possible for a priest to loose or bind anything, unless such loosing and binding takes place in heaven; second that for the

justification of the wicked man there is needed infinite power
by which God cleanses from spot and stain and grants
grace. . . .

The ignorant think that the priest binds and looses in time
first and after him God. It is folly to have this opinion.
God's act of binding or loosing is absolutely first. And it is
evident, it would be blasphemy to assert that a man may
remit an offense done to so great a Lord, without the Lord
himself approving the remission. For by the universal law
and practice followed by the Lord, He himself must loose or
bind first, if any vicar looses or binds. And for us no article
of the faith ought to be more certain than the impossibility
of any one of the church militant to absolve or bind except
in so far as he is conformed to the head of the church, our
Lord Jesus Christ.

Hence, the faithful should be on his guard against this
form of statement: "If the pope or any other pretends that
he binds or looses by a particular sign, then by that fact the
offender is loosed or bound." For by conceding this, they
have to concede that the pope is impeccable as is God, for
otherwise he is able to err and to misuse the key of Christ.
And it is certain that as impossible as it is for the figure of
a material key to open anything when the substance is wanting, so impossible is it for Christ's vicar to open or shut
except as he conforms himself to the key of Christ which
first opens or shuts. For just as Christ the firstborn of many
brethren and the first-fruits of them that sleep was the first
to enter the kingdom, so he alone and above all could have
had committed to him the spiritual kingdom. And the same
is to be said in regard to any opening or closing whatever
which pertains to the heavenly country. And it is plain that
every vicar of Christ, so long as he continues to walk in this
world, may err, even in those things which concern the faith
and the keys of the church, as those knew who wrote the

Chronicles; for Peter himself, Christ's first vicar, sinned in these regards.

Likewise, God is the only being who cannot be ignorant as to whose sins may be remitted, and He the only being who cannot be moved by a wrong motive and judge unjust judgment. But any vicar may be ignorant as to whose sins ought to be remitted, and he may be moved by a wrong motive in binding or loosing. Therefore, if he refuse to impart absolution to one truly penitent and confessing, moved by anger or greed, he cannot by his act bind such a person in guilt. Similar would be the case with the one who came with a lying confession, as happens very often, and the priest, not knowing his hypocrisy, should impart to him the words of absolution. Undoubtedly he does not thereby absolve, for the Scriptures say, Wisdom of Solomon 1 : 4: "The Holy Spirit evades a feigned act of worship." In the first case, just noted, the vicar alleges that he bound or forgave sins and did not; and in the second case he alleges that he loosed or remitted sins and did not. And it is evident how great the illusion may be of those who administer the keys and of those who do not truly repent. For it is necessary that a person, wishing to be absolved, be first so disposed in his will that he is sorry for his guilt, and then have the purpose to sin no more. Hence, all priests combined—who are at the same time vicars—are not able to absolve from sins him who wishes to go on sinning and who does not wish to lament his sins.

So all together are not able to bind a righteous man or retain his sins when he humbles himself with his whole heart and has a contrite heart, a thing which God does not despise. Wherefore St. Jerome, commenting on Matt. 16 : 19, "I will give unto thee the keys of the kingdom of heaven, and whatsoever thou shalt loose on earth shall be loosed in heaven," etc., says: "Some, not understanding this passage, appropriate something of the arrogance of the Pharisees so as to think

that they can damn the guiltless and loose offenders, for
with God not the judgment of priests is sought but the life
of the guilty." To these words the Master of Sentences adds:
"Here it is plainly shown, that God does not follow the
sentence of the church which judges in ignorance and deceit-
fully." He also adds, "Sometimes he who is sent out-
doors, that is, outside the holy church, by the priests is,
nevertheless, inside. And he who, by virtue of the truth,
is outside, seems to be kept inside by the priest's false sentence." And again he says: That the priest who binds and
looses others ought himself to be prudent and just, for otherwise he will put to death souls who do not die and revive souls
which do not live, and in this way he turns his power of pro-
nouncing judgment into an instrument of cursing—so that it
is said in Mal. 2 : 2: "I will bless your cursings and curse your
blessings." Therefore the vicars of Christ ought to take heed
that they do not lightly presume to bind or loose whenever it
pleases them. . . .

The aforesaid doctors* laid down in their writing that "the
pope is the head of the Roman church and the college of
cardinals the body, and that they are very successors and
princes of the apostle Peter and the college of Christ's other
apostles in ecclesiastical office for the purpose of defining all
catholic and church matters, correcting and purging all errors
in respect to them and, in all these matters, to have the care
of all the churches and of all the faithful of Christ. For in
order to govern the church throughout the whole world it is
fitting there should always continue to be such manifest and
true successors in the office of Peter, the prince of apostles,
and of the college of the other apostles of Christ. And such
successors cannot be found or procured on the earth other
than the pope, the existing head, and the college of cardinals,
the existing body, of the aforesaid Roman church."

These follies, long drawn out, which, I think, proceeded
for the most part from the brain of Stanislaus, overcome

* Antagonists of Huss, named in an omitted passage.

and terrified by the Roman curia, involve many points. And in regard to these, I note that in their writing the church is taken to mean all Christian pilgrims. They seem to admit this when they say that "the body of the clergy in the kingdom of Bohemia, not only with the whole body of clergy in the world but also with the whole body of Christendom, always feels and believes as the faith dictates, just as the Roman church does." Or, secondly, these doctors call the pope, together with his cardinals, alone the Roman church, when they say that they believe just as the Roman church believes and not otherwise, the pope being the head of the Roman church and the cardinals the body. In these ways only, so far as I can see, do the doctors designate the church in their writing.

I assume that the pope stands for that spiritual bishop who in the highest way and in the most similar way, occupies the place of Christ, just as Peter did after the ascension. But if any person whatsoever is to be called pope —whom the Western church accepts as Roman bishop— appointed to decide, as the final court, ecclesiastical cases and to teach the faithful whatever he wishes, then there is an abuse of the term, because according to this view it would be necessary in cases to concede that the most unlettered layman or a female, or a heretic and antichrist, may be pope. This is plain, for Constantine II, an unlettered layman, was suddenly ordained a priest and through ambition made pope and then was deposed and all the things which he ordained were declared invalid, about A. D. 707. And the same is plain from the case of Gregory, who was unlettered and consecrated another in addition to himself. And as the people were displeased with the act, a third pope was superinduced. Then these quarrelling among themselves, the emperor came to Rome and elected another as sole pope. . . .

As for a heretic occupying the papal chair we have an instance in Liberius, of whom Castrensis writes, that at Constantius's demand he was exiled for three years because he wished to favor the Arians. At the council of the same Constantius, the Roman clergy ordained Felix pope who, during the sessions of a synod condemned and cast out two Arian presbyters, Ursacius and Valens, and when this became known, Liberius was recalled from exile, and being wearied by his long exile and exhilarated by the reoccupation of the papal chair, he yielded to heretical depravity; and when Felix was cast down, Liberius with violence held the church of Peter and Paul and St. Lawrence so that the clergy and the priests who favored Felix were murdered in the church, and Felix was martyred, Liberius not preventing.

As for an antichrist occupying the papal chair, it is evident that a pope living contrary to Christ, like any other perverted person, is called by common consent antichrist. In accordance with John 2 : 22, many are become antichrists. And the faithful will not dare to deny persistently that it is possible for the man of sin to sit in the holy place. Of him the Saviour prophesied, which is spoken of by Daniel, "standing in the holy place," Matt. 24 : 15. The apostle also says: "Let no man beguile you in any wise, for it will not be except the falling away come first and the man of sin be revealed, the son of perdition; he that opposeth and exalteth himself against all that is called God or is worshipped; so that he sitteth in the temple of God setting himself forth as God," II Thess. 2 : 3-4. And it is apparent from the *Chronicles* how the papal dignity has sunk. . . .

In regard to these follies of the unlearned, I find these points: (1) The pope is the head of the holy Roman church. (2) The college of cardinals is the body of the holy Roman church. (3) The pope is manifestly and truly the successor of the prince of the apostles, Peter. (4) Cardinals are manifest and true successors of the college of Christ's other apostles. (5) For the government of the church throughout the whole world, there should always be manifest and true successors of the same kind in the office of the prince of the apostles and in the office of Christ's other apostles. (6) Such successors are not to be found or procured on the earth, other than the pope, the existing head and the college of cardinals, the existing body of the church.

Against all these six points, the argument in brief runs thus: all truth in the religion of Christ is to be followed and only that is truth which is known by the bodily senses, or discovered by an infallible intelligence or known through revelation, or laid down in divine Scripture. Therefore, none of these six points is truth in the religion of Jesus Christ. . . .

No pope is the manifest and true successor of Peter, the prince of the apostles, if in morals he lives at variance with the principles of Peter; and if he is avaricious, then is he the vicar of Judas, who loved the reward of iniquity and sold Jesus Christ. And by the same kind of proof the cardinals are not the manifest and true successors of the college of Christ's other apostles unless the cardinals live after the manner of the apostles and keep the commands and counsels of our Lord Jesus Christ. For, if they climb up by another way than by the door of our Lord Jesus Christ, then are they thieves and robbers, just as the Saviour himself declared when of all such he said: "All that came before me are thieves and robbers," John 10 : 8. Whosoever, therefore, say that they are Christ's true and manifest vicars, knowing that they are living in sin, lie. Therefore the apostle says: How "do they of the synagogue of Satan say that they are Jews, and they are not, but lie"? (Rev. 2 : 9.)

Hence if the cardinals heap up to themselves ecclesiastical livings and barter with them and take money for their sale either themselves or through others, and so devour and consume in luxurious living the goods of the poor, and if they do not do miracles or preach the Word of God to the people or pray sincerely or fill the place of deacons, whom the apostles appointed, Acts 6—by not performing their duties or living their lives—in how far, I ask, are they the vicars of the apostles? In *this*, that they heap up livings or, like Gehazi, seize upon gifts, or because very early in the morning they come into the pope's presence clad in the most splendid apparel, and attended with the most sumptuous retinue of horsemen—thus attended, not on account of the distance of place or difficulty of the journey but to show their magnificence to the world and their contrariety to Christ and his apostles, who went about among the towns, cities and castles clad in humble garb, on foot, preaching the kingdom of God. . . .

Concerning the testimony of the doctors who treat of the pope's power, it is alleged, that all who thus magnify the pope's power and say that he can do without guilt whatsoever he wills and that nobody has the right to ask why he does this or that—all these are mendacious rhetoricians, leading the people of our Lord Jesus Christ astray. Nor ought such to be believed except as their words are founded in Scripture. For thus the great doctor, Augustine, often asserted of himself that he ought to be believed only so far as he had grounded himself in Scripture. It is evident, that God may give other successors of the apostles than the pope and the cardinals, just as he was able to give others in the place of the pontiffs of the old law, the scribes and the Pharisees with their traditions. And to these, who did not keep God's law, the Lord said: "I say unto you the kingdom of heaven shall be taken away from you and shall be given to a nation bringing forth the fruits thereof," Matt. 21 : 43. These words the Saviour spoke to the priests when they alone bore sentence against themselves in that they said: "He will miserably destroy these wicked men and will let out the vineyard to other husbandmen who shall render him the fruits in their seasons." How, therefore, is the hand of the Lord shortened that He is not able to cast out the pope and the cardinals and appoint others in their places who, though they have no titles, will build up the church as the Lord did with the apostles?

Likewise all bishops of Christ's church who follow Christ in their lives, they are true vicars of the apostles and they are not pope or cardinals. Therefore, other true successors of the apostles can be found and given besides the pope and the cardinals. . . .

Here it becomes us to consider the two sects of the clergy, namely, the clergy of Christ and the clergy of antichrist. Christ's clergy rests in its head, Christ, and in his law; but antichrist's clergy rests wholly or chiefly on human laws and the laws of antichrist, and yet it is clothed upon, like the clergy of Christ and the church, with the design that the people may be led astray by its simulation. And so it is fitting that these two things which are so contrary to each other obey two contrary heads with their laws. The outward evidence teaches the class to which the members belong. Indeed, it is established that the clergy of the church falls away into two parts and for this reason laymen cannot help but waver who are borne along by those who are so different from Christ in opinion and in life.

But these parts may commonly be best discerned from the fact that the clergy of antichrist is zealously intent upon human traditions and rights which savor of pride and the greed of this world, and that it wishes to live ostentatiously and in pleasure in a way contrary to Christ, wholly neglecting the imitation of the Lord Jesus Christ in its living. But Christ's clergy labors diligently for Christ's laws and his rights, whereby spiritual good is acquired that it may be shown, and it flees pride and the pleasure of this world, and seeks to live in conformity with Christ, giving itself up most zealously, following the Lord Jesus Christ. Nor is it right for the faithful to doubt that this part is the true clergy, and the other part is the false. And although in the absence of revelation, the pilgrim is not able clearly and with certainty to determine who the holy pastor really is, nevertheless we ought to decide by his works, which are conformed to Christ's law, that he is such a pastor. . . .

As for the principal thing according to which they believe all their sayings to be necessary or true, the aforementioned doctors lay down that "obedience is due to the apostolic see and to prelates from inferiors in all things whatsoever, where the purely good is not prohibited or the purely evil commanded, but also in that which is intermediate, which, in view of the mode, place, time or person, may be either good or bad in accordance with the Saviour's statement, Matt. 23 : 2: 'Whatsoever they bid you, these do and observe.' "

And they add: "But some of the clergy in the kingdom of Bohemia refuse to agree to this, endeavoring, as much as in them lies, to lead the faithful people to disobedience towards prelates and to irreverence towards the papal, episcopal, sacerdotal and clerical dignities, not giving attention to that which St. Augustine says in the words (Sermon 8): 'If thou hast fasted, hast made prayer night and day, if thou hast been in ashes or begging, if thou hast done nothing else except what is prescribed for thee in the law and thou hast been wise in thine own sight and not obedient to thy father —understand, not bodily father, but spiritual—thou hast lost all virtues. Therefore obedience is worth more than all the other moral virtues.' "

By the combination of the above sayings the doctors mix up the false with the true, flattery with fear, and these three things are involved in these words: "Certain of the clergy" —here having in mind our party—"refuse to agree to this, endeavoring as much as in them lies to lead the faithful people to disobedience." See what a false lie this is, by which they indicate that we are become seducers of the people, when it is (1) not the purpose of our side to seduce the people from real obedience, but that the people may be one, governed harmoniously by the law of Christ. (2) The purpose of our side is that the rules of antichrist shall not seduce the people from Christ, but that the law of Christ shall honestly rule in connection with the customs of the people so far as they are approved by God's law. (3) The purpose of our side is that the clergy live honestly according to the doctrine of Jesus Christ, laying aside pomp, avarice and luxury. (4) Our side wishes and preaches that the church militant, in its different parts which God has ordained, be honestly commingled, namely, of Christ's priests those who administer his law in purity, and from the world the nobles who press for the observance of the ordinances of Christ and the common people, both these parts serving in accordance with Christ's law. Therefore, let the doctors bestow this wrong on our side. But the flattery which they show to prelates and the fear with which they would affright our side are involved in the words: "endeavouring to lead the faithful people to disobedience towards prelates, and irreverence towards the papal, episcopal, sacerdotal and clerical dignities." Blessed be Christ Jesus that they have not dared to lay on us the calumny of disobedience to Jesus Christ—or perhaps they have forgotten to do so, for to serve him is to reign, and obedience rendered to him avails so much that is of no advantage to obey any one except in so far as such obedience is obedience to our God. . . .

Therefore, Christ's faithful disciple ought to consider how a command emanates from the pope, whether it is the express command of any apostle or of Christ's law or whether it has its foundation in Christ's law, and this being known to be the case, he ought to obey a command of this kind reverently and humbly. But, if he truly knows that a pope's command is at variance with Christ's command or counsel or tends to any hurt of the church, then he ought boldly to resist it lest he become a partaker in crime by consent.

For this reason, trusting in the Lord and in Christ Jesus,

who mightily and wisely protects the professors of his truth and rewards them with the prize of never-ending glory, I withstood the bull of Alexander V, which Lord Zbynek, archbishop of Prague, secured, 1409, and in which he commands that there should be no more preaching of sermons to the people by any priest whatsoever—even though he might be fortified with an apostolic instrument taking precedence of such a mandate or by any other written instrument—except in cathedrals, parochial or cloistral churches or in their cemeteries. This mandate, being contrary to the words and deeds of Christ and his apostles, is not apostolic, for Christ preached to the people on the sea, in the desert, in the fields and houses, in synagogues, in villages and on the streets, and taught his disciples, saying: "Go ye into all the world and preach the Gospel to every creature," Mark 16 : 15. And these, going forth, preached everywhere, that is, in every place where the people were willing to listen, God working with them. Therefore, this command is to the hurt of the church, and binds the Word of God, that it should not run freely. And, in the third place, it is prejudicial to the chapels which are erected and have with reason been confirmed by diocesans, and have been furnished with privileges by the apostolic see for the preaching of God's Word in them. For no advantage whatever can be seen to accrue from that command, but it is a fallacious and faithless irony, because the places set apart for divine worship and furnished with privileges for the preaching of the divine Word are deprived of their lawful liberties on account of some personal feeling or of some injurious appeal or some importunity, or on account of some temporal good. Hence, I appealed from that command of Alexander to Alexander himself, better informed. And while I was prosecuting the appeal, that Lord pope suddenly died. And, no audience being allowed me in the Roman curia, the Lord Zbynek, archbishop of Prague, secured papers aggravating the censure against me, from which, A. D. 1410, I appealed to Pope John XXIII, and he during two years did not grant audience to my legal advocates and solicitors. In the meantime I was weighed down still more by ecclesiastical proceedings. When, therefore, my appeal from one pope to his successor did not profit me and to appeal from the pope to a council involves long waiting and because it is of uncertain advantage to beg for grace in the matter of a grievance and censure, therefore I appealed finally to the head of the church, Jesus Christ. For he is superior to any pope whatever in deciding a case: he cannot err, nor to a suppliant, rightfully begging, can he deny justice, nor is he able in view of his law to condemn a man who in the sight of his law is without demerit. . . .

It is clear that the pope may err, and the more grievously because, in a given case, he may sin more abundantly, intensely and irresistibly than others, as said Bernard in his book addressed to Pope Eugenius: "More abundantly if the sin extends to all Christendom, more intensely if his act concerns the cure of souls and involves the withdrawal of spiritual benefits, and more irresistibly if no one dares to gainsay him, now in view of his alliance with the secular arms, now in view of the cloaked censures which he fulminates against the children of obedience, now in view of promotions and ecclesiastical dignities which he provides for his accomplices. Hence, as the papal office, when it profits the church, is the most deserving, so, when the papal office is perverted in that man who abuses his office, if it do injury to the church, is most undeserving. The evidence of a pope's defect is if he put aside the law and a devout profession of the Gospel and give heed to human tradition." It was on this subject that Bernard was reasoning with Eugenius.

This is the first mark. The second is when the pope and ecclesiastical superiors abandon the manner of life Christ followed and are involved in a secular way in things of the world. The third mark is when the pope advances the traffickers of this world in the ministry of Christ and gives himself up chiefly to the continued pursuit of the secular life so that the poor churches are oppressed. The fourth mark is when, by his own command or through the appointment of incapable persons in the pastoral cure, he deprives souls that are to be saved of the Word of God. . . .

The killing and driving to perdition of Christ's sheep are the two worst sins, although they may be distinguished, even as the making alive of the sheep by grace and their glorification are the two best things for the sheep, although different, and to them the killing and the destroying are opposites. And as killing is the opposite of making alive and murder of glorification, it follows that by as much as these two sins are more serious by so much are they opposed to the good things which are more excellent. And, as God himself is the cause of these good things, it follows that by as much as the killers and murderers of the sheep are worse than others, by so much are the killing and murdering of the sheep the worse sins. And it is clear that those who kill souls are the worst servants of antichrist and Satan.

In view of these things it is to be held that to rebel against an erring pope is to obey Christ the Lord. . . .

All rational creatures, according to the method practiced by the Roman curia, are subject to the curia's command, for every human creature is subject to the Roman pontiff, so it is said in the *Extravagante* of Boniface VIII (the bull *Unam sanctum*), namely: "Further we declare, say and define that it is altogether necessary for salvation for every human creature to be subject to the Roman pontiff." Similarly, the angelic world is subject to the Roman pontiff, as appears in the bull of Pope Clement: "We command the angels of paradise that they lead to the glory of paradise the soul of him who has been wholly absolved from purgatory."

Since, therefore, according to this method of the curia, every rational creature—angel or man—is subject to the commands of the Roman pontiff, and since the method in the processes of the same curia states that "whatsoever place, privileged or unprivileged, to which John Huss shall go, and as long as he may be there, we do subject them to the ecclesiastical interdict," it follows that if, by the highest possibility, John Huss, according to God's absolute power, reached by death the heavenly Jerusalem, that city would be subject to the ecclesiastical interdict. But blessed be God Almighty, who has ordered that the angels and all the saints in that heavenly Jerusalem are not subject to an interdict of this sort! Blessed also be Christ, the chief Roman pontiff, who has given grace to his faithful ones that, when there is no Roman pontiff for a given time, they may, under Christ as their leader, arrive in the heavenly country! For who would say that while the woman Agnes, to all appearances, was for two years and five months the only pope, no one could be saved? Or again, who would say that after a pope's death and in the interval between the pope's death and the election of his successor, no man dying in that period could be saved? Blessed also be God Almighty, who ordains that His militant church shall have such life that, when a pope is dead, she is not on that account without a head or dead! Because not upon the pope but upon the head, Christ, does her life depend. And blessed be God that, when a pope is insane or becomes a heretic, the church militant remains the faithful spouse of the Lord Jesus Christ! Blessed also be the Lord, the one living head of the church, who preserves her so effectually in unity that, even now, while there are three so-called papal heads, she remains the one spouse of the Lord Jesus Christ!

The Church, by John Huss,
Translated by David S. Schoff.
New York: Chas. Scribner's Sons, 1915.

VARIOUS LETTERS

TO ZAWYSSIUS, HIS CALUMNIATOR

GRACE TO YOU AND PEACE FROM OUR LORD JESUS CHRIST. IT
has come to my ears that you have accused me of heresy. If
this be true, send me word, and you shall know then, by the
grace of God, what is the faith which I confess, which I defend, which I do not dissemble in the shade, but which I
profess as becomes a true Christian. And, would that your
eyes might be opened to the manner in which, for nearly
thirty years, you have shorn your flock in Praschatitz. Where
do you dwell? How do you labor? How do you feed your
flock? You have forgotten these words of the Lord:—"Woe
unto the shepherds, who only care for themselves, and do not
feed their sheep!" Tell me, I pray you, are you penetrated
with that part of the gospel of Christ, which says—
"The good shepherd goeth before his sheep, and his sheep
follow him; for they know his voice." The time will come
when you must render an account of your sheep and of your
numerous benefices, concerning which it is said in your own
ordinances, that he who can live upon one, cannot retain another without committing a mortal sin.

Meditate then, on these things, and accuse not your neighbor of heresy. If you know him to be a heretic, you ought to
warn him, according to the Apostle's precept, a first and a

second time; if he refuse to listen to you, avoid him; and even should you be chosen to condemn him, still you must demonstrate by the Scriptures, that you condemn him justly, and deliver over his books to the flames.

I write you these few lines, to warn you fraternally, according to the precept of Christ, which tells us:—"If thy brother has just sinned, warn him in secret." Receive, then, my words, and declare, if you have thus spoken of me. Prove that I am a heretic, and I will, with humility, correct myself, and you shall receive a reward for having rescued a man from error. Nevertheless, I hope by the grace of Almighty God, that my faith in our Lord Jesus Christ is as great as yours, and that I am not less prepared to die for it with humility.

TO HIS FRIENDS, CONCERNING
HIS FURIOUS RECEPTION BY
THE COUNCIL OF CONSTANCE
1415

I, Master John Huss, in hope, servant of Christ, and ardently believing that believers in Christ may not, when I shall have ceased to live, find in my death an opportunity for scandal, and look on me as an obstinate heretic, do take to witness Jesus Christ, for the sake of whose word I have wished to die; and I leave in writing the remembrance of these things for the friends of truth.

I had often declared, both in private, in public, and before the Council, that I would consent to an inquiry, and would submit myself to instruction, abjuration, and punishment, if it was demonstrated to me that I had written, taught, or disseminated, any thing contrary to the truth. But fifty doctors, who stated that they were deputed by the Council, having been frequently corrected by me, and even in public, for having falsely extracted articles from my works, refused me any private explanation, and declared that they would not confer with me, saying, You ought to submit yourself to the decision of the Council. And the Council mocked when, in the public audience, I quoted the words of Christ and the holy doctors; at one time they reproached me with misunderstanding them, and, at another, the doctors insulted me.

An English doctor, who had already said to me in private, that Wycliffe had wished to annihilate all science, and had filled his books and his logic with errors, began to discourse on the multiplication of the body of Christ in the consecrated host, and, as his arguments were weak, he was told to be silent; then he cried out: "This man deceives the Council; take care that the Council be not led into error as it was by Berenger." When he was silent, another discussed noisily concerning the created and common essence. All began to clamor against him. I then demanded that he might be heard, and said to him, "You argue well; I will answer you most willingly." He also broke down, and he added in a sullen voice: "This man is a heretic." The Seignior Wenceslaus Duba, John de Chlum, and Peter, the notary, valiant champions and friends of the truth, know what clamors, what unworthy raillery and blasphemies were poured upon me in this assembly. Stunned by so much, I said, "I thought there was to be found in this Council, more decency, more piety, and more discipline." All then began to listen, for the Emperor had commanded silence to be observed.

The cardinal who presided said to me—"You spoke more humbly in your prison." I answered—"It is true; for then no one clamored against me, and now they are all vociferous." He added—"Will you submit to an investigation?" "I consent to it," replied I, "within the limits which I have fixed." "Take this for the result of the inquiry," resumed the cardinal, "that the doctors have declared the articles extracted from your books to be errors, which you ought to efface, in abjuring those already testified against you by witnesses." The Emperor afterwards said—"This will soon be committed to writing for you, and you will answer it." "Let that be done at the next audience," said the cardinal; and the sitting closed. God knows how many trials I have suffered since!

TO HIS FRIENDS, CONCERNING HIS
INWARD STRUGGLES IN PRISON

1415

The Lord be with you! The warning of the Lord is more precious to me than gold and topaz. I hope, then, in the mercy of Jesus Christ, that he will grant me his spirit, that I may hold fast in the truth. Pray to the Lord; for the spirit is willing and the flesh is weak. May the Almighty God be the reward of my well-beloved Nobles, who with a constant, fervent, and faithful heart, persevere in justice. God will enable them to know the truth in the kingdom of Bohemia. But that they may cling to it, it is necessary they return to Bohemia, forgetting vainglory in order to attach themselves to a King who is neither mortal nor subject to our miseries, but who is the King of Glory, giving eternal life.

Oh! with what sweet pleasure did I press the hand of the Seignior John, who did not blush to offer it to me, an unfortunate man—to me, a heretic, in chains, despised and loudly condemned by all. I shall not much longer hold discourse with you; salute, therefore, our faithful Bohemians.

Paletz came to visit me in prison, and accosted me in my deep distress, by telling me, in presence of the Commissioners, that since the birth of Christ, there had risen no heretic more dangerous than Wycliffe and myself. He further declared, that all those who have listened to my preachings are infected with this heresy, which consists in affirming that the material bread remains in the sacrament of the altar. "O Paletz," I answered, "how cruel are these words! and how much thou sinnest against me. I am about to die; perhaps when I rise from my bed I shall be conducted to the stake.

What reward will they give thee in Bohemia?" I should have perhaps abstained from writing these things, for fear of appearing to hate them.

I have ever kept in mind these words, "Put not your trust in princes"; and this other text, which says, "Cursed is he who trusts in man only."

Be prudent, for the sake of God, whether you should remain in this place, or whether you return; do not carry about you any of my letters, but disperse my writings amongst all our friends.

Learn that I have had a great combat to sustain, in not wondering at my dreams. I dreamed of the Pope's evasion before it took place, and after the event being related, I heard, in the nighttime, the Seignior John say, "The Pope will return to you." I have dreamed of Master Jerome's captivity, but not in what way it should occur; and likewise of the different prisons to which I should be conducted, such as they were afterwards assigned to me, but without any particular details. . . . A multitude of serpents often presented themselves before me, rolled up into a circle, the head forming the tail. I have seen many other things besides.

I write this, not that I consider myself a prophet, or that I should exalt myself, but in order to tell you I have experienced both mental and bodily temptations, as well as great fear of transgressing the precepts of our Lord Jesus Christ. I think now of these words of Jerome, who said to me, "If I go to Constance, I do not believe I shall return thence." A worthy shoe-maker, Andre Polonus, said, whilst bidding me farewell, "May God be with you: I can hardly hope that you will return safe and sound, very dear Master John, you who cling with so much force to truth. May the King, not he of Hungary, but of heaven, bestow on you his blessings for the true and excellent doctrines I have learned from you."

TO HIS FAITHFUL FOLLOWERS
AT HOME IN BOHEMIA

1415

I, John Huss, in hope servant of God, desire, that the believers in Bohemia who love the Lord, may live and die in grace, and at last obtain eternal life.

You who are high in dignity, you who are rich, and you who are poor, you all who are the faithful and well-beloved disciples of the Lord, I conjure you all to obey God, to glorify his word, and to elevate yourselves by listening to his precepts. I conjure you to cling to the divine word, which I have preached according to the law and after the testimony of the saints; I conjure you, if any among you, either in public meetings or in private conversations, have heard any words from me, or read any writings of mine contrary to God's truth, not to attach yourselves to such, although my conscience does not reproach me with having said or written anything of the nature to which I refer. I conjure you besides, if any one has remarked any thing trifling, either in my discourses or my writings, not to imitate me in that, but to pray to God that he may pardon my frivolity; I conjure you to love priests of good morals, and to honor, in preference, those who exert themselves in diffusing the word of God; I conjure you to beware of deceitful men, especially impious priests, of whom the Lord has said, they are outwardly dressed in sheep's clothing, while within they are ravening wolves; I conjure the powerful to treat their poor servants with kindness, and to command them with justice; I conjure citizens to keep a good conscience in their profession, artizans to apply themselves carefully to their callings, and to keep before their eyes the fear of God, and domestics faithfully to serve their masters; I conjure the masters of arts to live honestly, to instruct their pupils faithfully; first of all, teaching them to fear God, afterwards exerting themselves for the glory of God, the good of their country, and their own salvation, and not to attach themselves strongly to mere rules of propriety, whether for the sake of riches, or for worldly honours; I conjure the pupils of the public school, and all scholars, to obey their masters in all lawful things, and to labour with the greatest zeal, in order to advance one day the kingdom of God, their own salvation, and that of other men. I conjure you all to bestow your thanks on the generous noblemen, Wenceslaus Duba, John of Chlum, Henry Plumlovic, Wylem Zagee, Nicholas, and the other Bohemian, Moravian, and Polish Seigniors, who, as zealous defenders of God's truth, opposed this Council with all their power, endeavoring to obtain my deliverance; in particular, I mention Wenceslaus Duba and John of Chlum. Believe all they may report to you, for they were present at the Council on the days when I replied. They know what Bohemians have risen against me; they are acquainted with the unworthy deeds which were imputed to me by them; they are aware how the whole assembly vociferated against me whilst I was answering all the questions that were asked. I conjure you to pray for the King of the Romans, and for your own, and for the Queen, in order that the God of mercy may dwell with them and with you, now and forever.

I write you this letter in my prison and with my fettered hand, expecting after tomorrow my sentence of death, and having an entire confidence in God that He will not forsake me; that He will not suffer me to renounce His word, or abjure errors wickedly ascribed to me by false witnesses. When we shall meet again in a happy eternity you will know with what clemency the Lord deigns to assist me in my cruel trials.

I know nothing concerning Jerome, my faithful friend, unless that he is detained in a wretched prison, waiting, like myself, for death, on account of that faith which he so courageously spread through Bohemia. But the Bohemians, our most cruel adversaries, have delivered us to the power of other enemies and to their chains. Pray to God for them. I conjure you, inhabitants of Prague, above all to love my Chapel of Bethlehem, and to have the word of God preached there, should God permit it. The fury of Satan is stirred up against that place. Seeing that the power of darkness has weakened in it, he has excited the parochial clergy against that temple. I hope God will protect it, and that His word will be preached there with more success by others than by me, a weak and infirm man. Lastly, I conjure you to love one another, to shut out no one from the path of divine truth, and to watch that the upright be not oppressed by violence. Amen.

Written on the night of the Monday before Saint Vitus, and sent by a good and faithful German.

Letters of John Huss, by Emile de Bonnechose,
Translated by Campbell Mackenzie, B. A.
Edinburgh: William Whyte & Co., MDCCCXLVI.

MARTIN LUTHER

1483 – 1546

ONLY BY GRADUAL STAGES DID MARTIN LUTHER COME TO THE full apprehension of the fact that he had precipitated a religious revolution. His profound personal conversion, when the saving truth of justification by faith dawned on him, probably occurred when he was about twenty-five years old. When he was twenty-eight he was a Professor of Sacred Theology, with his close friend, Staupitz, saying of him that he "should discharge for the rest of his life the lectureship at Wittenberg pertaining to him." He was thirty-four when he challenged Tetzel's sale of indulgences, and it was two years later, in his famous debate with the Catholic theologian, John Eck, that he made the definite statement that neither popes nor church councils are infallible.

Even then, however, he neither desired nor intended to disrupt the ancient church. His convinced hope was that the church in general and the pope in particular, when shown the crying evils of ecclesiastical corruption, would correct them. He was no vainglorious, cocksure reformer. Despite his courageous stand at the Diet of Worms, he reveals the anxious self-questioning which preceded his appearance there: "How often has my trembling heart palpitated—are you alone the wise one? Are all the others in error? Have so many centuries walked in ignorance? What if it should be you who err, and drag so many with you into error, to be eternally damned?"

Roman Catholicism, in Luther's day as always, had two aspects—not alone the vast ecclesiastical establishment with its elaborate apparatus of saving observances and sacraments, but the simple, evangelical piety of multitudes of plain people, who found in their faith personal resources of peace, power and hope. Luther had been bred in and was spiritually akin with this popular piety, and he was loyal to it, thought of the church in terms of it, and trusted the church to protect it from prevalent corruptions. Only by slow and reluctant stages did be come to the conviction that he faced a desperate fight, concerning which he wrote at last to Spalatin: "I beg of you, if you have a right feeling for the Gospel, do not think this matter can be carried through without tumult, scandal, or sedition. . . . This is God's war, who did not come to bring peace. . . . You ought to beware of thinking that Christ will achieve things in the earth quietly and softly, when you see that he fought with his own blood, and afterwards all the martyrs."

Luther's defiance of the papacy—he publicly burned the pope's Bull denouncing him—was greeted throughout Germany with tumultuous response, some of it inevitably adverse, but much of it enthusiastic. Aleander, the papal legate, was astonished and disturbed. "The whole of Germany is in full revolt," he wrote, "nine-tenths raise the war-cry, 'Luther!', while the watchword of the other tenth who are indifferent to Luther is 'Death to the Roman curia'."

The man who touched off this upheaval needed stout stuff in his constitution, and Luther measured up to the demand. He was a sturdy character, with immense natural vitality, often rough, rude, boisterous, his resilience inspiriting, his indignation explosive, his courage magnificent. He rightly described himself: "God uses coarse wedges for splitting coarse blocks." Comparing himself with the gentler Melanch-

thon, he said: "I am rough, boisterous, stormy and altogether warlike. I am born to fight against innumerable
monsters and devils. I must remove stumps and stones, cut
away thistles and thorns, and clear the wild forest; but
Master Philip comes along softly and gently, sowing and
watering with joy." There was, to be sure, another side to
Luther—a contagious joviality, sometimes breaking loose into
uproarious humor. He loved music. "I have no pleasure in
any man who despises music," he said. "It is no invention of
ours; it is the gift of God. I place it next to theology." He
was tender-hearted and affectionate, especially toward children: "Never be hard with children. Many a fine character
has been ruined by the stupid brutality of pedagogues. . . .
I was myself flogged fifteen times in one forenoon over the
conjugation of a verb. Punish, if you must, but be kind too,
and let the sugar-plum go with the rod." Deeper than all else
was his personal religious experience and a conscience which
refused compromise. The Roman hierarchy tried on him every device of conciliation and intimidation at its disposal, but
they confronted a resolute, burly, stubborn character who
would not budge.

The understanding of the problem which Luther faced involves emphasis on at least one major matter.

Luther's difficulty was not so much to get a reformation
started as to keep it under control and to save it from wild
extremes. When he returned to Wittenberg from his retreat
at the Wartburg, where his friends had immured him to
protect his life, he found the city in uproar—Carlstadt
and Zwilling teaching radical extravagances, violent image-
smashing afoot, and the Zwickau prophets claiming supernatural revelations which seemed to them infallible. It took
all Luther's powerful influence to bring order out of the
threatened chaos.

This type of problem came to its climax in the Peasants'
War. All Germany was in a revolutionary mood, and the
peasants, oppressed and rebellious, urged their demands

upon their rulers. At first, Luther was sympathetic with their requests but, when violence became imminent, he saw his whole cause in jeopardy. He toured the country pleading with the peasants for restraint, and when despite his efforts the revolt grew worse, he exploded in a vehement tract, *Against the Murdering, Thieving Hordes of Peasants.* Over against Thomas Müntzer's call to the rebels for bloody violence—"Heed not the groans of the godless; they will beg, weep, and entreat you for pity like children. Show them no mercy!"—Luther issued an equally bloodthirsty and pitiless call. "Let every one who can," he wrote, "smite, slay and stab, secretly or openly, remembering that nothing can be more poisonous, hurtful or devilish than a rebel. It is just as when one must kill a mad dog; if you don't strike him, he will strike you, and the whole land with you."

This outrageous tract left an indelible stain on Luther's reputation, and the Peasants' War itself, in which the rebels were mercilessly exterminated, put the fear of revolution—by many identified with the Reformation—into the minds of German rulers. The cause of religious reform was seriously injured, and in Luther's thinking a deep distrust of the common people was engendered which affected him throughout his life, and made Lutheranism for many years inimical to democracy in church and state.

This need which pressed on Luther—to keep his burgeoning reformation steady and to save it from extremes—explains in part his tragic controversy with Zwingli about the Lord's Supper. Zwingli held, as many Protestants hold today, that the Lord's Supper is a sacrament of commemoration, a symbol of Christ's sacrifice, not an actual partaking of his body and blood metaphysically present in the elements. Luther, however, feared this as too radical. He held that when Jesus said, "This is my body," he meant it literally, and by use of scholastic argument he convinced himself that, while the Roman dogma of Transubstantiation was false, so too was Zwingli's position. On the basis of this difference, along with his distrust of the democratic organization of the Swiss churches and his fear that alliance with the Swiss left wing might endanger alliance with the German right wing, Luther broke with Zwingli, and the Lutheran and Swiss movements of reformation were tragically separated.

This pressure which Luther felt to keep the Reformation from dangerous extremes accentuated in him a trend with which all the major Reformers were compelled to deal—dependence on the state to serve the purposes of religion. "The magistracy," said Luther, "has never been so praised since the days of the apostles as by me." If the Reformation were to proceed with decency and order, uncorrupted by wild fanaticisms such as the Anabaptists represented—so Luther thought—the godly prince must furnish the requisite authority. This does not mean that Luther idealized the German rulers. "From the beginning of the world a good prince has been a rare bird," he wrote, "and a pious prince a still rarer one. They are, as a rule, the greatest fools and worst knaves upon earth." Nevertheless, good or bad, he said, "They are the scourges and executioners of God, and He employs them to punish the wicked and to maintain external peace." Moreover, Luther had a strong nationalist strain in him. "I am the prophet of the Germans," he said, and on his lips the phrase "our Germany" was freighted with sincere emotion.

Luther, therefore, on the one side, declined to separate church and state, and, on the other, refusing anything like a theocracy where the church controlled the state, he chose a middle way where the prince should be the "nursing father of the Church," and in the end he placed the church dangerously under the dominion of the state. Nevertheless, Luther himself, seeing the danger, was not at peace about it and, after having often in unmitigated terms denied the right of rebellion against a duly constituted ruler, he qualified, if he did not reverse, his stand. "Since God will have us leave father and mother for his sake," he wrote, "certainly he will have us leave lords for his sake." Violent revolt still seemed to him not permissible, but so, too, was supine obedience to tyranny: "We recognize the authority, but we must rebuke our Pilates in their crime and self-confidence." This question concerning the attitude of Christians to the state and the right of rebellion and war against civil rulers tormented all the German Reformers. "My conscience," wrote Melanchthon, "is disquieted because of this thing; I am half dead with thinking about it."

The long and tangled story of Luther and early Lutheranism may be found in such books as Thomas M. Lindsay's *History of the Reformation*, Vol. I, and James Mackinnon's *Luther and the Reformation*. A *Compend of Luther's Theology*, edited by Hugh T. Kerr, Jr., presents a summary of his teaching; Roland H. Bainton's *Here I Stand* is the best biography of the Reformer which we have in English; and *Luther's Progress to the Diet of Worms*, by Ernest Gordon Rupp, and *Let God be God*, by P. S. Watson, are excellent. Luther has been inevitably a controversial figure. His limitations and mistakes are obvious. He was nothing if not forthright, candid, outspoken, explosive. When his detractors have said their last word, however, he stands out still as the greatest man of his generation. The extent and variety of his labors seem incredible. His powerful preaching, his trenchant and immensely influential writing, his endless achievements in education and organization, his constructive reforms in the church's liturgy, his contributions to hymnology, his invincible energy of character and, permeating all, his faith backed by an indubitable experience of God's presence and power, made him the major driving force in the Reformation's early days. When he died, the greater part of Germany had been won for Protestantism, although stormy days lay ahead.

Our first selection is Luther's famous address before the Diet of Worms. The Roman church, having failed in its endeavors to crush Luther by ecclesiastical censures, turned to the new Emperor, Charles V, for help. Luther was commanded to appear before the diet on April 16, 1521. He obeyed, believing, despite the imperial safe conduct, that he was going to his death. The emperor's hostility was unconcealed. "A single monk," he said, "led astray by private judgment, has set himself against the faith held by all Christians for a thousand years and more, and impudently concludes that all Christians up till now have erred. I have therefore resolved to stake upon this cause all my dominions, my friends, my body and my blood, my life and soul."

Nevertheless, the emperor faced stubborn opposition from many of the German deputies, in whose land, as Aleander, the papal legate said, "every stone and every tree cried out, 'Luther'." The population of Worms crowded the city's streets to welcome his arrival; he was the popular hero of the hour; and the next morning when, through thronged streets, he went to his first appearance before the diet, General Frundsberg, the outstanding soldier of Germany, clapped him on the shoulder, saying: "My poor monk! my little monk! Thou art on thy way to make a stand such as I and many of my knights have never done in our toughest battles."

At his first appearance before the diet he was faced with the charge of heresy, based on his writings, and was asked whether he would acknowledge that the books which bore his name were his and whether he would recant his errors. He acknowledged the books—"I will never deny any of them"— but, as for confessing errors, he asked time to consider, and was given until the next day. What he said then revealed the man, and made momentous history.

LUTHER'S REPLY AT THE

DIET OF WORMS

On the Second Day of His Appearance

MOST SERENE LORD EMPEROR, MOST ILLUSTRIOUS PRINCES, MOST
Clement Lords: I now present myself obediently at the time
set yesterday evening for my appearance. By the mercy of
God, Your Most Serene Majesty and Your Most Illustrious
Lordships, I pray that you will deign to listen leniently to
this my cause, which is, I hope, one of justice and truth.
Should I through my inexperience not accord to any one his
just titles, or should I err in any way in the matter of customs and courtly manners, may you benignly overlook such
mistakes in a man not brought up in palaces, but in monastic
seclusion. As concerns myself, I can bear witness to this
point only—that hitherto I have taught and written in simplicity of mind, having in view only the glory of God and
the sincere instruction of Christian believers.

Most Serene Emperor, and Most Illustrious Princes: As
to the two articles yesterday presented to me by Your Most
Serene Majesty—namely, whether I would acknowledge the
books edited and published in my name as mine, and
whether I wished to persevere in their defense or to revoke
them—I have given my ready and clear response to the first:
in that I still persist and shall persist forever; to wit, that
these books are mine, and have been made public by me, in
my name—unless meanwhile, haply, any matter in them has

been changed, or has been maliciously extracted, through the cunning or the perverse wisdom of my enemies. For clearly, I cannot acknowledge anything as mine, except what has been written of myself and by myself alone, to the exclusion of any explanation which may be the work of someone else.

To the second point, Your Most Serene Majesty and Your Lordships, I will reply by asking you to turn your minds condescendingly to this fact—that my books are not all of the same kind: for there is one group in which I have handled religious faith and conduct in a simple evangelical fashion; moreover, this class has been composed in such a spirit that my very adversaries are forced to recognize the works as useful, harmless, and explicitly worthy of a Christian's perusal. Even the Bull, fierce and cruel as it is, considers my books in part at least as harmless; although it condemns them as a whole, with an altogether unusual severity of judgment. Consider what I would be guilty of, were I to begin any revocation of this class of writings. Should I not be the sole one of all mortals to censure that very truth which is acknowledged by friend and foe equally? Should not I alone be contending against the accordant confession of the rest of the world?

There is another group of my books, which inveighs against the papacy, and the teaching of the papists. This class is directed against those who, by their extremely corrupt doctrine and example, lay waste our entire Christendom, with every evil that spirit and body can invent. For it cannot be denied, nor can anyone disguise the fact, attested as it is by the experience of all persons and by the complaints of the entire civilized world, that the consciences of believers are wretchedly entangled, vexed, and tortured, by papal laws and human teachings. Property and substance are devoured by an incredible tyranny, especially in this noble German nation, and will be devoured continuously without end, and by unworthy means. Yet Romanists, by their own edicts, caution us against the papal laws and doctrines which are contrary to the gospel and the opinions of the fathers, and declare that all such variants should be regarded as erroneous and unapproved.

If therefore I should recall these books, I should do nothing else than add to the strength of this tyranny, and should open, not windows only, but doors to this tremendous foe of religion. It would stalk abroad more freely than it has hitherto dared. Yes, from the proof of such a revocation, their wholly lawless and unrestrained kingdom of wickedness would become still more intolerable for the already wretched people; and their rule would be further strengthened and established, especially should it be reported that this evil deed had been done by me in virtue of the authority of Your Most Serene Majesty, and of the whole Roman Empire. Good God! what a covert for wickedness and tyranny I should become.

A third series of these books consists of such as I have written against certain private persons, whom people call distinguished; such, namely, as have tried to preserve the Roman tyranny, and to undermine that view of religion which I have inculcated. Toward those individuals I confess that I have been more bitter than befits a churchman and a monk. But then I do not set myself up as a saint; neither am I disputing about my own career, but about the teaching of Christ. It would not then be right for me to recall this class of works, because by such a withdrawal, despotism and irreligion would obtain sway, and that through my protection. It would rage against the people of Germany more violently than under any previous rule.

Nevertheless, because I am a man and not God, I cannot shield my practices with any other defense than that with which my Lord Jesus Christ himself vindicated his teaching. For when he had been asked about his doctrine before Annas, and had been smitten by the blow of a servant, he said, "If I have spoken evil, bear witness of the evil." If our Lord, who was always conscious of his inability to err, yet did not decline to hear any evidence against his doctrine even from the most contemptible menial—how much more ought I, who am of the dregs of the people, and powerless in everything save sin, to desire and expect the introduction of testimony against my teaching?

Therefore, Your Most Serene Majesty, Your Most Illustrious Lordships, I beseech you by the mercy of God, that whoever can, whether high or low, let him bring forward the proof, let him convince me of errors: let the Scriptures of Prophecy and Gospels triumph, for I will be wholly ready to revoke every error, if I can be persuasively taught; yes, I will be the first to cast my books into the fire.

From these considerations it has become manifest that the crisis and danger on the one hand, the zeal and the controversy on the other, which the occasion of my teaching has excited in the world, have been the object of anxious solicitude on my part, and have been thoroughly weighed. It was about this commotion that I was admonished so bravely and forcibly yesterday. Under these agitations, this to me is the most joyous feature of all—the sight of such zeal and dispute over the Word of God. For the course of that divine Word has just such a fortuity and consequence, in that Christ says: "I came not to send peace, but a sword; for I am come to set a man at variance against his father, and the daughter against her mother, and the daughter-in-law against her mother-in-law."

Moreover, we ought to reflect that since our God is wonderful and terrible in his counsels, he is probably testing us by so large an access of zeal, whether we will begin by condemning the Word of God. If so, we shall afterwards be precipitated into a more unendurable flood of evils. We should particularly avoid making the reign of this youthful and noble Prince Charles, in whom after God we place so much hope, unhappy and inauspicious. I could enforce this point very richly, through the examples furnished by Scripture, in the case of Pharaoh, the king of Babylon, and the kings of

Israel, who lost most when they were endeavoring to pacify and establish their kindoms by seemingly the wisest of counsels. Before they were aware, the Lord takes the crafty in their craftiness, and overturns mountains. Therefore we must fear God. I do not say this because it is necessary for such high authorities as you to be instructed by my teaching or admonition, but because I must not withhold the fealty due to my Germany. With these words I commend myself to Your Most Serene Majesty, and to Your Lordships; humbly begging you not to suffer me to be rendered odious without cause, by the persecution of my adversaries. I have spoken.

(To these words the same imperial orator replied with harshness that he ought not to have made such a response, nor were the subjects formally condemned and defined by the councils to be called in question; therefore he sought from him a simple answer, and one without horns: would he revoke or not? Then Luther said:—)

Therefore, Your Most Serene Majesty and Your Lordships, since they seek a simple reply, I will give one that is without horns or teeth, and in this fashion: I believe in neither pope nor councils alone; for it is perfectly well established that they have frequently erred, as well as contradicted themselves. Unless then I shall be convinced by the testimony of the Scriptures or by clear reason, I must be bound by those Scriptures which have been brought forward by me; yes, my conscience has been taken captive by these words of God. I cannot revoke anything, nor do I wish to; since to go against one's conscience is neither safe nor right: here I stand, I cannot do otherwise. God help me. Amen.

Library of the World's Best Literature,
Edited by Charles Dudley Warner, Vol. XXIII, Pp. 9328-9332.
J. A. Hill and Co., 1896.

From

CONCERNING CHRISTIAN
LIBERTY

CHRISTIAN FAITH HAS APPEARED TO MANY AN EASY THING; nay, not a few even reckon it among the social virtues, as it were; and this they do because they have not made proof of it experimentally, and have never tasted of what efficacy it is. For it is not possible for any man to write well about it, or to understand well what is rightly written, who has not at some time tasted of its spirit, under the pressure of tribulation; while he who has tasted of it, even to a very small extent, can never write, speak, think, or hear about it sufficiently. For it is a living fountain, springing up unto eternal life, as Christ calls it in John iv.

Now, though I cannot boast of my abundance, and though I know how poorly I am furnished, yet I hope that, after having been vexed by various temptations, I have attained some little drop of faith, and that I can speak of this matter, if not with more elegance, certainly with more solidity, than those literal and too subtle disputants who have hitherto discoursed upon it without understanding their own words. That I may open then an easier way for the ignorant—for these alone I am trying to serve—I first lay down two propositions, concerning spiritual liberty and servitude:—

A Christian man is the most free lord of all, and subject to none; a Christian man is the most dutiful servant of all, and subject to everyone.

Although these statements appear contradictory, yet, when they are found to agree together, they will do excellently for my purpose. They are both the statements of Paul himself, who says, "Though I be free from all men, yet have I made myself a servant unto all" (I Cor. ix. 19), and "Owe no man anything but to love one another" (Rom. xiii. 8). Now love is by its own nature dutiful and obedient to the beloved object. Thus even Christ, though Lord of all things, was yet made of a woman; made under the law; at once free and a servant; at once in the form of God and in the form of a servant.

Let us examine the subject on a deeper and less simple principle. Man is composed of a twofold nature, a spiritual and a bodily. As regards the spiritual nature, which they name the soul, he is called the spiritual, inward, new man; as regards the bodily nature, which they name the flesh, he is called the fleshly, outward, old man. The Apostle speaks of this: "Though our outward man perish, yet the inward man is renewed day by day" (II Corinthians iv. 16). The result of this diversity is that in the Scriptures opposing statements are made concerning the same man, the fact being that in the same man these two men are opposed to one another; the flesh lusting against the spirit, and the spirit against the flesh (Gal. v. 17).

We first approach the subject of the inward man, that we may see by what means a man becomes justified, free, and a true Christian; that is, a spiritual, new, and inward man. It is certain that absolutely none among outward things, under whatever name they may be reckoned, has any influence in producing Christian righteousness or liberty, nor, on the other hand, unrighteousness or slavery. This can be shown by an easy argument.

What can it profit to the soul that the body should be in good condition, free, and full of life; that it should eat, drink, and act according to its pleasure; when even the most impious slaves of every kind of vice are prosperous in these matters? Again, what harm can ill-health, bondage, hunger, thirst, or any other outward evil, do to the soul, when even the most pious of men, and the freest in the purity of their conscience, are harassed by these things? Neither of these states of things has to do with the liberty or the slavery of the soul.

And so it will profit nothing that the body should be adorned with sacred vestments, or dwell in holy places, or be occupied in sacred offices, or pray, fast, and abstain from certain meats, or do whatever works can be done through the body and in the body. Something widely different will be necessary for the justification and liberty of the soul, since the things I have spoken of can be done by an impious person, and only hypocrites are produced by devotion to these things. On the other hand, it will not at all injure the soul that the body should be clothed in profane raiment, should dwell in profane places, should eat and drink in the ordinary fashion, should not pray aloud, and should leave undone all the things above mentioned, which may be done by hypocrites.

And—to cast everything aside—even speculations, meditations, and whatever things can be performed by the exertions of the soul itself, are of no profit. One thing, and one alone, is necessary for life, justification, and Christian liberty; and that is the most holy word of God, the Gospel of Christ, as He says, "I am the resurrection and the life; he that believeth in Me shall not die eternally" (John xi. 25), and also, "If the Son shall make you free, ye shall be free indeed" (John viii. 36), and, "Man shall not live by bread alone, but by every word that proceedeth out of the mouth of God" (Matt. iv. 4).

Let us therefore hold it for certain and firmly established that the soul can do without everything except the word of God, without which none at all of its wants are provided for. But, having the word, it is rich and wants for nothing, since that is the word of life, of truth, of light, of peace, of

justification, of salvation, of joy, of liberty, of wisdom, of
virtue, of grace, of glory, and of every good thing. It is on
this account that the prophet in a whole Psalm (Psalm
cxix.), and in many other places, sighs for and calls upon
the word of God with so many groanings and words. . . .

But you will ask, What is this word, and by what means
is it to be used, since there are so many words of God? I
answer, The Apostle Paul (Rom. i.) explains what it is,
namely the Gospel of God, concerning His Son, incarnate,
suffering, risen, and glorified through the spirit, the Sancti-
fier. To preach Christ is to feed the soul, to justify it, to set
it free, and to save it, if it believes the preaching. For faith
alone, and the efficacious use of the word of God, bring salvation. "If thou shalt confess with thy mouth the Lord Jesus,
and shalt believe in thine heart that God hath raised Him
from the dead, thou shalt be saved" (Rom. x. 9); and again,
"Christ is the end of the law for righteousness to every one
that believeth" (Rom. x. 4), and "The just shall live by
faith" (Rom. i. 17). For the word of God cannot be received
and honoured by any works but by faith alone. Hence it is
clear that as the soul needs the word alone for life and justification, so it is justified by faith alone, and not by any
works. For if it could be justified by any other means, it
would have no need of the word, nor consequently of faith.

But this faith cannot consist at all with works; that is, if
you imagine that you can be justified by those works, whatever they are, along with it. For this would be to halt between two opinions, to worship Baal, and to kiss the hand to
him, which is a very great iniquity, as Job says. Therefore,
when you begin to believe, you learn at the same time that
all that is in you is utterly guilty, sinful, and damnable,
according to that saying, "All have sinned, and come short of
the glory of God" (Rom. iii. 23), and also: "There is none
righteous, no, not one; they are all gone out of the way; they
are together become unprofitable: there is none that doeth
good, no, not one" (Rom. iii. 10–12). When you have

learnt this, you will know that Christ is necessary for you, since He has suffered and risen again for you, that, believing on Him, you might by this faith become another man, all your sins being remitted, and you being justified by the merits of another, namely Christ alone.

Since then this faith can reign only in the inward man, as it is said, "With the heart man believeth unto righteousness" (Rom. x. 10); and since it alone justifies, it is evident that by no outward work or labour can the inward man be at all justified, made free, and saved; and that no works whatever have any relation to him. And so, on the other hand, it is solely by impiety and incredulity of heart that he becomes guilty and a slave of sin, deserving condemnation, not by any outward sin or work. Therefore the first care of every Christian ought to be to lay aside all reliance on works, and strengthen his faith alone more and more, and by it grow in the knowledge, not of works, but of Christ Jesus, who has suffered and risen again for him, as Peter teaches (I Peter v.) when he makes no other work to be a Christian one. Thus Christ, when the Jews asked Him what they should do that they might work the works of God, rejected the multitude of works, with which He saw that they were puffed up, and commanded them one thing only, saying, "This is the work of God: that ye believe on Him whom He hath sent, for Him hath God the Father sealed" (John vi. 27, 29). . . . .

Hence all we who believe on Christ are kings and priests in Christ, as it is said, "Ye are a chosen generation, a royal priesthood, a holy nation, a peculiar people, that ye should show forth the praises of Him who hath called you out of darkness into His marvellous light" (I Peter ii. 9).

These two things stand thus. First, as regards kingship, every Christian is by faith so exalted above all things that, in spiritual power, he is completely lord of all things, so that nothing whatever can do him any hurt; yea, all things are subject to him, and are compelled to be subservient to his salvation. Thus Paul says, "All things work together for good to them who are the called" (Rom. viii. 28), and also, "Whether life, or death, or things present, or things to come, all are yours; and ye are Christ's" (I Cor. iii. 22, 23).

Not that in the sense of corporeal power any one among the Christians has been appointed to possess and rule all things, according to the mad and senseless idea of certain ecclesiastics. That is the office of kings, princes, and men upon earth. In the experience of life we see that we are subjected to all things, and suffer many things, even death. Yea, the more of a Christian any man is, to so many the more evils, sufferings, and deaths is he subject, as we see in the first place in Christ the First-born, and in all His holy brethren.

This is a spiritual power, which rules in the midst of enemies, and is powerful in the midst of distresses. And this is nothing else than that strength is made perfect in my weakness, and that I can turn all things to the profit of my salvation; so that even the cross and death are compelled to serve me and to work together for my salvation. This a lofty and eminent dignity, a true and almighty dominion, a spiritual empire, in which there is nothing so good, nothing so bad, as not to work together for my good, if only I believe. And yet there is nothing of which I have need—for faith alone suffices for my salvation—unless that in it faith may exercise the power and empire of its liberty. This is the inestimable power and liberty of Christians.

Nor are we only kings and the freest of all men, but also priests forever, a dignity far higher than kingship, because by that priesthood we are worthy to appear before God, to pray for others, and to teach one another mutually the things which are of God. For these are the duties of priests, and they cannot possibly be permitted to any unbeliever. Christ has obtained for us this favour, if we believe in Him: that just as we are His brethren and co-heirs and fellow-kings with Him, so we should be also fellow-priests with Him, and venture with confidence, through the spirit of faith, to come into the presence of God, and cry, "Abba, Father!" and to pray for one another, and to do all things which we see done and figured in the visible and corporeal office of priesthood. But to an unbelieving person nothing renders service or works for good. He himself is in servitude to all things, and all things turn out for evil to him, because he uses all things in an impious way for his own advantage, and not for the glory of God. And thus he is not a priest, but a profane person, whose prayers are turned into sin, nor does he ever appear in the presence of God, because God does not hear sinners. . . .

Here you will ask, "If all who are in the Church are priests, by what character are those whom we now call priests to be distinguished from the laity?" I reply, By the use of these words, "priest," "clergy," "spiritual person," "ecclesiastic," an injustice has been done, since they have been transferred from the remaining body of Christians to those few who are now, by a hurtful custom, called ecclesiastics. For Holy Scripture makes no distinction between them, except that those who are now boastfully called popes, bishops, and lords, it calls ministers, servants, and stewards, who are to serve the rest in the ministry of the word, for teaching the faith of Christ and the liberty of believers. For though it is true that we are all equally priests, yet we cannot, nor, if we could, ought we all to, minister and teach publicly. Thus Paul says, "Let a man so account of us as of the ministers of Christ and stewards of the mysteries of God" (I Cor. iv. 1).

This bad system has now issued in such a pompous display of power and such a terrible tyranny that no earthly government can be compared to it, as if the laity were something else than Christians. Through this perversion of things it has happened that the knowledge of Christian grace, of faith, of liberty, and altogether of Christ, has utterly perished, and has been succeeded by an intolerable bondage to human works and laws; and, according to the Lamentations of

Jeremiah, we have become slaves of the vilest men on earth, who abuse our misery to all the disgraceful and ignominious purposes of their own will. . . .

And now let us turn to the other part: to the outward man. Here we shall give an answer to all those who, taking offense at the word of faith and at what I have asserted, say, "If faith does everything, and by itself suffices for justification, why then are good works commanded? Are we then to take our ease and do no works, content with faith?" Not so, impious men, I reply; not so. That would indeed really be the case, if we were thoroughly and completely inner and spiritual persons; but that will not happen until the last day, when the dead shall be raised. As long as we live in the flesh, we are but beginning and making advances in that which shall be completed in a future life. On this account the Apostle calls that which we have in this life the firstfruits of the Spirit (Rom. viii. 23). In future we shall have the tenths, and the fulness of the Spirit. To this part belongs the fact I have stated before: that the Christian is the servant of all and subject to all. For in that part in which he is free he does no works, but in that in which he is a servant he does all works. Let us see on what principle this is so.

Although, as I have said, inwardly, and according to the spirit, a man is amply enough justified by faith, having all that he requires to have, except that this very faith and abundance ought to increase from day to day, even till the future life, still he remains in this mortal life upon earth, in which it is necessary that he should rule his own body and have intercourse with men. Here then works begin; here he must not take his ease; here he must give heed to exercise his body by fastings, watchings, labour, and other regular discipline, so that it may be subdued to the spirit, and obey and conform itself to the inner man and faith, and not rebel against them nor hinder them, as is its nature to do if it is not kept under. For the inner man, being conformed to God and created after the image of God through faith, rejoices

and delights itself in Christ, in whom such blessings have
been conferred on it, and hence has only this task before it:
to serve God with joy and for nought in free love.

But in doing this he comes into collision with that contrary will in his own flesh, which is striving to serve the
world and to seek its own gratification. This the spirit of
faith cannot and will not bear, but applies itself with cheer-
fulness and zeal to keep it down and restrain it, as Paul
says, "I delight in the law of God after the inward man; but
I see another law in my members, warring against the law of
my mind and bringing me into captivity to the law of sin"
(Rom. vii. 22, 23), and again, "I keep under my body,
and bring it into subjection lest that by any means, when I
have preached to others, I myself should be a castaway"
(I Cor. ix. 27), and "They that are Christ's have crucified
the flesh, with the affections and lusts" (Gal. v. 24).

These works, however, must not be done with any notion
that by them a man can be justified before God—for faith,
which alone is righteousness before God, will not bear with
this false notion—but solely with this purpose: that the body
may be brought into subjection, and be purified from its evil
lusts, so that our eyes may be turned only to purging away
those lusts. For when the soul has been cleansed by faith
and made to love God, it would have all things to be cleansed
in like manner, and especially its own body, so that all things
might unite with it in the love and praise of God. Thus it
comes that, from the requirements of his own body, a man
cannot take his ease, but is compelled on its account to do
many good works, that he may bring it into subjection. Yet
these works are not the means of his justification before
God; he does them out of disinterested love to the service of
God; looking to no other end than to do what is well-
pleasing to Him whom he desires to obey most dutifully in
all things.

On this principle every man may easily instruct himself in
what measure, and with what distinctions, he ought to chas-

ten his own body. He will fast, watch, and labour, just as much as he sees to suffice for keeping down the wantonness and concupiscence of the body. But those who pretend to be justified by works are looking, not to the mortification of their lusts, but only to the works themselves; thinking that, if they can accomplish as many works and as great ones as possible, all is well with them, and they are justified. Sometimes they even injure their brain, and extinguish nature, or at least make it useless. This is enormous folly, and ignorance of Christian life and faith, when a man seeks, without faith, to be justified and saved by works. . . .

A bishop, when he consecrates a church, confirms children, or performs any other duty of his office, is not consecrated as a bishop by these works; nay, unless he had been previously consecrated as bishop, not one of those works would have any validity; they would be foolish, childish, and ridiculous. Thus a Christian, being consecrated by his faith, does good works; but he is not by these works made a more sacred person, or more a Christian. That is the effect of faith alone; nay, unless he were previously a believer and a Christian, none of his works would have any value at all; they would really be impious and damnable sins.

True, then, are these two sayings: "Good works do not make a good man, but a good man does good works"; thus it is always necessary that the substance or person should be good before any good works can be done, and that good works should follow and proceed from a good person. As Christ says, "A good tree cannot bring forth evil fruit, neither can a corrupt tree bring forth good fruit" (Matt. vii. 18). Now it is clear that the fruit does not bear the tree, nor does the tree grow on the fruit; but, on the contrary, the trees bear the fruit, and the fruit grows on the trees.

As then trees must exist before their fruit, and as the fruit does not make the tree either good or bad, but, on the contrary, a tree of either kind produces fruit of the same kind, so must first the person of the man be good or bad before he can do either a good or a bad work; and his works do not make him bad or good, but he himself makes his works either bad or good.

We may see the same thing in all handicrafts. A bad or good house does not make a bad or good builder, but a good or bad builder makes a good or bad house. And in general no work makes the workman such as it is itself; but the workman makes the work such as he is himself. Such is the case, too, with the works of men. Such as the man himself is, whether in faith or in unbelief, such is his work: good if it be done in faith; bad if in unbelief. For as works do not make a believing man, so neither do they make a justified man; but faith, as it makes a man a believer and justified, so also it makes his works good.

Since then works justify no man, but a man must be justified before he can do any good work, it is most evident that it is faith alone which, by the mere mercy of God through Christ, and by means of His word, can worthily and sufficiently justify and save the person; and that a Christian man needs no work, no law, for his salvation; for by faith he is free from all law, and in perfect freedom does gratuitously all that he does, seeking nothing either of profit or of salvation—since by the grace of God he is already saved and rich in all things through his faith—but solely that which is well-pleasing to God.

So, too, no good work can profit an unbeliever to justification and salvation; and, on the other hand, no evil work makes him an evil and condemned person, but that unbelief, which makes the person and the tree bad, makes his works evil and condemned. Wherefore, when any man is good or bad, this does not arise from his works, but from his faith or unbelief, as the wise man says, "The beginning of sin is to fall away from God"; that is, not to believe. Paul says, "He that cometh to God must believe" (Heb. xi. 6): and Christ says the same thing: "Either make the tree good, and his fruit good, or else make the tree corrupt, and his fruit corrupt" (Matt. xii. 33)—as much as to say, He who wishes to have good fruit will begin with the tree, and plant a good one; even so he who wishes to do good work must begin, not by working, but by believing, since it is this which makes the person good. For nothing makes the person good but faith, nor bad but unbelief. . . .

From all this it is easy to perceive on what principle good works are to be cast aside or embraced, and by what rule all teachings put forth concerning works are to be understood. For if works are brought forward as grounds of justification, and are done under false persuasion that we can pretend to be justified by them, they lay on us the yoke of necessity, and extinguish liberty along with faith, and by this very addition to their use they become no longer good, but really worthy of condemnation. For such works are not free, but blaspheme the grace of God, to which alone it belongs to justify and save through faith. Works cannot accomplish this, and yet, with impious presumption, through our folly, they take it upon themselves to do so; and thus break in with violence upon the office and glory of grace.

We do not then reject good works; nay we embrace them and teach them in the highest degree. It is not on their own account that we condemn them, but on account of this impious addition to them and the perverse notion of seeking justification by them. These things cause them to be only good in outward show, but in reality not good, since by them men are deceived and deceive others, like ravening wolves in sheep's clothing. . . .

Lastly, we will speak also of those works which he performs towards his neighbour. For man does not live for himself alone in this mortal body, in order to work on its account, but also for all men on earth; nay, he lives only for others, and not for himself. For it is to this end that he brings his own body into subjection, that he may be able to serve others more sincerely and more freely, as Paul says,

"None of us liveth to himself, and no man dieth to himself. For whether we live, we live unto the Lord; and whether we die, we die unto the Lord" (Rom. xiv. 7, 8). Thus it is impossible that he should take his ease in this life, and not work for the good of his neighbours, since he must needs speak, act, and converse among men, just as Christ was made in the likeness of men and found in fashion as a man, and had His conservation among men.

Yet a Christian has need of none of these things for justification and salvation, but in all his works he ought to entertain this view and look only to this object—that he may serve and be useful to others in all that he does; having nothing before his eyes but the necessities and the advantage of his neighbour. Thus the Apostle commands us to work with our own hands, that we may have to give to those that need. He might have said, that we may support ourselves; but he tells us to give to those that need. It is the part of a Christian to take care of his own body for the very purpose that, by its soundness and well-being, he may be enabled to labour, and to acquire and preserve property, for the aid of those who are in want, that thus the stronger member may serve the weaker member, and we may be children of God, thoughtful and busy one for another, bearing one another's burdens, and so fulfilling the law of Christ.

Here is the truly Christian life, here is faith really working by love, when a man applies himself with joy and love to the works of that freest servitude in which he serves others voluntarily and for nought, himself abundantly satisfied in the fulness and riches of his own faith.

Thus, when Paul had taught the Philippians how they had been made rich by that faith in Christ in which they had obtained all things, he teaches them further in these words: "If there be therefore any consolation in Christ, if any comfort of love, if any fellowship of the Spirit, if any bowels and mercies, fulfil ye my joy, that ye be like-minded, having the same love, being of one accord, of one mind. Let nothing be done through strife or vainglory; but in lowliness of mind let each esteem other better than himself. Look not every man on his own things, but every man also on the things of others" (Phil. ii. 1–4).

In this we see clearly that the Apostle lays down this rule for a Christian life: that all our works should be directed to the advantage of others, since every Christian has such abundance through his faith that all his other works and his whole life remain over and above wherewith to serve and benefit his neighbour of spontaneous goodwill. . . .

Finally, for the sake of those to whom nothing can be stated so well but that they misunderstand and distort it, we must add a word, in case they can understand even that. There are very many persons who, when they hear of this liberty of faith, straightway turn it into an occasion of licence. They think that everything is now lawful for them, and do not choose to show themselves free men and Christians in any other way than by their contempt and reprehension of ceremonies, of traditions, of human laws; as if they were Christians merely because they refuse to fast on stated days, or eat flesh when others fast, or omit the customary prayers; scoffing at the precepts of men, but utterly passing over all the rest that belongs to the Christian religion. On the other hand, they are most pertinaciously resisted by those who strive after salvation solely by their observance of and reverence for ceremonies, as if they would be saved merely because they fast on stated days, or abstain from flesh, or make formal prayers; talking loudly of the precepts of the Church and of the Fathers, and not caring a straw about those things which belong to our genuine faith. Both these parties are plainly culpable, in that, while they neglect matters which are of weight and necessary for salvation, they contend noisily about such as are without weight and not necessary.

How much more rightly does the Apostle Paul teach us to walk in the middle path, condemning either extreme and saying, "Let not him that eateth despise him that eateth not; and let not him which eateth not judge him that eateth" (Rom. xiv. 3)! You see here how the Apostle blames those who, not from religious feeling, but in mere contempt, neglect and rail at ceremonial observances, and teaches them not to despise, since this "knowledge puffeth up." Again, he teaches the pertinacious upholders of these things not to judge their opponents. For neither party observes towards the other that charity which edifieth. In this matter we must listen to Scripture, which teaches us to turn aside neither to the right hand nor to the left, but to follow those right precepts of the Lord which rejoice the heart. For just as a man is not righteous merely because he serves and is devoted to works and ceremonial rites, so neither will he be accounted righteous merely because he neglects and despises them. . . .

Luther's Primary Works,
Edited by Henry Wace and C. A. Buchheim.
London: Hodder and Stoughton, 1896.

ADDRESS TO THE CHRISTIAN
NOBILITY OF THE GERMAN
NATION

THE ROMANISTS HAVE, WITH GREAT ADROITNESS, DRAWN
three walls round themselves, with which they have hitherto
protected themselves, so that no one could reform them,
whereby all Christendom has fallen terribly.

Firstly, if pressed by the temporal power, they have affirmed and maintained that the temporal power has no jurisdiction over them, but, on the contrary, that the spiritual
power is above the temporal power.

Secondly, if it were proposed to admonish them with the
Scriptures, they objected that no one may interpret the Scriptures but the pope.

Thirdly, if they are threatened with a council, they pretend that no one may call a council but the pope.

Thus they have secretly stolen our three rods, so that they
may be unpunished, and intrenched themselves behind these
three walls, to act with all the wickedness and malice,
which we now witness. And whenever they have been compelled to call a council, they have made it of no avail by
binding the princes beforehand with an oath to leave them
as they were, and to give moreover to the pope full power
over the procedure of the council, so that it is all one
whether we have many councils or no councils, in addition to

which they deceive us with false pretenses and tricks. So grievously do they tremble for their skin before a true, free council; and thus they have overawed kings and princes, that these believe they would be offending God, if they were not to obey them in all such knavish, deceitful artifices.

Now may God help us, and give us one of those trumpets that overthrew the walls of Jericho, so that we may blow down these walls of straw and paper, and that we may set free our Christian rods for the chastisement of sin, and expose the craft and deceit of the devil, so that we may amend ourselves by punishment and again obtain God's favour.

a.   THE FIRST WALL
That the Temporal Power has no Jurisdiction over the Spirituality

Let us, in the first place, attack the first wall.

It has been devised that the pope, bishops, priests, and monks are called the *spiritual estate*, princes, lords, artificers, and peasants are the *temporal estate*. This is an artful lie and hypocritical device, but let no one be made afraid by it, and that for this reason: that all Christians are truly of the spiritual estate, and there is no difference among them, save of office alone. As St. Paul says (I Cor. xii), we are all one body, though each member does its own work, to serve the others. This is because we have one baptism, one Gospel, one faith, and are all Christians alike; for baptism, Gospel, and faith, these alone make spiritual and Christian people.

As for the unction by a pope or a bishop, tonsure, ordination, consecration, and clothes differing from those of laymen—all this may make a hypocrite or an anointed puppet, but never a Christian or a spiritual man. Thus we are all consecrated as priests by baptism, as St. Peter says: "Ye are a royal priesthood, a holy nation" (I Peter ii. 9); and in the book of Revelations: "And hast made us unto our God (by Thy blood) kings and priests" (Rev. v. 10). For,

if we had not a higher consecration in us than pope or
bishop can give, no priest could ever be made by the consecration of pope or bishop, nor could he say mass, or
preach, or absolve. Therefore the bishop's consecration is
just as if in the name of the whole congregation he took one
person out of the community, each member of which has
equal power, and commanded him to exercise this power
for the rest; in the same way as if ten brothers, co-heirs as
king's sons, were to choose one from among them to rule
over their inheritance, they would all of them still remain
kings and have equal power, although one is ordered to
govern.

And to put the matter more plainly, if a little company of
pious Christian laymen were taken prisoners and carried away to a desert, and had not among them a priest
consecrated by a bishop, and were there to agree to elect one
of them, born in wedlock or not, and were to order him to
baptize, to celebrate the mass, to absolve, and to preach, this
man would as truly be a priest, as if all the bishops and all
the popes had consecrated him. That is why in cases of necessity every man can baptize and absolve, which would not
be possible if we were not all priests. This great grace and
virtue of baptism and of the Christian estate they have quite
destroyed and made us forget by their ecclesiastical law. In
this way the Christians used to choose their bishops and
priests out of the community; these being afterwards confirmed by other bishops, without the pomp that now pre-
vails. So was it that St. Augustine, Ambrose, Cyprian, were
bishops.

Since, then, the temporal power is baptized as we are,
and has the same faith and Gospel, we must allow it to be
priest and bishop, and account its office an office that is
proper and useful to the Christian community. For whatever
issues from baptism may boast that it has been consecrated
priest, bishop, and pope, although it does not beseem every
one to exercise these offices. For, since we are all priests,

alike, no man may put himself forward or take upon himself, without our consent and election, to do that which we have all alike power to do. For, if a thing is common to all, no man may take it to himself without the wish and command of the community. And if it should happen that a man were appointed to one of these offices and deposed for abuses, he would be just what he was before. Therefore a priest should be nothing in Christendom but a functionary; as long as he holds his office, he has precedence of others; if he is deprived of it, he is a peasant or citizen like the rest. Therefore a priest is verily no longer a priest after deposition. But now they have invented *characteres indelibiles*, and pretend that a priest after deprivation still differs from a simple layman. They even imagine that a priest can never be anything but a priest—that is, that he can never become a layman. All this is nothing but mere talk and ordinance of human invention.

It follows then that between laymen and priests, princes and bishops, or, as they call it, between spiritual and temporal persons, the only real difference is one of office and function, and not of estate; for they are all of the same spiritual estate, true priests, bishops, and popes, though their functions are not the same—just as among priests and monks every man has not the same functions. And this, as I said above, St. Paul says (Rom. xii.; I Cor. xii.), and St. Peter (I Peter ii.): "We, being many, are one body in Christ, and severally members one of another." Christ's body is not double or twofold, one temporal, the other spiritual. He is one Head, and He has one body.

We see, then, that just as those that we call spiritual, or priests, bishops, or popes, do not differ from other Christians in any other or higher degree but in that they are to be concerned with the word of God and the sacraments—that being their work and office—in the same way the temporal authorities hold the sword and the rod in their hands to punish the wicked and to protect the good. A cobbler, a smith, a peasant, every man, has the office and function of his calling, and yet all alike are consecrated priests and bishops, and every man should by his office or function be useful and beneficial to the rest, so that various kinds of work may all be united for the furtherance of body and soul, just as the members of the body all serve one another.

Now see what a Christian doctrine is this: that the temporal authority is not above the clergy, and may not punish it. This is as if one were to say the hand may not help, though the eye is in grievous suffering. Is it not unnatural, not to say unchristian, that one member may not help another, or guard it against harm? Nay, the nobler the member, the more the rest are bound to help it. Therefore I say, Forasmuch as the temporal power has been ordained by God for the punishment of the bad and the protection of the good, therefore we must let it do its duty throughout the whole Christian body, without respect of persons, whether it strike popes, bishops, priests, monks, nuns, or whoever it may be. If it were sufficient reason for fettering the temporal power that it is inferior among the offices of Christianity to the offices of priest or confessor, or to the spiritual estate—if this were so, then we ought to restrain tailors, cobblers, masons, carpenters, cooks, cellarmen, peasants, and all secular workmen, from providing the pope or bishops, priests and monks, with shoes, clothes, houses, or victuals, or from paying them tithes. But if these laymen are allowed to do their work without restraint, what do the Romanist scribes mean by their laws? They mean that they withdraw themselves from the operation of temporal Christian power, simply in order that they may be free to do evil, and thus fulfil what St. Peter said: "There shall be false teachers among you . . . and in covetousness shall they with feigned words make merchandise of you" (II Peter ii. 1, etc.).

Therefore the temporal Christian power must exercise its office without let or hindrance, without considering whom it may strike, whether pope, or bishop, or priest: whoever is guilty, let him suffer for it.

7243

Whatever the ecclesiastical law has said in opposition to this is merely the invention of Roman arrogance. For this is what St. Paul says to all Christians: "Let every soul" (I presume including the popes) "be subject unto the higher powers; for they bear not the sword in vain: they serve the Lord therewith, for vengeance on evildoers and for praise to them that do well" (Rom. xiii. 1–4). Also St. Peter: "Submit yourselves to every ordinance of man for the Lord's sake . . . for so is the will of God" (I Peter ii. 13, 15). He has also foretold that men would come who should despise government (II Peter ii.), as has come to pass through ecclesiastical law.

Now, I imagine, the first paper wall is overthrown, inasmuch as the temporal power has become a member of the Christian body; although its work relates to the body, yet does it belong to the spiritual estate. Therefore it must do its duty without let or hindrance upon all members of the whole body, to punish or urge, as guilt may deserve, or need may require, without respect of pope, bishops, or priests, let them threaten or excommunicate as they will. That is why a guilty priest is deprived of his priesthood before being given over to the secular arm; whereas this would not be right, if the secular sword had not authority over him already by divine ordinance.

It is, indeed, past bearing that the spiritual law should esteem so highly the liberty, life and property of the clergy, as if laymen were not as good spiritual Christians, or not equally members of the Church. Why should your body, life, goods, and honour be free, and not mine, seeing that we are equal as Christians, and have received alike baptism, faith, spirit, and all things? If a priest is killed, the country is laid under an interdict: why not also if a peasant is killed? Whence comes this great difference among equal Christians? Simply from human laws and inventions.

It can have been no good spirit, either, that devised these evasions and made sin to go unpunished. For if, as Christ and the Apostles bid us, it is our duty to oppose the evil one and all his works and words, and to drive him away as well as may be, how then should we remain quiet and be silent when the pope and his followers are guilty of devilish works and words? Are we for the sake of men to allow the commandments and the truth of God to be defeated, which at our baptism we vowed to support with body and soul? Truly we should have to answer for all souls that would thus be abandoned and led astray.

Therefore it must have been the arch-devil himself who said, as we read in the ecclesiastical law, If the pope were so perniciously wicked, as to be dragging souls in crowds to the devil, yet he could not be deposed. This is the accursed and devilish foundation on which they build at Rome, and think that the whole world is to be allowed to go to the devil rather than they should be opposed in their knavery. If a man were to escape punishment simply because he is above the rest, then no Christian might punish another, since Christ had commanded each of us to esteem himself the lowest and the humblest (Matt. xviii. 4; Luke ix. 48).

b.   THE SECOND WALL
That no one may interpret the Scriptures but the pope

The second wall is even more tottering and weak: that they alone pretend to be considered masters of the Scriptures; although they learn nothing of them all their life. They assume authority, and juggle before us with impudent words, saying that the pope cannot err in matters of faith, whether he be evil or good, albeit they cannot prove it by a single letter. That is why the canon law contains so many heretical and unchristian, nay unnatural, laws; but of these we need not speak now. For whereas they imagine the Holy Ghost never leaves them, however unlearned and wicked they must be, they grow bold enough to decree whatever they like. But were this true, where were the need and use of the Holy Scriptures? Let us burn them, and content ourselves with the unlearned gentlemen at Rome, in whom the Holy Ghost dwells, who, however, can dwell in pious souls only. If I had not read it, I could never have believed that the devil should have put forth such follies at Rome and find a following.

But not to fight them with our own words, we will quote the Scriptures. St. Paul says, "If anything be revealed to another that sitteth by, let the first hold his peace" (I Cor. xiv. 30). What would be the use of this commandment, if we were to believe him alone that teaches or has the highest seat? Christ Himself says, "And they shall be all taught of God" (St. John vi. 45). Thus it may come to pass that the pope and his followers are wicked and not true Christians, and not being taught by God, have no true understanding, whereas a common man may have true understanding. Why should we then not follow him? Has not the pope often erred? Who could help Christianity, in case the pope errs, if we do not rather believe another who has the Scriptures for him?

Therefore it is a wickedly devised fable—and they cannot quote a single letter to confirm it—that it is for the pope alone to interpret the Scriptures or to confirm the interpretation of them. They have assumed the authority of their own selves. And though they say that this authority was given to St. Peter when the keys were given to him, it is plain enough that the keys were not given to St. Peter alone, but to the whole community. Besides, the keys were not ordained for doctrine or authority, but for sin, to bind or loose; and what they claim besides this from the keys is mere invention. But what Christ said to St. Peter: "I have prayed for thee that thy faith fail not" (St. Luke xxii. 32), cannot relate to the pope, inasmuch as the greater part of the popes have been without faith, as they are themselves forced to acknowledge; nor did Christ pray for Peter alone, but for all the Apostles and all Christians, as He says, "Neither pray I for these alone, but for them also which shall believe on Me through their word" (St. John xvii.). Is not this plain enough?

Only consider the matter. They must needs acknowledge that there are pious Christians among us that have the true faith, spirit, understanding, word, and mind of Christ; why then should we reject their word, and understanding, and follow a pope who has neither understanding nor spirit? Surely this were to deny our whole faith and the Christian Church. Moreover, if the article of our faith is right, "I believe in the holy Christian Church," the pope cannot alone be right; else we must say, 'I believe in the pope of Rome,' and reduce the Christian Church to one man, which is a devilish and damnable heresy. Besides that, we are all priests, as I have said, and have all one faith, one Gospel, one Sacrament; how then should we not have the power of discerning and judging what is right or wrong in matters of faith? What becomes of St. Paul's words, "But he that is spiritual judgeth all things, yet he himself is judged of no man" (I Cor. ii. 15), and also, "We having the same spirit of faith"? (II Cor. iv. 13). Why then should we not perceive as well as an unbelieving pope what agrees or disagrees with our faith?

By these and many other texts we should gain courage and freedom, and should not let the spirit of liberty (as St. Paul has it) be frightened away by the inventions of the popes; we should boldly judge what they do and what they leave undone by our own believing understanding of the Scriptures, and force them to follow the better understanding, and not their own. Did not Abraham in old days have to obey his Sarah, who was in stricter bondage to him than we are to any one on earth? Thus, too, Balaam's ass was wiser than the prophet. If God spoke by an ass against a prophet, why should He not speak by a pious man against the pope? Besides, St. Paul withstood St. Peter as being in error (Gal. ii). Therefore it behooves every Christian to aid the faith by understanding and defending it and by condemning all errors.

c. THE THIRD WALL
That no one may call a council but the pope

The third wall falls of itself, as soon as the first two have
fallen; for if the pope acts contrary to the Scriptures, we
are bound to stand by the Scriptures, to punish and to constrain him, according to Christ's commandment, "Moreover,
if thy brother shall trespass against thee, go and tell him his
fault between thee and him alone; if he shall hear thee, thou
hast gained thy brother. But if he will not hear thee, then
take with thee one or two more, that in the mouth of two or
three witnesses every word may be established. And if he
shall neglect to hear them, tell it unto the church; but if
he neglect to hear the church, let him be unto thee as a
heathen man and a publican" (St. Matt. xviii. 15–17). Here
each member is commanded to take care for the other; much
more then should we do this, if it is a ruling member of the
community that does evil, which by its evildoing causes great
harm and offence to the others. If then I am to accuse him
before the church, I must collect the church together. Moreover, they can show nothing in the Scriptures giving the pope
sole power to call and confirm councils; they have nothing
but their own laws; but these hold good only so long as they
are not injurious to Christianity and the laws of God. Therefore, if the pope deserves punishment, these laws cease to
bind us, since Christendom would suffer, if he were not punished by a council. Thus we read (Acts xv.) that the council
of the Apostles was not called by St. Peter but by all the
Apostles and the elders. But if the right to call it had lain
with St. Peter alone, it would not have been a Christian
council, but a heretical *conciliabulum*. Moreover, the most
celebrated council of all—that of Nicaea—was neither called
nor confirmed by the Bishop of Rome, but by the Emperor
Constantine; and after him many other emperors have done
the same, and yet the councils called by them were accounted
most Christian. But if the pope alone had the power, they

must all have been heretical. Moreover, if I consider the councils that the pope has called, I do not find that they produced any notable results.

Therefore when need requires, and the pope is a cause of offence to Christendom, in these cases whoever can best do so, as a faithful member of the whole body, must do what he can to procure a true free council. This no one can do so well as the temporal authorities, especially since they are fellow-Christians, fellow-priests, sharing one spirit and one power in all things, and since they should exercise the office that they have received from God without hindrance, whenever it is necessary and useful that it should be exercised. Would it not be most unnatural, if a fire were to break out in a city, and every one were to keep still and let it burn on and on, whatever might be burnt, simply because they had not the mayor's authority, or because the fire perchance broke out in the mayor's house? Is not every citizen bound in this case to rouse and call in the rest? How much more should this be done in the spiritual city of Christ, if a fire of offence breaks out, either at the pope's government or wherever it may! The like happens if an enemy attacks a town. The first to rouse up the rest earns glory and thanks. Why then should not he earn glory that descries the coming of our enemies from hell and rouses and summons all Christians?

But as for their boasts of their authority, that no one must oppose it, this is idle talk. No one in Christendom has any authority to do harm, or to forbid others to prevent harm being done. There is no authority in the church but for reformation. Therefore if the pope wished to use his power to prevent the calling of a free council, so as to prevent the reformation of the church, we must not respect him or his power; and if he should begin to excommunicate and fulminate, we must despise this as the doings of a madman, and, trusting in God, excommunicate and repel him as best we may. For this his usurped power is nothing; he does not possess it, and he is at once overthrown by a text from the Scriptures. For St. Paul says to the Corinthians "that God has given us authority for edification, and not for destruction" (II Cor. x. 8). Who will set this text at nought? It is the power of the devil and of antichrist that prevents what would serve for the reformation of Christendom. Therefore we must not follow it, but oppose it with our body, our goods, and all that we have. And even if a miracle were to happen in favour of the pope against the temporal power, or if some were to be stricken by a plague, as they sometimes boast has happened, all this is to be held as having been done by the devil in order to injure our faith in God, as was foretold by Christ: "There shall arise false Christs and false prophets, and shall show great signs and wonders, insomuch that, if it were possible, they shall deceive the very elect" (Matt. xxiv. 23); and St. Paul tells the Thessalonians that the coming of antichrist shall be "after the working of Satan with all power and signs and lying wonders" (II Thess. ii. 9).

Therefore let us hold fast to this: that Christian power can do nothing against Christ, as St. Paul says, "For we can do nothing against Christ, but for Christ" (II Cor. xiii. 8). But if it does anything against Christ, it is the power of antichrist and the devil, even if it rained and hailed wonders and plagues. Wonders and plagues prove nothing, especially in these latter evil days, of which false wonders are foretold in all the Scriptures. Therefore we must hold fast to the words of God with an assured faith; then the devil will soon cease his wonders.

And now I hope the false, lying spectre will be laid with which the Romanists have long terrified and stupefied our consciences. And it will be seen that, like all the rest of us, they are subject to the temporal sword; that they have no authority to interpret the Scriptures by force without skill; and that they have no power to prevent a council, or to pledge it in accordance with their pleasure, or to bind it beforehand, and deprive it of its freedom; and that if they do this, they are verily of the fellowship of antichrist and the devil, and have nothing of Christ but the name. . . .

Luther's Primary Works,
Edited by Henry Wace and C. A. Buchheim.
London: Hodder and Stoughton, 1896.

ADDRESS TO THE
CHRISTIAN NOBILITY
OF THE GERMAN NATION

OF THE MATTERS TO BE CONSIDERED IN THE COUNCILS

LET US NOW CONSIDER THE MATTERS WHICH SHOULD BE treated in the councils, and with which popes, cardinals, bishops, and all learned men should occupy themselves day and night, if they love Christ and His Church. But if they do not do so, the people at large and the temporal powers must do so, without considering the thunders of their excommunications. For an unjust excommunication is better than ten just absolutions, and an unjust absolution is worse than ten just excommunications. Therefore let us rouse ourselves, fellow-Germans, and fear God more than man, that we be not answerable for all the poor souls that are so miserably lost through the wicked, devilish government of the Romanists, and that the dominion of the devil should not grow day by day, if indeed this hellish government can grow any worse, which, for my part, I can neither conceive nor believe.

1. It is a distressing and terrible thing to see that the head of Christendom, who boasts of being the vicar of Christ and the successor of St. Peter, lives in a worldly pomp that no king or emperor can equal, so that in him that calls himself most holy and most spiritual there is more worldliness than in the world itself. He wears a triple crown, whereas the mightiest kings only wear one crown. If this resembles the

poverty of Christ and St. Peter, it is a new sort of resemblance. They prate of its being heretical to object to this; nay, they will not even hear how unchristian and ungodly it is. But I think that if he should have to pray to God with tears, he would have to lay down his crowns; for God will not endure any arrogance. His office should be nothing else than to weep and pray constantly for Christendom and to be an example of all humility.

However this may be, this pomp is a stumbling-block, and the pope, for the very salvation of his soul, ought to put it off, for St. Paul says, "Abstain from all appearance of evil" (I Thess. v. 21), and again, "Provide things honest in the sight of all men" (II Cor. viii. 21). A simple mitre would be enough for the pope: wisdom and sanctity should raise him above the rest; the crown of pride he should leave to antichrist, as his predecessors did some hundreds of years ago. They say, He is the ruler of the world. This is false; for Christ, whose viceregent and vicar he claims to be, said to Pilate, "My kingdom is not of this world" (John xviii. 36). But no viceregent can have a wider dominion than his Lord, nor is he a viceregent of Christ in His glory, but of Christ crucified, as St. Paul says, "For I determined not to know anything among you save Jesus Christ, and Him crucified" (II Cor. ii. 2), and "Let this mind be in you, which was also in Christ Jesus, who made Himself of no reputation, and took upon Himself the form of a servant" (Phil. ii. 5, 7). Again, "We preach Christ crucified" (I Cor. i.). Now they make the pope a viceregent of Christ exalted in heaven, and some have let the devil rule them so thoroughly that they have maintained that the pope is above the angels in heaven and has power over them, which is precisely the true work of the true antichrist.

2. What is the use in Christendom of the people called "cardinals"? I will tell you. In Italy and Germany there are many rich convents, endowments, fiefs, and benefices, and as the best way of getting these into the hands of Rome, they

created cardinals, and gave them the sees, convents, and prelacies, and thus destroyed the service of God. That is why Italy is almost a desert now: the convents are destroyed, the sees consumed, the revenues of the prelacies and of all the churches drawn to Rome; towns are decayed, the country and the people ruined, because there is no more any worship of God or preaching; why? Because the cardinals must have all the wealth. No Turk could have thus desolated Italy and overthrown the worship of God.

Now that Italy is sucked dry, they come to Germany and begin very quietly; but if we look on quietly Germany will soon be brought into the same state as Italy. We have a few cardinals already. What the Romanists mean thereby the drunken Germans are not to see until they have lost everything—bishoprics, convents, benefices, fiefs, even to their last farthing. Antichrist must take the riches of the earth, as it is written (Dan. xi. 8, 39, 43). They begin by taking off the cream of the bishoprics, convents, and fiefs; and as they do not dare to destroy everything as they have done in Italy, they employ such holy cunning to join together ten or twenty prelacies, and take such a portion of each annually that the total amounts to a considerable sum. The priory of Würzburg gives one thousand guilders; those of Bamberg, Mayence, Treves, and others also contribute. In this way they collect one thousand or ten thousand guilders, in order that a cardinal may live at Rome in a state like that of a wealthy monarch.

After we have gained this, we will create thirty or forty cardinals on one day, and give one St. Michael's Mount, near Bamberg, and likewise the see of Würzburg, to which belong some rich benefices, until the churches and the cities are desolated; and then we shall say, We are the vicars of Christ, the shepherds of Christ's flocks; those mad, drunken Germans must submit to it. I advise, however, that there be made fewer cardinals, or that the pope should have to support them out of his own purse. It would be amply sufficient if there were twelve, and if each of them had an annual income of one thousand guilders.

What has brought us Germans to such a pass that we have to suffer this robbery and this destruction of our property by the pope? If the kingdom of France has resisted it, why do we Germans suffer ourselves to be fooled and deceived? It would be more endurable if they did nothing but rob us of our property; but they destroy the church and deprive Christ's flock of their good shepherds, and overthrow the service and word of God. Even if there were no cardinals at all, the church would not perish, for they do nothing for the good of Christendom; all they do is to traffic in and quarrel about prelacies and bishoprics, which any robber could do as well.

3. If we took away ninety-nine parts of the pope's court and only left one hundredth, it would still be large enough to answer questions on matters of belief. Now there is such a swarm of vermin at Rome, all called papal, that Babylon itself never saw the like. There are more than three thousand papal secretaries alone; but who shall count the other office-bearers, since there are so many offices that we can scarcely count them, and all waiting for German benefices, as wolves wait for a flock of sheep? I think Germany now pays more to the pope than it formerly paid the emperors; nay, some think more than three hundred thousand guilders are sent from Germany to Rome every year, for nothing whatever; and in return we are scoffed at and put to shame. Do we still wonder why princes, noblemen, cities, foundations, convents, and people grow poor? We should rather wonder that we have anything left to eat.

Now that we have got well into our game, let us pause a while and show that the Germans are not such fools as not to perceive or understand this Romish trickery. I do not here complain that God's commandments and Christian justice are despised at Rome; for the state of things in Christendom, especially at Rome, is too bad for us to complain of such high matters. Nor do I even complain that no account is taken of natural or secular justice and reason. The mischief lies still deeper. I complain that they do not observe their own fabricated canon law, though this is in itself rather mere tyranny, avarice, and worldly pomp, than a law. This we shall now show.

Long ago the emperors and princes of Germany allowed the pope to claim the *annates* from all German benefices; that is, half of the first year's income from every benefice. The object of this concession was that the pope should collect a fund with all this money to fight against the Turks and infidels, and to protect Christendom, so that the nobility should not have to bear the burden of the struggle alone, and that the priests should also contribute. The popes have made such use of this good simple piety of the Germans that they have taken this money for more than one hundred years, and have now made of it a regular tax and duty; and not only have they accumulated nothing, but they have founded out of it many posts and offices at Rome, which are paid by it yearly, as out of a ground-rent.

Whenever there is any pretence of fighting the Turks, they send out some commission for collecting money, and often send out indulgences under the same pretext of fighting the Turks. They think we Germans will always remain such great and inveterate fools that we will go on giving money to satisfy their unspeakable greed, though we see plainly that neither *annates*, nor absolution money, nor any other—not one farthing—goes against the Turks, but all goes into the bottomless sack. They lie and deceive, form and make covenants with us, of which they do not mean to keep one jot. And all this is done in the holy name of Christ and St. Peter.

This being so, the German nation, the bishops and princes, should remember that they are Christians, and should defend the people, who are committed to their government and protection in temporal and spiritual affairs, from these ravenous wolves in sheep's clothing, that profess to be shepherds and rulers; and since the *annates* are so shamefully abused, and the covenants concerning them not carried out, they should not suffer their lands and people to be so piteously and unrighteously flayed and ruined; but by an imperial or a national law they should either retain the *annates* in the country, or abolish them altogether. For since they do not keep to the covenants, they have no right to the *annates*; therefore bishops and princes are bound to punish this thievery and robbery, or prevent it, as justice demands. And herein should they assist and strengthen the pope, who is perchance too weak to prevent this scandal by himself or, if he wishes to protect or support it, restrain and oppose him as a wolf and tyrant; for he has no authority to do evil or to protect evil-doers. Even if it were proposed to collect any such treasure for use against the Turks, we should be wise in future, and remember that the German nation is more fitted to take charge of it than the pope, seeing that the German nation by itself is able to provide men enough, if the money is forthcoming. This matter of the *annates* is like many other Romish pretexts. . . .

This precious Roman avarice has also invented the practice of selling and lending prebends and benefices on condition that the seller or lender has the reversion, so that if the incumbent dies, the benefice falls to him that has sold it, lent it, or abandoned it; in this way they have made benefices heritable property, so that none can come to hold them unless the seller sells them to him, or leaves them to him at his death. Then there are many that give a benefice to another in name only, and on condition that he shall not receive a farthing. It is now, too, an old practice for a man to give another a benefice and to receive a certain annual sum, which proceeding was formerly called simony. And there are many other such little things which I cannot recount; and so they deal worse with the benefices than the heathens by the cross dealt with Christ's clothes.

But all this that I have spoken of is old and common at

Rome. Their avarice has invented another device, which I hope will be the last and choke it. The pope has made a noble discovery, called *Pectoralis Reservatio*, that is, "mental reservation"—*et propius motus*, that is, "and his own will and power." The matter is managed in this way: Suppose a man obtains a benefice at Rome, which is confirmed to him in due form; then comes another, who brings money, or who has done some other service of which the less said the better, and requests the pope to give him the same benefice: then the pope will take it from the first and give it him. If you say, that is wrong, the Most Holy Father must then excuse himself, that he may not be openly blamed for having violated justice; and he says "that in his heart and mind he reserved his authority over the said benefice," whilst he never had heard of or thought of the same in all his life. Thus he has devised a *gloss* which allows him in his proper person to lie and cheat and fool us all, and all this impudently and in open daylight, and nevertheless he claims to be the head of Christendom, letting the evil spirit rule him with manifest lies.

This wantonness and lying reservation of the popes has brought about an unutterable state of things at Rome. There is a buying and a selling, a changing, blustering and bargaining, cheating and lying, robbing and stealing, debauchery and villainy, and all kinds of contempt of God, that antichrist himself could not rule worse. Venice, Antwerp, Cairo, are nothing to this fair and market at Rome, except that there things are done with some reason and justice, whilst here things are done as the devil himself could wish. And out of this ocean a like virtue overflows all the world. Is it not natural that such people should dread a reformation and a free council, and should rather embroil all kings and princes than that their unity should bring about a council? Who would like his villainy to be exposed?

Finally, the pope has built a special house for this fine traffic—that is, the house of the *Datarius* at Rome. Thither all must come that bargain in this way for prebends and benefices; from him they must buy the *glosses* and obtain the right to practise such prime villainy. In former days it was fairly well at Rome, when justice had to be bought, or could only be put down by money; but now she has become so fastidious that she does not allow any one to commit villainies unless he has first bought the right to do it with great sums. If this is not a house of prostitution, worse than all houses of prostitution that can be conceived, I do not know what houses of prostitution really are.

If you bring money to this house, you can arrive at all that I have mentioned; and more than this, any sort of usury is made legitimate for money; property got by theft or robbery is here made legal. Here vows are annulled; here a monk obtains leave to quit his order; here priests can enter married life for money; here bastards can become legitimate; and dishonour and shame may arrive at high honours; all evil repute and disgrace is knighted and ennobled; here a marriage is suffered that is in a forbidden degree, or has some other defect. Oh, what a trafficking and plundering is there! one would think that the canon laws were only so many money-snares, from which he must free himself who would become a Christian man. Nay, there the devil becomes a saint, and a god besides. What heaven and earth might not do may be done by this house. Their ordinances are called *compositions* —compositions, forsooth! confusions rather. Oh, what a poor treasury is the toll on the Rhine compared with this holy house!

Let no one think that I say too much. It is all notorious, so that even at Rome they are forced to own that it is more terrible and worse than one can say. I have said and will say nothing of the infernal dregs of private vices. I only speak of well-known public matters, and yet my words do not suffice. Bishops, priests, and especially the doctors of the universities, who are paid to do it, ought to have unanimously written and exclaimed against it. Yea, if you will turn the leaf, you will discover the truth. . . .

Meanwhile, since this devilish state of things is not only an open robbery, deceit, and tyranny of the gates of hell, but also destroys Christianity body and soul, we are bound to use all our diligence to prevent this misery and destruction of Christendom. If we wish to fight the Turks, let us begin here, where they are worst. If we justly hang thieves and behead robbers, why do we leave the greed of Rome so unpunished, that is the greatest thief and robber that has appeared or can appear on earth, and does all this in the holy name of Christ and St. Peter? Who can suffer this and be silent about it? Almost everything that they possess has been stolen or got by robbery, as we learn from all histories. Why, the pope never bought those great possessions, so as to be able to raise well-nigh ten hundred thousand ducats from his ecclesiastical offices, without counting his gold mines described above and his land. He did not inherit it from Christ and St. Peter; no one gave it or lent it him; he has not acquired it by prescription. Tell me, where can he have got it? You can learn from this what their object is when they send out legates to collect money to be used against the Turk. . . .

Luther's Primary Works, Together with His Shorter and Larger Catechisms,
Edited by Henry Wace, D.D. and C. A. Buchheim, Ph.D.
London: Hodder and Stoughton, MDCCCXCVI.

PREFACE TO ST. PAUL'S
EPISTLE TO THE ROMANS

THIS EPISTLE IS IN TRUTH THE PRINCIPAL PART OF THE NEW Testament and the very purest Gospel. It fully deserves that every Christian should know it by heart, word for word, and should feed upon it every day, as daily bread for his soul. It cannot be read too often nor too deeply pondered, and the more it is studied the more precious and sweet to the taste does it become.

Therefore will I also do my part, with all the power that God has given me, to prepare the way by this little Preface, so that everyone may come to a right understanding of this Epistle. For it has hitherto been miserably obscured by glosses and all manner of idle talk, although it is in itself a shining light, almost sufficient to illuminate every part of the Holy Scriptures.

In the first place, we must learn to understand the language which is here used, and must know what St. Paul means by the words Law, Sin, Grace, Faith, Righteousness, Flesh, Spirit, and the like. Otherwise, all our reading of the Epistle will be in vain.

The little word, LAW, is not to be understood here in the ordinary sense, as teaching what things are to be done and what things are not to be done, as in the case of human laws, whose demands are met by outward works, with which the heart may have nothing to do. God judges according to the depths of the heart. His law, therefore, requires the whole heart, and is not satisfied with outward works, but, on the contrary, condemns as hypocrisy and lies the works which are done without the whole heart. Therefore, all men are called liars (Ps. cxvi. 11), because no one keeps the law of God, or can keep it, with the whole heart; for everyone finds in himself an aversion to that which is good, and an inclination toward that which is evil. Now where there is no free inclination toward that which is good, there the heart is not fully devoted to the law of God, and there also are certainly to be found sin and an incurring of the wrath of God, even though there may be outwardly the appearance of many good works and an honorable life. . . .

For although thou dost outwardly keep the law by thy works from fear of punishment or love or reward, yet thou doest it all without free inclination toward the law or love for it, but with aversion and under constraint and wouldst rather do otherwise if it were not for the law. It follows from this that thou art at heart an enemy of the law. What does it profit, then, that thou teachest others not to steal, whilst thou art thyself at heart a thief, and wouldst gladly be one outwardly if thou wast not afraid?—although even the outward works are not commonly performed for any length of time by such hypocrites. Thus thou teachest others, but not thyself. Thou dost not even thyself know what thou teachest, and hast never yet rightly understood the law. Yea, further—the law but increases sin, as the apostle says in chapter five (v. 20), because a man but grows the more hostile to the law the more it requires of him that which he cannot perform.

Therefore St. Paul says, in the seventh chapter (vii. 14), that the law is spiritual. What does this mean? If the law were carnal (bodily), it could be satisfied with works. But now, since it is spiritual, no one can meet its requirements, unless everything which he does proceeds from the depths of his heart. But such a heart can no one give but the Spirit of God, who conforms man to the law, so that he becomes cordially inclined toward the law, and thenceforth does all things, not from fear or compulsion, but with a willing heart. It is thus that the law is spiritual, because it must be loved and obeyed by such a spiritual heart and demands such a spirit. Where this spirit does not dwell in the heart, there remains sin, with aversion and hostility toward the law, although the law is good and just and holy.

Accustom thyself, therefore, to the thought, that it is one thing to do the works of the law, and a very different thing to fulfill the law. The works of the law consist in everything which man does, or can do, in conformity to the law by his free will and in his own strength. But since, along with and beneath such works, there remain in the heart aversion to the law and only a compulsory submission to it, such works are all of no avail nor benefit. This is what St. Paul means when he says, in chapter iii, verse 20; "By the works of the law no man becomes righteous before God."

Thou seest from this that the Scholastics and Sophists are deceivers, when they teach men that they can by works prepare themselves for grace. How can he by works prepare himself for that which is good, who performs no good work without unwillingness and aversion in his heart? How can the work which proceeds from an unwilling and rebellious heart be pleasing to God?

But to fulfill the law is to do with willingness and love the works which the law requires, and freely and without constraint of the law to lead an upright and godly life, as if there were no law and no penalty for disobedience. But such a willingness and free love for the law is bestowed upon the heart by the Holy Spirit, as the apostle says in the fifth chapter (v. 5). But the Spirit is not given, as he declares in the introduction to the Epistle, except in, with, and through faith in Jesus Christ. So likewise faith cometh not, except only through the Word of God, or the Gospel, which preaches Christ, teaching that He is the Son of God and Son of Man, slain and risen from the dead for our sakes. This is declared in chapter iii, verse 25: "Whom God hath set forth to be a propitiation through faith in his blood;" in chapter iv, verse 25: "Who was delivered for our offences, and was raised again for our justification;" and in chapter x, verse 9: "And that if thou shalt confess with thy mouth the Lord Jesus, and shalt believe in thine heart that God hath raised him from the dead, thou shalt be saved."

Hence it is that faith alone makes righteous (justifies) and fulfills the law, for it brings the Spirit through the merits of Christ. But the Spirit makes the heart free and willing, as the law requires; and then good works proceed of themselves from faith. This is what he means in chapter three, where, after having entirely rejected the works of the law, it sounds as though he would abolish the law itself through faith. No, says he (v. 31), we establish the law through faith; that is, we fulfill it through faith. . . .

FAITH is not the human fancy and dream which some people mistake for faith. When such persons see that no amendment of the life and no good works follow, although they may hear and talk much about faith, they fall into error and declare that faith is not enough, but we must perform good works if we would be pious and attain salvation. In consequence of this, when they hear the Gospel, they fall to work and frame for themselves by their own powers a notion in their hearts which says, I believe. This they then consider true faith. But as it is a human invention and notion, of which the heart in its depths finds out nothing, it accomplishes also nothing and no amendment of the life follows.

But faith is a divine work in us, which transforms us and begets us anew from God (John 1:13), which crucifies the old Adam, makes us in heart, temper, disposition, and in all our powers entirely different men, and brings with it the Holy Spirit. O, this faith is a living, busy, active, powerful thing! It is impossible that it should not be ceaselessly doing that which is good. It does not even ask whether good works should be done; but before the question can be asked, it has done them, and it is constantly engaged in doing them. But he who does not do such works, is a man without faith. He gropes and casts about him to find faith and good works, not knowing what either of them is, and yet prattles and idly multiplies words about faith and good works.

Faith is a living, well-founded confidence in the grace of God, so perfectly certain that it would die a thousand times rather than surrender its conviction. Such confidence and personal knowledge of divine grace makes its possessor joyful, bold, and full of warm affection toward God and all created things—all of which the Holy Spirit works in faith. Hence, such a man becomes without constraint willing and eager to do good to everyone, to serve everyone, to suffer all manner of ills, in order to please and to glorify God, who has shown toward him such grace. It is thus impossible to separate works from faith—yea, just as impossible as to separate burning and shining from fire. Therefore be on your guard against your own false notions and unprofitable babblings, ye who would be so wise in your opinions about faith and good works, although you are the greatest fools. Pray God that He may work faith in you; otherwise you must remain forever without faith, whatever fancies you may invent and whatever works you may be able to perform.

Preface to St. Paul's Epistle to the Romans,
Translated by Dr. Charles E. Hay.
Philadelphia: Lutheran Publication Society, 1903.

PHILIP MELANCH-THON

1497 – 1560

ON

PHILIP MELANCHTHON

A YOUNG MAN, TWENTY-ONE YEARS OLD, PHILIP MELANCH-
thon joined the faculty at the University of Wittenberg, as
Professor of Greek. He already was a Humanist scholar of
wide renown, and he brought distinction to the institution
where he and Martin Luther formed a lifelong friendship.
Luther was the more forceful character and Melanchthon fell
under his spell, adopted his views, became the literary scribe
of the early Lutheran movement, and in his *Loci Communes*
produced the first treatise on systematic theology written by
a Protestant.

Luther was robust, stormy, sometimes crude; Melanchthon
was gracious, gentle, conciliatory. They made a strange team
but, despite tensions and differences, their affectionate friendship held firm until Luther's death. How impossible it is to
take literally and seriously everything that Luther said in
his boisterous hours, as some of his detractors have done,
is illustrated in his dealing with his friend. Asked how he
thought St. Paul looked, Luther laughingly answered: "I
think he was a scrawny shrimp like Melanchthon," and once,
making uproarious fun of his quiet, ascetic friend he cried,
"Sin for all you are worth! God can forgive only a lusty
sinner."

Nevertheless, while Melanchthon, especially in his early years, was dominated by Luther, his own contribution to the Reformation was of first-class significance. He was a great teacher and his classroom was crowded with eager youths. He was a master of style and was called on repeatedly to put into telling form what needed to be said. He was the most renowned negotiator the German Protestants had, and in one conference and diet after another he displayed his diplomatic powers.

The *Loci Communes* is not exciting reading now, but it presents with clarity the Protestant position which, when the book was written, was new and challenging. Luther's major service to theology was to slough off the old scholastic approach to dogma and to found doctrine primarily on the Scriptures. Melanchthon with systematic thoroughness presented the results of this startling innovation, and what his book meant to those who first read it modern minds cannot readily imagine. At least seventeen editions of it in Latin appeared between 1521 and 1525, besides several reprints of a German translation; Luther called it "an invincible book, worthy not only of immortality, but of being placed in the Canon"; and for half a century it held first place as the theological textbook in the universities.

If one is to understand Melanchthon's theological emphases, one must see what the Reformers were fighting against. They confronted a vast system of "works," by which the soul's salvation could be assured. To multitudes Roman Catholicism had become an elaborate apparatus of performances by which the horrors of hell could be avoided and the pains of purgatory mitigated and shortened. When Zwingli, for example, became parish priest of the great convent of Einsiedeln, he found himself dealing with a statue of the Virgin Mary, reputed to possess miraculous powers, to pray before which a hundred thousand pilgrims came annually. Over the portal of the shrine stood the inscription: "Here is complete forgiveness of all possible transgressions."

Against this entire apparatus of salvation by "works"—masses, pilgrimages, image-worship, auricular confession, penances, etc.—the Reformers set themselves, often with such fury that their extravagant utterances are difficult for moderns to understand. The fallacy of seeking salvation by outward deeds which man can perform was founded, they were sure, on a shallow idea of human wickedness, and they portrayed man's sinfulness as so dark and desperate that no "works" of his could cure it. They went out to achieve what Calvin called "the utter destruction of human glory, that God might be all in all." They called the best that man by himself alone can do "filthy rags." Good works without faith—that is, goodness motived by fear of punishment or selfish desire for reward—are, said Luther, "idle, damnable sins." They saw man as so desperately wicked that no dilly-dallying with outward observances or legalistic morality could save him. Only God's grace could bring salvation, cleansing and regenerating the soul until, being now a "good tree," the man could bear "good fruit." They stressed, underlined and played up man's hopeless estate as a sinner that they might achieve in him, first a sense of great need, then an acceptance of a great salvation through God's regenerating grace, and then an experience of great gratitude, overflowing in good works spontaneously rising from a heart made right with God.

When in Melanchthon we run on shocking sayings about human goodness—"How stinking are the moral virtues, how bloody are the rags of righteousness of the saints!"—his meaning can be grasped only if we understand what he is attacking. He wants real goodness. He lauds and extols it. But he is furious against the vulgar ideas and superstitious practices of churchmen who suppose that real goodness can be achieved by outward performances and pious legalisms, while their inward lives are uncleansed, unregenerate, undedicated.

On fundamental matters like this, Melanchthon and Luther

always saw eye to eye but, as the years passed, in successive editions of *Loci Communes*, Melanchthon's more individual, independent judgments appeared. He always meant by faith what Luther meant, not mere intellectual assent but vital, personal self-committal; he was, however, more of an intellectualist than Luther, and one of his major contributions was his reassertion of the rights of natural reason, and his insistence that reason and revelation cannot be out of harmony. His theology, therefore, became more and more an ordered, well-integrated system, and one of the main emphases of historic Protestantism finds in him its earliest expression, that the church is composed "of those who hold pure doctrine and agree in it." For a very competent treatment of this and similar developments the reader is referred to Arthur Cushman McGiffert's *Protestant Thought Before Kant*.

In one central matter Melanchthon's thought showed marked growth—he broke free from Luther's stern acceptance of predestination. Luther had had a stormy struggle concerning the doctrine, which he himself described:

Common sense and natural reason are highly offended that God by his mere will deserts, hardens and damns, as if he delighted in sins and in such eternal torments, he who is said to be of such mercy and goodness. Such a concept of God appears wicked, cruel and intolerable, and by it many men have been revolted in all ages. I myself was once offended to the very depth of the abyss of desperation, so that I wished I had never been created. There is no use trying to get away from this by ingenious distinctions. Natural reason, however much it is offended, must admit the consequences of the omniscience and omnipotence of God.

Melanchthon, nevertheless, did get away from it, although at first he had accepted it. If God predestines everything and man's free will is an illusion, then God himself is responsible for all the evil men do; men are not responsible since they have no choice, and to exhort them, instruct them, praise them when good and blame them when evil is insane—this logic Melanchthon accepted despite Augustine and Luther. He taught at last, in 1543, that a man's final destiny is not predestined from all eternity, but that, while God's grace comes first, man has power to accept or reject it. "God is not the cause of sin," he said. "Contingence must evidently be conceded, because sin, properly speaking, arises from the will of the devil and of man, and is committed without the approbation of God and without his forcing our wills. Hence it is not by any means committed necessarily by absolute necessity."

Melanchthon, therefore, was no mere copy of Luther, but made his own distinctive contribution to Protestant theology. His most notable service, however, sprang from his desire to hold Christendom together and to prevent a final disruption. He had an ecumenical spirit, and passionately wished to find common grounds of agreement on which to base Christian unity. To be sure, he could not foresee the future and, turning his back on his Swiss brethren, disliking and fearing Zwingli and all his ways, he sought instead some ground of mutual understanding with Rome, where it was not to be found. This endeavor came to its climax at the Diet of Augsburg (1530), where Melanchthon was chosen to prepare the statement of the Protestants for presentation to the Emperor —one of the most influential pronouncements of the Reformation. It was sufficiently firm and uncompromising so that Calvin signed it, and Luther rejoiced that he had "lived to see the hour when Christ was confessed by such great confessors in such a glorious Confession." But its irenic and conciliatory spirit—it did not openly condemn the papacy, it did not mention Scripture as the sole authority, nor did it assert the universal priesthood of all believers—is indicated in its opening sentence:

Inasmuch as the Churches among us dissent in no articles of faith from the Holy Scriptures nor the Church Catholic, and only omit a few of certain abuses, which are novel, and have crept in with time partly and in part have been introduced by violence, and contrary to the purport of the canons, we beg that your

Imperial Majesty would clemently hear both what ought to be changed, and what are the reasons why people ought not to be forced against their consciences to observe these abuses.

Melanchthon's ecumenical endeavor failed in its major purpose. The "abuses"—enforced celibacy of the priesthood, the sacrificial character of the Mass, the necessity of auricular confession, monastic vows, and the episcopate's assumption of both spiritual and secular authority—were too precious to the Roman system to be surrendered. But the Augsburg Confession did rally the united support of German Protestantism, and remains still the doctrinal statement in which millions of Protestants affirm their faith.

Melanchthon's later years were disturbed by unhappy controversies. His "supreme determination" was undoubtedly, as he said, "to preserve purity of doctrine and the true worship of God in the churches committed to our faith," but he tried to achieve that end by a kind of conciliation unacceptable to many of Luther's followers, insisting on the acceptance of whatever the Scriptures demanded and on refusing whatever the Scriptures denied, but on consenting also to observances about which the Scriptures said nothing. It was a dangerous and mistaken attempt at compromise. It opened the door, so his enemies saw clearly, to some of the "abuses." He was accused of trimming, of vacillation, of weak surrender, until once he prayed for death that he might escape the "madness of the theologians."

Nevertheless, Melanchthon stands out now as one of the most admirable figures of the Reformation, and could his gracious, conciliatory, pacific spirit, searching for mutual understanding and unity, wherever they might be found, have prevailed within Protestantism, and between Protestantism and the reformers within Roman Catholicism, history would have a less contentious and bloodthirsty tale to tell.

An excellent biography of the Reformer is James William Richard's *Philip Melanchthon, The Protestant Preceptor of Germany.*

MELANCHTHON'S ORATION
AT THE FUNERAL OF
MARTIN LUTHER

WHAT, THEN, ARE THE GREAT AND SPLENDID THINGS DIS-closed by Luther which render his life illustrious? Many are crying out that confusion has come upon the church, and that inexplicable controversies have arisen. I reply that this belongs to the regulation of the church. When the Holy Spirit reproves the world, disorders arise on account of the obstinacy of the wicked. The fault is with those who will not hear the Son of God, of whom the Heavenly Father says: 'Hear ye him.' Luther brought to light the true and necessary doctrine. That the densest darkness existed touching the doctrine of repentance, is evident. In his discussions he showed what true repentance is, and that is, the refuge and the sure comfort of the soul which quails under the sense of the wrath of God. He expounded Paul's doctrine, which says that man is justified by faith. He showed the difference between the Law and the Gospel, between the righteousness of faith and civil righteousness. He also showed what the true worship of God is, and recalled the church from heathenish superstition, which imagines that God is worshipped, even though the mind, agitated by some academic doubt, turns away from God. He bade us worship in faith and with a good conscience, and led us to the one Mediator, the Son of God, who sits at the right hand of the Eternal Father and makes intercession for us—not to images or dead men, that by a shocking superstition impious men might worship images and dead men.

He also pointed out other services acceptable to God, and so adorned and guarded civil life, as it had never been adorned and guarded by any other man's writings. Then from necessary services he separated the puerilities of human ceremonies, the rites and institutions which hinder the true worship of God. And that the heavenly truth might be handed down to posterity he translated the Prophetical and Apostolic Scriptures into the German language with so much accuracy that his version is more easily understood by the reader than most commentaries.

He also published many expositions, which Erasmus was wont to say excelled all others. And as it is recorded respecting the rebuilding of Jerusalem that with one hand they builded and with the other they held the sword, so he fought with the enemies of the true doctrine, and at the same time composed annotations replete with heavenly truth, and by his pious counsel brought assistance to the consciences of many.

Inasmuch as a large part of the doctrine cannot be understood by human reason, as the doctrine of the remission of sins and of faith, it must be acknowledged that he was taught of God; and many of us witnessed the struggles through which he passed, in establishing the principle that by faith are we received and heard of God.

Hence throughout eternity pious souls will magnify the benefits which God has bestowed on the church through Luther. First they will give thanks to God. Then they will own that they owe much to the labours of this man, even though atheists who mock the church declare that these splendid achievements are empty and superstitious nothings.

It is not true, as some falsely affirm, that intricate disputes have arisen, that the apple of discord has been thrown into the church, that the riddles of the Sphynx have been proposed. It is an easy matter for discreet and pious persons, and for those who do not judge maliciously to see by a comparison of views which accord with heavenly doctrine, and which do not. Yea, without doubt these controversies have already been settled in the minds of all pious persons. For since God wills to reveal himself and his purposes in the language of the Prophets and Apostles, it is not to be imagined that that language is as ambiguous as the leaves of the Sibyl, which, when disturbed, fly away, the sport of the winds.

Some, by no means evil-minded persons, have complained that Luther displayed too much severity. I will not deny this. But I answer in the language of Erasmus: 'Because of the magnitude of the disorders God gave this age a violent physician.' When God raised up this instrument against the proud and impudent enemies of the truth, he spoke as he did to Jeremiah: 'Behold I place my words in thy mouth; destroy and build.' Over against these enemies God set this mighty destroyer. In vain do they find fault with God. Moreover, God does not govern the church by human counsels; nor does he choose instruments very like those of men. It is natural for mediocre and inferior minds to dislike those of more ardent character, whether good or bad. When Aristides saw Themistocles by the mighty impulse of genius undertake and successfully accomplish great achievements, though he congratulated the state, he sought to turn the zealous mind of Themistocles from its course.

I do not deny that the more ardent characters sometimes make mistakes, for amid the weakness of human nature no one is without fault. But we may say of such a one what the ancients said of Hercules, Cimon, and others: 'rough indeed, but worthy of all praise.' And in the church, if, as Paul says, he wars a good warfare, holding faith and a good conscience, he is to be held in the highest esteem by us.

That Luther was such we do know, for he constantly defended purity of doctrine and kept a good conscience. There is no one who knew him, who does not know that he was possessed of the greatest kindness, and of the greatest affability in the society of his friends, and that he was in no sense contentious or quarrelsome. He also exhibited, as such a man ought, the greatest dignity of demeanour. He possessed

'An upright character, a gracious speech.'

Rather may we apply to him the words of Paul: 'Whatsoever things are true, whatsoever things are honest, whatsoever things are just, whatsoever things are pure, whatsoever things are lovely, whatsoever things are of good report.' If he was severe, it was the severity of zeal for the truth, not the love of strife, or of harshness. Of these things we and many others are witnesses. To his sixty-third year he spent his life in the most ardent study of religion and of all the liberal arts. No speech of mine can worthily set forth the praises of such a man. No lewd passions were ever detected in him, no seditious counsels. He was emphatically the advocate of peace. He never mingled the arts of politics with the affairs of the church for the purpose of augmenting his own authority, or that of his friends. Such wisdom and virtue, I am persuaded, do not arise from mere human diligence. Brave, lofty, ardent souls, such as Luther had, must be divinely guided.

What shall I say of his other virtues? Often have I found him weeping and praying for the whole church. He spent a part of almost every day reading the Psalms, with which he mingled his own supplications amid tears and groans. Often did he express his indignation at those who through indifference or pretence of other occupations, are indifferent in the matter of prayer. On this account, he said, Divine Wisdom has prescribed forms of prayer, that by reading them our minds may be quickened, and the voice ever may proclaim the God we worship.

In the many grave deliberations incident to the public perils, we observed the transcendent vigour of his mind, his valour, his unshaken courage, where terror reigned. God was his anchor, and faith never failed him.

As regards the penetration of his mind, in the midst of uncertainties he alone saw what was to be done. Nor was he indifferent, as many suppose, to the public weal. On the contrary he knew the wants of the state, and clearly understood the feelings and wishes of his fellow-citizens. And though his genius was so extraordinary, yet he read with the greatest eagerness both ancient and modern ecclesiastical writings and all histories, that he might find in them examples applicable to present conditions.

The immortal monuments of his eloquence remain, nor has the power of his oratory ever been surpassed.

The removal of such a man from our midst, a man of the most transcendent genius, skilled in learning, trained by long experience, adorned with many superb and heroic virtues, chosen of God for the reformation of the church, loving us all with a paternal affection—the removal of such a man from our midst calls for tears and lamentations. We are like orphans bereft of a distinguished and faithful father. But though we must bow to God, yet let us not permit the memory of his virtues and of his good offices to perish from among us. And let us rejoice that he now holds that familiar and delightful intercourse with God and his Son, our Lord Jesus Christ, which by faith in the Son of God he always sought and expected, where, by the manifestations of God, and by the testimony of the whole church in heaven, he not only hears the applause of his toils in the service of the Gospel, but is also delivered from the mortal body as from a prison, and has entered that vastly higher school, where he can contemplate the essence of God, the two natures joined in Christ, and the whole purpose set forth in founding and redeeming the church—which great things, contained and set forth in the sacred oracles, he contemplated by faith; but seeing them now face to face, he rejoices with unspeakable joy; and with his whole soul he ardently pours forth thanks to God for his great goodness.

Philip Melanchthon, The Protestant Preceptor of Germany,
by James William Richard.
New York: G. P. Putnam's Sons, 1898.

THE LOCI COMMUNES

OF THE WHOLE SCRIPTURE THERE ARE TWO PARTS: THE LAW and the gospel. The law indicates the sickness, the gospel the remedy. To use Paul's words, the law is a minister of death, while the gospel is a minister of life and peace. "The strength of sin is the law," I Cor. 15:56; the gospel is the power or strength of salvation to everyone that believes. Nor has the Scripture so narrated the law and gospel in such a manner that one would regard as gospel what Matthew, Mark, Luke and John have written, and as law what Moses has recorded. But the plan of the gospel is scattered; there are promises in both the Old and the New Testaments. And again, laws are scattered throughout all the books of the Old and the New Testaments. Nor are the periods of law and gospel to be discriminated as is commonly thought, although sometimes law, sometimes gospel one after the other have been revealed. Every period that occurs to my mind is a period of law and gospel just as men in every period are justified in the same way: sin being revealed by the law, and grace through a promise or the gospel. . . .

Just as the law is that by which the right is enjoined, and by which sin is made manifest, so also the gospel is the promise of the grace or mercy of God, and therefore the forgiveness of sin and the testimony of God's benevolence toward us. Our minds assured of God's benevolence by this testimony believe that He has forgiven all guilt; and being thus elevated, love and praise God and are exceedingly joyful and rejoice in God. . . . Moreover Christ is the pledge of all these promises; wherefore all scriptural promises must be referred to him, who at first obscurely, but later more clearly has been revealed in them. . . .

The prophets teach the law when they censure hypocrisy, impiety, carnal security and the like. For they especially condemn hidden vices or hypocrisy. They declare the gospel also as often as they incite, animate and fill shattered consciences with the lively promise of Christ in such a manner that that Apostolic expression resounds: "Who shall separate us from the love of God?" Rom. 8:35. The gospels of Matthew, Mark, Luke and John, treat after a fashion, now of law and now of promises, and in these give examples both of the grace and of the wrath of God. . . .

I have advised these things chiefly for this reason: to destroy the current error which the impious sophistical professors of theology have produced about the distinction between law and gospel, and the Old and the New Testaments. It is this: that Moses was succeeded by Christ who gave a new law called the gospel, which is contained in Matt. 5 and 6. And further that between the law of Moses and that of Christ there is this difference: the Mosaic law demands only external works while that of Christ demands the affections; indeed the Mosaic law teaches a sort of hypocritical and Pharisaic righteousness. For what is the simulation of external works but Pharisaism?

Moreover the prophets testify that the Mosaic law demands the affections also, when they so often enjoin upon man to recognize and to fear God, to do judgment and righteousness. These things the Sophists will no doubt tell me were not taught before the incarnation of Christ and the men of their own age. However what sentence is better known than that of Jeremiah? The Sophists, though unwillingly, ought to refer it to the law of Moses. For in chapter 7:22 he says: "I did not speak with your fathers nor order precepts upon them concerning holocausts and victims, in the day that I led them out of Egypt: but this word I did enjoin saying: Hear ye my voice and I will be to you a God and ye shall be to me a people." Tell me, Thomas, what has entered your mind that you should teach that the Mosaic law demands nothing but Pharisaism that is, external works, when Moses himself so often demands the affections in no obscure words. And to pass over many places, he surely forbids the coveting of another's property, etc. Ex. 20:17. He had beforehand already interdicted "work" when he forbade stealing and adultery. Therefore you will grant that the following words were stipulated with reference to the affection: "Thou shalt covet not thy neighbor's wife, nor his manservant, etc.," and in Deut. 10:12: "And now, O Israel, what does the Lord thy God, demand of thee but to fear the Lord thy God, and walk in his ways and love him, and serve the Lord thy God, with thy whole heart and with thy whole mind, and keep the mandates of the Lord and his ceremonies, which I this day enjoin upon thee, that it may be well with thee." And again in Deut. 5:16: "Circumcise the foreskin of your heart and harden not your neck, etc." You can find in Moses 600 pages of this nature, so that it is not doubtful but that the law of Moses demands both affections and works.

Christ in like manner explains the law, for grace cannot be proclaimed without the law. And he rebukes the interpretation of the Pharisees and Scribes from the beginning when he says that we shall not enter the kingdom of heaven unless our righteousness shall exceed the righteousness of the Pharisees and the Scribes. The Pharisees interpreted the law thus: you satisfy the law, "Thou shalt not kill", if you do not kill with the hand; you satisfy the law, "Thou shalt commit no adultery" if you do not seduce another man's wife. Christ however teaches that the law demands the affections of the heart and not only an external simulation of works. For the law forbade concupiscence. The law even forbade vindication and in the same manner demanded that one love his enemies. Leviticus 19:17: "Thou shalt not hate thy brother in thy heart, but publicly accuse him lest you carry sin against him. Do not vindicate nor be mindful of an injury of the sons of your people, and love thy neighbor as thyself."

Therefore law and gospel ought to be declared at the same time and both sin and grace ought to be shown. Two cherubim have been placed in the Ark, law and gospel; wherefore it happens that you cannot rightly and successfully teach the gospel without the law or the law without the gospel. And as Christ has joined the law with the gospel, so also the prophets joined the gospel with the law. . . .

Now it remains to teach, however it may be, what is the power of the law and what that of the gospel. For in some degree it may be learned from this, what is the distinction between law and gospel. Indeed, in the first place, the Scripture differs with human reason on the power of the law. Scripture calls the law the power of wrath and of sin, the scepter of an executioner, lightning, thunder. Human reason calls it a correction for crimes, a principle of living. For this language Cicero uses when he speaks of laws. Nothing is more universally celebrated than the praises of laws. So much so that to the flesh Paul might seem crazy to call the law "the strength of sin." I Cor. 15:56. Thus the Jews (John 9:28) who professed to be disciples of Moses were unwilling to recognize Christ. Wherefore, in order to discuss the power of the law with exactness, I shall compare the two classes of mankind.

To the first class belong those who carnally understand the law, but do not perceive that it demands the impossible. These are blind and see neither sin, nor law, nor righteousness. Moreover, they are the hypocritical Sophists of all ages. Paul calls the righteousness of this class "the righteousness by the works of the law." He especially means those who hear the law and control their hands, their feet, and their mouth, but not their hearts. For they would prefer to be without the law, no matter how holy they may seem to themselves. This class takes joy in pleasures, wealth, and honor. Of what sort these are, none has said better than the Spirit of God. In the first place, they are without faith, that is, their heart understands nothing about God. As Scripture says: "It does not seek God," meaning thereby that their heart does not magnify but despises God. Then, too, according to Psalm 13, "they turn aside," that is, since they neither fear nor believe God, they turn off to their own counsels. In addition, they even try to justify themselves by their own works. The Scripture has often reproved this class of men, calling them "workers of iniquity." In Psalm 5:10, David thus describes hypocrites: "In whose mouth there is no right or candor, whose inward parts are vanity, whose throat is an open abyss." To this class of men, there is no difficulty in the law. For they live according to a false and carnal knowledge of the law. Therefore, the law cannot accomplish in them what it ought, but they devise unto themselves idols, images of man and the shadows of carnal virtues. Moreover, they are impelled to simulate good works by a carnal affection, either from the fear of punishment, or the pursuit of gain; and are foolishly secure, since they do not see the sickness of their own mind.

The pride, haughtiness, and pertinacity of this class of men are incredible. They are so far from satisfying the law that there are none that are farther. The Pharisee in Luke 18:11 who says—"I am not like other men."—belongs to this class. And Isa. 28:15 describes the drunkards of Ephraim in the following language: "We have made league with death, and with hell have we made a pact." And in Jeremiah we read "They knew not to blush." Matt. 7:23: "Ye workers of iniquity." Paul witnesses that he was such before his conversion, in Rom. 7:8: "I have once lived without the law," that is, there was a time when I seemed to exceed illustriously the law, a time when I surpassed all my equals in the hypocrisy of works. For the law did not then condemn, nor accuse, nor arraign me. And such indeed are all men, who attempt to exhibit the law through natural powers according to the capacity of reason, when they do not understand either the law or their own powers. These are they who behold only the back of Moses, who see only his veiled face, as Paul says in II Cor. 3:17, when he asserts that the Jews cannot understand evangelical righteousness because they behold Moses with veiled hearts. He means that the Jews cannot see what the law demands, as we can who are nothing but sin and an accursed thing. . . .

To the second class of mankind, belong all those to whom pertain these words of Paul: "The law is the strength of wrath," etc. God reveals the law to these, and shows them the condition of their hearts. Indeed, God terrifies and confounds them by the sense of their sin. These are precisely the ones in whom God works through the law. The law does nothing in hypocrites; but they of themselves reproduce a sort of shadow of the law, by means of a kind of hypocritical righteousness. In these the law does its true and proper work. It shows them sin. This is truly done because it is done by God. And Scripture calls this work: "Judgment, the wrath of God, the fury of God, the aspect and face of wrath," etc. Psalm 96:2 ff. says "Judgment is the correction of his throne, fire will go before him and burn up his enemies round about. His lightnings shown upon the earth, the earth saw and was moved. The mountains melted like wax from before the face of the Lord, the whole earth from before the face of the Lord." Psalm 75:9: "From heaven thou hast made judgment to be heard, the earth trembled and shook." And Zech. 2:13: "Let all flesh keep silence before the Lord." Isa. 13:13: "He will shake the earth by the strength of his mouth, and with the wrath of his lips will he kill the impious." Habk. 3:6: "He looked upon and dissolved the nations, and the mountains were forever removed." But what profit is there in heaping up many passages, since there is plainly another part of Scripture, the law, and its function is to kill and to condemn, to show the root of our sin and to confound us? It not only mortifies avarice or lust, but it mortifies the very head of all evil, self-love, and the judgment of reason, and whatever nature possesses that may seem to be good in itself. From this it will appear, how stinking are the moral virtues, how bloody are the rags of the righteousness of the saints! To be sure, even Moses should exclaim in Ex. 34:7: "Before thy face not even the innocent is innocent." And Nah. 1:3: "Cleansing he will not make innocent." And David in Ps. 142:2: "Enter not into judgment with thy servant"; and Ps. 6:2: "Lord, try me not in thy fury." In Isaiah 38:13, Hezekiah says: "As a lion he breaketh all my bones." And this is what John has said in a few words, as is his custom in all things, 1:17: "The law was given by Moses, but grace and truth came through Jesus Christ." . . .

Those whom conscience has terrorized to such a degree, would be driven doubtless to despair as usually happens in the case of condemned individuals, unless they were consoled and encouraged by the promise of the grace and mercy of God, which is rightly called the gospel. If an afflicted conscience believes the promise of grace in Christ, it is revived and vivified by faith, as is wonderfully declared by various examples. . . .

Sometime ago, I mentioned how confused David was by the word of Nathan. And he would have utterly perished had he not heard at once the gospel: "The Lord hath taken away thy sin, thou shalt not die," II Chron. 12:13. Some are of the opinion, that we are to seek nothing but allegories in the histories of the Old Testament. But here you can see how much instruction there is in this one example of David, even if you consider the letter alone. Nay more, this alone is to be seen, in that by which the spirit of God has largely exhibited the works both of wrath and also of mercy. What

word could be more evangelically conceived than this: "The
Lord hath taken away thy sin?" Is this not the sum of the
gospel or of the preaching of the New Testament: sin has
been taken away? You may add to these, if you will, a heap
of gospel traditions. For instance, Luke 7:37 ff. A woman
sinner washes the Lord's feet with her tears, and he consoles
her with these words: "Thy sins are remitted unto thee."
And what story is more commonly known than that of the
prodigal son, in Luke 15, who confesses his sin, and upon
his confession, the father lovingly receives, embraces, and
kisses him. Luke 5: Peter dumfounded by a miracle and
therefore shocked at heart, exclaims: "Depart from me, O
Lord, for I am a sinful man." Christ consoles and restores
him with these words: "Fear not," etc.

From these examples, I believe it can be understood just
what is the difference between the law and the gospel, and
what is the power of the law and what that of the gospel.
The law terrorizes, the gospel consoles. The law is the voice
of wrath and of death, the gospel that of peace and life, or
as the prophet says, the voice of the bridegroom and bride.
And he who is thus encouraged by the voice of the gospel and believes in God is already justified, as I shall sub-
sequently show. It is not a thing unknown to Christians,
how much joy, how much gladness this consolation af-
fords. Those joyful words of the prophets by which they
describe Christ and the church, pertain to this. Isa. 32:13:
"And my people will dwell in the beauty of peace and the
tabernacles of trust and in rich repose." Likewise: "Joy and
gladness will be found in it, and the voice of praise." In
Jer. 33:6: "I will reveal to them the declaration of peace
and truth. And it will be to me for a name and joy
and praise and exultation to all the nations of the earth."
Zephaniah 3:9: "I shall give the people an elect lip that all
may call on the name of the Lord." Psal. 20:7: "Thou wilt
rejoice him with gladness, etc." And Psal. 96:11: "Light

has arisen unto the just, and gladness in the heart of the righteous."

But what is to be gained from the multiplication of incidents, seeing that both from the promulgation of the gospel and the advent of Christ alike, the power of the law and of the gospel is made sufficiently clear.

We are justified when, mortified by the law, we are raised up by the word of grace that is promised in Christ, or in the gospel that forgives sins; and when we cling to Christ nothing doubting but that the righteousness of Christ is our righteousness, that his satisfaction is our expiation, that his resurrection is ours. In a word, nothing doubting that our sins are forgiven and that God loves and cherishes us. Our works however good they may be do not constitute our righteousness. For righteousness is faith alone in the mercy and grace of God in Jesus Christ. That is what Paul means when he says: "The just live by faith." Rom. 3:22 reads: "Righteousness of God is by the faith of Jesus Christ.". . .

Faith is nothing other than reliance upon the divine mercy promised in Christ. . . . This reliance on the benevolence or mercy of God first pacifies the heart, and then incites us to give thanks to God for his mercy, so that we of our own accord and joyfully do the law. . . .

For this reason, it is most beautifully said in the book of Ecclesiasticus 32:17: "In all thy work believe with faith in thy mind. For this is the keeping of the commandments." Whatsoever kind the works may be: eating, drinking, working with the hand, teaching, I add that even they are plainly sins. You should not look at works: look at the promise of the mercy of God with trust in him doubting nothing, but that you have in heaven not a judge, but a father that cares for you just as human parents care for their children. But if there were no signification of the divine will toward us other than the fact that he has willed to be called father in that prayer which we daily pray, this alone should be sufficient argument that nothing is demanded of us before our faith. Now since God so often demands faith, since he so often approves of it alone, since he has commended it unto us by rich promises and in addition by the death of his son, why do we not commit ourselves to such a great mercy as this, and believe it? Scholastic theology has taught human works and satisfactions, for faith, for an anchor of consciences. May God destroy that scandal of his church! . . .

Now this fact must be considered also: that just as works are the fruits of the Spirit, they are also indications, testimonies, and signs of it. Christ says as much in Matt. 7:16: "By their fruits ye shall know them." For hypocrisy cannot forever be dissembled, and faith unable to assert itself to most eagerly serve God as a pious son serves a pious father. For when by faith we have tasted of the mercy of God, and have known the divine goodness through the word of the gospel which pardons our sins and promises grace, the soul cannot but love God in return and be joyful, and express its gratitude by some mutual kindness as it were for such great mercy. Paul has most graphically said the same (Rom. 8:15): "By faith we cry: Abba, father." Now because such a mind subjects itself to God, false ambition, jealousy, malice, envy, avarice, pleasures, and their fruits, are banished and it knows things that are humble; it hates itself and abominates all its own cupidities; in a word, a Paul (Rom. 6:21) says: "Now are we ashamed of those things which we aforetime enjoyed." Therefore it imparts itself to all its neighbors and serves them, placing itself at their disposal, considering their wants as its own, doing all things with everyone candidly, sincerely, without self-seeking and with no malice. Such is the efficacy of faith as it appears from the works of those whose hearts are possessed by true faith.

Concerning such a faith as this, Paul (Gal: 5:6) says: "In Christ Jesus circumcision profiteth nothing nor uncircumcision, but faith which is powerful through love." He

says faith in Christ is powerful and then this faith is of the
type that imparts itself through love in the use of a neighbor. I John 4:7: "Everyone that loveth his brother is born of
God and knows God. Who does not love, does not know
God, for God is love." And II Peter 1:5-8: "Add to your faith
virtue, to virtue knowledge, to knowledge temperance, to
temperance patience, to patience piety, to piety brotherly
love, to brotherly love, love." Now if we possess these things,
they will cause the knowledge of our Lord Jesus Christ to be
by no means unfruitful. Now by this gradation, Peter has
ingrafted the remaining virtues to faith as though beautiful
branches to a root, so that virtue, that is the vehemence and
passion of a mortified flesh, follows faith. But this vehemence
is ruled by knowledge, so that its duty to the body is performed. . . .

It is evident from this, how the love of God and the love
of neighbor which they call "Caritas", proceed from faith.
For the very knowledge of the mercy of God causes us to
love God in return. It causes us of our own accord to subject
ourselves to all creatures and this is "love of neighbor."

It will not be useless to point out that concerning which I
perceive there are contentions everywhere, namely: "How
may man know whether he is in the favor of God, and how
can it be ascertained whether there is faith in his heart?" The
question is a two-fold one. For in the former the question
is concerning the will of God toward us, and not of our affections; whereas in the latter, the question concerns our
affections alone. Now the Scholastics indeed taught—and it
was a most foul error—that neither could be known. And it
is clearly evident that the whole bunch of them possessed
nothing of the Spirit. Now in reference to the flesh I ask,
how can it know what the divine will toward it is, since it is
entirely ignorant of God? And moreover, how will the flesh
which does not fully understand its own affections judge of
spiritual affections? Jer. 17:9: "The heart of man is

depraved and inscrutable." Therefore, the Scholastics simply imagined that there were several qualities in the soul of man of which we ourselves are ignorant. Besides, they taught that God wishes that we do not seek to know so that the conscience may forever fluctuate in uncertainty with itself. Now what is this but teaching despair? Indeed that is my opinion.

In the first place, as touching the divine will, faith is nothing but a sure and constant reliance on the divine benevolence toward us. The will of God is known, but by faith from the promise of the gospel. For you do not attribute true glory to God if you do not believe that God wills himself to be manifested by the gospel. They know themselves to be in the favor of God who estimate the will of God in accordance with his own word, and not from human merits. Thus Paul in Rom. 4, when he teaches by several arguments that righteousness is by faith, finally adds this most powerful reason! If justification were by our works rather than by faith, the conscience would never be at rest, longing now for this and now for that in life and labor; and the result would be nothing but despair. Consequently (in Rom. 4: 13-6) he says: "Therefore not by works, that the promise may be firm according to grace." And how often do the prophets glory in security! Hosea: 2:10: "I shall cause them to sleep with confidence." Jer. 23:6: "In those days shall Judah be safe and Israel shall dwell in confidence". . . .

Moreover what security would there be if our consciences are forever in doubt as to the will of God? It is necessary therefore that we be certain of the grace and benevolence of God toward us. That is what the Lord says in Jer. 9:24: "Let him that glorieth glory in this, that he understandeth and knoweth me." God wishes that his will be known and that we glory in his will. What is more impious than to deny that the divine will either ought not or cannot be known? Especially so when he has already expressed it by his own word?

So far, I have said that we ought to be certain of the benevolence of God toward us. What now about the works of God in us? Can we know whether we have conceived the Spirit of God in our heart? I answer: The fruits of the Spirit bear us witness as to what has transacted in our hearts. Gal. 5:24: "They who are of Christ have crucified the flesh." Moreover each person knows whether he hates and abominates sin truly from his heart, and that is the "crucifixion of the flesh." Each person knows whether he fears God, whether he believes God. Hypocrisy indeed emulates the Spirit of God, but temptation discerns it, during which only the fruitful endure. Whatsoever you do, see to it that you first believe. For God wills that true glory be attributed to him. Moreover, I shall bring together under several heads, this whole discussion on the law, gospel, and faith.

SUMMATION: LAW, GOSPEL, FAITH

1 Law is that teaching which prescribes what ought and what ought not to be done.

2 The gospel is the promise of the grace of God.

3 The law demands the impossible: Love of God and neighbor. Rom. 8.

4 They who attempt to express the law through human powers and free will, only feign external works and fail to express the affections which the law demands.

5 Therefore they do not satisfy the law but are hypocrites: "White-washed sepulchres without," as Christ calls them in Matt. 23:27, and Gal. 3:10: "Those who are of the works of the law, are under the curse."

6 Hence it is not the function of the law to justify.

7 But the proper function of the law is to reveal sin and therefore to confound the conscience, Rom. 3:20. "The knowledge of sin is by the law."

8 To the conscience which now knows sin and is confused by the law, Christ is revealed by the gospel.

9 Thus when John preaches repentance, at the same time

he shows Christ: "Behold the Lamb of God that taketh away the sins of the world." John 1:29.

10 Faith, by which we believe the gospel showing us Christ, and by which Christ is received as the one who has placated the father, which through grace is given, constitutes our righteousness, John 1:12: "As many as received him, to them gave he the power to become the children of God."

11 If indeed such faith alone justifies us, there is plainly no respect for our merits or our works, but only of Christ's merits.

12 Such a faith pacifies and exhilarates the heart, Rom. 5:1: "Being justified by faith we have peace."

13 And it results that for such kindness, for the fact that sin is forgiven for Christ's sake, God is loved in return and thus the love of God is the fruit of faith.

14 This same faith causes us to be ashamed of the fact that we have offended such a kind and liberal father.

15 And in addition, it causes us to abominate our flesh together with its concupiscences.

16 Human reason neither fears nor believes God but is utterly ignorant of him and despises him, according to Ps. 13:1: "The fool hath said in his heart there is no God." And Luke 16:31: "If they do not hear Moses and the prophets they will not believe even if one would get up from the dead." By this Christ means that the human heart does not believe the word of God. This madness of the human heart Solomon (as instanced by Ecclesiastes 8:11) has reproached "Because no judgment is quickly brought against evil, and the sons of man without any fear perpetrate evil things."

17 Because the human heart is utterly ignorant of God, it therefore turns aside to its own counsels and cupidities and sets itself up in the place of God.

18 When God confounds the human heart through the law by a knowledge of sin, it does not yet know God and certainly not his goodness, and therefore it hates God as though he were an executioner.

19 When God arouses and consoles the human heart by showing Christ through the gospel, precisely then does it know God; or it knows both his power and goodness. This is what Jeremiah means when he says in 9:24: "Let him glory in this, that he knoweth me."

20 He who has believed the gospel and knows the goodness of God, his heart is now made erect so that he trusts God and fears him, and consequently abominates the counsels of the human heart.

21 Peter has most aptly said in Acts 15:9: "Hearts are purified by faith."

22 Mercy is revealed by promises.

23 Sometimes these promises are corporal, sometimes spiritual.

24 In the law corporal things are promised such as: the land of Canaan, the kingdom, etc.

25 The gospel is the promise of grace or the forgiveness of sins through Christ.

26 All corporal promises depend on the promise of Christ.

27 For the first promise was of grace or the promise of Christ. Gen. 3:15: "Her seed shall bruise thy head," that is, the seed of Eve should bruise the kingdom of the serpent lying in wait for our heel, that is, sin and death.

28 This promise was renewed in the one made to Abraham, Gen. 12:3 and 18:18: "In thy seed shall all nations be blessed."

29 Wherefore since Christ should be born of Abraham's posterity, the promises which were added to the law concerning the possession of the land, etc., are obscure promises of the coming of Christ. For these corporal things were promised to the people lest they should die before the promised seed would come, and also that God might in the meantime indicate his mercy and try the people's faith by these corporal things.

30 Upon the birth of Christ, the promises which had been made were consummated and the remission of sins was

openly accomplished, for which purpose Christ was to be born.

31 The promises of the Old Testament are signs of the coming of Christ and therefore of the promise of grace that was to be published in the future.

32 Just as he does not really know God who merely knows that God exists but does not know his power and mercy, in like manner he does not truly believe who merely believes in the existence of God but not his power and mercy.

33 Therefore he truly believes who in addition to threats believes the gospel also; who turns his face to the mercy of God or to Christ who is the pledge of divine mercy. . . .

The Loci Communes, by Philip Melanchthon,
Edited by Charles L. Hill.
Boston: Meador Publishing Co., 1944.

HULDREICH ZWINGLI

1484 – 1531

HULDREICH ZWINGLI

ZWINGLI WAS BORN IN GERMAN SWITZERLAND ONLY SEVEN months after Luther's birth, and came into the reformed faith by a route quite independently his own. His uncle and other relatives were clergymen, and from his precocious youth his parents planned that he should be a priest. He received an excellent education at the Universities of Vienna and of Basle. He studied under men of liberal culture, devoted himself to the new learning in the classics, was a Humanist, full of admiration for men like Erasmus, and at the age of twenty-two became a parish priest, with no more apparent ambition than to enjoy the opportunity which the priesthood afforded to pursue his scholarly studies.

He was a faithful priest, however, intensely interested in his people, deeply concerned about their problems, and winning their devotion by his personal quality even more than by his brilliant intellect, so that when he left his first parish after ten years, one of his pupils wrote: "What could possibly have happened more saddening for our Glarus than to be bereft of so great a man?"

His scholarly Humanism had long since alienated him from many current practices in the church, and when as priest at the popular shrine of Einsiedeln, he faced fla-

grant supersitition, he began speaking out. He experienced
no such inner moral and spiritual struggle as Luther had
undergone. His major concern was not with his own soul's
salvation but with the condition of his people—their religious illiteracy, their gross superstition, their maltreated
souls abused by the corruptions of the church. He spoke at
first as any Roman Catholic Humanist might have spoken,
endeavoring to correct ignorance and credulity without disturbing the people's established loyalties. But he soon was
presenting the Bible as the sole basis of Christian truth,
Christ as the only mediator between God and man, and
God's grace as man's only hope of salvation. As he himself
said, "I began to preach the gospel of Christ in the year
1516, before anyone in my locality had so much as heard the
name of Luther." Zwingli deserves much greater credit than
commonly is given him as one of the original pioneers of
the Reformation.

During his stay in Einsiedeln, however, and even after his
call to the Great Minster of Zurich in 1518, he evidently
foresaw no open break with Rome. He still was a Humanist,
like Erasmus, fully intending to continue within the ancient
church and to labor for its gradual improvement. Early in
his priesthood he had accepted a papal pension, and even
after he began his serious criticism of the papacy he retained
it, surrendering it only in 1520 when it had become a
scandalous impediment to his reforming work. In 1522
he wrote: "My connection with the pope of Rome is now a
thing of several years back. At the time it began it seemed to
me a proper thing to take his money and to defend his opinions, but when I realized my sin I parted company with him
entirely."

Roman Catholic anxiety regarding Zwingli, which had begun while he was at Einsiedeln, deepened at Zurich, and
with good reason. The hierarchy tempted him with financial
bribes, promises of ecclesiastical preferment and threats, but
to no purpose. He became increasingly forthright and un-

compromising. A papal peddler of indulgences was driven from Zurich. Zwingli's preaching in the Minster, magnetic in its drawing power and persuasive in its impact on the citizens, was centered in a systematic exposition of the Bible, and was based on the startling proposition which Zwingli later made explicit in *The First Helvetic Confession:* "Canonic Scripture, the Word of God, given by the Holy Spirit and set forth to the world by the Prophets and Apostles, the most perfect and ancient of all philosophies, alone contains perfectly all piety and the whole rule of life." On this basis Zwingli attacked traditional ideas and practices which the Scriptures did not mention or confirm—abstinence from meat in Lent, pilgrimages, adoration of relics and images, masses for the dead, the invocation of Mary and the saints, the celibacy of monks and priests. Finally, in 1522 and 1523, the Council of Zurich, after public disputation, supported Zwingli, removed the canton from the bishopric of Constance, and officially established the Reformation.

Zurich was the most democratically governed municipality in Switzerland. Its Council was composed of the Masters of the thirteen guilds—twelve representing the various trades and one the patricians. Even before Zwingli came, ecclesiastical as well as secular property was taxed by the municipality, and monasteries and convents were subject to civil inspection and control. On this democratic foundation Zwingli built. Religion was a prime concern of the state; the majority could enforce its will in that realm as in all others; magistrates were responsible for the administration of religious affairs and, if they proved unworthy, it was the right and duty of the people to depose them. So began in Zurich a type of Protestant church-structure, based on representative democracy in the state, which Calvin took over and developed, but in which Luther, with his distrust of the common people, profoundly disbelieved.

Zwingli's acceptance of the Swiss system was all the more hearty because he was such an ardent patriot. "When I was a child," he wrote, "if anyone said a word against our fatherland, I bristled up instantly." While he was at Glarus he went as chaplain with the Swiss army on three Italian campaigns. One of his first clashes with the *status quo* was his attack on the prevalent system of hiring out Swiss troops to the pope and to other sovereigns as mercenaries in their campaigns. Against this vicious custom he spoke and wrote, determined "utterly to root out the traffic," until, so far as Zurich was concerned, it was abolished.

His ardent patriotism undoubtedly increased Zwingli's influence with his fellow-citizens, so that by 1524, the Reformation was firmly established in his canton. Saints' days were no longer observed; masses for the dead, payment for confession, extreme unction, blessing of candles and holy water, were ended; pictures, statues and images were removed from churches and relics were buried; priests could marry; and the convents and monasteries were transformed into hospitals, orphanages and poor-houses.

Meanwhile Zwingli himself had found deeper levels in his own religious experience. While he was on vacation in 1519 the plague struck Zurich, and Zwingli, returning to minister to his parishioners, fell victim to it and nearly died. This experience, along with the influence of Luther's books—concerning which he said, "What I have read of his writings I find based on the Word of God, and no creature can overthrow that"—issued in a deeper note in Zwingli's life and teaching. As Professor Lang puts it, he "ceased to be merely an Erasmian Reformer and became an evangelical Reformer in the full sense of the term."

Because Zwingli and Luther agreed so well on central matters—the sovereignty and precedent grace of God, the sole mediatorship of Christ, justification by faith and the Scriptures as the authoritative test of truth—their tragic controversy and separation were the more deplorable. At the Colloquy of Marburg, where in 1529 the two men met for the first and only time, Luther himself says that "Zwingli begged with tears in his eyes before the Landgrave and all of them, saying 'There are no people on earth with whom I would rather be in harmony than with the Wittenbergers.'" He would not, however, surrender his position that the Lord's Supper, instead of being a repetition of Christ's sacrifice, was simply the grateful remembrance of it by faithful souls in the manner which Christ had appointed. On that point Luther was adamant—"impudent and obstinate," Zwingli called him—and, in the end, brushed his Swiss brethren off. "You have a different spirit from ours," Luther said.

It is a pity that he said it. Could he have foreseen the future, he would not have said it. There was truth in it, however, for beneath the controversy concerning the Lord's Supper were differences of temperament, of religious experience, of attitude toward the common people, and of doctrinal emphasis which made mutual understanding difficult. In Arthur Cushman McGiffert's *Protestant Thought Before Kant*, the reader may find a concise statement of the presuppositions and conclusions of Zwinglian theology which makes clear its diversity from Luther and Melanchthon.

Zwingli is reported to have said that the trouble he had with Roman Catholics in Zurich was child's play compared with his strife with the Anabaptists. In one respect, at least, they were far ahead of their time. They wanted complete separation of church and state, and they wanted it at once. They were insistent and clamorous in their denial of infant baptism, and in their demand for a church composed only of regenerate persons who voluntarily, at a responsible age, had chosen to confess their faith. When private conference and public disputation availed nothing in quieting these radical schismatics, the Council of Zurich used force. In the end, most of the leading Swiss Anabaptists faced martyrdom. Grebel was banished and later died of the plague; Manz was drowned in the Lake of Zurich; Blaurock was flogged and banished under penalty of death if he returned; Hübmaier was burned at the stake in Vienna.

In 1529 Zwingli was at the peak of his power, with followers in all parts of German Switzerland, and with Zurich thoroughly reformed. His labors in education, in church organization, in preaching and writing, and in the formulation of civil policies were immensely influential until, at the age of forty-seven, he fell in battle, when the army of the Roman Catholic cantons invaded Zurich. The story of his life is best told, in English, in *Hüldreich Zwingli, The Reformer of German Switzerland*, by Samuel Macauley Jackson.

In this anthology we present excerpts from Zwingli's major work, *On True and False Religion*, and from his statement of his position prepared, at the Emperor's request, for the Diet of Augsburg.

ON TRUE AND FALSE
RELIGION

RELIGION

HERE, THEREFORE, WE SEE MORE CLEARLY THAN DAY THAT religion took its rise when God called runaway man back to Him, when otherwise he would have been a deserter forever. For he saw that his nakedness, that is, his guilt, was of such kind and degree that he despaired of a return to favor. But a merciful God pitied his persistence in flight and his bewildered soul; and, like a devoted father who indeed hates the folly or recklessness of his son yet cannot hate the son, He gently calls to him in his desolation and despair, asking him how matters stand: "Adam, where art thou?" Oh, wonderful and unspeakable graciousness of the Heavenly Father! He who places all things where they are—or they would be nowhere—asks him where he is; but He asks for the sake of the unhappy man, that He may show him the more plainly the depth of his guilt; for he did not know where in the world he was. For, frightened by his consciousness of guilt, he saw that it was all up with his home and happy hearth, saw that the words of his Lord were only too true: "In the day that thou eatest thereof thou shalt surely die." He felt how his heart fluttered, how his mind in its distracted state fluctuated between many plans, all unpromising and illusory; and at the same time he feared the destined death was at hand every moment. The Heavenly Father, therefore, asks him where he is, that man may be mindful for ever in what position, in what condition of his affairs, he was when God gently called to him. Here, I say, is the cradle of religion, or rather loyal devotion (for this is the established relation between parents and children, between God and man). The unhappy man saw that he deserved nothing but wrath; therefore he despairs and flees from God. Now see the loyal devotion of the father to his undutiful son. He runs to him in spite of his obstinacy and overbears him amidst his rash designs. What is this but loyal devotion to the son? Loyal devotion, therefore, springs from God even to our day, but for our benefit; for what are we to suppose that God would have lacked even if Adam had immediately expired by the destined death? But pious devotion is complete only when we turn to the one who calls us away from ourselves and our designs.

Unhappy, indeed, is the parent (the human parent, I mean) who pursues his son with constant kindness, only to find him constantly resisting or retreating; for his devotion to his son is in vain. But such defeat cannot happen to God; for he whom He calls is forced to respond whether he will or not. This is shown by the prevaricating Adam, the adulterer and murderer David, the persecutor Paul. Pious devotion, therefore, or religion, is this: God reveals man to himself, that he may recognize his disobedience, treason, and wretchedness as fully as Adam did. The result is that man utterly despairs of himself, but at the same time God shows the ample store of His own bounty, so that he who had despaired of himself may see that he has with his Creator and Father an abundance of grace so sure and ready that he cannot possibly be torn away from Him on whose grace he leans. This clinging to God, therefore, with an unshaken trust in Him as the only good, as the only one who has the knowledge and the power to relieve our troubles and to turn away all evils or to turn them to His own glory and the benefit of His people, and with filial dependence upon Him as a father—this is piety, is religion. For as those who are thus minded enjoy God's fatherly care, so they in their turn anxiously and unceasingly pore over, study, and consider the ways in which they can please Him and deserve well of Him. Piety, therefore, is recognized as surely present where there is an eagerness to live according to the will of God, just as, likewise, perfect devotion between parents and children requires that the son shall study to obey the father as much as the father to benefit the son. Again, true piety is born only when man not only thinks that he lacks many things, but sees that he has absolutely no means of pleasing God, whereas his Creator and Father so abounds in all things that no one in His hands can lack anything, and His bounty and love to man are so great that He can refuse no man anything.

And this can be so abundantly confirmed by the testimony of Scripture that all its teaching, in the Old Testament as well as in the New, and all the pious really sing no other song than that we have nothing, God lacks nothing, by Him nothing is denied. For with the Lord is mercy in exceeding abundance. "With him is the fountain of life" [Ps. 36:9]. "The earth is his and the fulness thereof" [Ps. 24:1]. "Salvation is his, and that so ready that he manifests his blessing, *i.e.*, his bounty and kindness, freely to his people" [Ps. 3:8]. . . .

REPENTANCE

We have till now* regarded repentance as a forced and feigned pain for sins committed, and as the paying of the penalty set upon the sin by the judge, *i.e.*, the father confessor. We repented of our evil doing only when the pope ordered, or when the celebration of Easter was approaching, or when our health demanded it. What was this but hypocrisy? Or whence came it except from ignorance of our-

---

* *i.e.* till the Reformation

selves? For he who has attained to knowledge of himself
sees such a vast slough of wickedness that he is driven not
only to grieve, but to shudder, to despair, to die. For what
lust is so filthy, what greed so bold, what self-esteem so high,
that every man does not see it in his own heart, scheming or
working or hiding something? And as no one can deny this,
how has it happened that we have not felt the pain that is
born thereof? It has happened from the fact that, as was
said above, no one tries to go down into himself, no one.
When, therefore, we do so go down, real pain and shame
immediately follow. But this was by no means the case before in the repentance of the popes. For how should any one
be disgusted with himself when no one knew himself, but
thought rather that he was righteous either through his own
works or through hired efforts?

The second part of the gospel, then, is repentance: not
that which takes place for a time, but that which makes a
man who knows himself blush and be ashamed of his old
life, for one reason because he is greatly dissatisfied
and pained at himself, and for another because he sees it
ought to be altogether foreign to a Christian to waste away
in those sins from which he rejoiced to believe that he had
been delivered. When, therefore, Christ and John and the
Apostles preached, saying, "Repent," they certainly did not
speak of that feigned and counterfeit repentance which I
mentioned in the first place; nor of that which is felt once
for all and straightway thinks license to sin given it, for this
kind, as has been sufficiently set forth, is just as much a
counterfeit as that performed by order of the popes. But
they spoke of the repentance in which a man goes into himself and diligently investigates the reason of all his acts, his
concealments, pretences, and dissimulations. When he has
done this honestly, he is driven by the vast extent of his
disease to despair of his own righteousness and salvation,
just as a man who has received a mortal wound keeps expecting black and everlasting night. Then, if some Machaon

should bid him be of good cheer, that the wound could be sewed up and all made good again, I think nothing more acceptable and cheering could happen to him. So our sinner betakes himself to begging for mercy, and presently after seeing Christ understands that all things are to be hoped for (for "if God is for us, who is against us?" [Rom. 8:31]. He rises up who had lain prostrate. He lives who had learned and felt to his horror that he was dead. But neither Christ, nor John, nor the Apostles spoke of this side of repentance in such a way as to imply that it is to last a certain time and then can be put aside. It is to last permanently, as long as we carry about this pitiful burden of the body. For this is so given over to vanities that it never stops teeming with evil growths, which, as soon as they spring up, must be crushed, cut off, stifled, as things highly unbecoming a Christian. And this labor, this struggle, this watchfulness—what is it if not repentance? Therefore when Christ and John and the Apostles preach saying, "Repent," they are simply calling us to a new life quite unlike our life before; and those who had undertaken to enter upon this were marked by an initiatory sacrament, baptism to wit, by which they gave public testimony that they were going to enter upon a new life. . . .

SACRAMENTS

So I am brought to see that a sacrament is nothing else than an initiatory ceremony or a pledging. For just as those who were about to enter upon litigation deposited a certain amount of money, which could not be taken away except by the winner, so those who are initiated by sacraments bind and pledge themselves, and, as it were, seal a contract not to draw back. . . . When this has been accomplished the person initiated is bound to perform for the office, order, or institution to which he has devoted himself what the institution or office demands. A sacrament, therefore, since it cannot be anything more than an initiation or public inauguration, cannot have any power to free the conscience. That can be freed by God alone; for it is known to Him alone, for He alone can penetrate to it, as has been abundantly shown in considering man and the gospel. How, therefore, could water, fire, oil, milk, salt, and such crude things make their way to the mind? Not having that power, how will they be able to cleanse it? In fact, what is the cleansing of the mind? Is it a sort of contact with some clean thing? But what can the mind touch, or what touch the mind? Since, therefore, no creature can know a man within to the core, but only God, it remains that no one can purge the conscience save God alone. Solomon, in II Chron. 6:30, is a witness: "For thou only knowest the hearts of the children of men." Also the Pharisees, in Luke 5:21: "Who can forgive sins, but God alone?" And lest anyone should wonder about this latter testimony, I will remark that testimony from an opponent is the strongest. They are wrong, therefore, by the whole width of heaven who think that sacraments have any cleansing power.

The second group, seeing this, taught that sacraments are signs which when they are performed make a man sure about what is performed within him. But this was a vain invention; as if, forsooth, when a man is wet with the water something happens in him which he could not possibly have known unless water had been poured over him at the same time! They did not know, if they will allow me to say so, what faith is or how it is born in a man. I said some time back that faith is a matter of fact, not of knowledge or opinion or imagination. A man, therefore, feels faith within, in his heart; for it is born only when a man begins to despair of himself, and to see that he must trust in God alone. And it is perfected when a man wholly casts himself off and prostrates himself before the mercy of God alone, but in such fashion as to have entire trust in it because of Christ who was given for us. What man of faith can be unaware of this? For then only are you free from sin when the mind trusts itself unwaveringly to the death of Christ and finds rest there. And if meanwhile you had been deluged with the whole Jordan and a sacred formula been repeated a thousand times, your mind would yet have had no feeling of being in a better state, except in so far as this trivial and fleeting notion that the sacraments purify, so persistently beaten into it, gave a false impression of having persuaded it. For they that have not faith gape with wonder at anything applied to them that is said to have any power, and fancy they have found, nay, actually felt, salvation, when they have not felt anything at all within, as is shown by their subsequent lives. For if we become new men, that is to say, if we love God and our neighbor, we shrink from sin, put on Christ and daily grow more and more into the perfect man, are changed by the action of the Holy Spirit. But who would not feel this change?

If, however, pleasing ourselves for a time with the freedom from guilt we have acquired, we presently, when this hallucination has worn off, return to the old life, like a dog to his vomit [cf. Prov. 26:11], it is evident that we have not felt any change of heart, but only the awe of the water. Many are baptized, therefore, who during baptism feel nothing beyond awe of the water, and not also remission of sins, that is, the deliverance of the heart. And this was generally the case with those who were baptized by John and those who after the ascension of Christ at the preaching of the Apostles and disciples received baptism before they were sure of salvation through Christ or were fully taught in regard to it, as in Acts 19:2–6 and 10:44. Cornelius and his house had received the Holy Spirit before they were baptized: they had, therefore, been sure of the grace of God before baptism. Therefore this second view has no value, which supposes that the sacraments are signs of such a kind that, when they are applied to a man, the thing signified by the sacraments at once takes place within him. For in this way the liberty of the divine Spirit which distributes itself to individuals as it will, that is, to whom it will, when it will, where it will, would be bound. For if it were compelled to act within when we employ the signs externally, it would be absolutely bound by the signs, whereas we see that really the opposite takes place, as has been made clear by the testimony above.

Consequently, in the third place, there came forward men who, seeing clearly that the sacraments cannot purify, nor the operation of the divine Spirit be such a slave to the sacraments that, when they are performed, it is compelled at the same time to operate within (for it is established that the Holy Spirit was sometimes given before baptism, sometimes afterwards, as in Acts 10:44–48 and 19:2–6), taught that the sacraments are signs which make a man sure of the thing that has been accomplished within him. Hence, for example, they refuse baptism to all who have not previously so well learned and confessed the faith that they can respond to all its articles. Their view is just as far from the truth as was the preceding. For those who have so learned and confessed the faith have been sure for some time already of salvation, as was made plain a little while ago in the refutation of the error of the second group. For if the heart already trusts, it cannot be unaware of its trust. What need, therefore, has he of baptism who has already for some time been sure through his faith in God of the remission of his sins? The sacraments are, then, signs or ceremonials—let me say it with the good permission of all both of the new school and the old—by which a man proves to the church that he either aims to be, or is, a soldier of Christ, and which inform the whole church rather than yourself of your faith. For if your faith is not so perfect as not to need a ceremonial sign to confirm it, it is not faith. For faith is that by which we rely on the mercy of God unwaveringly, firmly, and single-heartedly, as Paul shows us in many passages.

So much for the meaning of the name. Christ left us two sacraments and no more, Baptism and the Lord's Supper. By these we are initiated, giving the name with the one, and showing by the other that we are mindful of Christ's victory

and are members of His church. In Baptism we receive a
token that we are to fashion our lives according to the rule
of Christ; by the Lord's Supper we give proof that we trust
in the death of Christ, glad and thankful to be in that company which gives thanks to the Lord for the blessing of redemption which He freely gave us by dying for us. The
other sacraments are rather ceremonials, for they have no
initiatory function in the church of God. Hence it is not improper to exclude them; for they were not instituted by God
to help us initiate anything in the church.

CONFESSION

The truly sacred writings know of no other confession than
that by which a man comes to know himself and to throw
himself upon the mercy of God, according to the word of
the prophet, Ps. 32:5: "I said, I will confess my transgressions unto the Lord; and thou forgavest the iniquity of my
sin." As, therefore, it is God alone who remits sins and puts
the heart at rest, so to Him alone ought we to ascribe the
healing of our wounds, to Him alone display them to be
healed. For who ever uncovered a wound to any other than
the physician or the person who he hoped could give him
helpful advice? Just so it is with confession: it is God alone
that heals our hearts; to Him alone, therefore, is the wound
to be disclosed. But if you do not yet quite know the physician or are not sure where he dwells, no one forbids your
unbinding your wound before a wise counsellor and begging
him to give you advice. And if he is a wise and faithful man,
he will be sure to send you to a physician who is so skilled
in his profession that he can sew up your wound. I will now
explain the parable. The man who knows not the physician
is he that has not yet come to a right knowledge of grace
through Christ, and yet, such is the nemesis of conscience,
is seeking to lay down the burden by which he is oppressed.
The sage and faithful counsellor is the minister of the word
of God, who, like the good Samaritan, pours wine and oil

into the wounds [Lk. 10:34]. The wine signifies the sharpness of repentance, to which he leads the man when he sets him before his own eyes so that he may learn to know himself, or sometimes drags him in spite of his resistance to a knowledge of his hypocrisy. It is a bitter and sharp thing that you are thoroughly bad within to the very core; it is a still more bitter thing that you cannot deny your wickedness; it is the most bitter thing when you realize that you are dead and that your hopes have failed. Then the world begins to burn. Presently, therefore, the minister of the word should pour in oil, that is, Christ, who is anointed beyond all with the oil of gladness, that is, he should show what grace has bestowed upon us through Him. When the man has learned this, he can no longer be kept from hastening to Him.

Auricular confession, then, is nothing but a consultation in which we receive, from him whom God has appointed to the end that we may seek the law from his lips, advice as to how we can secure peace of mind. Behold the Keys, therefore, behold the Gospel, of which enough has been said. The minister of the word, therefore, evangelizes you; and when you have been evangelized, that is, when you have received Christ, you are absolved and delivered from the burden of sin, and this relief you feel in your heart, even if no pontiff pronounces the words of any formula over you. Nonsense and sheer trumpery, therefore, are the promises of the Papalists concerning the Keys. Unless he is sure within through faith, you will say in vain, "Thou art free." For you can no more make him sure by your words than you can make an elephant of a fly by saying, "You are an elephant." You may teach and expound the meaning of the Gospel, but you do it in vain, unless the Lord give inward teaching. For how many are there who hear and do not receive it [cf. Mk. 4:15]! What is the reason they do not receive it? God hath not drawn them [cf. Jn. 6:44]. As soon as He draws them, they leap over to Him without your help. Unless a man has this certainty of faith, he will be absolved a thousand times by the

priest in vain, for he will always go from him in despair and
unbelief. And the things concerning confession that have
been invented and handed down are as the ocean and Cim-
merian darkness, so that it is not at all worth while to refute
them.

If you examine properly the few things that I add here,
you will sail safely through the whole of Scripture, as far
as confession is concerned, easily perceiving that of the auricular confession we have hitherto practiced absolutely no
mention is made therein. [I.] To confess is, first, to praise
and to give thanks to the Lord; as, "Confess unto the Lord,
for he is good," as the children of Israel sang when Pharaoh
was drowned. [II.] Next, to confess is to trust in the Lord,
to confess that He is our rock and refuge, as Ps. 105:1–25
and I John 4: 15–16: "Every one that confesseth that Jesus
is the Son of God, etc." [III.] Further, to confess is to acknowledge that of which you are reproached or accused; as
those whose consciences were pricked by the preaching of
John acknowledged that the case was as he taught. So today
those confess their sins who when they hear the word of God
are conscience stricken so that they recognize their trouble,
and straightway betake themselves to the physician. [IV.]
Finally, we confess our sins when we inform our neighbor or
some learned scholar of our secret guilt, in order that he
may join us in asking forgiveness of the Heavenly Father,
or may find counsel, as has been said, that will enable us to
resist evil thereafter. Of this confession, James, 5:16, says:
"Confess your sins one to another, and pray for one another,
that ye may be healed; for the continual prayer of a
righteous man availeth much." Relying upon this passage,
the Papalists have defended auricular confession hitherto,
though St. James is not speaking of that, but of the confession which every man makes to his neighbor when he
discloses to him some internal and hitherto hidden wound.
Hence, nothing more can be wrung from this passage than
that every man should go to his neighbor and ask him to

pray with him for his shortcomings. And in order that he may do this more earnestly, he exposes the foulness of his wound. In a word, he makes sufficient confession who trusts in God, as was said in the second article above; who praises Him and gives thanks for blessings bestowed, as in the first article; who acknowledges his sins and deplores them before the Lord, as in the third; who fervently prays for forgiveness with the help of brethren, as in the last. He, I say, makes sufficient confession who is so minded, and he has no need of any priest. But he who has not been taught after this fashion certainly has very great need of a priest. But of what sort of priest? Not of one who gets into the treasure chest with false keys, but of one who by the word of God teaches men to recognize their misery, and grace as well. Secret confession, therefore, is a consultation, the Keys are the expounding of the gospel, and all else is mere windy gabble of the Papalists.

But there are those who say that many persons will perpetrate many misdeeds when they are not obliged to confess. To such I answer: You are either inexperienced or hypocrites; inexperienced, because you have not learned that nobody ever refrained from misdoing on account of confession, whereas we know that, on the contrary, if they were ashamed to confess, many have refrained from confessing what they had done; hypocrites, because no person can help knowing how recklessly he conceals things and even feigns righteousness where he wishes to give the impression that he has made a clean breast of everything and has felt sincere sorrow. Yet, we still venture to defend a thing which has been nothing but a means of getting men's goods away from them; for unless the Lord of Hosts had left us the seed [cf. Isa. 6:13], *i.e.*, had brought back again the light of the gospel, it would have been all over with everybody's goods, earnings, and possessions. Was not the pope of Rome saying that all realms are his? We have ourselves seen the legate of the pope of Rome putting up the claim at Zurich that a certain house belonging to the priory, as they call it, was his. Let us, therefore, confess frequently to the Lord, let us begin a new life frequently, and if there is anything not clear let us go frequently to a wise scholar who looks not at the pocket-book but at the conscience! . . .

PURGATORY

Holy Scripture knows nothing of the fire of purgatory in the sense used by the theologians, but the mind of man knows it well, for by means of this false notion of the fire of purgatory, such wealth has been heaped up that the riches of Croesus and the Hyperboreans and the gems of India are cheap in comparison. For this is what the mind of man thought up, as you may see somewhere in Origen: Some men go hence who are not utterly bad; why, then, should they be thrust into everlasting punishment? Others go hence who are not wholly good; why, then, should they be admitted at once into the company of the blessed? This argument has some appearance of soundness and, according to Paul's words, Col. 2:23, some show of wisdom, but in will-worship, *i.e.*, the religion which is the product of the human will. But if you confront it with the word of God, it will vanish like dust before the face of the wind [cf. Wisdom of Solomon 5:15]. If we do not do this, we shall be abandoned by the Lord just as the people of Israel were once left to their own devices and perished in them, as in Psalm 81:12–13 David indicates, speaking in the character of God: "But my people heard not my voice, and Israel hearkened not to me. So I let them go according to the desires of their heart: they shall walk in their own inventions." But what greater presumption can there be than to declare that in the other world things are just as you have happened to picture them to yourself? We should listen to what the Lord God says within us, not to what presumptuous reason invents within us, which, as soon as it has cunningly produced anything that it hopes will seem probable to everybody, immediately sallies forth to win glory. This state of mind we ought to leave to the Gentiles, as Paul has finely taught, Eph. 4:17, in this fashion: "This I say therefore, and testify in the Lord, that ye henceforth walk not as other Gentiles walk in the vanity of their mind." See how he calls our devices the vanity of the mind. There follows: "Being darkened in their understanding, alienated from the life of God, because of the ignorance that is in them, because of the blindness of their heart," etc. We should not, therefore, walk in the way of our minds and devices.

Since, then, a purgatory (for the custom has long prevailed of so naming this illusory expiation in fire) can nowhere be affirmed from the Word of God, how is it that we are so stupid as to believe in such vapid and suspicious nonsense, when we see, forsooth, that those who affirm a purgatory teach in what ways its fires can be quenched, and in the same breath offer their aid for hire? They bid you give gold, for by this especially is the flame weakened if the man who receives the gold devoutly celebrates mass, prays, and sings psalms; and at the same time he holds out his hand for the gold. Why are we not as shrewd as Lucian's Timon, who in such fine style used his spade upon some philosopher or other who advised him to throw the gold he had found into the sea, but not too far from the shore, since he doubtless had the scheme of gathering it up from there at night and carrying it off? Purgatory is very much like certain quack medicines that are carried about by peddlers. They mount a platform in the midst of the marketplace, and tell about some sickness or disease that is committing ravages all about, and say they have themselves suffered from it but by the blessing of the gods have recovered in spite of the malady, thanks to medicine exhibited before the eyes of all. They add that the disease is not far off; that, in fact, it is already raging in neighboring places. See how, first of all, they produce here expectation and fear of the disease, and then promise a remedy. So those who affirmed a purgatory—what bonds,

good God! what snakes, fires, what rivers running fire, sul-
phur, naphtha, or glowing iron, did they not bellow about!
What tales of the poets did they not outdo! And the minds
of the stupid were just as much dumfounded by this as
when an unexpected and cruel enemy is reported to be before the city walls, firing the farms, killing the farmers, and
destroying everything. The blockheads stood thunderstruck at
this nonsense, just as if they thought they already felt the
woe. But a remedy was at hand, marked at an exorbitant
price in the beginning (for that was most necessary), in order to make a raid first upon the pocket-books of the rich.
"Do you want to free a soul? You can do it for a piece of
gold." But when the wealthy souls had been set free from
their prison-cells, they turned to the paltry souls of the humble, but under a pretence that should prevent the rich from
suspecting that they were being made sport of. They pretended that the mercy of God ought not to be denied to any-
body; that, consequently, the poor, quite as well as the rich,
might free souls from purgatory (that is, their bit of coin
from their purse), but on condition that no one should say
he was poor, so as to be able to get so great a boon cheaper
(for in that way the soul was hurt rather than helped), and
that everyone should give as much as he could. And did they
not cheat both high and low with this transparent nonsense?
Who, pray, is so senseless as not to see that such utter blindness could not have been so widespread unless the Lord had
inflicted it upon us because of our unbelief? Since, therefore,
we have now recovered our sight, so that we see plainly that
those who trust in Christ are the sons of God and come not
into judgment [cf. Jn. 5:24], let us no longer suffer ourselves to be held captive by such foolish lies.

EXCOMMUNICATION

Christ, in order that the church, His bride, might be kept
guiltless [cf. Eph. 5:27], commanded, Matt. 18: 15-17:
"And if thy brother sin against thee, go and show him his

fault between thee and him alone: if he hear thee, thou hast gained thy brother. But if he hear thee not, take with thee one or two more, that at the mouth of two or three witnesses every word may be established. And if he shall refuse to hear them, tell it unto the church; and if he refuse to hear the church, let him be unto thee as the Gentile man and a publican." In the first place, here we see excommunication inflicted for a sin, not for interest and other debts, which are to be collected by the power of the courts when you are unwilling to remit them. Here fall to the ground the bulls, briefs, and diplomas with which the Roman Pontiff (and in naming him I mean the whole papal hierarchy, *i.e.*, whatever has sworn to obey his laws) has worried the whole church of Christ; for these have chiefly been used because of pecuniary disagreements and differences in regard to property, not because of the offence caused by sin.

Second, it is required that you meet the sinner alone and admonish him in a friendly way. Here the pontifical crowd sin again. For as soon as it pleases them, they summon to their tribunal before the whole congregation some unsuspecting person, very often an innocent one. See what an atrocious exercise of power! No king or presiding officer but first calls the offender before himself; but these fellows cover with shame before the whole congregation an innocent man, or one who has suspected nothing of the sort, and thunder out: "Judge So-and-So admonishes this person to satisfy this other within a fortnight, or he will be excommunicated!" There the eyes of all were instantly turned upon the poor astounded fellow, and he was not allowed to utter a syllable or to plead his case, to protest against the wrong or to defend his innocence; for if so much as even the feeblest sound had escaped him, it would have been all up with the poor wretch. And I am inclined to think that the great king of the Persians dealt with his subjects less roughly and barbarously; whose habit they tell us it was from early times to compel all who approached him first to brush and to kiss the dust with their lips, and then to plead their case. But this poor fellow of ours is more than prostrated to the earth in the sight and hearing of all: with his case unheard, he is forced to depart convicted and condemned in the judgment of all. Or if ever he is permitted to plead his cause, it happens in a corner, not in the public assembly, where he had received the blow.

Third, it is required that before you cast off your brother you try speaking to him in the presence of witnesses; so reluctantly does the church of Christ resort to public punishment. On the other hand, pettifoggers of the market place aim at making the greatest possible haste without any regard for mercy, and at causing the greatest amount of loss instead of sparing; for the number of fees increases with the number of summonses and judgments. Finally, the judgment of the whole church is required; not of the Church Universal, for that can never assemble in this world, but of the church in which the accused is a member and communicant. Here the dominion, or rather despotism, of the Roman Pontiff shows itself in its true character. Excommunication is effected only when the church has rejected him who displeases her; but the pope casts out of the church the very man she herself most desires to be saved to her; nor does he consult the church, but commands her to treat as excommunicated the man whom he himself hates or proposes to ruin. But if we ought to interpret laws by the intention of the lawgiver, as we certainly ought, and not judge that a man has infringed the law who has not infringed it, it follows that those who are excommunicated by the popes in this fashion are not guilty in the sight of God. For, as far as this form of fixing guilt is concerned, excommunication belongs to the church and to no one else; and unless she excommunicates, the man is not cast off or held guilty in heaven whom the pope holds guilty [cf. Mt. 16:19].

Hence all the artifices of excommunications and censures must fall to the ground. And we must see to it that the true rod of discipline be restored to the church of Christ, that it may smite the shameless sinner, and when he has changed his heart, admit him into fellowship again. This will keep in the path, even in spite of themselves, some who walk not after the Spirit. But even if it does not profit them, yet those who desire to live honestly and peaceably in this world will profit from not being forced to see sin reaping a harvest unmolested. This power of excommunication, I say, is not that of a magistrate, for it belongs to the whole church; and it belongs to the church so completely that unless she casts out a man he is not cast out. I say this the more willingly, in order that these impostors may no longer be able to shelter themselves by saying: "How, pray, can the dominion of the Roman Pontiff be denied? Did not Christ Himself institute excommunication?" He did not institute it as the pope uses it. Nay, neither he nor any individual can use it, but only the particular church concerned. For the name itself shows clearly enough what it is, even if we had not so plain an utterance on the subject. For to excommunicate is to remove from the company of those who communicate together. And if you say, "Cannot the pope cast out of the church?" I say that he cannot, for that belongs to the church alone, and not to the pope. For Christ never said, "Tell it to the pope." Hence it came about that persons excommunicated by the pope did not in like manner seem to the church worthy of such rejection; and so it followed that few shunned those whom he ordered men to abhor. Let them, therefore, fulminate, thunder, storm, and thrust us down to hell with their formulas, but let us not be moved one whit. On the other hand, let us fear exceedingly to tempt the severity of the church by our wantonness. This will be pleasing in the sight of the Most High. . . .

The Latin Works of Huldreich Zwingli, Vol. III,
Edited by Clarence Nevin Heller.
Philadelphia: The Heidelberg Press, 1929.

AN ACCOUNT OF THE FAITH

WE WHO ARE PREACHING THE GOSPEL IN THE CITIES OF A Christian state were anxiously awaiting, O Charles, holy Emperor of justice, the time when an account of our faith, which we both have and confess, would be asked of us also.

While we are standing in readiness for this, there comes to us the report, more by rumor than by definite announcement, that many have already prepared an outline and summary of their religion and faith, which they are offering you. Here we are in a great dilemma; for, on the one hand, love of truth and desire for public peace urge us all the more to do ourselves what we see others doing; but, on the other hand, the shortness of the time deters us, not only because all things must be done very speedily and as it were superficially, on account of your haste (for this also rumor announces); but also because we, who are acting as preachers of the Divine Word in the cities and country districts of the state already mentioned, are settled and separated too far apart to be able to assemble in so brief a time, and deliberate as to what is most fitting to write to your Highness. Moreover, as we have already seen the confession of the others and even their refutation by their opponents, which seem to have been prepared even before a demand was made for them, I believed that it would not be improper if I alone should forthwith submit an account of my faith, without anticipating the judgment of my people. For if in any business one must make haste slowly, here we must certainly make haste swiftly, since by handling this matter with careless neglect we run into the danger of being suspected because of silence or of being arrogant because of negligence.

To you then, O Emperor, I offer a summary of my faith, with this condition, that at the same time I declare solemnly, that I entrust and permit the judgment not only of these articles, but of all that I have ever written or, by the grace of God, shall yet write, not to one man only, nor to a few merely, but to the whole Church of God, as far as it speaks by the command and inspiration of the Word and spirit of God.

First of all, I both believe and know that God is one and He alone is God, and that He is by nature good, true, powerful, just, wise, the Creator and Preserver of all things, visible and invisible; that Father, Son and Holy Spirit are indeed three persons, but that their essence is one and single. And I think altogether in accordance with the Creed, the Nicene and also the Athanasian, in all their details concerning the Godhead himself, the names of the three persons.

I believe and understand that the Son assumed flesh, the human nature, indeed the whole man, consisting of body and soul which He truly assumed of the immaculate and perpetual virgin Mary; but this in such a manner, that the whole man was so assumed into the unity of the hypostasis or person of the Son of God, that the man did not constitute a separate person, but was assumed into the inseparable, indivisible and indissoluble person of the Son of God. . . . So God and man is one in Christ, the Son of God from eternity and the Son of Man from the time appointed; one person, one Christ, perfect God and perfect man; not because one nature becomes the other, or because the natures are fused together, but because each remains its peculiar self; and yet, the unity of this person is not broken by this retention of the peculiarities.

Hence one and the same Christ, according to the character of the human nature, cries in infancy, grows, increases in wisdom [Luke 2:52], hungers, thirsts, eats, drinks, is warm, is cold, is scourged, sweats, is wounded, is cruelly slain, fears, is sad and endures what else pertains to the penalty and punishment of sin, though from sin itself He is most remote. But according to the peculiarity of the divine nature, with the Father He controls the highest and the lowest (*i.e.*, heaven and earth) He pervades, sustains and preserves all things, gives sight to the blind, restores the lame, calls to life the dead, prostrates His enemies with His word, when dead resumes life, ascends to heaven and sends from His home the Holy Spirit. All these things, however diverse in nature and character, the one and the same Christ does, remaining the one person of the Son of God, in such a way that even those things that pertain to His divine nature are sometimes ascribed, on account of the unity and perfection of the person, to the human nature, and those things that pertain to the human nature are sometimes attributed to the divine. . . .

Secondly—I know that this supreme Deity, which is my God, freely determines all things, so that His counsel does not depend upon the contingency of any creature. For it is peculiar to defective human wisdom to reach a decision because of preceding discussion or example. God, however, who from eternity to eternity surveys the universe with a single, simple look, has no need of any reasoning process or waiting for events; but being equally wise, prudent, good, etc., He freely determines and disposes of all things, for whatever is, is His. Hence it is that, although having knowledge and wisdom, He in the beginning formed man who should fall, but at the same time determined to clothe in human nature His Son, who should restore him when fallen. For by this means His goodness was in every way manifested.

Since this goodness contained mercy and justice within it, He exercised justice when He expelled the transgressor

from the happy home of Paradise, when He bound him to
the mill of human misery and by fetters of disease, when
He shackled him with the law, which, although it was holy,
he was never able to fulfill. Here, twice miserable, man
learned that not only his flesh had fallen into tribulation, but
that his mind also was tortured by the dread of the law he
had transgressed. For he saw that, according to its intent, the
law is holy and just and a declaration of the divine mind, so
that it enjoined nothing but what equity taught, yet he saw
at the same time that by his deeds he could not satisfy the
intent of the law. Being thus condemned by his own judgment, having abandoned all hope of attaining happiness, and
departing in despair from God's sight, he had no prospect
but that of enduring the pains of eternal punishment. All
this was a manifestation of the justice of God.

Then, when the time came to reveal His goodness, which
He had determined from eternity to display no less than His
justice, God sent His Son to assume our nature in every part,
except as far as it inclined to sin, in order that, being our
brother and equal, He could be a mediator, to make a sacrifice for us to divine justice, which must remain holy and in-
violate, no less than to His goodness. Thereby the world
might be sure both of the appeasing of the justice and of the
presence of the goodness of God. For since He has given His
Son to us and for us, how will He not with Him and because
of Him give us all things [Rom. 8:32]? What is it that we
ought not to promise ourselves from Him, who so far humbled himself as not only to be our equal but also to be altogether ours? Who can sufficiently marvel at the riches and
grace of the divine goodness, whereby He so loved the world,
i.e., the human race, as to give up His Son for its life [John
3:16].

This I regard as the heart and life of the Gospel; this is
the only medicine for the fainting soul, whereby it is restored
to God and itself. For none but God himself can give it the
assurance of God's grace. But now God has liberally, abun-

dantly and wisely lavished it upon us that nothing further remains which could be desired; unless someone would dare to seek something that is beyond the highest and beyond overflowing abundance.

Thirdly—I know that there is no other victim for expiating sin than Christ (for not even was Paul crucified for us); no other pledge of divine goodness and mercy more certain and undisputable (for nothing is as certain as God); no other name under heaven whereby we must be saved than that of Jesus Christ [Acts 4:12]. Hence there is left neither justification nor satisfaction based on our works, nor any expiation nor intercession of all saints, whether on earth or in heaven, who live by the goodness and mercy of God. For this is the one, sole Mediator between God and men, the God-man Christ Jesus. But the election of God remains firm and unchangeable. Those whom He elected before the foundation of the world He elected in such a manner as to make them His own through His Son; for as He is kind and merciful, so also is He holy and just. All His works, therefore, savor of mercy and justice. Hence His election also justly savors of both. It is goodness to elect whom He will; it is justice to make the elect His own and to unite them to Himself through His son, who for us has become the victim to satisfy divine justice. . . .

Fourthly—I think of original sin as follows: An act is called sin when it is committed against the law; for where there is no law there is no transgression, and where there is no transgression there is no sin in the proper sense, since sin is plainly an offense, a crime, a misdeed or guilt. I confess, therefore, that our father [Adam] committed what was truly a sin, namely an atrocious deed, a crime, an impiety. But his descendants have not sinned in this manner, for who among us crushed with his teeth the forbidden apple in Paradise? Hence, willing or unwilling, we are forced to admit that original sin, as it is in the children of Adam, is not properly sin, as has been explained; for it is not a misdeed

contrary to law. It is, therefore, properly a disease and condition—a disease, because just as he fell through self-love, so
do we also; a condition, because just as he became a slave
and liable to death, so also are we born slaves and children
of wrath [Eph. 2:3] and liable to death. However, I have
no objection to this disease and condition being called, after
the habit of Paul, a sin; indeed it is a sin inasmuch as those
born therein are God's enemies and opponents, for they are
drawn into it by the condition of birth, not by the perpetra-
tion of a definite crime, except as far as their first parent has
committed one. . . . I acknowledge that this original sin,
through condition and contagion, belongs by birth to all who
are born from the love of man and woman; and I know that
we are by nature children of wrath, but I doubt not that we
are received among the sons of God by grace, which through
the second Adam, Christ, has repaired the fall. This takes
place in the following manner:

Fifthly—It is evident, if in Christ, the second Adam, we
are restored to life, as in the first Adam we were delivered to
death, that in condemning children born of Christian parents, nay even the children of the heathen, we act rashly. For
if Adam by sinning could ruin the entire race, and Christ
by His death did not quicken and redeem the entire race
from the calamity inflicted by the former, then the salvation
conferred by Christ is no longer a match for sin. Moreover
(which God forbid) the word is not true: "As in Adam all
die, even so in Christ shall all be made alive" [I Cor.
15:22]. But, whatever must be the decision about the
children of heathen, this we must certainly maintain that, in
view of the efficacy of the salvation procured through Christ,
those go astray who pronounce them subject to an eternal
curse, not only on account of Christ's reparation already
mentioned, but also on account of God's free election, which
does not follow faith, but faith follows election. . . . For
those who have been elected from eternity have undoubtedly
been elected before faith. Therefore those who because of

their age have not faith should not be rashly condemned by us; for although they do not as yet have it, yet God's election is hidden from us. If before Him they are elect, we judge rashly about things unknown to us. However, regarding the children of Christians we judge differently—namely, that all children of Christians belong to the church of God's people and are parts and members of His church. . . .

Sixthly—Of the church, therefore, we thus think, namely, that the word "church" in the Scriptures is to be taken in various meanings. It is used for the elect, who have been predestined by God's will to eternal life. Of this church Paul speaks when he says that it has neither wrinkle or spot [Eph. 5:27]. This is known to God alone, for according to the word of Solomon [Prov. 15:11], He alone knows the hearts of the children of men. Nevertheless those who are members of this church, since they have faith, know that they themselves are elect and are members of this first church, but are ignorant about members other than themselves. For thus it is written in Acts [13:48]: "And as many as were ordained to eternal life believed." Those, therefore, that believe are ordained to eternal life. But no one, save he who believes, knows who truly believe. He is already certain that he is elect of God. For, according to the apostle's word [II Cor. 1:22], he has the seal of the Spirit, by which, pledged and sealed, he knows that he has become truly free, a son of the family, and not a slave. For the Spirit cannot deceive. If He tell us that God is our Father, and we confidently and fearlessly call Him Father, untroubled because we shall enter upon the eternal inheritance, then it is certain that God's Spirit has been shed abroad in our hearts. It is therefore settled that he is elect who had this security and certainty, for they who believe are ordained to eternal life. . . .

Again, the "church" is taken in a general sense for all who are rated as Christians, *i.e.*, those who have enlisted under His name, a large number of whom acknowl-

edge Christ publicly by confession or participation in the
sacraments, and yet at heart shrink back from Him or are
ignorant of Him. To this church, we believe, belong all those
who confess Christ's name. Thus Judas belonged to the
church of Christ and all those who turned away from Christ.
For by the apostles Judas was regarded as belonging to the
church of Christ no less than Peter and John, although it
was by no means the case. Christ knew who were His and
who were the devil's. This church, therefore, is visible, albeit
it does not assemble in this world. It consists of all who confess Christ, even though among them are many reprobates.
Christ has depicted it in the charming allegory of the ten
virgins, some of whom were wise and others foolish [Matth.
25]. This church is also sometimes called elect, although it
is not like the first without spot. But as it is considered by
men the church of God, because of known confession, so for
the same reason it is styled elect. For we judge that they who
have enlisted under Christ are believers and elect. Thus Peter spoke to "the elect scattered abroad throughout Pontus,"
etc. [I Pet. 1:1]. Here he means by "elect" all who belonged
to the churches to which he is writing, and not those only
who were properly elected of God; for as they were unknown
to Peter, he could not have written to them.

Finally, the "church" is taken for every particular congregation of this universal and visible church, as the Church of
Rome, of Augsburg, of Lyons. There are still other meanings
of the word "church," which it is not necessary to enumerate
at present. Hence I believe that there is one church of those
who have the same Spirit, through whom they are made certain that they are the true children of the family of God; and
this is the first fruits of the church. I believe that this church
does not err in regard to truth, namely in those fundamental
matters of faith upon which everything depends. I believe
also that the universal, visible church is one, while it maintains that true confession, of which we have already spoken.
I believe that to this church belong Isaac, Jacob, Judah and

all who were of the seed of Abraham, and also those infants whose parents in the first beginnings of the Christian church, through the preaching of the apostles, were won to the cause of Christ. . . .

Seventhly—I believe, indeed I know, that all the sacraments are so far from conferring grace that they do not even convey or dispense it. In this matter, most powerful Emperor, I may seem to thee perhaps too bold. But my opinion is firm. For as grace comes from or is given by the Divine Spirit (when I speak of grace I use the Latin term for pardon, *i.e.*, indulgence or spontaneous favor), so this gift pertains to the Spirit alone. Moreover, a channel or vehicle is not necessary to the Spirit, for He Himself is the virtue and energy whereby all things are borne, and has no need of being borne; neither do we read in the Holy Scriptures that visible things, as are the sacraments, carry certainly with them the Spirit, but if visible things have ever been borne with the Spirit, it has been the Spirit, not the visible things that have done the bearing. . . .

Therefore, the Spirit of grace is conveyed not by this immersion, not by this drinking, not by this anointing. For if it were thus, it would be known how, where, whence and whither the Spirit is borne. If the presence and efficacy of grace are bound to the sacraments, they work whithersoever they are carried; and where they are not used, everything becomes feeble. Nor can theologians plead that the proper disposition of the subject is demanded as a prerequisite [for the right use of the sacraments]. For example, the grace of baptism or of the Eucharist (so they say) is conferred upon him who is first prepared for it. For he who according to their opinion receives grace through the sacraments, either prepares himself for it or is prepared by the Spirit. If he prepares himself, we can do something of ourselves and prevenient grace is nothing. If he is prepared by the Spirit for the reception of grace, I ask whether this be done through the sacraments as a channel or independent of the sacraments?

If the sacraments mediate, man is prepared by the sacrament for the sacrament, and thus there will be a process ad infinitum; for a sacrament will be required as a preparation for a sacrament. But if we be prepared without the sacrament for the reception of sacramental grace, the Spirit is present in His goodness before the sacrament, and hence grace has been shown and is present before the sacrament is administered.

From this it follows (as I willingly and gladly admit in regard to the subject of the sacraments) that the sacraments are given as a public testimony of that grace which is previously present to every individual. Thus baptism is administered in the presence of the church to one who before receiving it either confessed the religion of Christ or has the word of promise, whereby he is known to belong to the church. Hence it is that when we baptize an adult we ask him whether he believes. And only when he answers "yes," then he receives baptism. Faith therefore, has been present before he receives baptism, and is not given by baptism. But when an infant is offered, the question is asked whether its parents offer it for baptism. When they have answered through witnesses that they wish it baptized, then the infant is baptized. Here the promise of God precedes, that He regards our infants, no less than those of the Hebrews, as belonging to the church. For when members of the church offer it, the infant is baptized under the law that, since it has been born of Christians, it is regarded by the divine promise among the members of the church. By baptism, therefore, the church publicly receives one who has previously been received through grace. Hence baptism does not convey grace but the church certifies that grace has been given to him to whom it is administered.

I believe therefore, O Emperor, that a sacrament is a sign of a sacred thing, i. e., of grace that has been given. I believe that it is a visible figure or form of the invisible grace, provided and bestowed by God's bounty, i.e., a visible example

which presents an analogy to something done by the Spirit. I
believe that it is a public testimony. Thus when we are baptized the body is washed with the purest element; by this it
is signified that by the grace of divine goodness we have been
gathered into the assembly of the church and of God's people, wherein we should live upright and pure. Thus Paul explains the mystery of Romans VI. The recipient of baptism
testifies, therefore, that he belongs to the church of God,
which worships its Lord in soundness of faith and purity of
life. For this reason the sacraments, which are sacred ceremonies (for the Word is added to the element and it becomes
a sacrament) should be religiously cherished, *i.e.*, highly
valued and treated with honor. For though they are unable
to bestow grace, they nevertheless associate visibly with the
church us who have previously been received into it invisi-
bly; and this should be regarded with the highest veneration,
since with their administration the words of the divine promise are declared and pronounced. . . .

Eighthly—I believe that in the holy Eucharist, *i.e.*, the
supper of thanksgiving, the true body of Christ is present
by the contemplation of faith. This means that they who
thank the Lord for the benefits bestowed on us in His Son
acknowledge that He assumed true flesh, in it truly suffered,
truly washed away our sins by His blood; and thus everything done by Christ becomes as it were present to them by
the contemplation of faith. But that the body of Christ in
essence and really, *i.e.*, the natural body itself, is either present in the supper or masticated with our mouth and teeth, as
the Papists or some who look back to the fleshpots of
Egypt assert, we not only deny, but constantly maintain to
be an error, contrary to the Word of God. This, with the
divine assistance, I will in a few words, make as clear as the
sun to your majesty, O Emperor. First, by citing the divine
oracles; secondly, by attacking the opponents with arguments
derived therefrom, as with military engines; lastly, by showing that the ancient theologians held our opinion. Meanwhile,

thou Creator, thou Spirit, be present, enlighten the minds
of thy people, and fill with grace and light the hearts that
thou hast created! . . .

Let them who wish go now and condemn us for heresy,
only let them know that by the same process they are condemning the opinions of the theologians, contrary to the decrees of the pontiffs. For from these facts it becomes very
evident that the ancients always spoke figuratively when they
attributed so much to the eating of the body of Christ in the
Supper; meaning, not that sacramental eating could cleanse
the soul but faith in God through Jesus Christ, which is spiritual eating, whereof this external eating is but symbol and
shadow. And as bread sustains the body and wine enlivens
and exhilarates, thus it strengthens the soul and assures it of
God's mercy that He has given us His Son; thus it renews
the mind by the confidence that, by His blood, the sins with
which it was being consumed were destroyed. . . .

Ninthly—I believe that ceremonies which are not through
superstitious use contrary either to faith or to God's word
(although I do not know whether such be found) can be
tolerated by charity until the light of day shines clearer and
clearer. But at the same time I believe that by virtue of
the same charity the ceremonies mentioned should be abolished when it can be done without great offense, however much the evilminded may clamor. For Christ did not
forbid Mary Magdalene to pour out the ointment, although
the dishonest and evilminded Judas made an ugly disturbance. Images, however, which are misused for worship, I do
not count among ceremonies, but among the number of those
things which are diametrically opposed to the Word of God.
But those which do not serve for worship and in whose cases
there exists no danger of future worship, I am so far from
condemning that I acknowledge both painting and statuary
as God's gifts.

Tenthly—I believe that the work of prophesying or
preaching is most sacred, so that it is a work most necessary,

above all others. For to speak scripturally or strictly, we see that among all nations the outward preaching of apostles, evangelists and bishops preceded faith, which nevertheless we attribute to the Spirit alone. For alas! We see very many who hear indeed the outward preaching of the Gospel, but believe not, because there is a lack of the Spirit. Whithersoever, then, prophets or preachers of the Word are sent, it is a sign of God's grace, that He wishes to manifest a knowledge of Himself to His elect; and to whom they [the preachers] are denied, it is a sign of His impending wrath. . . .

Eleventh—I know that the magistrate when lawfully installed, holds God's place no less than the prophet. For as the prophet is a minister of heavenly wisdom and goodness, as one who teaches faithfully and brings error to light, so the magistrate is the minister of goodness and justice. Of goodness, in that with fidelity and moderation, like God, he both hears and determines concerning the affairs of his people; of justice, in that he breaks the audacity of the wicked and protects the innocent. If a prince have these endowments, I believe that no fear need be entertained for his conscience. If he lack these, though he make himself an object of fear and terror, his conscience can in no way be cleared, upon the ground that he has been lawfully installed. Yet, at the same time I believe, that a Christian should obey such a tyrant, until that time comes whereof Paul says: "If thou canst become free, use it rather" [I Cor. 7:21]. Nevertheless, I believe that this time is indicated by God alone, and not by man; and this is done not obscurely but as openly as when Saul was rejected and David became his successor. Regarding tribute and taxes, to be paid for protection, I am of the same opinion as Paul, Romans 13.

Twelfthly—I believe that the figment of purgatorial fire is as much an affront to the redemption of Christ freely granted to us as it has been a lucrative business to its authors. For if it be necessary by punishments and tortures to expiate the guilt of our crimes, Christ will have died in vain and grace will have lost its meaning. Can anything more wicked be imagined in Christianity? Or what sort of a Christ do they have who wish to be called Christians and yet dread this fire, which is no longer fire, but smoke? . . .

The above [twelve points] I firmly believe, teach and maintain, not by my own utterances, but by those of the Word of God; and, God willing, I promise to do this as long as the mind controls these members, unless some one from the declarations of Holy Scripture, properly understood, explain and establish the reverse as clearly and plainly as we have established the above. For it is no less agreeable and delightful than fair and just for us to submit our judgment to the Holy Scriptures, and the church, deciding in harmony with these by virtue of the Spirit. . . .

The Latin Works of Huldreich Zwingli, Vol. II,
Edited by William John Hinke.
Philadelphia: The Heidelberg Press, 1922.

JOHN CALVIN

1509 - 1564

JOHN CALVIN

JC

JOHN CALVIN, WHO HAS BEEN CALLED "THE ONLY GENTLE-man among the Reformers," came from a good family in Noyon, France. He studiously availed himself of excellent educational opportunities in universities and seminaries at Paris, Orleans, Bruges, Poitiers and Basel. A precocious mind, he evidently thought hard and fast, so that his fellow-students said he was "all Logic and Latin," and gave him the nickname "the accusative case." Originally headed for the Roman Catholic priesthood, he turned to law to please his father, but persisted in his theological interests and, somewhere around his twenty-first year, by what he called a "sudden conversion" became a Protestant.

Falling under suspicion of the Parisian authorities, he went into hiding under an assumed name and, after finding asylum in various places, arrived in Basel in 1535. There in the following year, at the age of twenty-six, he published his great work, the most influential theological treatise of the Reformation, *The Institutes of the Christian Religion*. In later years he published revised editions of this early work, but essentially he never varied from the positions he stated and defended at the age of twenty-six.

Thinking of himself as a scholar, he says more than once

that his whole ambition for himself was a life of quiet study but, coming to Geneva in 1536, he was overborne by William Farel's insistence and accepted the position of teacher in the Genevan Church. "Farel kept me at Geneva," he wrote, "not so much by advice and entreaty as by a dreadful adjuration, as if God had stretched forth His hand upon me from on high to arrest me."

Geneva, like Basel, had already become officially Protestant before his arrival, and Calvin began at once to make it actually so. In physique he was a slight, frail figure; he suffered from ill health all his life; but he turned out to be an indefatigable teacher, writer, organizer, administrator and ecclesiastical statesman, unequalled in Protestant history.

Calvin had a high respect for the independent functions of the church as the custodian of God's will revealed in his Word, but along with this went a profound conviction that one of the major duties of the civil government was vigorous enforcement of what the church wanted done. While, therefore in Calvin's Geneva there was always a clear distinction in theory between church and state, in practical effect there emerged in the end a thoroughgoing theocracy, inspired and guided by Calvin and the ministers.

The development of this theocracy was uneven and stormy. Geneva was a cosmopolitan city, rejoicing in its recently achieved freedom from the House of Savoy and from the papal sovereignty. Liberty ran into libertinism; morals were undisciplined; the ministers needed training; the church needed instruction; the magistrates needed direction and invigoration; popular conduct needed drastic reformation. Calvin's endeavors to make everyone believe and behave as he desired met vehement opposition. At one point he faced complete defeat, was exiled from the city, and spent over three years as a minister in Strassburg. Having once tasted Calvin's leadership, however, Geneva could not get on without him, and he was called back again.

From our modern point of view Calvin's ruthless methods

in enforcing conformity to the church's rule are shocking. Prison for a burgher who smiled during a baptismal service, for a tired man who slept during a sermon, for two burghers who played skittles, for two others who played dice for a quarter-bottle of wine, for a man who insisted on naming his son Claude instead of Abraham—the record is full of such sentences. Calvin's regime became, as even one of his admirers puts it, "an inquisitorial, harsh, tyrannical system of legally inforced obedience." To criticize a sermon, to sing a worldly song, to adorn oneself with unpermitted finery, to dance, or in any way to break the strict Sabbath laws—all such conduct was punished as criminal. To be sure, Calvin was not responsible for such coercive uses of government; they were the common practice of mediaeval municipalities; but Calvin accepted them, believed in them, developed their efficiency, gave religious backing and direction to them, and ruthlessly demanded their extension and enforcement.

Calvin had no doubt that at least exile and more generally capital punishment were proper penalties for heretics. Geneva was a town of not more than sixteen thousand inhabitants, and yet between 1542 and 1546, when Calvin was in full control, fifty-eight people were executed and seventy-six banished. Moreover, torture was an accepted procedure, and Geneva's record, covering sixty years, is one hundred and fifty heretics burned at the stake. In saying this, however, one needs to remember that during the eighteen years of Torquemada's presidency of the Roman Catholic Inquisition, ten thousand two hundred and twenty persons were burned.

Historic attention has been focused on the burning of Servetus, condemned because he denied the orthodox doctrine of the Trinity. It is to Calvin's credit that he protested against the burning of Servetus and wanted him decapitated instead, but there is no doubt that he worked for the man's execution and hotly defended it afterward. When Calvin heard that Servetus might come to Geneva, he wrote to Farel, "If he should come and my authority avails aught, I shall never suffer him to depart alive," and while Servetus was on trial he wrote again to Farel, "I hope that the sentence of capital punishment will be pronounced against him. Yet I should like to have the horrors of torture mitigated for him."

Calvin, therefore, has become one of the most controversial figures in history. His support of mediaeval brutality toward heretics by appeal to Old Testament custom in early Israel was ruthless. Says Balzac, "Calvin's rabid religious intolerance was morally crueller than Robespierre's political intolerance; and if he had had a more extensive sphere of influence than Geneva, he would have shed more blood than the dread apostle of political equality." On the other hand the Reformer's defenders say that he was simply a man of his time. There is truth in that defense; the principle on which Calvin acted, that the government should by persecution and death suppress heresy, was almost universally accepted throughout Europe; when Servetus came to Geneva he had just escaped from prison in Vienna, where the Roman Catholics a few weeks later sentenced him to death by slow fire; the sentence of death for heresy was a commonplace, and even gentle Philip Melanchthon called Servetus' execution in Geneva "justly done." Nevertheless, in Calvin's day there were some men far ahead of their time. The Swiss Anabaptists had already taken their resolute stand against the whole hideous business of religious persecution; Sebastian Franck, Calvin's contemporary, had denounced religious intolerance *in toto*, even saying, "Wherefore my heart is alien to none. I have my brothers among the Turks, Papists, Jews and all peoples"; Castellio—whom Calvin hated as he hated few other men—sprang to Servetus' defense and published in Basel a magnificent plea for liberty of conscience against the persecutors, in his work, *Concerning Heretics*. "Christ would be a Moloch," said Castellio, "if he required that men be offered and burned alive."

How comes it, then, that Calvin must still be rated as one of the greatest, as he certainly was one of the most influential, of the Reformers? "To omit Calvin," said Lord Morley, "from the forces of Western Evolution is to read history with one eye shut."

Calvin was a complex character, full of inner contradictions and gifted with immense abilities, so that to center attention solely on his dogmatic intolerance and his acceptance of current ideas of persecution's use on behalf of religion is to misconceive him. He made Geneva a city of refuge for persecuted Protestants from all Europe. An endless stream of refugees flocked there, and either remained to strengthen Calvin's regime, or, like John Knox, returned to their own lands as militant reformers, so that Geneva became the major citadel of Protestantism. He was a great conciliator, laboring to bring together into unity Lutherans, Zwinglians and the Reformed Churches of France, England and the Low Countries. "I would cross ten seas," he wrote to Archbishop Cranmer, "if, by this means, holy communion might prevail among the members of Christ."

He was a great educator—the Academy has been called "the crown of Calvin's Genevan work"—and his ideas and methods in training ministers and in setting the standards of preaching and popular instruction were immensely influential. He was a consummate organizer, and the structure of the Calvinistic churches, which he planned, made Protestantism an independent and powerful force even in countries, such as France, where the civil governments were hostile. He was an able diplomatist and exercised a momentous influence on the policies both of states and churches in Western Europe, and he was a tireless missionary statesman, sending his emissaries far and wide to meet the needs of critical areas.

Through his correspondence, whose variety and extent are almost incredible, he brought inspiration, guidance and courage to thousands. One letter, written to five young Frenchmen facing death for their Protestantism in Lyons, is typical:

It is needful that you sustain hard conflicts, that that which was said to Peter be accomplished in you: "You shall be carried whither ye would not." But you know in what strength you have to fight; upon which all who rely shall never be surprised and still less confounded. Therefore, my brothers, be confident that you will be strengthened according to your need by the spirit of our Lord Jesus that you fail not under the burden of temptations, however pressing they may be, any more than he who had so glorious a victory that it is an infallible pledge to us of our triumph in the midst of our miseries. If he pleases to make use of you even to death in his battle, he will uphold you by his mighty hand to fight firmly, and will not suffer a single drop of your blood to remain useless.

Calvin's regime in Geneva illustrates the very opposite of political liberty, and yet Calvinism in the end was one of the major factors in achieving the political liberty which moderns enjoy. Lutheranism and Zwinglianism were dependent on the state, but Calvin's church was so organized that it had an independent status and claimed a divine right superior to the state's control. "We are subject to men who rule over us," wrote Calvin, "but subject only in the Lord. If they command anything against Him, let us not pay the least regard to it, nor be moved by all the dignity which they possess as magistrates." This basic principle, in the end, shook the foundations of the whole concept of the state's right to control consciences.

As for Calvin's theology, it has been popularly, and not untruthfully, conceived as centered in the doctrine of predestination. This dogma, however, was no unique specialty of Calvin; along with the Roman Catholics and with Luther and Zwingli he took it from Paul and Augustine, but his inexorable logic carried it to its ruthless conclusion and his mind refused to shrink from the most terrific statements of the result. If every man's eternal destiny is foreknown and fore-ordained by God from before the foundation of the world, then free will is an illusion and, as some are elected to be saved, so others are predestined to be damned. This dogma Calvin relentlessly taught, and some of his statements are bloodcurdling, as when, commenting on the command in Deuteronomy to destroy whole villages, killing even the children, he says: "We may rest assured that God would suffer only those infants to be destroyed whom he had already damned and destined to eternal death."

Rebellion against this brutal doctrine was already under way in Calvin's time. Melanchthon could not stomach its more horrid conclusions, and Calvin himself says: "The human mind, when it hears this doctrine of election, cannot restrain its petulance, but boils and rages as if aroused by the sound of a trumpet." The modern mind, shocked by the horror of this Calvinistic tenet, commonly fails to see what, in practical effect, the Calvinists got out of it. They had been eternally elected—*that* was its point of practical impact—they were predestined to do God's will, and therefore nothing on earth could stop them. Fearing God so much that they feared no one else at all, they went out in consequence to face "the wrath of devils and the scorn of men," sure that their vocation must never be betrayed and that their cause could never be defeated. The result is indicated in the remark of a seventeenth-century secularist: "I had rather meet coming against me a whole regiment with drawn swords than one Calvinist convinced that he is doing the will of God."

John Calvin, by Williston Walker, is a good, brief biography. *Calvin and the Reformation,* by James Mackinnon, gives a balanced estimate of the Reformer's work. *The Teaching of Calvin,* by A. Mitchell Hunter, is excellent, as is J. E. Harkness' *John Calvin: The Man and His Ethics.* For stimulating statements concerning Calvinism's influence on modern capitalism see Max Weber's *The Protestant Ethic and the Spirit of Capitalism,* and R. H. Tawney's *Religion and the Rise of Capitalism.* On contemporary protests against Calvin's intolerance, Roland H. Bainton has given us an admirable treatise in his book on Sebastian Castellio's *Concerning Heretics.*

In this anthology we quote, first, portions of Calvin's famous letter to Cardinal Sadolet, and then extracts from his *Instruction in Faith,* a compendium of his *Institutes,* which he himself prepared for purposes of popular indoctrination.

CALVIN'S LETTER TO
CARDINAL JAMES SADOLET*

YOU LATELY ADDRESSED A LETTER TO THE SENATE AND PEOPLE of Geneva, in which you sounded their inclination as to whether, after having once shaken off the yoke of the Roman Pontiff, they would submit to have it again imposed upon them. In that letter, as it was not expedient to wound the feelings of those whose favor you required to gain your cause, you acted the part of a good pleader; for you endeavored to soothe them by abundance of flattery, in order that you might gain them over to your views. Any thing of obloquy or bitterness you directed against those whose exertions had produced the revolt from that tyranny. And here (so help you) you bear down full sail upon those who, under pretence of the gospel, have by wicked arts urged on the city to what you deplore as the subversion of religion and of the church. I, however, Sadolet, profess to be one of those whom with so much enmity you assail and stigmatise. For though religion was already established, and the form of the church corrected, before I was invited to Geneva, yet having not only approved my suffrage, but studied as much as in me lay to preserve and confirm what had been done by Viret and Farel, I cannot separate my case from theirs. Still, if you had attacked me in my private character, I could easily have

* Dated, September 1, 1539, when Calvin was exiled from Geneva.

forgiven the attack in consideration of your learning, and in honour of your letters. But when I see that my ministry, which I feel assured is supported and sanctioned by a call from God, is wounded through my side, it would be perfidy, not patience, were I here to be silent and connive. . . .

For although I am for the present relieved of the charge of the Church of Geneva, that circumstance ought not to prevent me from embracing it with paternal affection—God, when he gave it to me in charge, having bound me to be faithful to it for ever. Now, then, when I see the worst snares laid for that church, whose safety it has pleased the Lord to make my highest care, and grievous peril impending if not obviated, who will advise me to await the issue silent and unconcerned? . . .

You are mistaken in supposing that we desire to lead away the people from that method of worshipping God which the Catholic Church always observed. You either labour under a delusion as to the term "church," or, at least, knowingly and willingly give it a gloss. I will immediately show the latter to be the case, though it may also be that you are somewhat in error. First, in defining the term, you omit what would have helped you, in no small degree, to the right understanding of it. When you describe it as that which in all parts, as well as at the present time, in every region of the earth, being united and consenting in Christ, has been always and everywhere directed by the One Spirit of Christ, what comes of the Word of the Lord, (i.e., the Holy Scripture), that clearest of all marks, and which the Lord himself, in pointing out the church, so often recommends to us? For seeing how dangerous it would be to boast of the Spirit without the Word, he declared that the church is indeed governed by the Holy Spirit, but in order that that government might not be vague and unstable, he annexed it to the Word. . . .

We are assailed by two sects, which seem to differ most widely from each other. For what similitude is there in appearance between the pope and the Anabaptists? And yet, that you may see that Satan never transforms himself so cunningly, as not in some measure to betray himself, the principal weapon with which they both assail us is the same. For when they boast extravagantly of the Spirit, the tendency certainly is to sink and bury the Word of God, that they may make room for their own falsehoods. And you, Sadolet, by stumbling on the very threshold, have paid the penalty of that affront which you offered to the Holy Spirit, when you separated him from the Word. For, as if those who seek the way of God were standing where two ways meet, and destitute of any certain sign, you are forced to introduce them as hesitating whether it be more expedient to follow the authority of the church, or to listen to those whom you call the inventors of new dogmas. Had you known, or been unwilling to disguise the fact, that the Spirit goes before the church, to enlighten her in understanding the Word, while the Word itself is like the Lydian Stone, by which she tests all doctrines, would you have taken refuge in that most perplexing and thorny question? Learn, then, by your own experience, that it is no less unreasonable to boast of the Spirit without the Word, than it would be absurd to bring forward the Word itself without the Spirit. Now, if you can bear to receive a truer definition of the church than your own, say, in future, that it is the society of all the saints, a society which spread over the whole world, and existing in all ages, yet bound together by the one doctrine, and the one Spirit of Christ, cultivates and observes unity of faith and brotherly concord. With this church we deny that we have any disagreement. Nay, rather, as we revere our mother, so we desire to remain in her bosom.

But here you bring a charge against us. For you teach that all which has been approved for fifteen hundred years or more, by the uniform consent of the faithful, is, by our headstrong rashness, torn up and destroyed. Here I will not require you to deal truly and candidly by us (though this should be spontaneously offered by a philosopher, not to say a Christian). I will only ask you not to stoop to an illiberal indulgence in calumny, which, even though we be silent, must be extremely injurious to your reputation with grave and honest men. You know, Sadolet, and if you venture to deny, I will make it palpable to all that you knew, yet cunningly and craftily disguised the fact, not only that our agreement with antiquity is far closer than yours, but that all we have attempted has been to renew that ancient form of the church, which, at first sullied and distorted by illiterate men of indifferent character, was afterwards flagitiously mangled and almost destroyed by the Roman Pontiff and his faction.

I will not press you so closely as to call you back to that form which the Apostles instituted (though in it we have the only model of a true church, and whosoever deviates from it in the smallest degree is in error), but to indulge you so far, place, I pray you, before your eyes, that ancient form of the church, such as their writings prove it to have been in the age of Chrysostom and Basil, among the Greeks, and of Cyprian, Ambrose, and Augustine, among the Latins; after so doing, contemplate the ruins of that church, as now surviving among yourselves. Assuredly, the difference will appear as great as that which the Prophets describe between the famous church which flourished under David and Solomon, and that which under Zedekiah and Jehoiakim had lapsed into every kind of superstition, and utterly vitiated the purity of divine worship. Will you here give the name of an enemy of antiquity to him who, zealous for ancient piety and holiness, and dissatisfied with the state of matters as existing in a dissolute and depraved church, attempts to ameliorate its condition, and restore it to pristine splendour?

Since there are three things on which the safety of the church is founded, viz., doctrine, discipline, and the sacraments, and to these a fourth is added, viz., ceremonies, by which to exercise the people in offices of piety, in order that we may be most sparing of the honour of your church, by which of these things would you have us to judge her? The truth of Prophetical and Evangelical doctrine, on which the church ought to be founded, has not only in a great measure perished in your church, but is violently driven away by fire and sword. Will you obtrude upon me, for the church, a body which furiously persecutes everything sanctioned by our religion, both as delivered by the oracles of God, and embodied in the writings of holy Fathers, and approved by ancient Councils? Where, pray, exist among you any vestiges of that true and holy discipline, which the ancient bishops exercised in the church? Have you not scorned all their institutions? Have you not trampled all the Canons under foot? Then, your nefarious profanation of the sacraments I cannot think of without the utmost horror. . . .

That I may altogether disarm you of the authority of the church, which, as your shield of Ajax, you ever and anon oppose to us, I will show, by some additional examples, how widely you differ from that holy antiquity.

We accuse you of overthrowing the ministry, of which the empty name remains with you, without the reality. As far as the office of feeding the people is concerned, the very children perceive that Bishops and Presbyters are dumb statues, while men of all ranks know by experience, that they are active only in robbing and devouring. We are indignant, that in the room of the sacred Supper has been substituted a sacrifice by which the death of Christ is emptied of its virtues. We exclaim against the execrable traffic in masses, and we complain, that the Supper of the Lord, as to one of its halves, has been stolen from the Christian people. We inveigh against the accursed worship of images. We show that the sacraments are vitiated by many profane notions. We tell how indulgences crept in with fearful dishonour to the cross of Christ. We lament, that by means of human traditions, Christian liberty has been crushed and destroyed. Of these and similar pests, we have been careful to purge the churches which the Lord has committed to us. Expostulate with us, if you can, for the injury which we inflicted on the Catholic church, by daring to violate its sacred sanctions. The fact is now too notorious for you to gain anything by denying it, viz., that in all these points, the ancient church is clearly on our side, and opposes you, not less than we ourselves do.

But here we are again met by what you say, when, in order to palliate matters, you allege that though your manners should be irregular, that is no reason why we should make a schism in the holy church. It is scarcely possible that the minds of the common people should not be greatly alienated from you by the many examples of cruelty, avarice, intemperance, arrogance, insolence, lust, and all sorts of wickedness, which are openly manifested by men of your order, but none of those things would have driven us to the attempt which we made under a much stronger necessity. That necessity was, that the light of divine truth had been extinguished, the word of God buried, the virtue of Christ left in profound oblivion, and the pastoral office subverted. Meanwhile impiety so stalked abroad, that almost no doctrine of religion was pure from admixture, no ceremony free from error, no part, however minute, of divine worship untarnished by supersitition. Do those who contend against such evils declare war against the church, and not rather assist her in her extreme distress? And yet you would take credit for your obedience and humility in refraining, through veneration for the church, from applying your hand to the removal of these abominations. What has a Christian man to do with that prevaricating obedience, which, while the word of God is licentiously contemned, yields its homage to human vanity? What has he to do with that contumacious and rude humility, which, despising the majesty of God, only looks up with reverence to men? Have done with empty names of virtue, employed merely as cloaks for vice, and let us exhibit the thing itself in its true colors. Ours be the humility, which, beginning with the lowest, and paying respect to each in his degree, yields the highest honour and respect to the church, in subordination, however, to Christ the church's head; ours the obedience, which, while it disposes us to listen to our elders and superiors, tests all obedience by the Word of God; in fine, ours the church, whose supreme care it is humbly and religiously to venerate the Word of God, and submit to its authority. . . .

Let us direct our thoughts and minds to that Judge who, by the mere brightness of his countenance, will disclose whatever lurks in darkness, lay open all the secrets of the human heart, and crush all the wicked by the mere breath of his mouth. Consider, now, what serious answer you are to make for yourself and your party: our cause, as it is supported by the truth of God, will be at no loss for complete defence. I speak not of our persons, whose safety will be found not in defence, but in humble confession and suppliant deprecation; but in so far as our ministry is concerned, there is none of us who will not be able thus to speak:—

"O Lord, I have, indeed, experienced how difficult and grievous it was to bear the invidious accusations with which I was harassed on earth; but with the same confidence with which I then appealed to thy tribunal, I now appear before thee because I know that in thy judgment truth always reigns —that truth by whose assurance supported I first ventured to attempt—with whose assistance provided I was able to accomplish whatever I have achieved in thy church. They charged me with two of the worst crimes—heresy and schism. And the heresy was, that I dared to protest against dogmas which they received. But what could I have done? I heard from thy mouth that there was no other light of truth which could direct our souls into the way of life, than that which was kindled by thy Word. I heard that whatever human minds of themselves conceive concerning thy Majesty, the worship of thy Deity, and the mysteries of thy religion, was vanity. I heard that their introducing into the church instead of thy Word, doctrines sprung from the human brain, was sacrilegious presumption. But when I turned my eyes towards men, I saw very different principles prevailing. Those who were regarded as the leaders of faith neither understood thy Word, nor greatly cared for it. They only drove unhappy people to and fro with strange doctrines, and deluded them with I know not what follies. Among the people themselves, the highest veneration paid to thy Word was to revere it at a distance, as a thing inaccessible, and abstain from all investigation of it. Owing to this supine state of the pastors, and this stupidity of the people, every place was filled with pernicious errors, falsehoods, and superstition. They, indeed, called thee the only God, but it was while transferring to others the glory which thou hast claimed for thy Majesty. They figured and had for themselves as many gods as they had saints, whom they chose to worship. Thy Christ was indeed worshipped as God, and retained the name of Saviour; but where he ought to have been honoured, he was left without honour. For, spoiled of his own virtue, he passed unnoticed among the crowd of saints, like one of the meanest of them. There was none who duly considered that one sacrifice which he offered on the cross, and by which he reconciled us to thyself—none who ever dreamed of thinking of his eternal priesthood, and the intercession depending upon it—none who trusted in his righteousness only. That confident hope of salvation which is both enjoined by thy Word, and founded upon it, had almost vanished. Nay, it was received as a kind of oracle, that it was foolish arrogance, and, as they termed it, presumption for any one trusting to thy goodness, and the righteousness of thy Son, to entertain a sure and unfaltering hope of salvation. Not a few profane opinions plucked up by the roots the first principles of that doctrine which thou hast delivered to us in thy Word. The true meaning of Baptism and the Lord's Supper, also, were corrupted by numerous falsehoods. And then, when all, with no small insult to thy mercy, put confidence in good works, when by good works they strove to merit thy favour, to procure justification, to expiate their sins, and make satisfaction to thee—each of these things obliterating and making void the virtue of Christ's cross—they were yet altogether ignorant wherein good works consisted. For, just as if they were not at all instructed in righteousness by thy law, they had fabricated for themselves many useless frivolities, as a means of procuring thy favour, and on these they so plumed themselves, that, in comparison of them, they almost contemned the standard of true righteousness which thy law recommended—to such a degree had human desires, after usurping the ascendancy, derogated, if not from the belief, at least from the authority, of thy precepts therein contained. That I might perceive these things, thou, O Lord, didst shine upon me with the brightness of thy Spirit; that I might comprehend how impious and noxious they were, thou didst bear before me the torch of thy Word; that I might abominate them as they deserved, thou didst stimulate my soul. But in rendering an account of my doctrine, thou seest (what my own conscience declares) that it was not my intention to stray beyond those limits which I saw had been fixed by all thy servants. Whatever I felt assured that I had learned from thy mouth, I desired to dispense faithfully to the church. Assuredly, the thing at which I chiefly aimed, and for which I most diligently laboured, was, that the glory of thy goodness and justice, after dispersing the mists by which it was formerly obscured, might shine forth conspicuous, that the virtue and blessings of thy Christ (all glosses being wiped away) might be fully displayed. For I thought it impious to leave in obscurity things which we were born to ponder and meditate. Nor did I think that truths, whose magnitude no language can express, were to be maliciously or falsely declared. I hesitated not to dwell at greater length on topics on which the salvation of my hearer depended. For the oracle could never deceive which declares (John xvii. 3), 'This is eternal life, to know thee the only true God, and Jesus Christ, whom thou has sent.'

"As to the charge of forsaking the church, which they were wont to bring against me, there is nothing of which my conscience accuses me, unless, indeed, he is to be considered a deserter, who, seeing the soldiers routed and scattered, and abandoning the ranks, raises the leader's standard, and recalls them to their posts. For this, O Lord, were all thy servants dispersed, so that they could not, by any possibility, hear the command, but had almost forgotten their leader, and their service, and their military oath. In order to bring them together, when thus scattered, I raised not a foreign standard, but that noble banner of thine whom we must follow, if we would be classed among thy people.

"Then I was assailed by those who, when they ought to have kept others in their ranks, had led them astray, and when I determined not to desist, opposed me with violence. On this grievous tumults arose, and the contest blazed and issued in disruption. With whom the blame rests it is for thee, O Lord, to decide. Always, both by word and deed, have I protested how eager I was for unity. Mine, however, was a unity of the church, which should begin with thee and end in thee. For as oft as thou didst recommend to us peace and concord, thou, at the same time, didst show that thou wert the only bond for preserving it. But if I desired to be at peace with those who boasted of being the heads of the church and pillars of faith, I needed to purchase it with the denial of thy truth. I thought that any thing was to be endured sooner than stoop to such a nefarious action. For Thine Anointed himself hath declared, that though heaven and earth should be confounded, yet thy word must endure for ever (Matt. cciv. 35). Nor did I think that I dissented from thy church, because I was at war with those leaders; for thou hast forewarned me both by thy Son and by the apostles, that that place would be occupied by persons to whom I ought by no means to consent. Christ had predicted not of strangers, but of men who should give themselves out for pastors, that they would be ravenous wolves and false prophets, and had, at the same time, cautioned to beware of them. Where Christ ordered me to beware, was I to lend my aid? And the apostles declared that there would be no enemies of thy church more pestilential than those from within, who should conceal themselves under the title of pastors (Matt. vii. 15; Acts xx. 29; II Pet. ii. 1; John ii. 18). Why should I have hesitated to separate myself from persons whom they fore-warned me to hold as enemies? I had before my eyes the examples of thy prophets, who I saw had a similar contest with the priests and prophets of their day, though these were undoubtedly the rulers of the church among the Israel-itish people. But thy prophets are not regarded as schismat-ics, because, when they wished to revive religion which had fallen into decay, they desisted not, although opposed with the utmost violence. They still remained in the unity of the church, though they were doomed to perdition by wicked priests, and deemed unworthy of a place among men, not to say saints. Confirmed by their example, I too persisted. Though denounced as a deserter of the church, and threat-ened, I was in no respect deterred, or induced to proceed less firmly and boldly in opposing those who, in the character of pastors, wasted thy church with a more than impious tyranny. My conscience told me how strong the zeal was with which I burned for the unity of thy church, provided thy truth were made the bond of concord. As the commotions which followed were not excited by me, so there is no ground for imputing them to me.

"Thou, O lord, knowest, and the fact itself has testified to me, that the only thing I asked was, that all controversies should be decided by thy word, that thus both parties might unite with one mind to establish thy kingdom; and I de-clined not to restore peace to the church at the expense of my head, if I were found to be unnecessarily the cause of tumult. But what did our opponents? Did they not instantly, and like madmen, fly to fires, swords, and gibbets? Did they not decide that their only security was in arms and cruelty?

Did they not instigate all ranks to the same fury? Did they not spurn all methods of pacification? To this it is owing that a matter, which might at one time have been settled amicably, has blazed into such a contest. But although, amidst the great confusion, the judgments of men were various, I am freed from all fear, now that we stand at thy tribunal, where equity, combined with truth, cannot but decide in favour of innocence."

Such, Sadolet, is our pleading, not the fictitious one which you, in order to aggravate our case, were pleased to devise, but that, the perfect truth of which is known to the good even now, and will be made manifest to all creatures on that day. . . .

Tracts Relating to the Reformation, by John Calvin,
Translated by Henry Beveridge.
Edinburgh: Vol. 1, 1844.

INSTRUCTION IN FAITH

ALL MEN ARE BORN IN ORDER TO KNOW GOD

AS NO MAN IS FOUND, HOWEVER BARBAROUS AND EVEN SAV-age he may be, who is not touched by some idea of religion, it is clear that we all are created in order that we may know the majesty of our Creator, that having known it, we may esteem it above all and honor it with all awe, love, and reverence.

But, leaving aside the unbelievers, who seek nothing but to efface from their memory that idea of God which is planted in their hearts, we, who make profession of personal religion, must reflect that this decrepit life of ours, which will soon end, must be nothing else but a meditation of immortality. Now, nowhere can eternal and immortal life be found except in God. It is necessary, therefore, that the principal care and solicitude of our life be to seek God, to aspire to him with all the affection of our heart, and to repose nowhere else but in him alone.

WHAT DIFFERENCE THERE IS BETWEEN TRUE AND FALSE RELIGION

Since it is commonly agreed that if our life is without religion we are most miserable and in no way better than brute animals, no one wishes to be considered as completely alien-

ated from piety and acknowledgment of God. There is, however, a great difference in the way of declaring one's religion,
because the majority of men are not truly touched by the
awe of God. Yet, willingly or not, they are bound by this
thought always coming anew to their minds that there is
some divinity by whose power they stand or fall. Hence,
being astonished by the thought of such a great power, they
revere it in some way in order not to provoke it against
themselves by too great a contempt. Yet, living in a disorderly way and rejecting all honesty, they exhibit a great
sense of security in despising the judgment of God. Moreover, they turn away from the true God because they estimate God not by his infinite majesty but by the foolish and
giddy vanity of their own mind. Hence, although they may
afterward strive to serve God with great care, that does not
profit them at all, because they do not worship the eternal
God, but the dreams and fancies of their own heart in place
of God. Now the gist of true piety does not consist in a fear
which would gladly flee the judgment of God but, being unable to do so, has horror of it. True piety consists rather in
a pure and true zeal which loves God altogether as Father,
and reveres him truly as Lord, embraces his justice and
dreads to offend him more than to die. All those who possess
this zeal do not undertake to forge for themselves a God as
their temerity wishes, but they seek the knowledge of the
true God from that very God and do not conceive him otherwise than he manifests and declares himself to them.

WHAT WE MUST KNOW OF GOD

Now since the majesty of God in itself goes beyond the capacity of human understanding and cannot be comprehended
by it, we must adore its loftiness rather than investigate it, so
that we do not remain overwhelmed by so great a splendor.
Hence, we must seek and consider God in his works, which,
for this reason the Scripture calls representations of the invisible things (Rom. 1:20; Heb. 11:1) because these works

represent to us that of the Lord which otherwise we cannot see. Now this does not keep our intellect up in the air through frivolous and vain speculations, but is a thing that we must know and that generates, nourishes, and confirms in us a true and solid piety, that is, faith united with reverential fear. We contemplate, therefore, in this universality of things, the immortality of our God, from which immortality have proceeded the beginning and origin of all things; his power which has created such a great system and now sustains it; his wisdom which has composed and rules with such a distinct order such a great and complex variety of beings and things; his goodness which has been the reason in itself why all these things have been created and now subsist; his justice which manifests itself in a marvelous way in the protection of good people and in the retribution of the bad; his mercy which endures our iniquities with such a great kindliness in order to call us to amendment. Certainly all this should abundantly teach us all of such a God as it is necessary to know, if we in our coarseness were not blind to such a great light. Yet here we sin not only by blindness, for our perversity is such that when it estimates the works of God there is nothing that it does not understand in an evil and perverse sense, so that it turns upside down all the heavenly wisdom which otherwise shines so clearly in those works. It is therefore necessary to come to the word [of God] where God is very well described to us through his workings, because in the Scripture these works are estimated not according to the perversity of our judgment, but by the standard of the eternal truth. From God's word, therefore, we learn that our only and eternal God is the spring and fountain of all life, justice, wisdom, virtue, goodness, and clemency. And, as every good without exception comes from him, so also every praise should rightly return to him. And although all these things appear clearly in each part of heaven and earth, yet only then do we at last understand truly that to which they tend, what their value is and at what end we must understand them, when we descend into ourselves and consider in what way the Lord manifests in us his life, wisdom, and power, and exercises toward us his justice, clemency, and goodness.

MAN

At first man was formed in the image and resemblance of God in order that man might admire his Author in the adornments with which he had been nobly vested by God and honor him with proper acknowledgment. But, having trusted such a great excellence of his nature and having forgotten from whom it had come and by whom it subsisted, man strove to raise himself up apart from the Lord. Hence man had to be stripped of all God's gifts of which he was foolishly proud, so that, denuded and deprived of all glory, he might know God whom man, after having been enriched by his liberalities, had dared to despise. As a result, this resemblance to God having been effaced in us, we all who descend from the seed of Adam are born flesh from flesh. For, though we are composed of a soul and a body, yet we feel nothing but the flesh, so that to whatever part of man we turn our eyes, it is impossible to see anything that is not impure, profane, and abominable to God. The intellect of man is indeed blinded, wrapped with infinite errors and always contrary to the wisdom of God; the will, bad and full of corrupt affections, hates nothing more than God's justice; and the bodily strength, incapable of all good deeds, tends furiously toward iniquity.

FREE WILL

The Scripture testifies often that man is a slave of sin. The Scripture means thereby that man's spirit is so alienated from the justice of God that man conceives, covets, and undertakes nothing that is not evil, perverse, iniquitous, and soiled. Because the heart, totally imbued with the poison of sin, can emit nothing but the fruits of sin. Yet one must not infer therefrom that man sins as constrained by violent necessity. For, man sins with the consent of a very prompt and inclined will. But because man, by the corruption of his affections, very strongly keeps hating the whole righteousness of God and, on the other hand, is fervent in all kinds of evil, it is said that he has not the free power of choosing between good and evil—which is called free will.

SIN AND DEATH

Sin means in the Scripture both the perversity of human nature, which is the fountain of all vices, and the evil desires which are born from it and the iniquitous transgressions which spring from these evil desires, such as murders, thefts, adulteries, and other things of this kind. Hence, being sinners from our mothers' wombs, we are all born subject to the wrath and retribution of God. And, having grown up, we pile upon ourselves an ever heavier judgment of God. Finally through all our life we tend ever more toward death. For there is no doubt that all iniquity is execrable to the justice of God. What can we expect in the face of God, we miserable ones who are oppressed by such a great load of sins and soiled by an infinite filth, except a very certain confusion such as his indignation brings? Though it fells man with terror and crushes him with despair, yet this thought is necessary for us in order that, being divested of our own righteousness, having given up faith in our own power, being rejected from all expectation of life, we may learn from the understanding of our poverty, misery, and infamy, to prostrate ourselves before the Lord and, by the acknowledgment of our iniquity, powerlessness, and utter ruin, give him all glory of holiness, might, and deliverance.

HOW WE ARE DELIVERED AND
RESTORED TO LIFE

If this knowledge of ourself, which shows us our nothingness, consciously enters into our hearts, an easy access to having the true knowledge of God is made to us. Or rather, God himself has opened to us, as it were, a first door to his kingdom when he has destroyed these two worst pests, which are self-assurance in front of his retribution and false confidence in ourselves. For we begin then to lift our eyes to heaven, those eyes that before were fixed and stopped on earth. And we, who once rested in ourselves, long for the Lord. On the other hand, though our iniquity should deserve something quite different, this merciful Father yet, according to his unspeakable benignity, shows himself voluntarily to us who are thus afflicted and perplexed. And by such means which he knows to be helpful in our weakness, he recalls us from error to the right way, from death to life, from ruin to salvation, from the kingdom of the devil to his own reign. As the Lord has therefore established this first preparation for all those whom he pleases to re-establish as heirs to heavenly life—that is to say, those who distressed by conscience and burdened by the weight of their sins feel themselves stung in the heart and stimulated reverently to fear him—God then first places his Law before us in order that it exercise us in this knowledge. . . . .

THE SUMMARY OF THE LAW

Now our Lord Jesus Christ has clearly enough declared to us the real purpose of all the commandments of the Law, when he taught that all the Law is comprised in two articles. The first article is that we should love the Lord our God with all our heart, with all our soul, and with all our strength. The second article is that we should love our neighbor as much as ourselves. And this interpretation, our Lord has taken from the Law itself. For the first part is found in Deut. 6:5, and the second is seen in Lev. 19:18.

WHAT COMES TO US FROM
THE LAW ALONE

Behold above, therefore, the standard of a just and holy life and even a very perfect image of justice or righteousness, so that if someone expresses the Law of God in his life, he will

lack nothing of the perfection required before the Lord. In
order to certify that, God promises to those who shall have
fulfilled the Law not only the grand blessings of the present
life, which are recited in Lev. 26:3-13 and in Deut. 27:1-14,
but also the recompense of eternal life (Lev. 18:5). On the
other hand, he pronounces retribution with eternal death
against those who shall not have accomplished by deeds that
which is commanded in the Law. Moses also, having published the law (Deut. 30:19), took heaven and earth as witnesses that he had proposed to the people good and evil,
life and death.

But although the Law shows the way of life, yet we must
see what this demonstration can avail us. Certainly if our
will be all formed and disposed to obedience toward the divine will, the mere knowledge of the Law would fully suffice
for salvation. But as our carnal and corrupt nature altogether wars against the spiritual Law of God and in nothing is mended by the teaching thereof, it results that the very
Law (which was given unto salvation if it had found good
and capable hearers) becomes on the contrary an occasion
of sin and death. For, since we are all convicted of being
transgressors of the Law, the more clearly the Law discloses
to us the justice of God, the more it uncovers on the other
hand our iniquity. And again, as the Law catches us in
greater transgression, so it renders us deserving of a heavier
judgment of God. And, the promise of eternal life being thus
taken away, the curse alone remains for us, which catches us
all by means of the Law.

THE LAW IS A PREPARATION
TO COME TO CHRIST

The testimony of the Law, however, which convinces us of
iniquity and transgression, is not made in order that we
should fall into despair, and, having lost courage, stumble
into ruin. Certainly the apostle (Rom. 3:19, 20) testifies
that by the judgment of the Law we all are condemned, in

order that every mouth be closed and the entire world be found guilty before God. Yet that very apostle elsewhere (Rom. 11:32) teaches that God has enclosed all under unbelief, not in order to ruin them or let them perish, but, on the contrary, in order that he may exercise mercy on all.

The Lord, therefore, after reminding us (by means of the Law) of our weakness and impurity, comforts us with the assurance of his power and his mercy. And it is in Christ his son that God shows himself to us benevolent and propitious. For, in the Law he appeared only as remunerator of perfect righteousness (of which we are completely destitute) and, on the other hand, as upright and severe judge of sins. But in Christ his face shines full of grace and kindliness even toward miserable and unworthy sinners; for, he gave this admirable example of his infinite love, when he exposed his own son for us, and in him opened to us all the treasure of his clemency and goodness.

WE APPREHEND CHRIST
THROUGH FAITH

Just as the merciful Father offers us the Son through the word of the Gospel, so we embrace him through faith and acknowledge him as given to us. It is true that the word of the Gospel calls all to participate in Christ, but a number, blinded and hardened by unbelief, despise such a unique grace. Hence, only believers enjoy Christ; they receive him as sent to them; they do not reject him when he is given, but follow him when he calls them.

ELECTION AND PREDESTINATION

Beyond this contrast of attitudes of believers and unbelievers, the great secret of God's counsel must necessarily be considered. For, the seed of the word of God takes root and brings forth fruit only in those whom the Lord, by his eternal election, has predestined to be children and heirs of the heavenly kingdom. To all the others (who by the same

counsel of God are rejected before the foundation of the
world) the clear and evident preaching of truth can be nothing but an odor of death unto death. Now, why does the
Lord use his mercy toward some and exercise the rigor of
his judgment on the others? We have to leave the reason of
this to be known by him alone. For, he, with a certainly
excellent intention, has willed to keep it hidden from us all.
The crudity of our mind could not indeed bear such a great
clarity, nor our smallness comprehend such a great wisdom.
And in fact all those who will attempt to rise to such a
height and will not repress the temerity of their spirit, shall
experience the truth of Solomon's saying (Prov. 25:27) that
he who will investigate the majesty shall be oppressed by the
glory. Only let us have this resolved in ourselves that the
dispensation of the Lord, although hidden from us, is nevertheless holy and just. For, if he willed to ruin all mankind,
he has the right to do it, and in those whom he rescues from
perdition one can contemplate nothing but his sovereign
goodness. We acknowledge, therefore, the elect to be recipients of his mercy (as truly they are) and the rejected to be
recipients of his wrath, a wrath, however, which is nothing
but just.

Let us take from the lot of both the elect and the others,
reasons for extolling his glory. On the other hand, let us not
seek (as many do), in order to confirm the certainty of our
salvation, to penetrate the very interior of heaven and to
investigate what God from his eternity has decided to do with
us. That can only worry us with a miserable distress and
perturbation. Let us be content, then, with the testimony by
which he has sufficiently and amply confirmed to us this certainty. For, as in Christ are elected all those who have been
preordained to life before the foundations of the world were
laid, so also he is he in whom the pledge of our election is
presented to us if we receive him and embrace him through
faith. For what do we seek in election except that we be
participants in the life eternal? And we have it in Christ,

who was the life since the beginning and who is offered as life to us in order that all those who believe in him may not perish but enjoy the life eternal. If, therefore, in possessing Christ through faith we possess in him likewise life, we need not further inquire beyond the eternal counsel of God. For Christ is not only a mirror by which the will of God is presented to us, but he is a pledge by which life is as sealed and confirmed to us.

WHAT TRUE FAITH IS

One must not imagine that the Christian faith is a bare and mere knowledge of God or an understanding of the Scripture which flutters in the brain without touching the heart, as is usually the case with the opinion about things which are confirmed by some probable reason. But faith is a firm and solid confidence of the heart, by means of which we rest surely in the mercy of God which is promised to us through the Gospel. For thus the definition of faith must be taken from the substance of the promise. Faith rests so much on this foundation that, if the latter be taken away, faith would collapse at once, or, rather, vanish away. Hence, when the Lord presents to us his mercy through the promise of the Gospel, if we certainly and without hesitation trust him who made the promise, we are said to apprehend his word through faith. And this definition is not different from that of the apostle (Heb. 11:1) in which he teaches that faith is the certainty of the things to be hoped for and the demonstration of the things not apparent; for he means a sure and secure possession of the things that God promises, and an evidence of the things that are not apparent, that is to say, the life eternal. And this we conceive through confidence in the divine goodness which is offered to us through the Gospel. Now, since all the promises of God are gathered together and confirmed in Christ, and are, so to speak, kept and accomplished in him, it appears without doubt that Christ is the perpetual object of faith. And in that object, faith contemplates all the riches of the divine mercy.

FAITH IS A GIFT OF GOD

If we honestly consider within ourselves how much our thought is blind to the heavenly secrets of God and how greatly our heart distrusts all things, we shall not doubt that faith greatly surpasses all the power of our nature and that faith is a unique and precious gift of God. For, as St. Paul maintains (I Cor. 2:11), if no one can witness the human will, except the spirit of man which is in man, how will man be certain of the divine will? And if the truth of God in us wavers even in things that we see by the eye, how will it be firm and stable where the Lord promises the things that the eye does not see and man's understanding does not comprehend?

Hence there is no doubt that faith is a light of the Holy Spirit through which our understandings are enlightened and our hearts are confirmed in a sure persuasion which is assured that the truth of God is so certain that he can but accomplish that which he has promised through his holy word that he will do. Hence (II Cor. 1:22; Eph. 1:13), the Holy Spirit is called like a guarantee which confirms in our hearts the certainty of the divine truth, and a seal by which our hearts are sealed in the expectation of the day of the Lord. For it is the Spirit indeed who witnesses to our spirit that God is our Father and that similarly we are his children (Rom. 8:16).

WE ARE JUSTIFIED IN CHRIST
THROUGH FAITH

Since it is clear that Christ is the perpetual object of faith, we cannot know what we receive through faith except by looking to him. For truly he has been given to us by the Father in order that we may obtain in him life eternal; as he says (John 17:3), life eternal is to know one God the Father and Jesus Christ whom he has sent. And again (John 11:26), he who comes to believe in me shall never die, and if he has died he shall live. Yet, in order that this might be done, it is necessary that we, who are contaminated by stains of sin, be cleansed in him, because nothing defiled shall enter the kingdom of God. Christ, therefore, makes us thus participants in himself in order that we, who are in ourselves sinners, may be, through Christ's righteousness, considered just before the throne of God. And in this manner being stripped of our own righteousness, we are clothed with the righteousness of Christ; and, being unjust by our own deeds, we are justified through the faith of Christ.

For we are said to be justified through faith, not in the sense, however, that we receive within us any righteousness, but because the righteousness of Christ is credited to us, entirely as if it were really ours, while our iniquity is not charged to us, so that one can truly call this righteousness simply the remission of sins. This the apostle evidently declares when he so often compares the righteousness that some imagine they obtain by means of good deeds with the righteousness that comes to us through faith, and teaches that the latter righteousness destroys the former (Rom. 10:3; Phil. 3:9). Now, we shall see in the Symbol in what manner Christ has deserved this righteousness for us and in what this righteousness consists, in which Symbol will indeed be recited in order all the thing on which our faith is founded and resting.

WE ARE SANCTIFIED THROUGH FAITH
IN ORDER TO OBEY THE LAW

Just as Christ by means of his righteousness intercedes for us with the Father in order that (he being as our guarantor) we may be considered as righteous, so by making us participants in his spirit, he sanctifies us unto all purity and innocence. For the spirit of the Lord has reposed on Christ without measure—the spirit (I say) of wisdom, of intelligence, of counsel, of strength, of knowledge and reverential fear of the Lord—in order that we all may draw from his fullness and receive grace through the grace that has been given to Christ. As a result, those who boast of having the faith of Christ and are completely destitute of sanctification by his spirit deceive themselves. For the Scripture teaches that Christ has been made for us not only righteousness but also sanctification. Hence, we cannot receive through faith his righteousness without embracing at the same time that sanctification, because the Lord in one same alliance, which he has made with us in Christ, promises that he will be propitious toward our iniquities and will write his Law in our hearts (Jer. 31:33; Heb. 8:10; 10:16).

Observance of the Law, therefore, is not a work that our power can accomplish, but it is a work of a spiritual power. Through this spiritual power it is brought about that our hearts are cleansed from their corruption and are softened to obey unto righteousness. Now the function of the Law is for Christians quite different from what it may be without faith; for, when and where the Lord has engraved in our hearts the love for his righteousness, the external teaching of the Law (which before was only charging us with weakness and transgression) is now a lamp to guide our feet, to the end that we may not deviate from the right path. It is now our wisdom through which we are formed, instructed, and encouraged to all integrity; it is our discipline which does not suffer us to be dissolute through evil licentiousness.

REPENTANCE AND REGENERATION

It is now easy from this to understand why repentance is always joined with the faith of Christ, and why the Lord affirms (John 3:3) that no one can enter the kingdom of heaven except he who has been regenerated. For repentance means conversion, turning over to, whereby, having left the perversity of this world, we return to and in the way of the Lord. Now, as Christ is no minister of sin, so, after having purged us from the stains of sin, he does not clothe us with the participation of his righteousness in order that we may afterward profane with new stains so grand a grace, but in order that, being adopted as children of God, we may consecrate our life course and days to come to the glory of our Father.

The effect of this repentance depends upon our regeneration, which has two aspects, that is to say: the mortification of our flesh, that is, a killing of our inborn corruption; and the spiritual vivification through which man's nature is restored to integrity. We must, therefore, meditate during all our life on the fact that, being dead unto sin and unto our former selves, we may live unto Christ and his righteousness. And since this regeneration is never accomplished as long as we are in the prison of this mortal body, it is necessary that the cure of repentance continues until we die. . . . .

PRAYER

The man rightly instructed in true faith first of all obviously perceives how indigent and denuded of all goods he is and how much he lacks all help of salvation. Hence, if he seeks some succor to assist him in his poverty, he must go out of himself to seek that succor elsewhere. On the other hand, he contemplates the Lord who liberally and out of his good will offers himself in Jesus Christ and in him opens all the heavenly treasures to the end that the whole faith of that man may stop to look at this beloved Son, all his expectation may depend on him, and all his hopes may rest and be fixed in him. Nothing therefore remains but that the man seek unto God and ask him in prayer what he has known to exist in God. Otherwise, to know that God is the Lord and distributor of all goods (who invites us to ask of him what we need), to pray to him and to invoke him profit nothing. This would be as if someone, knowing of a treasure hidden in the ground of

the earth, abandoned it there through indifference, being unwilling to take the trouble to unearth it.

Prayer is similar to a communication between God and us
whereby we expound to him our desires, our joys, our sighs,
in a word, all the thoughts of our hearts. Hence, each and
every time we invoke the Lord, we must diligently strive to
descend in the depth of our heart and from there seek him,
and not with the throat or the tongue only. For at times the
tongue helps in prayer, either in retaining the spirit more
attentive in the meditation of God or in occupying this part
of our body (which is especially destined to extol the
glory of God) along with the heart to meditate the goodness
of God. Yet, the Lord declares through his prophet (Isa.
29:13; Matt. 15:8,9) what prayer avails without the will,
when he has pronounced a very heavy punishment on all
those who honor him with their lips, while having their
hearts far from him. Moreover, if true prayer must be nothing else than a pure affection of our heart when we should
thereby approach God, we must dismiss all thought of our
own glory, all fancy of our own dignity and all self-
confidence. Thus indeed the prophet (Dan. 9:4-19; Baruch
2:11 ff.) admonishes us to pray, being founded not on our
own righteous deeds, but through the great mercies of the
Lord, in order that he may answer our prayers out of love
for himself, inasmuch as his name is invoked upon us. This
knowledge of our misery must not bar our access to God,
since prayer has not been instituted in order to raise us arro-
gantly before God, nor to extol our dignity, but to the end
that we confess with sighs our calamities, just as children
expound with familiarity their complaints to their fathers.
Such a sentiment should rather be like a spur to incite and
stimulate us to pray more. Now, there are two things that
must marvelously move us to pray. First, the instruction of

God by which he commands us to pray. Secondly, the promise whereby he assures us that we shall obtain all that which we will ask. For, those who invoke him, seek him, and depend on him, receive a singular consolation inasmuch as they know that, in doing that, they do a thing pleasing to him. Moreover, being assured of his truth, let them certainly trust that he will answer their prayer. "Ask" (he says: Matt. 7:7) "and it shall be given to you, knock and it will be opened to you; seek and you shall find." And in the psalm (Ps. 50:15): "Call upon me in the day of thy necessity, and I will free thee, and thou wilt glorify me." Here he has comprised or included the two kinds of prayer, which are invocation or request, and thanksgiving. By the former we disclose before God our hearts' desires. By the latter we acknowledge his benefits toward us. We must assiduously use both kinds of prayer, for we are pressed by such poverty and indigence that even the most perfect have sufficient matter to sigh and groan continually, and invoke the Lord with all humility. On the other hand, the liberalities which our Lord by his goodness pours forth upon us are so abundant, and wherever we turn our eyes the miracles of his works appear so great, that we can never lack matter for praise and thanksgiving.

PERSEVERANCE IN PRAYER

Finally we must well observe this: We must not wish to bind God to certain circumstances, because in this very prayer we are taught not to put on him any law, nor to impose upon him any condition. For, before making any prayer for ourselves, before all things, we ask that his will be done; whereby we submit beforehand our will to his, in order that, as if it were caught and retained by a rein, our will may not presume to wish to range and to submit him under our will. If, having the heart formed in this obedience, we permit ourselves to be governed according to the good pleasure of the divine providence, we shall easily learn to persevere in prayer and wait with patience upon the Lord, while deferring the fulfillment of our desires to the hour set by his will; being assured that, although he does not show himself to us, yet he is always present to us and at his own time will reveal that he did not at all have his ears deaf to our prayers, though they seemed to men to be despised by him. And even if at the end, after long waiting, our mind cannot understand the profit of our praying, and our senses feel no fruit thereof, nevertheless our faith will certify unto us what our mind and sense will not be able to perceive, that is, we shall have obtained [from God] all that which was good for us, for he will make us in poverty to possess abundance and in affliction to have consolation. For, even if all things should fail us, yet God will never leave us, inasmuch as he cannot disappoint the expectation and patience of his own. And he alone will be sufficient unto us for all things, inasmuch as he contains in himself all goods, which in the time to come he will fully reveal to us.

WHAT THE SACRAMENT IS

The sacrament therefore is an external sign through which the Lord presents and testifies to us his good will toward us in order to sustain us in the weakness of our faith. Or (to speak more briefly and more clearly) the sacrament is a testimony of the grace of God declared by an external sign. The Christian Church uses only two sacraments, which are Baptism and the Lord's Supper.

BAPTISM

Baptism has been given to us by God, to help, first, our faith in him, and, secondly, our profession of faith before men. Faith looks at the promise through which the merciful Father offers us the communication of his Christ, in order that, being clothed with him, we may be participants in all his goods. Yet baptism represents particularly two things: The first is the purgation which we obtain in the blood of Christ; the second is the mortification of our flesh, which we have had through his death. For the Lord has commanded his own to be baptized in the remission of sins (Matt. 28:19; Acts 2:38). And St. Paul (Eph. 5:26,27) teaches the Church to be sanctified through her bridegroom, and cleansed through the washing of water unto the word of life. And again (Rom. 6:3-11) St. Paul shows how we are baptized in the death of Christ; that is, we are buried in his death in order that we may walk in newness of life. By these things it is not signified, however, that the water is cause, not even instrument, of purgation and regeneration, but only that the knowledge of such gifts is received in this sacrament, since we are said to receive, to obtain, and to be appointed to that which we believe to be given by the Lord, be it that then for the first time we know him, or be it that, having known him before, we are more certainly persuaded of it.

Baptism serves likewise as our acknowledgment of faith in the sight of men; because it is a mark by which we publicly declare that we wish to be numbered among the people of God, to the end that we, together with all believers, may serve and honor, with one same religion, one God. Since, therefore, principally through baptism the alliance of the Lord is confirmed with us, we rightly baptize our children, since they are already participants in the eternal covenant through which the Lord promises (Gen. 17:1-14) that he will be God not only of us, but also of our posterity.

THE SUPPER OF THE LORD

The promise that is added to the mystery of the supper declares clearly to what purpose the supper has been instituted, and whither it tends. That is to say, it confirms to us that the body of the Lord has once for all been given in such a way for us, that it is now ours and will be ours perpetually. It confirms that his blood has once been shed in such a way for us that it [is and] will be always ours. The signs are the bread and the wine, under which the Lord presents to us the true yet spiritual communication of his body and his blood. This communication is content with the bond of his spirit, and does not require at all a presence of the flesh enclosed under the bread, or of the blood under the wine. For, although Christ, being elevated to heaven, has left his abode on earth in which we are still pilgrims, yet no distance can dissolve his power of nourishing his own with himself. He gives us in the supper an instruction concerning this matter so certain and manifest that without any doubt we must be assured that Christ with all his riches is there presented to us, not less than if he could be put in the presence of our eyes and be touched by our hands; and even he is present with so great a power and efficacy that he not only brings there to our spirits assured confidence of eternal life, but also renders us certain of the immortality of our flesh. For our flesh is already vivified by Christ's immortal flesh, and communicates in some way with his immortality.

Hence, under the bread and wine, the body and blood are presented, to the end that we may learn not only that they are ours, but that they are for us life and nourishment. So, when we see the bread set apart as the body of Christ, at once we must think of this simile: Just as the bread nourishes, sustains, and preserves the life of our body, so the body of Christ is the food and preservation of our spiritual life. And when the wine is presented to us as a sign of the blood, we must likewise think that such fruits as he brings to the body we receive spiritually from the blood of Christ.

Now, as this mystery is a teaching of God's liberality which is so great toward us, it must also admonish us not to be ungrateful toward such a generous kindliness, but rather to extol it with fitting praises and to celebrate it with thanksgiving. Moreover, it exhorts us to embrace each other mutually by such a unity as that which binds among themselves and conjoins together the members of one same body. For no harsher or more pricking spur could be given to move and to incite among us a mutual charity than when Christ, giving himself to us, invites us not only by his example to

give ourselves and to expose ourselves mutually one for the
other, but inasmuch as he makes himself common to all, he
makes us also all one in himself.

THE PASTORS OF THE CHURCH
AND THEIR POWER

Since the Lord has willed that both his word and his sacraments be dispensed through the ministry of men, it is necessary that there be pastors ordained to the churches, pastors
who teach the people both in public and in private the pure
doctrine, administer the sacraments, and by their good example instruct and form all to holiness and purity of life.
Those who despise this discipline and this order do injury
not only to men, but to God, and even, as heretics, withdraw
from the society of the church, which in no way can stand
together without such a ministry. For what the Lord has once
(Matt. 10:40) testified is of no little importance: It is that
when the pastors whom he sends are welcomed, he himself
is welcomed, and likewise he is rejected when they are rejected. And in order that their ministry be not contemptible,
pastors are furnished with a notable mandate: to bind and
to loose, having the added promise that whatever things they
shall have bound or loosed on earth, are bound or loosed in
heaven (Matt. 16:19). And Christ himself in another passage
(John 20:23) explains that to bind means to retain sins,
and to loose means to remit them. Now, the apostle declares
what is the mode of loosing when (Rom. 1:16) he teaches
the Gospel to be the power of God unto salvation for each
believer. And he tells also the way of binding when he declares (II Cor. 10:4-6) the apostles to have retribution ready
against any disobedience. For, the sum of the Gospel is that
we are slaves of sin and death, and that we are loosed and
freed by the redemption which is in Christ Jesus, while those
who do not receive him as redeemer are bound as by new
bonds of a graver condemnation.

But let us remember that this power (which in the Scripture is attributed to pastors) is wholly contained in and limited to the ministry of the word. For Christ has not given this power properly to these men but to his word, of which he has made these men ministers. Hence, let pastors boldly dare all things by the word of God, of which they have been constituted dispensators; let them constrain all the power, glory, and haughtiness of the world to make room for and to obey the majesty of that word; let them by means of that word command all from the greatest to the smallest; let them edify the house of Christ; let them demolish the reign of Satan; let them feed the sheep, kill the wolves, instruct and exhort the docile; let them rebuke, reprove, reproach, and convince the rebel—but all through and within the word of God. But if pastors turn away from the word to their dreams and to the inventions of their own minds, already they are no longer to be received as pastors, but being seen to be rather pernicious wolves, they are to be chased away. For Christ has commanded us to listen only to those who teach us that which they have taken from his word.

HUMAN TRADITIONS

As we have thus a general thought of St. Paul (that is, that all things in the churches must be done decently and in order) we must not count as human traditions the civic observances by which (as by some bonds of unity) order and honesty stand, and peace and concord are retained in the assemblies of Christians. But rather these observances must be referred to that rule of the apostle, provided that they be not thought necessary for salvation, nor binding consciences through religion, nor related to the service of God, and no piety whatever be put in them. But it is necessary greatly and manfully to resist those rules which, as if they were necessary to serve and to honor God, are made under the name of spiritual laws for binding the consciences, for they not only destroy the liberty which Christ has secured for us, but they obscure also the true religion and they violate the majesty of God, who wishes to reign alone in our consciences through and by means of his word. May this then remain firm and definite: All things are ours provided we belong to Christ (I Cor. 3:21-23); and God is served in vain where are taught doctrines which are merely commandments of men (Matt. 15:1-20).

EXCOMMUNICATION

Excommunication is the act whereby those who are manifestly fornicators, adulterers, thieves, homicides, misers, robbers, iniquitous, pernicious, voracious, drunkards, seditious, and prodigal (if they do not amend themselves after having been admonished) are, according to God's commandment, rejected from the company of believers. The church does not thereby cast them into perpetual ruin and despair. She simply condemns their ways of life and their manners, and, if they do not correct themselves, she makes them already certain of their condemnation. Now, this discipline is necessary among believers because, as the church is the body of Christ, she must not be polluted and contaminated by such stinking and rotten members who dishonor the head; moreover, in order that the saints be not (as it is usual to happen) corrupted and spoiled by the company of the bad. This discipline is profitable also to the latter themselves that their malice be thereby thus chastised; while tolerance would render them more obstinate, this disciplinary provision confuses them with shame and teaches them to amend themselves. When this result is obtained, the church with kindliness will receive them again in her communion and in the participation of that union from which they had been excluded. Now, in order that no one despise obstinately the judgment of the church, or think it to be of little account to have been condemned by the sentence of believers, the Lord testifies that such judgment of the faithful is nothing else than the pronouncement of his sentence, and that what they shall have done on earth is ratified in heaven (Matt. 18:

15-18). For they have the word of God, by which they can condemn the perverse, and they have the word by which they can receive in grace those who amend themselves.

THE MAGISTRATE OR CIVIC OFFICER

The Lord has not only testified that the status of magistrate or civic officer was approved by him and was pleasing to him, but also he has moreover greatly recommended it to us, having honored its dignity with very honorable titles. For the Lord affirms (Prov. 8:15-16) that the fact that kings rule, that counselors order just things, and that the great of the earth are judges, is a work of his wisdom. And elsewhere (Ps. 82:6-7), he calls them gods, because they do his work. In another place also (Deut. 1:17; II Chron. 19:5-7) they are said to exercise judgment for God, and not for man. And Saint Paul (Rom. 12:8) calls the higher offices gifts of God. But (Rom. 13:1-7) where he undertakes a greater discussion of the matter, he teaches very clearly that their power is ordered by God, and that they are ministers of God for praising those who do good and for accomplishing the retribution of God's wrath on the bad. Hence princes and magistrates must think of Him whom they serve in their office, and do nothing unworthy of ministers and lieutenants of God. All their solicitude must be in this: to keep in true purity the public form of religion, to establish and to guide the life of the people by very good laws, and to procure the welfare and the tranquillity of their subjects, both in public and in private. But this cannot be obtained except through justice and judgment, which two things are to them particularly recommended by the prophet (Jer. 22:1-9). Justice is to safeguard the innocent, to maintain, to keep and to free them; judgment is to resist the audacity of evil men, to repress violence, and to punish misdeeds.

On the other hand, the mutual duty of subjects and citizens is not only to honor and to revere their superiors, but to recommend by prayers to the Lord their salvation and prosperity, to submit willingly to their rule, to obey their laws and constitutions, and not to refuse the charges imposed by them: be they taxes, tolls, tributes, and other contributions, or be they offices, civic commissions, and all the like. So that we must not only render ourselves obedient to superiors who rightly and dutifully administer their higher office, but also it is fit to endure those who tyrannically abuse their power, until, through legitimate order, we be freed from their yoke. For, just as a good prince is a testimony of the divine beneficence for maintaining the salvation of men, so a bad and evil prince is a plague of God for chastising the sins of the people. Yet, let this generally be held as certain that to both the power is given by God, and we cannot resist them without our resisting the ordinance of God.

But from obedience to superiors we must always except one thing: that it does not draw us away from obedience to Him to whose edicts the commands of all kings must yield. The Lord, therefore, is the king of kings, and, once he has opened his sacred mouth, he must be listened to by all and above all. Only after that, we are subject to men who are constituted over us, but not otherwise than in him. If men command us to do something against him, we must do nothing, nor keep any account of such an order. On the contrary, let rather this sentence take place: that it is necessary to obey God rather than men (Acts 4:19).

Instruction in Faith (1537), by John Calvin,
Translated and Edited by Paul T. Fuhrmann.
Philadelphia: The Westminster Press, 1949.

JOHN KNOX

c. 1514 – 1572

JOHN KNOX

WHEN JOHN KNOX WAS BORN, ABOUT 1514, THE REFORMATION in Germany and Switzerland was a rising tide, but in Scotland its premonitions were mostly evident in martyrdoms. Knox probably began his student life at St. Andrews fairly soon after the execution of Patrick Hamilton—kinsman of a noble Scotch family and a disciple of Luther, who had studied in Europe—and Knox's words sound like a personal recollection: "When those cruel wolves had devoured their prey, there was none within St. Andrews who began not to enquire wherefore was Patrick Hamilton burnt?" Nevertheless it was in 1545, seventeen years after Hamilton's death, before evidence appears of Knox's public alliance with the Reformers.

Meanwhile he had entered the Roman Catholic priesthood and, like many Scotch priests at that time, had become a notary and a tutor. The martyrdom of George Wishart apparently was the catalyst which precipitated his decision to join the "new religion." Wishart—suspected of heresy because he read the Greek New Testament with his students!—had fled the country and, after six years in Germany, Switzerland, and England, had returned to Scotland determined to preach the reformed faith. He was, said Knox, "a man of such graces as before were never heard within this realm, yea, and are rare to be found yet in any man." Knox became his friend and disciple; when danger loomed attended him with a "two-handed sword" for his defense; was with him the last night before his arrest, leaving him only when dismissed by Wishart with the words, "One is sufficient for one sacrifice." The fire that burned Wishart at the stake lit a blaze in Knox which, in the end, destroyed the ascendancy of Roman Catholicism in Scotland.

What Wishart stood for is made evident in the testimony which he gave at his trial: the Holy Scriptures, rather than fallible ecclesiastical councils or the pope, the test of truth; salvation by personal faith, not by sacramental observances; all true believers priests, as against any exclusive ecclesiastical priesthood; the denial of purgatory, priestly celibacy, compulsory confession to a priest, the worship of saints and the power of exorcism and holy water; and, at the heart of all, the rejection of the Roman Catholic Mass as idolatrous. With some such equipment of ideas John Knox became a reformer.

Knox was a stern man in a stern age and in a rough and violent country. Says Dr. Thomas McCrie: "The corruptions by which the Christian religion was universally disfigured, before the Reformation, had grown to a greater height in Scotland than in any other nation within the pale of the Western Church. Supersitition and religious imposture, in their grossest forms, gained an easy admission among a rude and ignorant people." From the first, Knox's road was rough, and it took a rough man to travel it. When Cardinal Beaton, who had caused Wishart's martyrdom, was assassinated at St. Andrews—Knox condoned the assassination as a "Godly fact"—Knox, with his pupils, joined the company there of refugees from the gathering peril. There he was called for the first time to preach; and after the sermon the hearers said: "Others snipped the branches of the Papistry; but he strikes at the root, to destroy the whole."

In this experience at St. Andrews Knox discovered himself as a preacher, but within a year the castle fell to the French and Knox, along with other prisoners, was condemned to the galleys, in the "torment" of which he spent eighteen months. From then on Knox's life was toil and tumult. He was primarily a man of action; his personal contribution to the thinking of the Reformation is not significant; he welcomed and assimilated the ideas of others, especially Calvin, and interpreted them to his people; but more than any other of the Reformers he was plunged into the rough and tumble of politics, so that his major meaning lies in what he did, rather than in what he wrote. "I consider myself," he said, "rather called of my God to instruct the ignorant, comfort the sorrowful, confirm the weak, and rebuke the proud, by tongue and lively voice in these most corrupt days, than to compose books for the ages to come." Perhaps one reason for this choice lay in the fact that printing had first come to Scotland only seven years before Knox was born, and the "lively voice" was the most effective instrument in a largely illiterate population.

Released from the galleys he went to England, at that time under the reforming sovereignty of Edward VI, where he held pastorates at Berwick and Newcastle; he fled the country when Mary Tudor's bloody reign began; he served congregations of refugees in Frankfort and Geneva; he returned to Scotland for nine months, when Mary of Guise was Regent, to strengthen the growing Protestant cause; he went back to his flock in Geneva at their importunate call; and in 1559 made his final return to Scotland. There in 1560 the Queen Regent died, and the Protestants drew up the "Scots Confession" which the government pledged itself to maintain. Then Mary, Queen of Scots, came from France to Edinburgh, and the long tussle began to decide whether the Reform could hold its ground or Roman Catholicism would reassert its power.

It is a story of complex politics, of intrigue and deceit, of shifting loyalties among the noble families, of bitter rancor and hatred, vituperation and abuse, of murders, assassinations and civil war. No wonder that Knox, who was at the center of it all, is a controversial figure! Read *The Life of John Knox*, by Thomas McCrie, or *John Knox*, by Henry Cowan, and one sees the impressive strength and courage of his character; read *John Knox and the Reformation*, by Andrew Lang, or *John Knox, Portrait of a Calvinist*, by Edwin Muir, and one sees his harsh vehemence and intolerance; and now in the middle of the twentieth century Hugh Watt in *John Knox in Controversy* still endeavors to solve the problem. Nevertheless, even Lang says: "That Knox was a great man; a disinterested man; in his regard for the poor a truly Christian man; as a shepherd of Calvinistic souls a man fervent and considerate; of pure life; in friendship loyal; by jealousy untainted; in private character genial and amiable, I am entirely convinced."

One may not expect, however, to find in Knox any of those liberal ideas concerning the tolerant uses of government which now obtain in civilized lands. In his day they did not obtain anywhere. Two lively questions concerned all the Reformers: whether it was right to rebel violently against a duly constituted government and king, and whether it was right to persecute to the death heretics who denied the established religion of the realm. As to the first, Luther and Zwingli, having appealed from the church to the government and having devolved upon the government responsibility for correcting religious abuses, were strongly impressed with the sanctity of the civil order. Even Calvin once said, although it is not by any means his major emphasis: "One cannot resist magistrates without resisting God." Knox, however, facing a régime which cruelly persecuted the reformed faith, came to an opposite conclusion. If there was a "divine right of kings," Knox was sure that there was also a "divine right of presbyteries" and, when they were in contradiction, the latter had the divine right of decisive action. "Let it be here noted," he said of one Old Testament passage, "that the prophet of God sometimes may teach treason against kings, and yet neither he, nor such as obeys the word spoken in the Lord's name by him, offends God." When, therefore, the case seemed clear to him that the ruling régime was supporting idolatry—and to Knox the Roman Catholic Mass was idolatry—he counseled and supported any means, violent or otherwise, that would overthrow it. "The people," he said, "yes, or a part of the people, may execute God's judgments against their king, being an offender."

As to persecution for heresy, Knox shared the prevailing concepts of his time. To be sure, Luther, Zwingli and Melanchthon shrank from the death penalty for false doctrine. "I have little love for death sentences," wrote Luther in his early days, "even though well deserved; what alarms me in this matter is the example that is set. I can, therefore, by no means approve that false teachers shall be put to death. . . . Heretics must not be suppressed or held down by physical force, but only combated by the word of God. For heresy is a spiritual affair, which cannot be cleaned away by earthly fire or earthly water."

The Roman Catholic Inquisition was too brutally real and what Knox called "the bloody, butcherly brood" of persecutors was too horrible for the early Reformers to desire a Protestant imitation. Knox, however, like Calvin, was a man of his time, and the thesis, which had started innocently enough, that the government should support true religion, went through to its logical conclusion, that the government should destroy false religion and liquidate its adherents. Knox based this policy upon the most ruthless passages in the Old Testament, such as Deuteronomy 13: 6-11, arguing from them that even those who invite others to idolatry, that is, the Mass, must be put to death, that idolators must suffer regardless of their rank, and that the duty of inflicting the death penalty belongs not to "kings and chief rulers only, but also to the whole body of that people, and to every member of the same, according to that possiblity and occasion which God doth minister to avenge the injury done against His glory."

On this matter, Knox was adamant and his ideal was clear. "All dregs of Popery" were to be thrown out of the land; no "power or liberty be permitted to any, of what estate, degree or authority they be, either to live without the yoke of discipline by God's word commanded" or "to alter one jot in religion which from God's mouth thou hast received."

Any mitigation of our modern judgment on this fierce intolerance of Knox must rest on consideration of the barbarous situation by which he was confronted. In every Roman Catholic kingdom Protestants were being tortured, beheaded and burned, and, as for Scotland, even when the lords were disposed to conciliate Queen Mary, they exclaimed in her presence, "God forbid that the lives of the faithful stood in the power of the papists! For just experience has taught us what cruelty is in their hearts." One of the last sermons Knox preached followed news of the Massacre of St. Bartholomew. Some seventy thousand Protestants had been murdered in France in one week, and a solemn service of thanksgiving in honor of the great event was celebrated in Rome by order of the pope. So far as religious persecution was concerned, it was a barbarous age.

As to the basic idea of tolerance versus intolerance in religion one should recall that as late as 1832 Pope Gregory XVI, in his encyclical, *Marari Vos*, wrote:

. . . . that absurd and erroneous opinion, or better, that product of delirium, that it is necessary to extend and guarantee liberty of conscience to everyone. The path to this most pestilent error is being prepared by the full and unlimited freedom of opinions which is being widely diffused, to the misfortune of religion and civil society, while some keep saying with extreme impudence that religion will derive some advantage from it. . . . Experience has proved from earliest times that states distinguished for wealth, for power, for glory, have perished from this single evil, unrestrained freedom of thought, freedom of speech, and the love of novelties. To this is related that deadly freedom, never adequately to be execrated and detested, the liberty of the press.

As for Knox himself, his sternness, harshness, vehemence and intolerance were only one side of him. "Beloved brethren," he wrote, "two things we must avoid. The former that ye presume not to be revengers of your own cause, but that ye resign over vengeance unto Him who only is able to requite them, according to their malicious minds. Secondly, that ye hate not, with any carnal hatred, these blind, cruel and malicious tyrants; but that ye learn of Christ to pray for your persecutors, lamenting and bewailing that the devil should so prevail against them, that headlong they should run body and soul to perpetual perdition." These two sides of Knox— austerity and gentleness, harshness and grace, vehemence and conciliation—were never integrated. Especially in his thought of the proper relation of church and state he was a child of his time, and Roger Williams was yet to come.

His personality must have been compelling, magnetic; he bound friends to him in undying loyalty; when things were at their worst, his words caused "the minds of men . . . to be wonderfully erected"; and his courage was magnificent.

In the end Queen Mary defeated herself, so alienating her subjects that many who would naturally have supported her turned against her, and finally she fled to England, where Elizabeth imprisoned and at last executed her. Knox, meanwhile, stood his ground, sometimes in such despair that once he cried, "Lord Jesus, receive my spirit, and put an end, at thy good pleasure, to this my miserable life: for justice and truth are not to be found amongst the sons of men." Nevertheless he lived to see Protestantism established in his native land.

Here is a contemporary account of John Knox in his elder years by James Melville, then a student at St. Andrews:

But of all the benefits I had that year the greatest was the coming of that most notable prophet and apostle of our nation, Mr. John Knox. . . . I heard him teach there the prophecy of Daniel that summer and the winter following. I had my pen and my little book, and took away such things as I could comprehend. In the opening up of his text he was moderate the space of an half-hour; but when he enterred to application, he made me so to grew (shudder) and tremble, that I could not hold a pen to write. . . . Mr. Knox would sometimes come in and repose him in our College yard, and call us scholars unto him and bless us, and exhort us to know God and his work in our country, and stand by the good cause, to use our time well, and learn the good instructions and follow the good example of our masters. . . . I saw him every day of his doctrine go hulie and fear (carefully and slowly), with a furring of martriks (a fur of martin-skin) about his neck, a staff in one hand, and good Godly Richard Bannatyne, his servant, holding up the other oxter (armpit), from the Abbey to the parish kirk; and, by the said Richard and another servant, lifted up to the pulpit, where he behoved to lean at his first entry; but, ere he had done with his sermon, he was so active and vigorous that he was like to ding that pulpit in blads (break it in pieces) and fly out of it.

HISTORY OF THE
REFORMATION IN SCOTLAND

THE EARLY BEGINNINGS

IN THE SCROLLS OF GLASGOW IS FOUND MENTION OF ONE whose name is not expressed that, in the year of God 1422, was burnt for heresy; but what were his opinions, or by what order he was condemned, it appears not evidently. But our Chronicles make mention that, in the days of King James the First, about the year of God 1431, was apprehended in the University of Saint Andrews one named Paul Craw, a Bohemian, who was accused of heresy before such as then were called Doctors of Theology. His accusation consisted principally that he followed John Hus and Wycliffe in the opinion of the sacrament, who denied that the substance of bread and wine was changed by virtue of any words; or that confession should be made to priests; or yet prayers to saints departed. While that God gave unto him grace to resist them, and not to consent to their impiety, he was committed to the secular judge (for our bishops follow Pilate, who both did condemn and also wash his hands), who condemned him to the fire; in the which he was consumed in the said city of Saint Andrews about the time afore written. And to declare themselves to be the generation of Sathan who, from the beginning, hath been enemy to the truth, and he that desireth the same to be hid from the knowledge of men, they put a ball of brass in his mouth to the end that he should not give confession of his faith to the people, neither yet that they should understand the defence which he had against their unjust accusation and condemnation.

But their fathers' practice did not greatly advance their kingdom of darkness, neither yet was it able utterly to extinguish the truth. For albeit that in the days of King James the Second and Third we find small question of religion moved within this realm, yet in the time of King James the Fourth, in the sixth year of his reign, and in the twenty-second year of his age, which was in the year of God 1494, were summoned before the King and his Great Council, by Robert Blacader, called Archbishop of Glasgow, the number of thirty persons. These were called the Lollards of Kyle. They were accused of the Articles following, as we have received them forth of the Register of Glasgow:

1 First, That images are not to be had, nor yet to be worshipped.
2 That the relics of saints are not to be worshipped.
3 That laws and ordinances of men vary from time to time, and that by the pope.
4 That it is not lawful to fight, or to defend the faith. (We translate according to the barbarousness of their Latin and dictament.)
5 That Christ gave power to Peter only, and not to his successors, to bind and loose within the kirk.
6 That Christ ordained no priests to consecrate.
7 That after the consecration in the Mass, there remains bread; and that there is not the natural body of Christ.
8 That tithes ought not to be given to ecclesiastical men (as they were then called).
9 That Christ at his coming has taken away power from kings to judge. (This article we doubt not to be the venomous accusation of the enemies, whose practice has ever been to make the doctrine of Jesus Christ suspect to kings

and rulers, as that God thereby would depose them of their royal seats where, by the contrary, nothing confirms the power of magistrates more than does God's word—But to the Articles.)

10 That every faithful man or woman is a priest.

11 That the unction of kings ceased at the coming of Christ.

12 That the pope is not the successor of Peter, but where he said, "Go behind me, Sathan."

13 That the pope deceives the people by his Bulls and his Indulgences.

14 That the Mass profiteth not the souls that are in purgatory.

15 That the pope and the bishops deceive the people by their pardons.

16 That Indulgences ought not to be granted to fight against the Saracens.

17 That the pope exalts himself against God, and above God.

18 That the pope cannot remit the pains of purgatory.

19 That the blessings of the bishops (of dumb dogs they should have been styled) are of no value.

20 That the excommunication of the kirk is not to be feared.

21 That in no case is it lawful to swear.

22 That priests might have wives, according to the constitution of the law.

23 That true Christians receive the body of Jesus Christ every day.

24 That after matrimony be contracted, the kirk may make no divorcement.

25 That excommunication binds not.

26 That the pope forgives not sins, but only God.

27 That faith should not be given to miracles.

28 That we should not pray to the glorious Virgin Mary, but to God only.

29 That we are no more bound to pray in the kirk than in other places.

30 That we are not bound to believe all that the doctors of the kirk have written.

31 That such as worship the Sacrament of the kirk (we suppose they meant the Sacrament of the altar) commit idolatry.

32 That the pope is the head of the kirk of Antichrist.

33 That the pope and his ministers are murderers.

34 That they which are called principals in the Church, are thieves and robbers.

By these Articles, which God in his merciful providence caused the enemies of his truth to keep in their registers, may appear how mercifully God hath looked upon this realm, retaining within it some spunk of his light, even in the time of greatest darkness. Neither yet ought any man to wonder, albeit that some things be obscurely, and some scabrously spoken; but rather ought all faithful to magnify God's mercy who, without public doctrine, gave so great light.

THE FIRST PETITION TO THE QUEEN REGENT, MARY OF GUISE

While the Queen Regent practiced with the Prelates how that Jesus Christ his blessed Evangel might utterly be suppressed within Scotland, God so blessed the labours of his weak servants, that no small part of the Barons of this Realm began to abhor the tyranny of the Bishops: God did so open their eyes by the light of his word, that they could clearly discern betwixt idolatry and the true honouring of God. Yes, men almost universally began to doubt whether that they might (God not offended) give their bodily presence to the Mass, or yet offer their children to the papistical baptism. To the which doubts, when the most godly and the most learned in Europe had answered, both by word and writ, affirming, "That neither of both might we do, without the extreme peril of our souls," we began to be more troubled; for then also began men of estimation and that bare

rule among us, to examine themselves concerning their duties, as well towards Reformation of Religion, as towards the
just defence of their brethren most cruelly persecuted. And
so began divers questions to be moved, to wit, "If that with
safe conscience such as were judges, lords, and rulers of the
people, might serve the upper powers in maintaining idolatry, in persecuting their brethren, and in suppressing Christ's
truth?" Or, "Whether they, to whom God in some cases had
committed the sword of justice, might suffer the blood of
their brethren to be shed in their presence, without any
declaration that such tyranny displeased them?" By the plain
Scriptures it was found, "That a lively faith required a plain
confession, when Christ's truth is oppugned; that not only
are they guilty that do evil, but also they that assent to evil."
And plain it is, that they assent to evil who, seeing iniquity
openly committed, by their silence seem to justify and allow
whatsoever is done.

These things being resolved, and sufficiently proved by
evident Scriptures of God, we began every man to look more
diligently to his salvation: for the idolatry and tyranny of
the clergy (called the Churchmen) was and is so manifest,
that whosoever doth deny it, declares himself ignorant of
God, and enemy to Christ Jesus. We therefore, with humble
confession of our former offences, with fasting and supplication unto God, began to seek some remedy in so present a
danger. And first, it was concluded, "That the Brethren in
every town at certain times should assemble together, to Common Prayers, to exercise and reading of the Scriptures, till it
should please God to give the sermon of exhortation to some,
for comfort and instruction of the rest."

And this our weak beginning God did so bless, that within
few months the hearts of many were so strengthened, that we
sought to have the face of the church amongst us, and open
crimes to be punished without respect of person. And for
that purpose, by common election, were elders appointed, to
whom the whole brethren promised obedience. . . .

Yet because we would attempt nothing without the knowledge of the sacred authority, with one consent, after the deliberation of many days, it was concluded, that by our public and common Supplication, we should attempt the favours, support and assistance of the Queen, then Regent, to a godly Reformation. And for that purpose, after we had drawn our orisons and petitions, as followeth, we appointed from amongst us a man whose age and years deserved reverence, whose honesty and worship might have craved audience of any magistrate on earth, and whose faithful service to the authority at all times had been such, that in him could fall no suspicion of unlawful disobedience. This orator was that ancient and honourable father, Sir James Sandilands of Calder, knight, to whom we gave commission and power in all our names then present, before the Queen Regent thus to speak:

THE FIRST ORATION, AND PETITION, OF THE PROTESTANTS OF SCOTLAND TO THE QUEEN REGENT

Albeit we have of long time contained ourselves in that modesty (Most Noble Princess), that neither the exile of body, tynsall of goods, nor perishing of this mortal life, were able to convene us to ask at your Grace reformation and redress of those wrongs, and of that sore grief, patiently borne of us in bodies and minds of so long time; yet are we now, of very conscience and by the fear of our God, compelled to crave at your Grace's feet, remedy against the most unjust tyranny used against your Grace's most obedient subjects, by those that be called the Estate Ecclesiastical. Your Grace cannot be ignorant what controversy hath been, and yet is, concerning the true religion, and right worshipping of God, and how the Clergy (as they will be termed) usurp to themselves such empire above the consciences of men, that whatsoever they command must be obeyed, and whatsoever they forbid must be avoided, without further respect had to God's pleasure, commandment, or will, revealed to us in his most holy word;

or else there abideth nothing for us but faggot, fire, and sword; by the which many of our brethren, most cruelly and most unjustly, have been stricken of late years within this realm: which now we find to trouble and wound our consciences; for we acknowledge it to have been our bound duty before God, either to have defended our brethren from those cruel murderers (seeing we are part of that power which God hath established in this realm), or else to have given open testification of our faith with them, which now we offer ourselves to do, lest that by our continual silence we shall seem to justify their cruel tyranny; which doth not only displease us, but your Grace's wisdom most prudently doth foresee, that for the quieting of this intestine dissension, a public reformation, as well in the religion as in the temporal government, were most necessary; and to the performance thereof, most gravely and most godly (as we are informed), ye have exhorted as well the Clergy as the Nobility, to employ their study, diligence, and care. We therefore of conscience dare no longer dissemble in so weighty a matter, which concerneth the glory of God and our salvation: Neither now dare we withdraw our presence, nor conceal our petitions, lest that the adversaries hereafter shall object to us, that place was granted to Reformation, and yet no man suited for the same; and so shall our silence be prejudicial unto us in time to come. And therefore we, knowing no other order placed in this realm, but your Grace, in your grave Council, set to amend, as well the disorder ecclesiastical, as the defaults in the temporal regiment, most humbly prostrate ourselves before your feet, asking your justice, and your gracious help, against them that falsely traduce and accuse us, as that we were heretics and schismatics, under that colour seeking our destruction; for that we seek the amendment of their corrupted lives, and Christ's religion to be restored to the original purity. Further, we crave of your Grace, with open and patent ears, to hear these our subsequent requests; and to the joy and satisfaction of our trou-

bled consciences, mercifully to grant the same, unless by
God's plain word any be able to prove that justly they ought
to be denied.

THE FIRST PETITION

First, humbly we ask, that as we have, of the laws of this
realm, after long debate, obtained to read the holy books of
the Old and New Testaments in our common tongue, as spiritual food to our souls, so from henceforth it may be lawful
that we may convene, public or privately, to our Common
Prayers, in our vulgar tongue; to the end that we may increase and grow in knowledge, and be induced, in fervent
and oft prayer, to commend to God the holy church universal, the Queen of our Sovereign, her honourable and gracious husband, the ability of their succession, your Grace
Regent, the Nobility, and whole Estate of this Realm.

Secondly, if it should happen in our said conventions any
hard place of Scripture to be read, of the which no profit
ariseth to the conveners, that it shall be lawful to any qualified persons in knowledge, being present, to interpret and
open up the said hard places, to God's glory and to the profit
of the auditure. And if any think that this liberty should be
occasion of confusion, debate, or heresy; we are content that
it be provided, that the said interpretation shall underly the
judgment of the most godly and most learned within the
realm at this time.

Thirdly, That the holy sacrament of baptism may be used
in the vulgar tongue; that the godfathers and witnesses may
not only understand the points of the league and contract
made betwixt God and the infant, but also that the church
then assembled, more gravely may be informed and instructed of their duties, which at all times they owe to God,
according to that promise made unto Him when they were
ceived in his household by the lavachre of spiritual regeneration.

Fourthly, We desire, that the holy sacrament of the Lord's

Supper, or of his most blessed body and blood, may likewise be ministered unto us in the vulgar tongue; and in both kinds, according to the plain institution of our Saviour Christ Jesus.

And last, We most humbly require, that the wicked, slanderous, and detestable life of prelates, and of the State Ecclesiastical, may be so reformed, that the people by them have not occasion (as of many days they have had) to contemn their ministry, and the preaching whereof they should be messengers. And if they suspect that we, rather envying their honours, or coveting their riches and possessions, than zealously desiring their amendment and salvation, do travail and labour for this reformation; we are content not only that the rules and precepts of the New Testament, but also the writings of the ancient Fathers, and the godly approved laws of Justinian the Emperor, decide the controversy betwixt us and them: And if it shall be found, that either malevolently or ignorantly we ask more than these three forenamed have required, and continually do require of able and true ministers in Christ's Church, we refuse not correction, as your Grace, with right judgment, shall think meet. But and if all the forenamed shall damn that which we damn, and approve that which we require, then we most earnestly beseech your Grace, that notwithstanding the long consuetude which they have had to live as they list, that they be compelled either to desist from ecclesiastical administration, or to discharge their duties as becometh true ministers: So that the grave and godly face of the primitive church reduced [*i.e.* restored], ignorance may be expelled, true doctrine and good manners may once again appear in the church of this Realm. These things we, as most obedient subjects, require of your Grace, in the name of the Eternal God, and of his Son, Christ Jesus; in presence of whose throne judicial, ye and all others that here in earth bear authority, shall give accounts of your temporal regiment. The Spirit of the Lord Jesus move your Grace's heart to justice and equity. Amen.

These our Petitions being proposed, the Estate Ecclesiastical began to storm, and to devise all manner of lies to deface the equity of our cause. They bragged as that they would have public disputation, which also we most earnestly required, two things being provided: the former, that the plain and written Scriptures of God should decide all controversy; secondly, that our brethren, of whom some then were exiled, and by them unjustly damned, might have free access to the said disputation, and safe conduct to return to their dwelling places, notwithstanding any process which before had been led against them in matters concerning religion. But these being by them utterly denied (for no judge would they admit but themselves, their Councils, and Canon Law), they and their faction began to draw certain Articles of reconciliation, promising unto us, if we would admit the Mass to stand in her former reverence and estimation, grant Purgatory after this life, confess Prayer to Saints and for the dead, and suffer them to enjoy their accustomed rents, possession, and honour, that then they would grant unto us to pray and baptize in the vulgar tongue, so that it were done secretly, and not in the open assembly. But the grossness of these Articles was such, that with one voice we refused them; and constantly craved justice of the Queen Regent, and a reasonable answer of our former Petitions. . . .

John Knox's History of the Reformation in Scotland,
Edited by William Croft Dickinson, D.Lit. Vol. I.
New York: Philosophical Library, 1949.

KNOX MEETS MARY,
QUEEN OF SCOTS

THE NINETEENTH DAY OF AUGUST, THE YEAR OF GOD 1561, BE-twixt seven and eight hours before noon, arrived Marie, Queen of Scotland, then widow, with two galleys forth of France. In her company (besides her gentlewomen called the Maries), were her three uncles, the Duke d'Aumale, the Grand Prior, and the Marquis d'Elboeuf. There accompanied her also, Damville, son to the Constable of France, with other gentlemen of inferior condition, besides servants and officers. The very face of heaven, the time of her arrival, did manifestly speak what comfort was brought unto this country with her, to wit, sorrow, dolour, darkness, and all impiety. For, in the memory of man, that day of the year was never seen a more dolorous face of the heaven than was at her arrival, which two days after did continue so; for besides the surface wet, and corruption of the air, the mist was so thick and so dark that scarce might any man espy another the length of two pairs of boots. The sun was not seen to shine two days before, nor two days after. That fore-warning gave God unto us; but alas, the most part were blind. . . .

With great diligence the lords repaired unto her from all quarters. And so was nothing understood but mirth and quietness till the next Sunday, which was the XXIV of August, when preparation began to be made for that idol the

Mass to be said in the Chapel; which pierced the hearts of all. The godly began to bolden; and men began openly to speak, "Shall that idol be suffered again to take place within this realm? It shall not." The Lord Lindsay (then but Master), with the gentlemen of Fife, and others, plainly cried in the close, "The idolater priest should die the death," according to God's law. One that carried in the candle was evil effrayed; but then began flesh and blood to show itself. There durst no Papist, neither yet any that came out of France, whisper. But the Lord James (the man whom all the godly did most reverence) took upon him to keep the Chapel door. His best excuse was, that he would stop all Scottish men to enter in to the Mass. But it was, and is, sufficiently known that the door was kept that none should have entry to trouble the priest, who, after the Mass, was committed to the protection of Lord John of Coldingham and Lord Robert of Holyroodhouse, who then were both Protestants, and had communicated at the Table of the Lord. Betwixt them two was the priest convoyed to his chamber.

And so the godly departed with great grief of heart, and at afternoon repaired to the Abbey in great companies, and gave plain signification that they could not abide that the land which God by his power had purged from idolatry should in their eyes be polluted again. Which understood, there began complaint upon complaint. The old dountybours, and others that long had served in the Court and have no remission of sins but by virtue of the Mass, cried, "They would to France without delay; they could not live without the Mass." The same affirmed the Queen's uncles. And would to God that that menzie, together with the Mass, had taken good-night at this realm for ever; for so had Scotland been rid of an unprofitable burden of devouring strangers, and of the malediction of God that has stricken and yet will strike for idolatry.

The Council assembled, disputation was had of the next remedy. Politic heads were sent unto the gentlemen with these and the like persuasions, "Why, alas, will ye chase our Sovereign from us? She will incontinent return to her galleys; and what then shall all realms say of us? May we not suffer her a little while? We doubt not but she shall leave it. If we were not assured that she might be won, we should be as great enemies to her Mass as ye should be. Her uncles will depart, and then shall we rule all at our pleasure. Would not we be as sorry to hurt the Religion as any of you would be?"

With these and the like persuasions (we say) was the fervency of the Brethren quenched; and an Act was framed, the tenor of which followeth:

APUD EDINBURGH, XXV^to AUGUSTI ANNO &C. LXI°

Forsamekle as the Queen's Majesty has understood the great inconvenients that may come through the division presently standing in this Realm for the difference in matters of religion, that her Majesty is most desirous to see [it] pacified by a good order, to the honour of God, and tranquillity of her Realm, and means to take the same by advice of her Estates so soon as conveniently may be; and that her Majesty's godly resolution therein may be greatly hindered, in case any tumult or sedition be raised amongst the lieges if any sudden alteration or novation be pressed [at] or attempted before that the order may be established; Therefore, for eschewing of the said inconvenients, her Majesty ordains letters to be directed to charge all and sundry her lieges, by open proclamation at the Market Cross of Edinburgh, and other places needful, that they and every one of them, contain themselves in quietness, [and] keep peace and civil society among themselves: And in the meantime, while the Estates of this Realm may be assembled, and that her Majesty have taken a final order by their advice and public consent, which her Majesty hopes shall be to the contentment of the whole, that none of them take upon hand, privately or openly, to make alteration or innovation of the

state of religion, or attempt anything against the form which
her Majesty found publicly and universally standing at her
Majesty's arrival in this her Realm, under the pain of death:
With certification, that if any subject of the Realm shall come
in the contrary hereof, he shall be esteemed and held a sedi-
tions person and raiser of tumult, and the said pain shall be
executed upon him with all rigour, to the example of others.
Attour, her Majesty by the advice of the Lords of her Secret
Council, commands and charges all her lieges that none of
them take upon hand to molest or trouble any of her domes-
tical servants, or persons whatsomever, come forth of France
in her Grace's company at this time, in word, deed, or countenance, for any cause whatsomever, either within her palace
or without, or make any derision or invasion upon any of
them, under whatsomever colour or pretence, under the said
pain of death: Albeit her Majesty be sufficiently persuaded
that her good and loving subjects would do the same for
the reverence they bear to her person and authority, notwithstanding that no such commandment were published.

This Act and Proclamation, penned and put in form by
such as before professed Christ Jesus (for in the Council then
had Papists neither power nor vote), it was publicly proclaimed at the Market Cross of Edinburgh, upon Monday
foresaid. No man reclaimed, nor made repugnance to it, except the Earl of Arran only who, in open audience of the
Heralds and people protested, "That he dissented that any
protection or defence should be made to the Queen's domestics, or to any that came from France, to offend God's Majesty, and to violate the laws of the Realm, more than to any
other subject. For God's law had pronounced death against
the idolater, and the laws of the Realm had appointed punishment for sayers and hearers of Mass; which (said he) I
here protest, be universally observed and that none be exempted, until such time as a law, as publicly made, and as
consonant to the law of God, have disannulled the former." . . .

This boldness did somewhat exasperate the Queen, and such as favoured her in that point. As the Lords, called of the Congregation, repaired unto the town at the first coming they showed themselves wondrously offended that the Mass was permitted; so that every man as he came accused them that were before him; but after that they had remained a certain space, they were as quiet as were the former. Which thing perceived, a zealous and godly man, Robert Campbell of Kinzeancleuch, said unto the Lord Ochiltree, "My Lord, now ye are come, and almost the last of all the rest; and I perceive, by your anger, that the fire-edge is not off you yet; but I fear, that after that holy water of the Court be sprinkled upon you, that ye shall become as temperate as the rest. For I have been here now five days, and at the first I heard every man say, 'Let us hang the priest'; but after that they had been twice or thrice in the Abbey, all that fervency was past. I think there be some enchantment whereby men are bewitched." And in very deed so it came to pass. For the Queen's flattering words, upon the one part, ever still crying, "Conscience, conscience: it is a sore thing to constrain the conscience"; and the subtle persuasions of her supposts (we mean even of such as sometimes were judged most fervent with us) upon the other part, blinded all men, and put them in this opinion: she will be content to hear the preaching, and so no doubt but she may be won. And thus of all it was concluded to suffer her for a time.

The next Sunday, John Knox*, inveighing against idolatry, showed what terrible plagues God had taken upon realms and nations for the same; and added, "That one Mass (there was no more suffered at first) was more fearful to him than if ten thousand armed enemies were landed in any part of the realm, of purpose to suppress the whole religion. For (said he) in our God there is strength to resist and confound multitudes if we unfeignedly depend upon him; whereof heretofore we have had experience; but when we join hands with

* He habitually writes of himself in the third person.

idolatry, it is no doubt but that both God's amicable presence
and comfortable defence leaveth us, and what shall then become of us? Alas, I fear that experience shall teach us, to the
grief of many." At these words, the Guiders of the Court
mocked, and plainly spake, "That such fear was no point of
their faith; it was beside his text, and was a very untimely
admonition." But we heard this same John Knox, in the
audience of the same men, recite the same words again in the
midst of troubles; and in the audience of many, ask [of]
God mercy that he was not more vehement and upright in the
suppressing of that idol in the beginning. "For (said he) albeit that I spake that which offended some (which this day
they see and feel to be true), yet did I not [that] which I
might have done; for God had not only given unto me
knowledge and tongue to make the impiety of that idol
known unto this realm, but he had given unto me credit with
many, who would have put in execution God's judgments, if
I would only have consented thereto. But so careful was I of
that common tranquillity, and so loth was I to have offended
those of whom I had conceived a good opinion, that in secret
conference with earnest and zealous men, I travailed rather
to mitigate, yea, to slaken, that fervency that God had kindled in others, than to animate or encourage them to put
their hands to the Lord's work. Whereintill I unfeignedly
acknowledge myself to have done most wickedly; and from
the bottom of my heart, ask of my God grace and pardon, for
that I did not what in me lay to have suppressed that idol
in the beginning." These and other words did many hear him
speak in public place, in the month of December, the year
of God 1565, when such as at the Queen's arrival only maintained the Mass, were exiled the realm, summoned upon
treason, and decreet of forfeiture intended against them.
But to return from whence we have digressed.

Whether it was by counsel of others, or of the Queen's
own desire, we know not; but the Queen spake with John
Knox, and had long reasoning with him, none being present

except the Lord James (two gentlewomen stood in the other end of the house). The sum of their reasoning was this. The Queen accused him that he had raised a part of her subjects against her mother, and against herself: That he had written a book against her just authority (she meant the treatise against the Regiment of Women), which she had, and should cause the most learned in Europe to write against it: That he was the cause of great sedition and great slaughter in England: and That it was said to her that all which he did was by necromancy, &c.

To the which the said John answered, "Madam, it may please your Majesty patiently to hear my simple an-answers. And first (said he) if to teach the truth of God in sincerity, if to rebuke idolatry, and to will a people to worship God according to his word, be to raise subjects against their princes, then cannot I be excused; for it has pleased God of his mercy to make me one (amongst many) to disclose unto this realm the vanity of the Papistical religion, and the deceit, pride and tyranny of that Roman Antichrist. But, Madam, if the true knowledge of God, and his right worshipping be the chief causes that must move men from their heart to obey their just princes (as it is most certain that they are) wherein can I be reprehended? I think, and am surely persuaded, that your Grace has had, and presently has, an unfeigned obedience of such as profess Jesus Christ within this realm as ever your father or other progenitors had of those that were called bishops. And touching that book which seemeth so highly to offend your Majesty, it is most certain that I wrote it, and am content that all the learned of the world judge of it. I hear that an Englishman hath written against it, but I have not read him. If he have sufficiently improved my reasons, and established his contrary proposition, with as evident testimonies as I have done mine, I shall not be obstinate, but shall confess my error and ignorance. But to this hour I have thought, and yet think, myself alone to be more able to sustain the things affirmed in that my work than any ten in Europe shall be able to confute it."

"Ye think then (quod she), that I have no just authority?"

"Please your Majesty (said he) that learned men in all ages have had their judgments free, and most commonly disagreeing from the common judgment of the world; such also have they published, both with pen and tongue, and yet notwithstanding they themselves have lived in the common society with others, and have borne patiently the errors and imperfections which they could not amend. Plato, the philosopher, wrote his Books of the Commonwealth, in the which he damneth many things than then were maintained in the world, and required many things to have been reformed; and yet, notwithstanding, he lived even under such policies as then were universally received without further troubling of any estate. Even so, Madam, am I content to do, in uprightness of heart, and with a testimony of a good conscience. I have communicated my judgment to the world. If the realm finds no inconvenience from the regiment of a woman, that which they approve shall I not further disallow than within my own breast, but shall be as well content to live under your Grace as Paul was to live under Nero; and my hope is, that so long as that ye defile not your hands with the blood of the saints of God, that neither I nor that book shall either hurt you or your authority; for in very deed, Madam, that book was written most especially against that wicked Jezebel of England."

"But (said she), ye speak of women in general."

"Most true it is, Madam (said the other), and yet it appeareth to me that wisdom should persuade your Grace never to raise trouble for that which to this day hath not troubled your Majesty, neither in person nor yet in authority. For of late years many things which before were held stable have been called in doubt; yes they have been plainly impugned. But yet, Madam (said he), I am assured that nei-

ther Protestant nor Papist shall be able to prove that any
such question was at any time moved in public or in secret.
Now, Madam (said he), if I had intended to have troubled
your estate because ye are a woman, I might have chosen a
time more convenient for that purpose than I can do now,
when your own presence is within the realm.

"But now, Madam, shortly to answer to the other two accusations. I heartily praise my God, through Jesus Christ, that
Sathan, the enemy of mankind, and the wicked of the world,
hath no other crimes to lay to my charge than such as the
very world itself knoweth to be most false and vain. For in
England I was resident only the space of five years. The
places were Berwick, where I abode two years; so long in
the New Castle; and a year in London. Now, Madam, if in
any of these places, during the time that I was there, any
man shall be able to prove that there was either battle, sedition or mutiny I shall confess that I myself was the male-
factor and the shedder of blood. I ashame not, Madam, further to affirm that God so blessed my weak labours that in
Berwick (where commonly before there used to be slaughter
by reason of quarrels that used to arise amongst soldiers),
there was as great quietness all the time that I remained
there as there is this day in Edinburgh. And where they slander me of magic, necromancy, or of other art forbidden of
God, I have witnesses (besides my own conscience) all [the]
congregations that ever heard me, what I spake both against
such arts, and against those that use such impiety. But, seeing the wicked of the world said, That my Master, the Lord
Jesus, was possessed of Beelzebub, I must patiently bear, albeit that I, wretched sinner, be unjustly accused of those
that never delighted in the verity."

"But yet (said she), ye have taught the people to receive
another religion than their princes can allow. And how
can that doctrine be of God, seeing that God commands subjects to obey their princes?"

"Madam (said he), as right religion took neither original

strength nor authority from worldly princes but from the Eternal God alone, so are not subjects bound to frame their religion according to the appetites of their princes. For oft it is that princes are the most ignorant of all others in God's true religion, as we may read in the histories as well before the death of Christ Jesus, as after. If all the seed of Abraham should have been of the religion of Pharaoh, whom to they were long subjects, I pray you, Madam, what religion should there have been in the world? Or, if all men in the days of the Apostles should have been of the religion of the Roman Emperors, what religion should there have been upon the face of the earth? Daniel and his fellows were subjects to Nebuchadnezzar, and unto Darius, and yet, Madam, they would not be of their religion, neither of the one nor of the other. For the three children said, 'We make it known unto thee, O King, that we will not worship thy gods'; and Daniel did publicly pray unto his God against the expressed commandment of the King. And so, Madam, ye may perceive that subjects are not bound to the religion of their princes, albeit they are commanded to give them obedience."

"Yea (quod she), but none of those men raised the sword against their princes."

"Yet Madam (quod he), ye cannot deny but that they resisted: for those that obey not the commandments that are given, in some sort resist."

"But yet (said she), they resisted not by the sword?"

"God (said he), Madam, had not given unto them the power and the means."

"Think ye (quod she), that subjects having power may resist their princes?"

"If their princes exceed their bounds (quod he), Madam, and do against that wherefore they should be obeyed, it is no doubt that they may be resisted, even by power. For there is neither greater honour nor greater obedience to be given to kings or princes than God has commanded to be given unto father and mother. But so it is, Madam, that the father may be stricken with a frenzy, in which he would slay his own children. Now, Madam, if the children arise, join themselves together, apprehend the father, take the sword or other weapons from him, and finally bind his hands, and keep him in prison till that his frenzy be overpast; think ye, Madam, that the children do any wrong? Or, think ye, Madam, that God will be offended with them that have stayed their father to commit wickedness? It is even so (said he), Madam, with princes that would murder the children of God that are subject unto them. Their blind zeal is nothing but a very mad frenzy; and therefore, to take the sword from them, to bind their hands, and to cast themselves in prison till that they be brought to a more sober mind, is no disobedience against princes, but just obedience, because that it agreeth with the will of God."

At these words, the Queen stood as it were amazed, more than the quarter of an hour. Her countenance altered, so that Lord James began to entreat her, and to demand, "What has offended you, Madam?"

At length, she said, "Well, then, I perceive that my subjects shall obey you, and not me; and shall do what they list, and not what I command: and so must I be subject to them, and not they to me."

"God forbid (answered he), that ever I take upon me to command any to obey me, or yet to set subjects at liberty to do what pleaseth them. But my travail is that both princes and subjects obey God. And think not (said he), Madam, that wrong is done unto you when ye are willed to be subject unto God: for it is He that subjects people under princes, and causes obedience to be given unto them; yea, God craves of kings that they be as it were foster-fathers to his church, and commands queens to be nurses unto his people. And this subjection, Madam, to God, and unto his troubled church, is the greatest dignity that flesh can get upon the face of the earth, for it shall carry them to everlasting glory."

"Yea (quod she), but ye are not the kirk that I will

nourish. I will defend the Kirk of Rome for I think it is the true kirk of God."

"Your will (quod he), Madam, is no reason; neither doth your thought make that Roman harlot to be the true and immaculate spouse of Jesus Christ. And wonder not, Madam, that I call Rome a harlot; for that church is altogether polluted with all kind of spiritual fornication, as well in doctrine as in manners. Yea, Madam, I offer myself further to prove that the church of the Jews that crucified Christ Jesus was not so far degenerated from the ordinances and statutes which God gave by Moses and Aaron unto his people when that they manifestly denied the Son of God, as that the Church of Rome is declined, and more than five hundred years hath declined, from the purity of that religion which the Apostles taught and planted."

"My conscience (said she), is not so."

"Conscience, Madam (said he), requires knowledge; and I fear that right knowledge ye have none."

"But (said she), I have both heard and read."

"So (said he), Madam, did the Jews that crucified Christ Jesus read both the Law and the Prophets, and heard the same interpreted after their manner. Have ye heard (said he), any teach but such as the pope and his cardinals have allowed? And ye may be assured that such will speak nothing to offend their own estate."

"Ye interpret the Scriptures (said she), in one manner, and they interpret in another. Whom shall I believe? And who shall be judge?"

"Ye shall believe (said he), God that plainly speaketh in his word: and further than the word teaches you, ye neither shall believe the one or the other. The word of God is plain in the self; and if there appear any obscurity in one place, the Holy Ghost, which is never contrarious to himself, explains the same more clearly in other places: so that there can remain no doubt but unto such as obstinately remain ignorant. And now (said he), Madam, to take one of the chief

points which this day is in controversy betwixt the Papists
and us: for example, the Papists allege, and boldly have
affirmed, That the Mass is the ordinance of God, and the institution of Jesus Christ, and a sacrifice for the sins of the
quick and the dead. We deny both the one and the other,
and affirm that the Mass as it is now used is nothing but the
invention of man; and, therefore, is an abomination before
God, and no sacrifice that ever God commanded. Now,
Madam, who shall judge betwixt us two thus contending?
It is no reason that either of the parties be further believed
than they are able to prove by unsuspect witnessing. Let them
lay down the book of God, and by plain words thereof prove
their affirmatives, and we shall give unto them the plea
granted. But so long as they are bold to affirm, and yet do
prove nothing, we must say that, albeit all the world believed them, yet believe they not God, but receive the lies of
men for the truth of God. What our Master Jesus Christ did,
we know by his Evangelists: what the priest doth at his Mass,
the world seeth. Now, doth not the Word of God plainly
assure us that Christ Jesus neither said nor yet commanded
Mass to be said at his Last Supper, seeing that no such thing
as their Mass is made mention of within the whole Scriptures?"

"Ye are oure sair for me (said the Queen), but and if they
were here that I have heard, they would answer you."

"Madam (quod the other), would to God that the
learnedest Papist in Europe, and he that ye would best believe, were present with your Grace to sustain the argument;
and that ye would patiently abide to hear the matter reasoned
to the end. For then I doubt not, Madam, but that ye should
hear the vanity of the Papistical religion and how small
ground it hath within the word of God."

"Well (said she), ye may perchance get that sooner than
ye believe."

"Assuredly (said the other), if ever I get that in my life,
I get it sooner than I believe. For the ignorant Papists cannot

patiently reason, and the learned and crafty Papist will never come in your audience, Madam, to have the ground of their religion searched out; for they know that they are never able to sustain an argument, except fire and sword and their own laws be judges."

"So say ye," (quod the Queen).

"But I can believe that it has been so to this day, (quod he). For how oft have the Papists in this and other realms been required to come to conference, and yet could it never be obtained, unless that themselves were admitted for judges. And therefore, Madam, I must yet say again that they dare never dispute but where themselves are both judge and party. And whensoever that ye shall let me see the contrary, I shall grant myself to have been deceived in that point."

And with this the Queen was called upon to dinner, for it was after noon. At departing, John Knox said unto her, "I pray God, Madam, that ye may be as blessed within the Commonwealth of Scotland, if it be the pleasure of God, as ever Deborah was in the Commonwealth of Israel." . . .

The brethren universally offended, and espying that the Queen, by her proclamations, did but mock them, determined to put to their own hands, and to punish for example of others. And so some Priests in the westland were apprehended, intimation made unto others (as unto the Abbot of Crossraguel, the Parson of Sanquhar, and such), that they should neither complain to Queen nor Council, but should execute the punishment that God has appointed to idolaters in his law, by such means as they might, wherever they should be apprehended.

The Queen stormed at such freedom of speaking, but she could not amend it; for the Spirit of God, of boldness and of wisdom, had not then left the most part of such as God had used as instruments in the beginning. They were of one mind to maintain the truth of God, and to suppress idolatry. Particularities had not divided them; and therefore could not

the devil, working in the Queen and Papists, do then what
they would; and, therefore, she began to invent a new craft.
She sent for John Knox to come unto her, where she lay at
Lochleven. She travailed with him earnestly two hours before
her supper, that he would be the instrument to persuade the
people, and principally the gentlemen of the West, not to
put hands to punish any man for the using of themselves in
their religion as pleased them. The other, perceiving her
craft, willed her Grace to punish malefactors according to the
laws, and he durst promise quietness upon the part of all
them that professed the Lord Jesus within Scotland. But if
her Majesty thought to delude the laws, he said, he feared
that some would let the Papists understand that, without
punishment, they should not be suffered so manifestly to offend God's Majesty.

"Will ye," quod she, "allow that they shall take my sword
in their hand?"

"The sword of Justice," quod he, "Madam, is God's, and
is given to princes and rulers for one end, which, if they
transgress, sparing the wicked, and oppressing the innocents,
they that in the fear of God execute judgment where God has
commanded, offend not God, although kings do it not;
neither yet sin they that bridle kings to strike innocent men
in their rage. The examples are evident; for Samuel feared
not to slay Agag, the fat and delicate king of Amalek, whom
king Saul saved. Neither spared Elijah Jezebel's false prophets, and Baal's priests, albeit that king Ahab was present.
Phinehas was no magistrate, and yet feared he not to strike
Cozbi and Zimri in the very act of filthy fornication. And so,
Madam, your Grace may see that others than chief magistrates may lawfully punish, and have punished, the vice and
crimes that God commands to be punished. And in this case
I would earnestly pray your Majesty to take good advisement,
and that your Grace should let the Papists understand
that their attemptates will not be suffered unpunished. For
power, by Act of Parliament, is given to all judges within their

own bounds, to search [for] massmongers, or the hearers of the same and to punish them according to the law. And therefore it shall be profitable to your Majesty to consider what is the thing your Grace's subjects look to receive of your Majesty, and what it is that ye ought to do unto them by mutual contract. They are bound to obey you, and that not but in God. Ye are bound to keep laws unto them. Ye crave of them service: they crave of you protection and defence against wicked doers. Now, Madam, if ye shall deny your duty unto them (which especially craves that ye punish malefactors) think ye to receive full obedience of them? I fear, Madam, ye shall not.". . .

Before the Parliament dissolved, John Knox, in his sermon before the most part of the Nobility began to enter in a deep discourse of God's mercies which that Realm had felt, and of that ingratitude which he espied almost in the whole multitude, which God had marvellously delivered from the bondage and tyranny both of body and soul. "And now, my Lords," said he, "I praise my God, through Jesus Christ, that in your own presence I may pour forth the sorrows of my heart; yes, yourselves shall be witness, if that I shall make any lie in things that are bypast. From the beginning of God's mighty working within this Realm, I have been with you in your most desperate tentations. Ask your own consciences, and let them answer you before God, if that I (not I, but God's Spirit in me), in your greatest extremity willed you not ever to depend upon your God, and in his name promised unto you victory and preservation from your enemies, so that ye would only depend upon his protection, and prefer his glory to your own lives and worldly commodity. In your most extreme dangers I have been with you: Saint Johnston, Cupar Muir, and the Craigs of Edinburgh are yet recent in my heart; yea, that dark and dolorous night wherein ye all, my Lords, with shame and fear left this town, is yet in my mind; and God forbid that ever I forget it. What was (I say) my exhortation unto you by my mouth, ye yourselves yet live to testify. There is not one of you against whom was death and destruction threatened, perished in that danger. And how many of your enemies has God plagued before your eyes! Shall this be the thankfulness that ye shall render unto your God, to betray his cause, when ye have it in your own hands to establish it as ye please? The Queen, ye say, will not agree with us. Ask ye of her that which by God's word ye may justly require, and if she will not agree with you in God, ye are not bound to agree with her in the Devil. Let her plainly understand so far of your minds; and steal not from your former stoutness in God, and he shall prosper you in your enterprises. But I can see nothing but such a recoiling from Christ Jesus, as the man that first and most speedily flyeth from Christ's enseignzie, holding himself most happy. Yes, I hear that some say that we have nothing of our Religion established, neither by Law or Parliament. Albeit that the malicious words of such can neither hurt the truth of God, nor yet us that thereupon depend, yet the speaker for his treason against God committed, and against this poor Commonwealth, deserves the gallows. For our Religion being commanded and so established by God, is accepted within this Realm in public Parliament; and if they will say that was no Parliament, we must and will say, and also prove, that that Parliament was as lawful as ever any that passed before it within this Realm. Yea, if the King then living was King, and the Queen now in this Realm be lawful Queen, that Parliament cannot be denied.

"And now, my Lords, to put an end to all, I hear of the Queen's marriage: Dukes, brethren to Emperors, and Kings, strive all for the best game. But this, my Lords, will I say (note the day, and bear witness after), whensoever the Nobility of Scotland professing the Lord Jesus, consents that an infidel (and all Papists are infidels) shall be head to your Sovereign, ye do so far as in ye lieth to banish Christ Jesus from this Realm; ye bring God's vengeance upon the country, a plague upon yourself, and perchance ye shall do small comfort to your Sovereign."

These words, and this manner of speaking were judged intolerable. Papists and Protestants were both offended; yea, his most familiars disdained him for that speaking. Placeboes and flatterers posted to the Court to give advertisement that Knox had spoken against the Queen's marriage. The Provost of Lincluden, Douglas of Drumlanrig, by surname, was the man that gave the charge that the said John should present himself before the Queen: which he did soon after dinner. The Lord Ochiltree and divers of the faithful bore him company to the Abbey; but none passed into the Queen with him in the cabinet but John Erskine of Dun, then Superintendent of Angus and Mearns.

The Queen, in a vehement fume, began to cry out that never Prince was handled as she was. "I have," said she, "borne with you in all your rigorous manner of speaking, both against myself and against my uncles; yea, I have sought your favours by all possible means. I offered unto you presence and audience whensoever it pleased you to admonish me; and yet I cannot be quit of you. I avow to God, I shall be once revenged." And with these words, scarcely could Marnock, her secret chamber-boy, get napkins to hold her eyes dry for the tears, and the howling, besides womanly weeping, stayed her speech.

The said John did patiently abide all the first fume, and at opportunity answered, "True it is, Madam, your Grace and I have been at divers controversies, into the which I never perceived your Grace to be offended at me. But when it shall please God to deliver you from that bondage of darkness and error in the which ye have been nourished, for the lack of true doctrine, your Majesty will find the liberty of my tongue nothing offensive. Without the preaching place, Madam, I think few have occasion to be offended at me; and there, Madam, I am not master of myself, but must obey

Him who commands me to speak plain, and to flatter no flesh upon the face of the earth."

"But what have ye to do," said she, "with my marriage?"

"If it please your Majesty," said he, "patiently to hear me, I shall show the truth in plain words. I grant your Grace offered unto me more than ever I required; but my answer was then, as it is now, that God hath not sent me to await upon the courts of Princesses, nor upon the chambers of Ladies; but I am sent to preach the Evangel of Jesus Christ to such as please to hear it; and it hath two parts, Repentance and Faith. And now, Madam, in preaching repentance, of necessity it is that the sins of men be so noted that they may know wherein they offend; but so it is that the most part of your Nobility are so addicted to your affections, that neither God's word, nor yet their Commonwealth, are rightly regarded. And therefore it becomes me so to speak, that they may know their duty."

"What have ye to do," said she, "with my marriage? Or what are ye within this Commonwealth?"

"A subject born within the same," said he, "Madam. And albeit I neither be Earl, Lord, nor Baron within it, yet has God made me (how abject that ever I be in your eyes), a profitable member within the same: Yea, Madam, to me it appertains no less to forewarn of such things as may hurt it, if I foresee them, than it does to any of the Nobility; for both my vocation and conscience crave plainness of me. And therefore, Madame, to yourself I say that which I speak in public place: Whensoever that the Nobility of this Realm shall consent that ye be subject to an unfaithful husband, they do as much as in them lieth to renounce Christ, to banish his truth from them, to betray the freedom of this Realm, and perchance shall in the end do small comfort to yourself."

At these words, howling was heard, and tears might have been seen in greater abundance than the matter required. John Erskine of Dun, a man of meek and gentle spirit, stood beside and entreated what he could to mitigate her anger, and gave unto her many pleasing words of her beauty, of her excellence, and how that all the Princes of Europe would be glad to seek her favours. But all that was to cast oil in the flaming fire. The said John stood still, without any alteration of countenance for a long season, while that the Queen gave place to her inordinate passion; and in the end he said, "Madam, in God's presence I speak: I never delighted in the weeping of any of God's creatures; yea, I can scarcely well abide the tears of my own boys whom my own hand corrects, much less can I rejoice in your Majesty's weeping. But seeing that I have offered unto you no just occasion to be offended, but have spoken the truth, as my vocation craves of me, I must sustain (albeit unwillingly), your Majesty's tears rather than I dare hurt my conscience, or betray my Commonwealth through my silence."

John Knox's History of the Reformation in Scotland,
Edited by William Croft Dickinson, D.Lit. Vol. II.
New York: Philosophical Library, 1949.

THE
ANABAPTISTS

THE ANABAPTISTS

WHILE THE NICKNAME, ANABAPTIST, COVERS DIVERSE GROUPS with radically varied opinions, certain common convictions distinguished Anabaptists in general from the rest of the Protestant movement. They denounced the kind of reformation proposed by Luther, Zwingli and Calvin as a halfway affair. They believed in a national state church no more than they believed in the Roman church. To them religion was the intimate concern of each individual soul, and the church was a voluntary society of the regenerate, who had been saved by faith in Christ and were living obediently to Christ's principles.

On this basis they not only threw over the papacy and the whole Roman sacramental system, but they denied as well all state interference in matters of religion, demanded complete freedom for the church and for individual consciences, and commonly so far separated themselves from the state that they refused to accept offices, to bear arms, or even to take oaths.

Because of this stand, opposition to infant baptism became the obvious and visible crux of their contention. While all the major Reformers denied the Roman doctrine of infant baptism, they retained the practice of it, regarding it, after

the analogy of Jewish circumcision, as the sacramental means
by which children were incorporated into the state church.
To the Anabaptists, this was an impossible conception. To
them becoming a Christian was a matter of individual choice,
and joining the church could have no reality save as it was
the personal, voluntary, responsible decision of the one concerned. They argued that if supernatural saving power, such
as Roman doctrine ascribed to infant baptism, was denied,
the logical and Scriptural conclusion was to drop it altogether,
and to make baptism the outward symbol of a responsible
person's acceptance of Christ and of his decision to unite
with Christ's people.

Far from putting major stress on baptism, therefore, the
Anabaptists, as compared with the rest of the Protestant
movement, minimized it; it was, said Menno Simons, one of
the least of God's commandments. It was Luther, Zwingli,
Calvin, Knox, and their followers who, regarding infant baptism as an essential factor in their whole church-state pro-
gram, insisted on its indispensability, and denounced Anabaptist ideas as intolerable. Hans Denck, one of the Anabaptist
leaders, even said; "In themselves ceremonies are not useful,
and he who thinks thereby to obtain anything, whether
through baptism or the breaking of bread, is superstitious.
. . . He who makes ceremonies burdensome is not much of a
gainer thereby; for should one lose all ceremonies, he would
not suffer any injury, and indeed it is better to want them
than to misuse them."

The major stream of the Anabaptist movement took its rise
in Zurich among the followers of Zwingli. Men like Grebel,
Manz, Blaurock, Denck, Hätzer, Hübmaier had been disciples
of Luther and Zwingli but, convinced that these Reformers
were going neither fast enough nor far enough, they demanded that their own much more radical ideas be put at
once into operation. "It stands ill with the gospel in Zurich,"
wrote Grebel to a friend, "and Zwingli no longer acts a shepherd's part." What these Swiss Brethren wanted was a church

composed of believers only, complete freedom for the church from state control, strict discipline within the church, confining its membership to faithful and consistent Christians. Moreover, many of them would not bear arms, would take no oaths, would accept no magistracy.

Their attitude seemed to the major Reformers insufferable. How could the Reformation be maintained if, having thrown over the papal church, it now threw over the support of the state? The necessities of their dangerous situation pressed hard on men like Zwingli; they could hold their ground and make progress against the tremendous power of Rome, only as they carried along with them the consent and backing of their governments; they saw—and it may well be, truly—certain failure ahead if the church were reduced to a voluntary society of Christians, who even refused to be magistrates.

That day in Zurich, therefore, when George Blaurock entreated Conrad Grebel to baptize him with the right Christian baptism, and when Blaurock, himself baptized, then baptized the rest of the little group, started an irrepressible conflict. The Anabaptists developed astonishing influence. They spread widely and numerously across Europe. Commonly springing from the depressed and the poor, they appealed to motives which were powerful in the rank and file. All the more, however, because their popularity was dangerous, they were persecuted with a ruthlessness which in the end almost obliterated them. The importance attached to them is indicated by the fact that all the major Reformers published brochures against them—Luther, Zwingli, Bucer, Oecolampadius, Calvin, Knox and many others. They were exiled from Zurich under heavy penalties—"We are determined," the Zurich Council announced, "not to tolerate Anabaptists within our borders. There must be no fellowship with them whatever"—and in 1529 an imperial edict decreed "that every Anabaptist and rebaptized person, of whatever age or sex, be put to death by sword, or fire, or otherwise. All preachers and those who abet and conceal them, all who persist in Anabaptism, or relapse after retraction, must be put to death. In no case must they be pardoned."

The Anabaptists themselves provided excuse for such attack and persecution, because a left-wing group developed out of the movement which went to wild, fanatical extremes. In Wittenberg, while Luther was still in hiding at the Wartburg after his confrontation of the Emperor at Worms, Nicholas Storch, coming from Zwickau, launched a campaign which threatened to disrupt the community. He preached the speedy coming of the millennium, the duty of community of goods, and the authority of his own supernatural revelations, and the disturbance his followers caused called Luther home to quiet the tumult. Ever afterward he denounced the Anabaptists mercilessly and called for their suppression. Similarly, Melchior Hoffmann broke away from the Lutheranism with which he started, and became an extreme fanatic, announcing the coming of the millennium in Strassburg in 1533, and arousing a social and religious excitement so great that it has been estimated that for some years a majority of Evangelicals in the Netherlands were Hoffmannites. This type of fanaticism came to its tragic climax in the city of Münster, where Jan of Leyden seized control and, after a regime of almost incredible orgies, collapsed before opposing armies and carried down with him the strength of the movement which he had so hideously misrepresented.

These wild extremists, however, were so much an aberration from the main movement which had begun with men like Grebel and Hübmaier, and the main movement contained such valuable truth, that it could not be utterly crushed out. Faithful Anabaptists still preserved their original ideas: a voluntary, purified church of believers only, a suffering, cross-bearing, sacrificial church, a strict discipline within the Christian society, stern censures and excommunications for all offenses, a strong sense of brotherhood and social obligation, a refusal to persecute or to take part in war, complete separation of church and state, and complete freedom of worship.

Menno Simons, converted from Roman Catholicism, left his priesthood, and gathered up the remnants of the scattered Anabaptists in the Low Countries. The Mennonites thus became the lineal descendants of the original Swiss Brethren; and English Baptists and Quakers so obviously show the influence of Anabaptist ideas as to leave no doubt that the continental movement was reflected in them by way of Anabaptist refugees who fled to England and English refugees who fled to the Low Countries.

No one person can be chosen in this anthology to represent such varied opinions as Anabaptism presents. Balthasar Hübmaier was an able scholar and a devoted Christian, his ideal to live in the spirit and by the principles of Jesus, but he did not agree with his brethren about accepting the magistrate's office or about rightful use of the sword. Han Denck was a Humanist scholar, but he was primarily a mystic and all his writings which have survived stress that approach to Christian experience. In Menno Simons' writings we have, on the whole, the most balanced picture of the Anabaptist position at its best.

The human side of the movement is well presented in such biographies as *Conrad Grebel,* by Harold S. Bender; *Balthasar Hübmaier,* by Henry C. Vedder; *Hans Denck,* by Alfred Coutts. *The Anabaptists in Switzerland,* by Henry S. Burrage is a valuable history, as is *The Anabaptists,* by Robert J. Smithson. *The Rise and Fall of the Anabaptists,* by E. Belfort Bax, while out of balance in its stressing of Anabaptist socialism, is a noteworthy volume. For a condensed summary, the article, *Anabaptism* in the *Encyclopaedia of Religion and Ethics* is excellent.

From

THE SCHLEITHEIM
CONFESSION OF FAITH

BROTHERLY UNION OF A NUMBER OF CHILDREN OF GOD
CONCERNING SEVEN ARTICLES*

MAY JOY, PEACE AND MERCY FROM OUR FATHER THROUGH THE atonement of the blood of Christ Jesus, together with the gifts of the Spirit—Who is sent from the Father to all believers for their strength and comfort and for their perseverance in all tribulation until the end, Amen—be to all those who love God, who are the children of light, and who are scattered everywhere as it has been ordained of God our Father, where they are with one mind assembled together in one God and Father of us all: Grace and peace of heart be with you all, Amen.

Beloved brethren and sisters in the Lord: First and supremely we are always concerned for your consolation and the assurance of your conscience (which was previously misled) so that you may not always remain foreigners to us and by right almost completely excluded, but that you may turn again to the true implanted members of Christ, who have been armed through patience and knowledge of themselves, and have therefore again been united with us in the strength of a godly Christian spirit and zeal for God.

* The so-called Schleitheim Confession of Faith, prepared at a conference of Anabaptist Swiss Brethren, 1527

It is also apparent with what cunning the devil has turned us aside, so that he might destroy and bring to an end the work of God which in mercy and grace has been partly begun in us. But Christ, the true Shepherd of our souls, Who has begun this in us, will certainly direct the same and teach [us] to His honor and our salvation, Amen.

Dear brethren and sisters, we who have been assembled in the Lord at Schleitheim on the Border, make known in points and articles to all who love God that as concerns us we are of one mind to abide in the Lord as God's obedient children, [His] sons and daughters, we who have been and shall be separated from the world in everything, [and] completely at peace. To God alone be praise and glory without the contradiction of any brethren. In this we have perceived the oneness of the Spirit of our Father and of our common Christ with us. For the Lord is the Lord of peace and not of quarreling, as Paul points out. That you may understand in what articles this has been formulated you should observe and note [the following].

A very great offense has been introduced by certain false brethren among us, so that some have turned aside from the faith, in the way they intend to practice and observe the freedom of the Spirit and of Christ. But such have missed the truth and to their condemnation are given over to the lasciviousness and self-indulgence of the flesh. They think faith and love may do and permit everything, and nothing will harm them nor condemn them, since they are believers.

Observe, you who are God's members in Christ Jesus, that faith in the Heavenly Father through Jesus Christ does not take such form. It does not produce and result in such things as these false brethren and sisters do and teach. Guard yourselves and be warned of such people, for they do not serve our Father, but their father, the devil.

But you are not that way. For they that are Christ's have crucified the flesh with its passions and lusts. You understand me well and [know] the brethren whom we mean. Separate yourselves from them for they are perverted. Petition the Lord that they may have the knowledge which leads to repentance, and [pray] for us that we may have constancy to persevere in the way which we have espoused, for the honor of God and of Christ, His Son, Amen.

The articles which we discussed and on which we were of one mind are these 1. Baptism; 2. The Ban [Excommunication]; 3. Breaking of Bread; 4. Separation from the Abomination; 5. Pastors in the Church; 6. The Sword; and 7. The Oath.

First. Observe concerning baptism: Baptism shall be given to all those who have learned repentance and amendment of life, and who believe truly that their sins are taken away by Christ, and to all those who walk in the resurrection of Jesus Christ, and wish to be buried with Him in death, so that they may be resurrected with Him, and to all those who with this significance request it [baptism] of us and demand it for themselves. This excludes all infant baptism, the highest and chief abomination of the pope. In this you have the foundation and testimony of the apostles. Mt. 28, Mk. 16, Acts 2, 8, 16, 19. This we wish to hold simply, yet firmly and with assurance.

Second. We are agreed as follows on the ban: The ban shall be employed with all those who have given themselves to the Lord, to walk in His commandments, and with all those who are baptized into the one body of Christ and who are called brethren or sisters, and yet who slip sometimes and fall into error and sin, being inadvertently overtaken. The same shall be admonished twice in secret and the third time openly disciplined or banned according to the command of Christ. Mt. 18. But this shall be done according to the regulation of the Spirit (Mt. 5) before the breaking of bread, so that we may break and eat one bread, with one mind and in one love, and may drink of one cup.

Third. In the breaking of bread we are of one mind and are agreed [as follows]: All those who wish to break one bread in remembrance of the broken body of Christ, and all who wish to drink of one drink as a remembrance of the shed blood of Christ, shall be united beforehand by baptism in one body of Christ which is the church of God and whose Head is Christ. For as Paul points out we cannot at the same time be partakers of the Lord's table and the table of devils; we cannot at the same time drink the cup of the Lord and the cup of the devil. That is, all those who have fellowship with the dead works of darkness have no part in the light. Therefore all who follow the devil and the world have no part with those who are called unto God out of the world. All who lie in evil have no part in the good.

Therefore it is and must be [thus]: Whoever has not been called by one God to one faith, to one baptism, to one Spirit, to one body, with all the children of God's church, cannot be made [into] one bread with them, as indeed must be done if one is truly to break bread according to the command of Christ.

Fourth. We are agreed [as follows] on separation: A separation shall be made from the evil and from the wickedness which the devil planted in the world; in this manner, simply that we shall not have fellowship with them [the wicked] and not run with them in the multitude of their abominations. This is the way it is: Since all who do not walk in the obedience of faith, and have not united themselves with God so that they wish to do His will, are a great abomination before God, it is not possible for anything to grow or issue from them except abominable things. For truly all creatures are in but two classes, good and bad, believing and unbelieving, darkness and light, the world and those who [have come] out of the world, God's temple and idols, Christ and Belial; and none can have part with the other.

To us then the command of the Lord is clear when He calls upon us to be separate from the evil and thus He will be our God and we shall be His sons and daughters.

He further admonishes us to withdraw from Babylon and

the earthly Egypt that we may not be partakers of the pain and suffering which the Lord will bring upon them.

From all this we should learn that everything which is not united with our God and Christ cannot be other than an abomination which we should shun and flee from. By this is meant all popish and antipopish works and church services, meetings and church attendance, drinking houses, civic affairs, the commitments [made in] unbelief and other things of that kind, which are highly regarded by the world and yet are carried on in flat contradiction to the command of God, in accordance with all the unrighteousness which is in the world. From all these things we shall be separated and have no part with them for they are nothing but an abomination, and they are the cause of our being hated before our Christ Jesus, Who has set us free from the slavery of the flesh and fitted us for the service of God through the Spirit Whom He has given us.

Therefore there will also unquestionably fall from us the unchristian, devilish weapons of force—such as sword, armor and the like, and all their use [either] for friends or against one's enemies—by virtue of the word of Christ, Resist not [him that is] evil.

Fifth. We are agreed as follows on pastors in the church of God: The pastor in the church of God shall, as Paul has prescribed, be one who out-and-out has a good report of those who are outside the faith. This office shall be to read, to admonish and teach, to warn, to discipline, to ban in the church, to lead out in prayer for the advancement of all the brethren and sisters, to lift up the bread when it is to be broken, and in all things to see to the care of the body of Christ, in order that it may be built up and developed, and the mouth of the slanderer be stopped.

This one moreover shall be supported of the church which has chosen him, wherein he may be in need, so that he who serves the Gospel may live of the Gospel as the Lord has ordained. But if a pastor should do something requiring discipline, he shall not be dealt with except [on the testimony of] two or three witnesses. And when they sin they shall be disciplined before all in order that the others may fear.

But should it happen that through the cross this pastor should be banished or led to the Lord [through martyrdom] another shall be ordained in his place in the same hour so that God's little flock and people may not be destroyed.

Sixth. We are agreed as follows concerning the sword: The sword is ordained of God outside the perfection of Christ. It punishes and puts to death the wicked, and guards and protects the good. In the Law the sword was ordained for the punishment of the wicked and for their death, and the same [sword] is [now] ordained to be used by the worldly magistrates.

In the perfection of Christ, however, only the ban is used for a warning and for the excommunication of the one who has sinned, without putting the flesh to death—simply the warning and the command to sin no more.

Now it will be asked by many who do not recognize [this as] the will of Christ for us, whether a Christian may or should employ the sword against the wicked for the defense and protection of the good, or for the sake of love.

Our reply is unanimously as follows: Christ teaches and commands us to learn of Him, for He is meek and lowly in heart and so shall we find rest to our souls. Also Christ says to the heathenish woman who was taken in adultery, not that one should stone her according to the law of His Father (and yet He says, As the Father has commanded me, thus I do), but in mercy and forgiveness and warning, to sin no more. Such [an attitude] we also ought to take completely according to the rule of the ban.

Secondly, it will be asked concerning the sword, whether a Christian shall pass sentence in worldly dispute and strife such as unbelievers have with one another. This is our united answer: Christ did not wish to decide or pass judgment between brother and brother in the case of the inheritance, but refused to do so. Therefore we should do likewise.

Thirdly, it will be asked concerning the sword, Shall one be a magistrate if one should be chosen as such? The answer is as follows: They wished to make Christ king, but He fled and did not view it as the arrangement of His Father. Thus shall we do as He did, and follow Him, and so shall we not walk in darkness. For he Himself says, He who wishes to come after me, let him deny himself and take up his cross and follow me. Also, He Himself forbids the [employment of] the force of the sword saying, The worldly princes lord it over them, etc., but not so shall it be with you. Further, Paul says, Whom God did foreknow He also did predestinate to be comforted to the image of His Son, etc. Also Peter says, Christ has suffered (not ruled) and left us an example, that ye should follow His steps.

Finally it will be observed that it is not appropriate for a Christian to serve as a magistrate because of these points: The government magistracy is according to the flesh, but the Christians' is according to the Spirit; their houses and dwelling remain in this world, but the Christians' are in heaven; their citizenship is in this world, but the Christians' citizenship is in heaven; the weapons of their conflict and war are carnal and against the flesh only, but the Christians' weapons are spiritual, against the fortification of the devil. The worldlings are armed with steel and iron, but the Christians are armed with the armor of God, with truth, righteousness, peace, faith, salvation and the Word of God. In brief, as is the mind of Christ toward us, so shall the mind of the members of the body of Christ be through Him in all things, that there may be no schism in the body through which it would be destroyed. For every kingdom divided against itself will be destroyed. Now since Christ is as it is written of Him, His members must also be the same, that His body may remain complete and united to its own advancement and up-building.

Seventh. We are agreed as follows concerning the oath: The oath is a confirmation among those who are quarreling or making promises. In the Law it is commanded to be performed in God's Name, but only in truth, not falsely. Christ, who teaches the perfection of the Law, prohibits all swearing to His [followers], whether true or false—neither by heaven, nor by the earth, nor by Jerusalem, nor by our head, —and that for the reason which He shortly thereafter gives, For you are not able to make one hair white or black. So you see it is for this reason that all swearing is forbidden: we cannot fulfill that which we promise when we swear, for we cannot change [even] the very least thing on us.

Now there are some who do not give credence to the simple command of God, but object with this question: Well now, did not God swear to Abraham by Himself (since He was God) when He promised him that He would be with him and that He would be his God if he would keep His commandments—why then should I not also swear when I promise to someone? Answer: Hear what the Scripture says: God, since He wished more abundantly to show unto the heirs the immutability of His counsel, inserted an oath, that by two immutable things (in which it is impossible for God to lie) we might have a strong consolation. Observe the meaning of this Scripture: What God forbids you to do, He has power to do, for everything is possible for Him. God swore an oath to Abraham, says the Scripture, so that He might show that His counsel is immutable. That is, no one can withstand nor thwart His will; therefore He can keep His oath. But we can do nothing, as is said above by Christ, to keep or perform [our oaths]: therefore we shall not swear at all.

Then others further say as follows: It is not forbidden of God to swear in the New Testament, when it is actually com-

manded in the Old, but it is forbidden only to swear by
heaven, earth, Jerusalem and our head. Answer: Hear the
Scripture, He who swears by heaven swears by God's throne
and by Him who sitteth thereon. Observe: it is forbidden to
swear by heaven, which is only the throne of God: how much
more is it forbidden [to swear] by God himself! Ye fools
and blind, which is greater, the throne or Him that sitteth
thereon?

Further some say, Because evil is now [in the world, and]
because man needs God for [the establishment of] the truth,
so did the apostles Peter and Paul also swear. Answer: Peter
and Paul only testify of that which God promised to Abraham with the oath. They themselves promise nothing, as the
example indicates clearly. Testifying and swearing are two
different things. For when a person swears he is in the first
place promising future things, as Christ was promised to
Abraham Whom we a long time afterwards received. But
when a person bears testimony he is testifying about the
present, whether it is good or evil, as Simeon spoke to Mary
about Christ and testified, Behold this (child) is set for the
fall and rising of many in Israel, and for a sign which shall
be spoken against.

Christ also taught us along the same line when He said, Let
your communication be Yea, yea; Nay, nay; for whatsoever
is more than these cometh of evil. He says, Your speech or
word shall be yea and nay. (However) when one does not
wish to understand, he remains closed to the meaning. Christ
is simply Yea and Nay, and all those who seek Him simply
will understand His Word. Amen.

Dear brethren and sisters in the Lord: These are the articles of certain brethren who had heretofore been in error
and who had failed to agree in the true understanding, so
that many weaker consciences were perplexed, causing the
Name of God to be greatly slandered. Therefore there has

been a great need for us to become of one mind in the Lord, which has come to pass. To God be praise and glory!

Now since you have so well understood the will of God which has been made known by us, it will be necessary for you to achieve perseveringly, without interruption, the known will of God. For you know well what the servant who sinned knowingly heard as his recompense.

Everything which you have unwittingly done and confessed as evil doing is forgiven you through the believing prayer which is offered by us in our meeting for all our shortcomings and guilt. [This state is yours] through the gracious forgiveness of God and through the blood of Jesus Christ. Amen.

Keep watch on all who do not walk according to the simplicity of the divine truth which is stated in this letter from [the decisions of] our meeting, so that everyone among us will be governed by the rule of the ban and henceforth the entry of false brethren and sisters among us may be prevented.

The Mennonite Quarterly Review,
October, 1945.
Translation by Dr. John C. Wenger.

From

TWO KINDS OF OBEDIENCE

OBEDIENCE IS OF TWO KINDS,* SERVILE AND FILIAL. THE FILIAL has its source in the love of the Father, even though no other reward should follow, yea even if the Father should wish to damn His child; the servile has its source in a love of reward or of oneself. The filial ever does as much as possible, apart from any command; the servile does as little as possible, yea nothing except by command. The filial is never able to do enough for Him; but he who renders servile obedience thinks he is constantly doing too much for Him. The filial rejoices in the chastisement of the Father although he may not have transgressed in anything; the servile wishes to be without chastisement although he may do nothing right. The filial has its treasure and righteousness in the Father whom it obeys only to manifest His righteousness; the servile person's treasure and piety are the works which he does in order to be pious. The filial remains in the house and inherits all the Father has; the servile wishes to reject this and receive his lawful reward. The servile looks to the external and to the prescribed command of his Lord; the filial is concerned about the inner witness and the Spirit. The servile is imperfect and therefore his Lord finds no pleasure in him; the filial strives for and attains perfection, and for that reason the Father cannot reject him.

The filial is not contrary to the servile, as it might appear,

* Anonymous Anabaptist statement from within The Swiss Brethren. Probable date between 1525 and 1530.

but is better and higher. And therefore let him who is servile seek for the better, the filial; he dare not be servile at all.

The servile is Moses and produces Pharisees and scribes the filial is Christ and makes children of God. The servile is either occupied with the ceremonies which Moses commanded or with those which people themselves have invented; the filial is active in the love of God and one's neighbor; yet he also submits himself to the ceremonies for the sake of the servants that he may instruct them in that which is better and lead them to sonship. The servile produces self-willed and vindictive people; the filial creates peaceable and mild-natured persons; the servile is severe and gladly arrives quickly at the end of the work; the filial is light and directs its gaze to that which endures. The servile is malevolent and wishes no one well but himself; the filial would gladly have all men to be as himself. The servile is the Old Covenant, and had the promise of temporal happiness; the filial is the New Covenant, and has the promise of eternal happiness, namely, the Creator Himself. The servile is a beginning and preparation for happiness; the filial is the end and completion itself. The servile endured for a time; the filial will last forever. The servile was a figure and shadow; the filial is the body and truth.

The servile was established to reveal and increase sin; the filial follows to do away with and extirpate the revealed and increased sin. For if a man wish to escape from sin he must first hate it, and if he would hate it he must first know it, and if he would know it there must be something to stir up and make known his hidden sin. Now it is Law or Scripture which does this: for as much as the Law demands, that much more the man turns from God to that which he has done, justifies himself therein, by his accomplishments, clings thereto as to his treasure and the greater such love becomes the more and the greater will grow his hatred for God and for his neighbor. For the more and the closer a man clings to the creature the farther he is from God. The more he desires the creature the less he will have of the Creator. Moreover the law gives occasion to people to depart farther from God, not because of itself (for it is good) but because of the sin which is in man. This is also the reason why Paul says that the law was given that it might increase sin, that sin might thereby become known. Yea, the law is the strength of sin and therefore it is just like the servile obedience, that is, obedience to law, which leads people into the most intense hatred of God and of one's neighbor. Therefore filial obedience is a certain way through which man escapes from such hatred and receives the love of God and of one's neighbor. Therefore as one administers death, the other administers life. The one is the Old Testament; the other, the New.

According to the Old Testament only he who murdered was guilty of judgment; but in the New, he also who is angry with his brother. The Old gave permission for a man to separate from his wife for every reason; but not at all in the New, except for adultery. The Old permitted swearing if one swore truly, but the New will know of no swearing. The Old has its stipulated punishment, but the New does not resist the evil.

The Old permitted hatred for the enemy; the New loves him who hates, blesses him who curses, prays for those who wish one evil; gives alms in this manner that the left hand does not know what the right has done; says his prayer secretly without evident and excessive babbling of mouth; judges and condemns no one; takes the mote out of the eye of one's brother after having first cast the beam out of one's own eye; fasts without any outward pomp and show; is like a light which is set on a candlestick and lightens everyone in the house; is like a city built on a hill, being everywhere visible; is like good salt that does not become tasteless, being pleasing not to man but to God alone; is like a good eye which illuminates the whole body; takes no anxious thought about clothing or food, but performs his daily and upright tasks; does not cast pearls before swine, nor that which is holy before dogs; seeks, asks and knocks; finding, receiving and having the door opened for him; enters through the narrow way and the small gate; guards himself from the Pharisees and scribes as from false prophets; is a good tree and brings forth good fruit; does the will of his Father, hearing what he should do, and then doing it.

The church of true believers is built upon Christ the chief cornerstone; stands against all the gates of hell, that is, against the wrathful judgment of the Pharisees, of the mighty ones of earth, and of the scribes; is a house and temple of God, against which no wind and no water may do anything, standing secure, so that everything else which withstands the teaching which proceeds from it, denying its truth, may itself finally give evidence that it is a dwelling of God—although it is now maligned by the Pharisees and scribes as a habitation of the devil: yea, finally they shall hear, Behold, the tabernacle of God is with men, and He will dwell with them, and they shall be His people, and God Himself shall be with them, and be their God, etc. But of the house of the Pharisees and scribes, it shall be said, Babylon the great is fallen, is fallen, and is become the habitation of devils, and the hold of every foul spirit, and a cage of every unclean and hateful bird, etc. But to God (through whom everything which boasts that is not, may be manifested that it is) be all honor, praise and glory through His beloved Son, our Lord and Brother Jesus Christ, Amen.

The Mennonite Quarterly Review,
January, 1947.
Translation by Dr. John C. Wenger.

From

THE WRITINGS OF
HANS DENCK*
1495 – 1527

I KNOW FOR CERTAIN THAT THIS VOICE OF CONSCIENCE AND religious feeling tells me the truth. I will therefore listen to it, whatever it may say to me. I shall not allow anyone to take it from me. And when I find it in any creature high or low, I will listen to it once more. Where it directs me I shall go as it desires, and what it warns me against, that I shall avoid. . . .

Where God is not he never can be brought. The Kingdom of God is within you, says the truth. It does not come to him who looks for it outside himself. He who really seeks God really has God, for without God we can neither seek nor find God. . . .

We should not deny the word that is in the heart, but should diligently and earnestly listen to what God in us wants to say. On the other hand, we should not absolutely reject all outward testimony, but should listen to everything and test everything. In this way our mind becomes clearer every day we live, till we hear God speak to us quite plainly, and we become certain of his will. . . .

I esteem the Holy Scriptures above all human treasure: yet not so much as I do the Word of God which is living,

* Typical paragraphs from Denck's writings, translated by various authors.

potent, eternal, free and independent of all elements of this world: for it is God Himself, it is Spirit and not letter, written without pen or paper so that it can never be blotted out. Therefore salvation is not bound up with the Scriptures, however good and useful they may be for that purpose. The reason is this. It is not possible for the Scriptures to make a bad heart good. But a good heart illumined with the light of God (a heart with a Divine spark in it) is improved by everything. The Scriptures are for the good and salvation of believers, but for unbelievers they are like everything else, only for their damnation. Therefore the elect of God can be saved without preaching and without Scriptures. Otherwise, how could the unlearned who cannot read, or whole towns and countries which have had no preachers sent to them by God be saved? . . .

The true scholar of Christ is free from all law, because the law of love is written on his heart by God: and according to this law he knows how to judge his actions, even if God had not written anything. Where there is a part that he cannot understand from the whole, he does not despise the testimony of any writing, but looks for it diligently. Still, he does not accept it, unless it is interpreted beforehand through the unction of the Holy Spirit. If he does not perceive a thing in his mind, then he abstains from judgment, and awaits the revelation of God, for a belief or a judgment that has not been opened by the Key of David (enlightened reason) cannot be accepted without great error. . . .

The word which is in the heart we must not deny, but listen diligently and earnestly to what God wishes to say to us, and at the same time not absolutely reject any outward testimony, but listen to and test everything, and then go on in the fear of the Spirit. Then the mind will become clearer and clearer every day until we hear God speaking to us in the plainest fashion, and we become certain of His will, which is that we should renounce all self-will and give ourselves up to freedom, which is God. It is then that we resemble God, and aim at attaining the character of God, as sons of God and joint-heirs with Christ. We live as God would have us live, and as Christ lived. But it is not we that live, but Christ that lives in us. . . .

O, who will give me a voice that I might cry out so loudly that all the world might hear me, that God the Lord, the All-Highest, is and waits in the deepest depths, till those who should be turned to Him are turned! Lord, my God, how is it that things are so in this miserable, wicked world, that Thou art so great and no one finds Thee, that Thou speakest so loudly and no one hears Thee: that Thou art so near to every one, and there is no one who knows Thee by name? . . .

No one can satisfy the law unless he knows and loves Christ. He who fulfils the law through Him has merit, but no ground for boasting before God. It is through God's grace that a way has been opened, which it was impossible for the whole world to open, and for this reason merit belongs not to man but to Jesus Christ, through whom everything that man has, has been granted by God. Whoever boasts of his own merit, as if he had it of himself, destroys the grace of Christ. . . .

To be a Christian is to be in measure like Christ, and to be ready to be offered as He gave Himself to be offered. I do not say that we are perfect as Christ was perfect, but I say rather that we are to seek the perfection which Christ never lost. Christ calls Himself the Light of the World, but He also tells His disciples that they are the light of the world. All Christians in whom the Holy Spirit lives, that is, all real Christians, are one with Christ in God and are like Christ. They will therefore have experiences like His, and what Christ did they will also do. . . .

See that you seek God where He is to be sought, in the temple and dwelling-place of the Divine glory, which is your heart and your soul.

A PROTEST FROM THE
ANABAPTISTS OF MORAVIA
AGAINST DEPORTATION

WE BRETHREN, WHO LOVE GOD AND HIS WORD, THE TRUE
witnesses of our Lord Jesus Christ, banished from many
countries for the name of God and for the cause of divine
truth, and have come hither to the land of Moravia, having assembled together and abode under your jurisdiction,
through the favor and protection of the Most High God, to
whom alone be praise and honour and laud for ever: we
beg you to know, honoured ruler of Moravia, that your officers have come to us and have delivered your message and
command, as indeed is well known to you. Already we have
given a verbal answer, and now we reply in writing: viz.,
that we have forsaken the world, an unholy life, and all
iniquity. We believe in Almighty God, and in his Son our
Lord Jesus Christ, who will protect us henceforth and forever in every peril, and to whom we have devoted our entire
selves, our life, and all that we possess, to keep his commandments, and to forsake all unrighteousness and sin.
Therefore we are persecuted and despised by the whole
world, and robbed of all our property, as was done aforetime to the holy prophets, and even to Christ himself. By
King Ferdinand, the prince of darkness, that cruel tyrant
and enemy of divine truth and righteousness, many of our

brethren have been slaughtered and put to death without mercy, our property seized, our fields and homes laid waste, ourselves driven into exile, and most fearfully persecuted.

After these things we came into Moravia, and for some time have dwelt here in quietness and tranquillity, under your protection. We have injured no one, we have occupied ourselves in heavy toil, which all men can testify. Notwithstanding, with your permission, we are driven by force from our possessions and our homes. We are now in the desert, in woods, and under the open canopy of heaven; but this we patiently endure, and praise God that we are counted worthy to suffer for his name. Yet for your sakes we grieve that you should thus so wickedly deal with the children of God. The righteous are called to suffer; but alas! woe, woe to all those who without reason persecute us for the cause of divine truth, and inflict upon us so many and so great injuries, and drive us from them as dogs and brute beasts! Their destruction, punishment and condemnation draw near, and will come upon them in terror and dismay, both in this life and in that which is to come. For God will require at their hands the innocent blood which they have shed, and will terribly vindicate his saints according to the words of the prophets.

And now that you have with violence bidden us forthwith to depart into exile, let this be our answer: We know not any place where we may securely live; nor can we longer dare remain here for hunger and fear. If we turn to the territories of this or that sovereign, everywhere we find an enemy. If we go forward, we fall into the jaws of tyrants and robbers, like sheep before the ravening wolf and the raging lion. With us are many widows, and babes in their cradle, whose parents that most cruel tyrant and enemy of divine righteousness, Ferdinand, gave to the slaughter, and whose property he seized. These widows and orphans and sick children, committed to our charge by God, and whom the Almighty has commanded us to feed, to clothe, to cher-

ish, and to supply all their need, who cannot journey with
us, nor, unless otherwise provided for, can long live—these
we dare not abandon. We may not overthrow God's law to
observe man's law, although it cost gold, and body and
life. On their account we cannot depart; but rather than
they should suffer injury we will endure any extremity, even
to the shedding of our blood.

Besides, here we have houses and farms, the property that
we have gained by the sweat of our brow, which in the sight
of God and men are our just possession: to sell them we
need time and delay. Of this property we have urgent need
in order to support our wives, widows, orphans and children, of whom we have a great number, lest they die of
hunger. Now we lie in the broad forest, and if God will,
without hurt. Let but our own be restored to us, and we will
live as we have hitherto done, in peace and tranquillity.
We desire to molest no one; not to prejudice our foes, not
even King Ferdinand. Our manner of life, our customs and
conversation, are known everywhere to all. Rather than
wrong any man of a single penny, we would suffer the loss
of a hundred gulden; and sooner than strike our enemy with
the hand, much less with the spear, or sword, or halbert, as
the world does, we would die and surrender life. We carry
no weapon, neither spear nor gun, as is clear as the open
day; and they who say that we have gone forth by thousands to fight, they lie and impiously traduce us to our rulers. We complain of this injury before God and man, and
grieve greatly that the number of the virtuous is so small.
We would that all the world were as we are, and that we
could bring and convert all men to the same belief; then
should all war and unrighteousness have an end.

We answer further: that if driven from this land there remains no refuge for us, unless God shall show us some
special place whither to flee. We cannot go. This land, and
all that is therein, belongs to the God of heaven; and if we
were to give a promise to depart, perhaps we should not

be able to keep it; for we are in the hand of God, who does with us what he wills. By him we were brought hither, and peradventure he would have us dwell here and not elsewhere, to try our faith and our constancy by persecution and adversity. But if it should appear to be his will that we depart hence, since we are persecuted and driven away, then, even without your command, not tardily but with alacrity, we will go whither God shall send us. Day and night we pray unto him that he will guide our steps to the place where he would have us dwell. We cannot and dare not withstand his holy will; nor is it possible for you, however much you may strive. Grant us but a brief space: peradventure our heavenly Father will make known to us his will, whether we are to remain here, or whither we must go. If this be done, you shall see that no difficulty, however great it may be, shall deter us from the path.

Woe, woe, unto you, O ye Moravian rulers, who have sworn to that cruel tyrant and enemy of God's truth, Ferdinand, to drive away his pious and faithful servants! Woe, we say to you! who fear more that frail and mortal man than the living, omnipotent and eternal God, and chase from you, suddenly and inhumanely, the children of God, the afflicted widow, the desolate orphan, and scatter them abroad. Not with impunity will you do this; your oaths will not excuse you, or afford you any subterfuge. The same punishment and torments that Pilate endured will overtake you: who, unwilling to crucify the Lord, yet from fear of Caesar adjudged him to death. God, by the mouth of the prophet, proclaims that he will fearfully and terribly avenge the shedding of innocent blood, and will not pass by such as fear not to pollute and contaminate their hands therewith. Therefore great slaughter, much misery and anguish, sorrow, and adversity, yea, everlasting groaning, pain and torment, are daily appointed you. The Most High will lift his hand against you, now and eternally. This we announce to you in the name of our Lord Jesus Christ, for verily it will not tarry, and shortly you shall see that we have told you nothing but the truth of God, in the name of our Lord Jesus Christ, and are witnesses against you, and against all who set at nought his commandments. We beseech you to forsake iniquity, and to turn to the living God with weeping and lamentation, that you may escape all these woes.

We earnestly entreat you, submissively and with prayers, that you take in good part all these our words. For we testify and speak what we know, and have learned to be true in the sight of God, and from that true Christian affection which we follow after before God and men. Farewell.

Martyrology, The Hanserd Knollys Society, i., 149-153, 1850.

"GOD HAS MERCY ON WHOM HE WILL HAVE MERCY, AND whom he will he hardens" (Rom. ix., 18). These words are the utterances of the almighty and secret will of God, which is pledged to no one, nor anything, and therefore he can without injustice have mercy on whom he will, or condemn whom he will. This will the schoolmen call the 'omnipotent' will, a will that no one can resist. Yes, God has the power and the right to make of us a vessel, either for honour or dishonour, without our being able to reply and say, 'Why hast thou made us so?' Besides this will, however, we find another revealed will of God, according to which God wills that all men should be redeemed and come to the knowledge of the truth. Christ himself has plainly made known this will in the words, "For God so loved the world that he gave his only-begotten Son, that whosoever believes in him might not perish, but have eternal life" (John iii., 16). "He suffered for our sins, and not for our sins only, but for the sins of the whole world. He is also the true light, that lights every man that comes into the world. To them that received him he gave power to become sons of God." Therefore he has commanded us to preach the gospel to every creature, that every one who receives it, who believes and is baptized, may be saved. Hence it follows that according to his revealed will God hardens, darkens or condemns no one and nobody, unless it be one who of his own will and wickedness will be hardened, darkened and condemned, and that is those people to whom Christ comes as to his own and they receive him not. When, therefore, it is said in the Scriptures that no one can resist God's will, the reference is not to the revealed, but to the secret will of God. But any one who does not observe this distinction gets into many difficulties and errors.

The revealed will of God the schoolmen call the "ordered" will, not as though the secret will were without order, for everything that God wills and does is right and good, but he himself is subject to no rule, but his will itself is the rule of all things. The schoolmen call that will ordered, because it is fulfilled according to the word of Scripture, in which he has revealed his will; and so we speak also of the "secret" and "revealed" will of God, not as though there were a double will in God, but the Scripture speaks so in order to accommodate itself to human weakness, that we may know that although God is almighty and can do all things by his power, yet he will not deal with us poor creatures according to his omnipotence, but according to his mercy, which he has shown by his Son. God wills that all men should be saved (I Tim. ii., 4). Who then can resist the will of God? "Nay, but, O man, who art thou that repliest against God? Shall the thing formed say to him who formed it, Why hast thou made me thus?" (Rom. ix., 20). If then God wills that all men should be saved, it must be done according to his will, and therefore the question is whether we will or not. . . .

Only a foolish king could place a goal before his subjects and then say "Now run that you may get there," when he already knows beforehand that they are bound in iron and they cannot run. It were certainly a cunning God, who invites all men to the supper, and really offers his mercy to every one, if he after all did not wish the invited to come.

It were a false God who should say in words, "Come here," and yet in secret in his heart should think, "Sit yonder." It would be an unfaithful God who should publicly offer grace to man, and should clothe him in new raiment, yet in secret take it away from him and prepare hell for him. Cursed be he who maintains that God has commanded us impossible things, for everything that is impossible to our strength is possible by the word which God has sent. . . . As the human eye is capable of seeing light, and yet cannot see it unless the light streams into the eye, likewise man has the power to see the light of faith through the word of God, yet he cannot see this light unless by the heavenly illumination it is borne into his soul. . . . Whoever denies the freedom of the human will, denies and rejects more than half of the Holy Scriptures.

Balthasar Hübmaier, by Henry C. Vedder,
Pp. 186-188; 197.
New York: G. P. Putnam's Sons, 1905.

From

A FORM FOR THE CELEBRATION OF THE LORD'S SUPPER

by

BALTHASAR HÜBMAIER

THE MEANING OF THE LORD'S SUPPER

FIRST—THAT THE MAN WHOLLY AND CERTAINLY BELIEVE THAT Christ has offered and poured out his body and his rose-colored blood for him on the cross in the power of his word as he said, "that is my body which is given for you and that is my blood which is poured out for you for the forgiveness of your sins."

Second—Let a man prove himself whether he has a true, inward and ardent hunger and thirst after the bread that came down from heaven in which truly man lives, and after the drink that flows into eternal life—to eat and drink both in the spirit, faith and truth as Christ teaches us. . . .

Third—Let the man prove himself in thankfulness: That with words and works he is thankful toward God for his great, superabundant and unspeakable love and goodness which he has shown him through his beloved Son and Lord Jesus Christ, especially that he now with the heart gives God praise and thanks. Moreover that he has a mind and will in-

clined to do for Christ his God and Lord as he (Christ)
has done for him. But Christ is not in need of our good
deeds, is not hungry, nor thirsty, is neither naked nor in
prison, but heaven and earth are his and all that is therein;
and so he points us to our neighbors, especially to our
fellow-members of the household of faith that we may fulfill on them the work of this thankfulness in a bodily and
spiritual way; by feeding the hungry, giving drink to the
thirsty, clothing the naked, comforting those in prison, giving
shelter to the suffering. Indeed he will receive this work of
pity from us just as if we had done it to himself. Yes, he
will say on the last day "I was hungry and ye gave me to
eat; I was thirsty and ye gave me to drink; I was naked,
in prison and without shelter and ye have clothed, visited
and housed me," Mat. XXV. He says I, I, I, me, me, me.
From that we learn certainly that all which we do to the
least of his, we do to Christ himself. Indeed he will not allow a single cool drink of water to go unrewarded, Mat. 10.
Whoever then is so minded toward his neighbor, he is in the
true communion of Christ, a member of his body, and
a fellow-member with all saved men.

Fourth—But in order that the church also may have
knowledge of his heart and will, the man now holds communion with her in the breaking of bread in which he gives
to her a public testimonial, yes makes for her a sacrament
or oath and gives her his plighted troth that henceforth he
will offer his body and pour out his blood also for his
brethren in the faith. And this he does not of human wantonness as Peter, but in reliance on the grace and power of
the suffering and bleeding of our Lord Jesus Christ his own
Savior, a living memorial of whose sufferings and death is
now made clear to men by the breaking of this bread and
the administering of the cup.

Fifth—That is the true communion of the saints, which is
not a communion because the bread is broken; but where
the bread is broken because the communion has preceded

and been enclosed in the heart since Christ has come in the flesh. For not all who break the bread are partakers of the body and blood of Christ, which I prove by the traitor Judas. But those who are now in communion inwardly and in spirit, they may also use this bread and wine worthily in an outward way . . .

Sixth—Since now this ceremony and sign pertains wholly to brotherly love, and yet a man who loves his brother as himself is a rare bird, in fact an Indian phoenix now on earth, who can with good conscience take a seat at the supper? Answer. The man who is so minded, so formed in his spirit and heart, inwardly sensible that he truly and from his heart can say, "the love of God which he has proven to me in offering his only begotten and dearly beloved son in payment of my sins as I have heard in his holy word and am certainly assured, has so moved, softened and permeated my spirit and soul, that I also am likewise disposed and willing to offer my flesh and blood, to rule over it and so master it that it must be obedient to me against its own will; further not to take advantage of, deceive or injure my neighbor in any way in body, soul, honor or goods, nor offend his wife or children, but rather for him go into the fire and die and as Paul even desired to be a curse for his brethren and Moses to be rooted out of the book of the living for his people."

Such a man may well take a seat at the supper of Christ with a good conscience and worthiness. . . .

Seventh—Since now the men are inwardly and wholly devoted to their fellow-members with honor, goods, body and life, even to the stretching their souls into hell for them with the help of God; hereupon it is indeed necessary again heartily to groan and pray to God that he would increase the faith of these new men, also to kindle in them the fire of brotherly love still better; so that they may increase more and more, grow up and persevere until the end in those two articles signified by water baptism and the

supper. Here there should be a common silence in order
that everyone who wishes to come to the table of God may
meditate upon the sufferings of Christ and so therein rest
with Saint John upon the Lord's breast. After this silence
the Lord's prayer is repeated by the church with devotion
and with hearts that desire grace. . . .

Eighth—Let the priest carefully explain that here bread is
bread and wine is wine and not flesh and blood as men have
for a long time believed.

Whoever would eat of this bread and drink of this drink
of the supper, let him stand up and repeat with heart and
mouth the following covenant:

THE COVENANT

Brethren and sisters, will you love God in the power of his
holy and living word, before, in and above all things, serve,
honor and pray to him alone and henceforth follow his
name; (will you) also subject your fleshly and sinful will
to his divine will which he has worked in you through his
living word, for life and death? Let each one separately say,
I WILL. Will you love your neighbor and fulfill on him the
works of brotherly love, offer your flesh and pour out your
blood for him, (will you) be obedient to father, mother
and all magistracy according to the will of God, and this in
the power of our Lord Jesus Christ who also offered his
flesh and poured out his blood for us? Let us each one separately say, I WILL. Will you use brotherly chastisement toward your brethren and sisters, make peace and harmony
between them, also reconcile yourself with all those who
have offended you, drop envy, hate and all evil will toward
any; willingly desist from all actions and dealings which injure, damage or vex your neighbor, also love your enemies
and do good to them; (and will you) exclude (from the
church) all those who are not willing so to do according to
the order of Christ, Mat. XVIII, c. Let each one separately say, I WILL. Do you desire hereon in the supper of

Christ by the eating of the bread and the drinking of the wine to confirm publicly before the church this covenant which you have just now made and to testify to the power of the living memorial of the suffering and death of Jesus Christ our Lord? Let each one separately say, I DESIRE it in the power of God.

Therefore eat and drink with one another in the name of God, Father, Son and Holy Ghost. May he give us all power and strength that we spend the time according to his holy will (and) worthy of salvation. The Lord communicate to us his grace. Amen.

The Baptist Review and Expositor, Jan'y, 1906,
"An Anabaptist Liturgy of the Lord's Supper,"
Translated by W. J. McGlothlin, Ph. D.

THE WRITINGS OF

MENNO SIMONS

1 4 9 6 – 1 5 6 1

CHRIST'S CHURCH CONSISTS OF THE CHOSEN OF GOD, HIS saints and beloved who have washed their robes in the blood of the Lamb, who are born of God and led by Christ's Spirit, who are in Christ and Christ in them, who hear and believe His word, live in their weakness according to His commandments and in patience and meekness follow in His footsteps, who hate evil and love the good, earnestly desiring to apprehend Christ as they are apprehended of Him. For all who are in Christ are new creatures, flesh of His flesh, bone of His bone and members of His body. . . .

Some of the parables, as of the net in which good and bad fishes are caught; of the wise and foolish virgins and their lamps; of the wedding of the king's son and the guests, and of the threshing floor with wheat and chaff, although the Lord spoke them in allusion to the church, yet they were not spoken for the purpose that the church should knowingly and willfully accept and suffer open transgressors in its communion; because in that case Christ and Paul would differ in doctrine, for Paul says that such should be disciplined and avoided. But they were spoken because many intermingle with the Christians in a Christian semblance, and place themselves under the Word and its sacraments who in fact are no Christians, but are hypocrites and dissemblers before their God; and these are likened unto the refuse fish which will be cast out by the angels at the day of Christ; unto the foolish virgins who had no oil in their lamps; unto the guest without a wedding garment and unto the chaff. For they pretend that they fear God and seek Christ; they receive baptism and the Lord's Supper and outwardly have a good appearance, but do not have faith, repentance, true fear and love of God, Spirit, power, fruit, works and deeds. . . .

Some of them charge and assert that we have our property in common. We reply that this charge is false and altogether without foundation. We do not teach nor practice the doctrine of having all property in common. But we teach and maintain by the word of the Lord that all true believers are members of one body, are baptized by one Spirit into one body (I Cor. 10:18) and have one Lord and one God (Eph. 4: 5, 6).

Inasmuch as they are thus one, therefore it is Christian and reasonable that they truly love one another and that the one member be solicitous for the welfare of the other, for both the Scriptures and nature teach it. All Scripture urges charity and love, and it is the one sign by which a true Christian may be known, as the Lord says, "By this shall all men know that ye are my disciples (that is, that ye are Christians) if ye have love one to another" (John 13:35).

Beloved reader, it has not been heard of that an intelligent person clothes and cares for one part of his body and leaves the rest destitute and naked. O no, it is but natural to care for all the members. Thus it must be with those who are the Lord's church or body. All who are born of God, are partakers of the Spirit of the Lord, and are called into one body of love, according to the Scriptures, are ready by such love to serve their neighbors, not only with money and goods, but also, according to the example of their Lord and Head, Jesus Christ, in an evangelical manner, with life and blood.

They practice charity and love as much as they have ability; they suffer no one to be a beggar among them; they distribute to the necessity of the saints, receive the miserable, take the stranger into their houses, console the afflicted, assist the needy, clothe the naked, feed the hungry, do not turn their faces from the poor, and do not despise their own suffering members—their own flesh. Isa. 58: 7, 8. . . .

We are not regenerated because we have been baptized, . . . but we are baptized because we have been regenerated by faith and the Word of God (I Pet. 1:23). Regeneration is not the result of baptism, but baptism the result of regeneration. This can indeed not be controverted by any man, or disproved by the Scriptures.

The Scriptures know of only one remedy, which is Christ with His merits, death and blood. Hence, he who seeks the remission of his sins through baptism, rejects the blood of the Lord and makes water his idol. Therefore let every one have a care, lest he ascribe the honor and glory due to Christ to the outward ceremonies and visible elements.

The believing receive remission of sins not through baptism, but in baptism, in the following manner: as with their whole heart they believe the precious Gospel of Jesus Christ which has been preached and taught to them, namely the glad tidings of grace, remission of sins, peace, favor, mercy and eternal life through Jesus Christ, our Lord, they experience a change of mind, renounce self, bitterly repent of their old sinful life, and with all diligence give attendance to the Word of the Lord, who has shown them such great love; and fulfill all that He has taught and commanded in His holy Gospel. Their confidence is firmly established upon the word of grace promising the remission of sins through the precious blood and merits of our Lord Jesus Christ. They therefore receive holy baptism as a token of obedience which proceeds from faith, an evidence before God and His church that they firmly believe in the remission of sins through Christ Jesus, as has been preached and taught them from the Word of God.

This baptism is the very least of all the commandments which He has given. It is a much greater commandment to love your enemies, to do good to those who do evil to you, to pray in spirit and in truth for those who persecute you, to subjugate the flesh under God's word, to tread under your feet all pride, covetousness, impurity, hate, envy and intemperance, to serve your neighbor with gold, silver, with house and possessions, with your hard labor, with counsel and deed, with life and death, nay to be free from all evil desire, unbecoming words and evil works, to love God and His righteousness, His will and commandments with all your heart, and to bear the cross of the Lord Jesus Christ with a joyous heart. Can the commandment of baptism be compared with any of these? I say again, it is the least of all the commandments that were given us, for it is not more than a little outward work, namely the application of a handful of water. Now he who has obtained the most important matter, namely the inward, will nevermore say, "What can water avail me," but will readily with a thankful and obedient heart hear and fulfill the words of God. But as long as he has not the inward work, he may well say, what can water avail me! . . .

Since, then, we do not find in all Scripture a single word by which Christ has ordained the baptism of infants, or that His apostles taught and practiced it, we say and confess rightly that infant baptism is but a human invention, an opinion of men, a perversion of the ordinance of Christ. . . .

To baptize before that which is required for baptism, namely faith, is found is as if one would place the cart before the horse, to sow before plowing, to build before the lumber is at hand, or to seal the letter before it is written. . . .

They appeal to Origen and Augustine and say that these assert that they have obtained infant baptism from the apostles. To this we reply and inquire whether Origen and Augustine have proved it from Scripture. If they have done so, we desire to hear it. But if not, we must hear and believe Christ and His apostles and not Augustine and Origen. . . .

Again, if the infant baptists assert that infant baptism is not forbidden and that therefore it is right, I reply that it is not expressly forbidden in the Holy Scriptures to bless, as they call it, holy water, candles, palms, goblets, and robes, to hold mass and other ceremonies, yet we say rightfully that it is wrong, first because people put their trust in these things, secondly because it is done without the commandment of God, for He has commanded us not a word thereof, and never should any commandment be observed which is not contained or implied in His holy Word, either in letter or spirit. . . .

I know that Luther teaches that faith is present in infants, just as in a believing, sleeping man. To this I reply, first, that if there were such a sleeping faith in little unconscious infants (which however is nothing but human sophistry), it would notwithstanding be improper to baptize such children so long as they would not verbally confess it and show the required fruits. For the holy apostles did not baptize any believers while they were asleep, as we have shown in our former writings. . . .

And although infants have neither faith nor baptism, think not therefore that they are lost. O no! they are saved, for they have the Lord's own promise of the Kingdom of God; not indeed through any element, ceremony or external rites, but only by grace through Jesus Christ. And therefore we do truly believe that grace is extended to them, yea that they are acceptable to God, pure and holy, heirs of God and of eternal life. On the ground of this promise all Christian believers may be assured of and rejoice in the truth that their children are saved. . . .

Zwingli taught that the will of God actuated a thief to steal and a murderer to kill, and that their punishment was also brought about by the will of God—which in my opinion is an abomination above all abominations. . . .

What shall I say, dear Lord? Shall I say that Thou hast ordained the wicked to wickedness, as some have said? Be that far from me. I know, O Lord, that Thou art good and nothing evil can be found in Thee. We are the works of Thy hand, created in Christ Jesus unto good works, that we should walk therein. Life and death hast Thou left to our choice. Thou willest not the death of the sinner, but that he should repent and live. Thou art the eternal light, therefore hatest Thou all darkness; Thou desirest not that any should perish, but that all repent, come to a knowledge of Thy truth and be saved. O dear Lord, so grievously have they blasphemed Thine unspeakably great love, Thy mercy and majesty that they have made Thee, the God of all grace and Creator of all things, a very devil, saying that Thou art the cause of all evil—Thou who art called the Father of lights. Of a surety evil can not come from good, nor light from darkness, nor life from death; yet do they ascribe their stubborn hearts and carnal minds to Thy will, in order that they may continue upon the broad way and have a cover for their sins. . . .

The regenerated do not go to war nor fight. They are the children of peace who have beaten their swords into plowshares and their spears into pruning hooks and know of no war. They give to Caesar the things that are Caesar's and to God the things that are God's. Their sword is the word of the Spirit which they wield with a good conscience through the Holy Ghost. . . .

Since we are to be conformed to the image of Christ (Rom. 8:29), how can we, then, fight our enemies with the sword? Does not the apostle Peter say: "For even hereunto were ye called, because Christ also suffered for us, leaving us an example, that ye should follow his steps; who did no sin neither was guile found in his mouth; who, when he was reviled, reviled not again; when he suffered he threatened not; but committed himself to him that judgeth righteously" (I Pet. 2:21-23; Matt. 16-24). And this accords with the words of John who says: "He that saith he abideth in him ought himself also so to walk, even as he walked" (I John 2:6). And Christ Himself says: "Whosoever will come after me, let him deny himself, and take up his cross and follow me" (Mark 8:34; Luke 9:23). Again: "My sheep hear my voice . . . and they follow me" (John 10:27). . . .

My dear reader, if the poor, ignorant world with an honest heart accepted this our hated and despised doctrine, which is not of us but of Christ, and faithfully obeyed it, they could well change their deadly swords into plowshares and their spears into pruning hooks, level their gates and walls, dismiss their executioners and henchmen. For all who accept our doctrine in its power, will by God's grace not have any ill will to any one upon earth, and not against their most bitter enemies, much less wrong and harm them by deeds and actions; for they are children of the Most High who from their hearts love that which is good and in their weakness avoid that which is evil; nay, hate it and are inimical thereto. . . .

O man! man! look upon the irrational creatures and learn wisdom. All roaring lions, all frightful bears, all devouring wolves, live in peace among themselves with their own species. But you, poor, helpless creatures, created in God's own image and called rational beings, are born without teeth, claws, and horns and with a feeble nature, speechless and strengthless, yea neither able to walk nor stand,

but have to depend entirely upon maternal care—to teach
you that you should be men of peace and not of strife. . . .

Peter was commanded to put his sword into the sheath.
All Christians are bidden to love their enemies, do good to
those who do them evil, and pray for those who abuse and
persecute them; to give the cloak also if any one sue them
at law for the coat; if they are stricken on the right cheek
to turn to him who abuses them the other also. Say, beloved, how can a Christian, according to the Scriptures,
consistently retaliate, rebel, war, murder, slay, torture, steal,
rob and burn cities and conquer countries? Matt. 26:52,
John 18:10; Matt. 5:12, 39, 40. . . .

I am well aware that the tyrants who boast themselves
Christians attempt to justify their horrible wars and shedding of blood, and would make a good work of it, by re-
ferring us to Moses, Joshua, etc. But they do not reflect that
Moses and his successors, with their iron sword, have served
out their time, and that Jesus Christ has now given us a new
commandment and has girded our loins with another sword.
They do not consider that they use the sword of war,
which they wield, contrary to all evangelical Scripture,
against their own brethren, namely those of like faith with
them who have received the same baptism and have broken
the same bread with them and are thus members of the
same body. . . .

Again, our fortress is Christ, our defence is patience, our
sword is the Word of God, and our victory is the sincere,
firm, unfeigned faith in Jesus Christ. Spears and swords of
iron we leave to those who, alas, consider human blood and
swine's blood of well nigh equal value. He that is wise, let
him judge what I mean. . . .

Captains, knights, soldiers and such like bloody men are
offering to sell soul and body for money, and swear with
uplifted hand that they will destroy cities and countries, apprehend and kill the citizens and inhabitants and rob them
of their possessions, although they have never harmed

them nor given them any provocation. O what an accursed, wicked, abominable business! And yet it is said that they protect the country and people and assist in administering justice. . . .

Christ says, "Ye have heard that it has been said to them of old time: Thou shalt not forswear thyself, but shalt perform unto the Lord thine oaths. But I say unto you: Swear not at all, neither by heaven, for it is God's throne, nor by the earth, for it is his footstool," etc. (Matt. 5:33-35).

The oath is required for no other purpose than to obtain truthful statement and testimony. Can, then, the truth not be told without an oath? Do all tell the truth who are under oath? You will admit that the first question is to be answered in the affirmative and the second in the negative.

Is, then, the oath itself the truth of the testimony, or does the truth depend upon him who swears the oath? Why then do not the authorities require the truth to be told with yea and nay, as ordained of God, rather than with an oath which God has forbidden? For they can notwithstanding punish those who are found false in their yea and nay, the same as those who commit perjury. . . .

That yea is yea and nay nay with all true Christians, is fully proved by those who, in our Netherlands, are so tyrannically visited with imprisonment, confiscation and torture, with fire, the stake and the sword, when indeed with one word they could escape all this, if they would misuse their yea and nay. But as they are born of the truth, therefore they walk in the truth, and testify to the truth unto death, as may abundantly be seen in Flanders, Brabant, Holland, West Friesland, etc. . . .

Tell me, kind reader, where have you, in all the days of your life read in the apostolic Scriptures, or heard, that Christ or the apostles called upon the power of the magistracy against those who would not hear their doctrine or obey their words? Yea, reader, I know to a certainty that wherever the government is to perform the ban with the sword, there is not the true knowledge, Spirit, word and church of Christ. . . .

Faith is a gift of God, therefore it cannot be forced upon any one by worldly authorities or by the sword; alone through the pure doctrine of the holy Word and with humble ardent prayer it must be obtained of the Holy Ghost as a gift of grace. Moreover it is not the will of the Master of the house that the tares should be rooted up as long as the day of reaping is not at hand, as the Scriptural parable teaches and shows with great clearness.

Now if our persecutors are Christians, as they think, and accept the word of God, why do they not heed and follow the word and commandment of Christ? Why do they root up the tares before the time? Why do they not fear, lest they root up the good wheat, and not the tares? Why do they undertake to do the duty of angels who, at the proper time, shall bind the tares in bundles and cast them into the furnace of everlasting fire? . . .

Further I say: If the government rightly knew Christ and His kingdom, they would in my opinion, rather choose death, than with their worldly power and sword undertake to settle spiritual matters, which are not subject to the authority of man but to that of the great and Almighty God alone. But now they [the magistrates] are taught by their theologians that they should arrest, imprison, torture and slay those who are not obedient to their doctrine, as may, alas, be seen, in many cities and countries. . . .

Beloved rulers and judges, if you take to heart these cited Scriptures, and diligently reflect upon them, you will observe that your office is not your own, but God's office and service; and it is in your place to humble yourselves before His majesty, fear His great and adorable name and rightly and reasonably perform your ordained office; further that you should not so unscrupulously, with your earthly and temporal power, undertake to adjust that which belongs to the jurisdiction and kingdom of Christ, the Prince of all princes, you should not by your iron sword judge and punish that which is reserved solely for the judgment of the Most High, namely the faith and matters pertaining thereto, as also Luther and others maintained in the beginning of his labors, but after they had come to a higher and more exalted station, they have forgotten it all.

How many pious children of God have they for the testimony of God and their conscience' sake within a few years deprived of their homes and possessions, have confiscated their needed property, and committed it to the bottomless money chests of the Emperor; how many have they betrayed, driven out of cities and countries and put them to the stocks and torture, turning the poor orphans naked into the streets. Some they have hanged, some they have tortured with inhuman tyranny and afterwards choked them with cords at the stake. Some they have roasted and burned alive. Some they have killed with the sword and given them to the fowls of the air to devour. Some they have cast to the fishes; some had their houses destroyed; some have been cast into slimy bogs. Some had their feet cut off, one of whom I have seen and conversed with. Others wander about here and there, in want, homelessness and affliction in mountains and deserts, in holes and caves of the earth, as Paul says. They must flee with their wives and little children from one country to another, from one city to another. They are hated, abused, slandered and belied by all men. By the theologians and the magistrates they are denounced. They are deprived of their food, are driven forth in the cold winter and pointed at with the finger of scorn; yea whoever can assist in the persecution of the poor oppressed Christians, thinks he has done God service, as Christ says, John 16:2. . . .

However lamentably we may here be persecuted, oppressed, smitten, robbed, burned at the stake, drowned in the water by the hellish Pharoah and his cruel, unmerciful servants, yet soon shall come the day of our refreshing and all the tears shall be wiped from our eyes and we shall be arrayed in the white silken robes of righteousness, follow the Lamb, and with Abraham, Isaac and Jacob sit down in the kingdom of God and possess the precious, pleasant land of eternal, imperishable joy. Praise God and lift up your heads, ye who suffer for Jesus' sake; the time is near when ye shall hear, "Come ye blessed" and ye shall rejoice with Him for ever more.

Menno Simons' Life and Writings, by Harold S. Bender.
Scottdale, Pennsylvania: Mennonite Publishing House, 1936.

RICHARD
HOOKER

1553 – 1600

RICHARD HOOKER

RH

THE PROTESTANT REFORMATION FOUND UNIQUE EXPRESSION in the Church of England. When Henry VIII broke with the pope and assumed the headship of the English church, he had behind him a strong body of popular support. The influence of Wycliffe had never died out; the Lollards had persisted, so that the Bishop of London arrested five hundred of them in 1521; and public protest had grown against the papal hierarchy, the covetous exactions of the priests, the manifold abuses of the monasteries, and the degenerate condition of the local parishes. While, however, it is utterly superficial to ascribe the English Reformation to Henry VIII's desire for a divorce from Catherine and to his further matrimonial difficulties, the fact that the open rupture between England and the papacy was precipitated by the king, for personal and political reasons, strongly affected the outcome.

So far as theological dogma was concerned, Henry VIII was a good Romanist. He had reacted vehemently against Lutheranism; Pope Leo X entitled him "Defender of the Faith" as a reward for his book against Luther; and, after the English clergy had confirmed the king's judgment "that the Bishop of Rome has not, in Scripture, any greater

jurisdiction in the kingdom of England than any other foreign bishop," one of his early pronouncements affirmed "Six
Articles," to be held and observed, with heavy penalties
named for any disregard of them. These articles affirmed the
Roman doctrine of the Mass, the refusal to the laity of
"communion in both kinds," the celibacy of the clergy, the
binding nature of vows of chastity or widowhood, the
lawfulness of private masses, and the necessity of auricular
confession to a priest.

While, therefore, Henry VIII decisively denied the pope's
supremacy, assumed for himself the headship of the English
church, took over the adjudication of all ecclesiastical appeals, which formerly had gone to Rome, and otherwise
acted for his own profit and convenience, as in his seizure of
the monasteries and their wealth, he left the episcopal structure of the Church of England and its basic dogmas for the
most part unchanged. The Bible, the Apostles', Nicene and
Athanasian creeds, and the dogmas of the first four Ecumenical Councils were still the norm of orthodoxy; the
sacrament of penance, with confession, was retained as necessary; baptism was declared essential to salvation—infants
shall "undoubtedly be saved thereby, and *else not;*" and
the saints and the Virgin Mary were to be invoked as inter-
cessors.

To be sure, men like Thomas Cranmer had done their
best to lead the king toward a more thorough reformation,
and their influence is seen in such Injunctions (1538) as
that "one whole Bible *of the largest volume* in English" is
to be placed in every church where the people most readily
can read it, "for it is the lively word of God that every
Christian man is bound to embrace and follow." Only when
Edward VI succeeded Henry VIII, however, did the government come under the control of men who were committed to
a more decisive policy of reformation. The *Act of the Six
Articles* was dropped from the statute books; the Lord's
Supper was ordered served to communicants in both kinds;

all laws against the marriage of the clergy were declared void; images in the churches, which had been "abused" as objects of pilgrimage were ordered destroyed; many Romanist bishops, deprived of their sees, were replaced by Reformers; and *The Boke of Common Praier* was introduced to give uniformity to the worship of the church.

When Mary Tudor succeeded Edward VI, however, the hope of restoring the papal supremacy was far from dead. If persecution could have achieved that end, Mary would have succeeded. Two hundred and eighty-eight persons were burnt in her reign, Strype estimates, "besides those that dyed of famine in sondry prisons." The country was religiously split asunder, and when Queen Elizabeth succeeded Mary Tudor, she faced a situation which demanded all the great statesmanship she possessed.

Elizabeth steered a middle course. Above all else she wanted a united England. To gain it she surrendered neither to the Romanists on one side nor to the Puritans upon the other, but held to a mediating policy, which ever since has been one of the distinctive characteristics of the Church of England. She decisively set the direction which the English church was to follow, despite the internal dissensions under James I, Charles I, the Cromwellian interlude, and the controversial reigns of Charles II and James II. The story of this stormy development and of the consequences of the church's mediating course can be found in such books as *A History of the Church of England,* by M. W. Patterson; *The Reformation in England,* by L. Elliott Burns; *The History of the Church of England,* by Richard Watson Dixon; *Documents Illustrative of English Church History,* by Henry Gee and William John Hardy; *Anglicanism,* by Paul Elmer More and Frank Leslie Cross; and *Cranmer and the Reformation,* by F. E. Hutchinson.

For the purposes of this anthology, a few keynotes of the Church of England may be especially stressed.

She held stoutly to the orthodoxy of the ancient creeds—

as, indeed, did all the primary Protestant Reformers—but she minimized anything that she could possibly regard as non-essential. As Jeremy Taylor put it, men should "not make more necessities than God made, which indeed are not many." What Protestant Reformer could go further than William Chillingworth did? "I am fully assured that God does not and therefore that men ought not to require any more of any man than this, to believe Scripture to be God's Word, to endeavor to find the true sense of it, and to live according to it."

She displayed in some of her outstanding leaders a strong tendency thus to simplify the faith, without thinning it out. Said Ralph Cudworth, "The Gospel is nothing else but God descending into the world in our form and conversing with us in our likeness . . . that He might deify us, that is (as St. Peter expresses it) make us *partakers of the divine Nature*." If, on one side, the English church threw over many Roman dogmas, on the other, her outstanding leaders repudiated the whole Calvinistic doctrine of predestination, "which doctrine," said William Laud, "my very soul abominates; for it makes God, the God of all mercies, to be the most fierce and unreasonable tyrant in the world."

Earnestly desiring to make religion a unifying and not a divisive force in England, the church became increasingly inclusive. To be sure, she shut out faithful Romanists on one side and stalwart Puritans on the other, but she reached out so far in both directions that many who else would have remained Romanists and Puritans came into her communion.

She emphasized the external form and order of the church —its episcopacy, its sacraments, its uniform worship through the enforced employment of the *Book of Common Prayer*, its ceremonies, festivals and ritual traditions. Indeed, the distinctive quality of the English church is revealed in the fact that her unique contribution was not an outstanding prophetic voice or a revolutionary theologian, but a prayer book. She had a flair for the practical. Whatever differences of opinion might divide her people, she wanted them united in worship. It is typical that the first important theological treatise from an English churchman was on a practical subject, *The Laws of Ecclesiastical Polity*, by Richard Hooker.

While, in her sometimes desperate endeavors to unify England religiously, she did her full share of persecution, after the manner of her times, she claimed no infallibility herself and she disclaimed it in everybody else. Said Richard Hooker: "Two things there are which trouble greatly these later times: one that the Church of Rome cannot, another that Geneva will not, err."

The Church of England is unique among the major movements of the Reformation in that no man's name is associated with her. She had no Luther or Zwingli, no Calvin or John Knox. It is the more difficult, therefore, for the anthologist to discover in any single writer an adequate expression of the English church's position. Richard Hooker, however, has a status which few would dispute. Trained at Oxford to good purpose, he was made an Oxford Fellow at the age of twenty-four, and a few years later was appointed to the mastership of the Temple, where he preached at the morning service. It is typical of Elizabethan times that his disappointed rival for the position, Walter Travers, a Presbyterian, who preached at the evening service, was accustomed to refute at night what Hooker had said in the morning, with Hooker replying the next Sunday, so that the saying gained currency, "The forenoon sermon spake Canterbury, the afternoon Geneva." It may have been this debate, accompanied by dissatisfaction with its fragmentary character, which led Hooker to his life work. He petitioned for removal to a country pastorate, and there he devoted the remainder of his life to writing his masterpiece, *The Laws of Ecclesiastical Polity*. Its aim was not only to refute the claims of Roman Catholicism, but especially to answer the attacks of the Presbyterians on Episcopalian polity and customs, and in particular to correct their too strict legalism in their treatment of the Scriptures. Its many excellencies of substance, spirit and style have gained it a permanent place in the literature of the church, and no brief excerpts can do it justice.

Richard Hooker, by L. S. Thornton, and *Richard Hooker and Contemporary Religious Ideas*, by F. J. Shirley, are important interpretations of the man and his times.

From

THE LAWS OF

ECCLESIASTICAL POLITY

HAVING FOUND THIS THE HEAD THEOREM OF ALL THEIR DIS-
courses, who plead for the change of Ecclesiastical Government in England, namely, "That the Scripture of God is in
such sort the rule of human actions, that simply whatsoever
we do, and are not by it directed thereunto, the same is
sin"; we hold it necessary that the proofs hereof be
weighed. Be they of weight sufficient or otherwise, it is not
ours to judge and determine; only what difficulties there
are which as yet withhold our assent till we be further and
better satisfied, I hope, no indifferent amongst them will
scorn or refuse to hear. First, therefore, whereas they allege, "That Wisdom" doth teach men "every good way";
(Prov. ii. 9.) and have thereupon inferred that no way is
good in any kind of action unless Wisdom do by Scripture
lead unto it; see they not plainly how they restrain the
manifold ways which Wisdom hath to teach men by, to
one only way of teaching, which is by Scripture? The
bounds of Wisdom are large, and within them much is contained. Wisdom was Adam's instructor in Paradise; Wisdom indued the Fathers who lived before the Law with the
knowledge of holy things; by the Wisdom of the Law of
God, David attained to excel others in understanding, and
Solomon likewise to excel David by the self-same Wisdom of
God, teaching him many things besides the Law. The ways

337

of well-doing are in number even as many, as are the kinds of voluntary actions; so that whatsoever we do in this world, and may do it ill, we shew ourselves therein by well-doing to be wise. Now if Wisdom did teach men by Scripture not only all the ways that are right and good in some certain kind, according to that of St. Paul concerning the use of Scripture, but did simply, without any manner of exception, restraint, or distinction, teach every way of doing well, there is no art but Scripture should teach it, because every art doth teach the way how to do something or other well. To teach men, therefore, Wisdom professeth, and to teach them every good way; but not every good way by one way of teaching. Whatsoever either Men on Earth, or the Angels of Heaven do know, it is as a drop of that unemptiable Fountain of Wisdom; which Wisdom hath diversely imparted her treasures unto the world. As her ways are of sundry kinds, so her manner of teaching is not merely one and the same. Some things she openeth by the Sacred Books of Scripture; some things by the glorious works of Nature; with some things she inspireth them from above by spiritual influence; in some things she leadeth and traineth them only by worldly experience and practice. We may not so in any one special kind admire her, that we disgrace her in any other; but let all her ways be according unto their place and degree adored. . . .

God may be glorified by obedience, and obeyed by performance of his will, and his will be performed with an actual intelligent desire to fulfill that Law which maketh known what his will is, although no special clause or sentence of Scripture be in every such action set before men's eyes to warrant it. For Scripture is not the only Law whereby God hath opened his will touching all things that may be done; but there are other kinds of Laws which notify the will of God, as in the former Book hath been proved at large; nor is there any Law of God, whereunto he doth not account our obedience his glory. "Do therefore all things unto the glory of God (saith the Apostle), be inoffensive both to the Jews and Grecians, and the Church of God; even as I please all men in all things, not seeking mine own commodity, but many's, that they may be saved." In the least thing done disobediently towards God, or offensively against the good of men, whose benefit we ought to seek for as for our own, we plainly shew that we do not acknowledge God to be such as indeed he is, and consequently that we glorify him not. This the blessed Apostle teacheth; but doth any Apostle teach, that we cannot glorify God otherwise than only in doing what we find that God in Scripture commandeth us to do? . . .

An earnest desire to draw all things unto the determination of bare and naked Scripture, hath caused here much pains to be taken in abating the estimation and credit of man. Which if we labour to maintain as far as truth and reason will bear, let us not think that we travail about a matter not greatly needful. For the scope of all their pleadings against Man's Authority, is to overthrow such Orders, Laws, and Constitutions in the Church, as depending thereupon, if they should therefore be taken away, would peradventure leave neither face nor memory of Church to continue long in the world, the world especially being such as now it is. That which they have in this case spoken, I would for brevity's sake let pass; but that the drift of their speech being so dangerous, their words are not to be neglected. Wherefore to say that simply an argument taken from Man's Authority doth hold no way, neither affirmatively nor negatively, is hard. By a man's authority we here understand the force which his word hath for the assurance of another's mind that buildeth upon it; as the Apostle somewhat did upon their report of the house of Chloe; and the Samaritans in a matter of far greater moment upon the report of a simple woman. For so it is said in St. John's Gospel, "Many of the Samaritans of that city believed in him for the saying of the woman, which testi-

fied, He hath told me all things that ever I did." The
strength of man's authority is affirmatively such, that the
weightiest affairs in the world depend thereon. . . .

For whatsoever we believe concerning salvation by Christ,
although the Scripture be therein the ground of our belief;
yet the authority of man is, if we mark it, the key which
openeth the door of entrance into the knowledge of the
Scripture. The Scripture doth not teach us the things that
are of God, unless we did credit men who have taught us
that the words of Scripture do signify those things. Some
way therefore, notwithstanding man's infirmity, yet his authority may enforce assent. Upon better advice and deliberation so much is perceived, and at the length confest, that
arguments taken from the authority of men, may not only
so far forth as hath been declared, but further also be of
some force in "human sciences"; which force be it never so
small, doth shew that they are not utterly naught. But in
"matters divine" it is still maintained stiffly, that they have
no manner of force at all. Howbeit, the very self-same reason, which causeth to yield that they are of some force in
the one, will at the length constrain also to acknowledge
that they are not in the other altogether unforcible. For if
the natural strength of man's wit may by experience and
study attain unto such ripeness in the knowledge of things
human, that men in this respect may presume to build
somewhat upon their judgment; what reason have we to
think but that even in matters divine, the like wits furnisht
with necessary helps, exercised in Scripture with like diligence, and assisted with the grace of Almighty God, may
grow unto so much perfection of knowledge, that men
should have just cause, when any thing pertinent unto faith
and religion is doubted of, the more willingly to in-
cline their minds towards that which the sentence of so
grave, wise, and learned in that faculty shall judge most
sound? . . .

The testimonies of God are true, the testimonies of God

are perfect, the testimonies of God are all-sufficient unto that end for which they were given. Therefore accordingly do we receive them; we do not think that in them God hath omitted any thing needful unto his purpose, and left his intent to be accomplished by our devisings. What the Scripture purposeth, the same in all points it doth perform. Howbeit, that here we swerve not in judgment, one thing especially we must observe, namely, that the absolute perfection of Scripture is seen by relation unto that end whereto it tendeth. And even hereby it cometh to pass, that first such as imagine the general and main drift of the body of sacred Scripture not to be so large as it is, nor that God did thereby intend to deliver, as in truth he doth, a full instruction of all things unto salvation necessary, the knowledge whereof man by nature could not otherwise in this life attain unto; they are by this very mean induced either still to look for new revelations from Heaven, or else dangerously to add to the Word of God uncertain Tradition, that so the doctrine of man's salvation may be complete; which doctrine we constantly hold in all respects without any such thing added to be so complete, that we utterly refuse as much as once to acquaint ourselves with any thing further. Whatsoever, to make up the doctrine of man's salvation, is added as in supply of the Scripture's unsufficiency, we reject it. Scripture purposing this, hath perfectly and fully done it. Again, the scope and purpose of God in delivering the Holy Scripture, such as do take more largely than behoveth, they on the contrary side, racking and stretching it further than by him was meant, are drawn into sundry as great inconveniences. These, pretending the Scripture's perfection, infer thereupon, that in Scripture all things lawful to be done must needs be contained. We count those things perfect which want nothing requisite for the end whereto they were instituted. As, therefore, God created every part and particle of man exactly perfect, that is to say, in all points sufficient unto that use for which he appointed it; so the

Scripture, yea, every sentence thereof, is perfect, and wanteth nothing requisite unto that purpose for which God
delivered the same. So that if hereupon we conclude, that
because the Scripture is perfect, therefore all things lawful to
be done are comprehended in the Scripture; we may even as
well conclude so of every sentence, as of the whole sum and
body thereof, unless we first of all prove that it was the
drift, scope, and purpose of Almighty God in Holy Scripture to comprise all things which man may practise. But
admit this, and mark, I beseech you, what would follow.
God in delivering Scripture to his Church should clean
have abrogated amongst them the Law of Nature, which is
an infallible knowledge imprinted in the minds of all the
children of men, whereby both general principles for direct-
ing of human actions are comprehended, and conclusions
derived from them; upon which conclusions groweth in par-
ticularity the choice of good and evil in the daily affairs
of this life. Admit this, and what shall the Scripture be but
a snare and a torment to weak consciences, filling them with
infinite perplexities, scrupulosities, doubts insoluble, and extreme despairs. Not that the Scripture itself doth cause any
such thing (for it tendeth to the clean contrary, and the
fruit thereof is resolute assurance and certainty in that it
teacheth), but the necessities of this life urging men to do
that which the light of Nature, common discretion, and
judgment of itself directeth them unto; on the other side,
this doctrine teaching them that so to do were to sin against
their own souls, and that they put forth their hands to iniquity whatsoever they go about and have not first the sacred Scripture of God for direction; how can it choose but
bring the simple a thousand times to their wits' end? how
can it choose but vex and amaze them? For in every action
of common life, to find out some sentence clearly and infallibly setting before our eyes what we ought to do (seem
we in Scripture never so expert), would trouble us more
than we are aware. In weak and tender minds we little

know what misery this strict opinion would breed, besides
the stops it would make in the whole course of all men's lives
and actions. Make all things sin which we do by direction
of Nature's light, and by the rule of common discretion,
without thinking at all upon Scripture; admit this position, and parents shall cause their children to sin as oft as
they cause them to do any thing before they come to years
of capacity, and be ripe for knowledge in the Scripture: admit this, and it shall not be with masters as it was with
him in the Gospel; but servants "being commanded to go,"
shall stand still till they have their errand warranted unto
them by Scripture. Which, as it standeth with Christian
duty in some cases, so in common affairs to require it were
most unfit. Two opinions therefore there are concerning sufficiency of Holy Scripture, each extremely opposite unto
the other, and both repugnant unto truth. The schools of
Rome teach Scripture to be unsufficient, as if, except Traditions were added, it did not contain all revealed and supernatural truth which absolutely is necessary for the children
of men in this life to know, that they may in the next be
saved. Others justly condemning this opinion, grow likewise
unto a dangerous extremity, as if Scripture did not only
contain all things in that kind necessary, but all things simply, and in such sort, that to do any thing according to any
other Law, were not only unnecessary, but even opposite
unto salvation, unlawful and sinful. Whatsoever is spoken of
God, or things appertaining to God, otherwise than as the
truth is, though it seem an honour, it is an injury. And as
incredible praises given unto men do often abate and impair
the credit of their deserved commendation; so we must likewise take great heed, lest, in attributing unto Scripture more
than it can have, the incredibility of that do cause even
those things which indeed it hath most abundantly, to be
less reverendly esteemed. I therefore leave it to themselves
to consider, Whether they have in this first point or
not overshot themselves; which, God doth know, is quickly

done, even when our meaning is most sincere, as I am verily persuaded theirs in this case was. . . .

But we must note, that he which affirmeth speech to be necessary amongst all men throughout the world, doth not thereby import that all men must necessarily speak one kind of language; even so the necessity of Polity and Regiment in all Churches may be held without holding any one certain Form to be necessary in them all. Nor is it possible that any Form of Polity, much less of Polity Ecclesiastical, should be good, unless God himself be author of it. "Those things that are not of God (saith Tertullian), they can have no other than God's adversary for their author." Be it whatsoever in the Church of God, if it be not of God, we hate it. Of God it must be; either as those things sometime were, which God supernaturally revealed, and so delivered them unto Moses for government of the commonwealth of Israel; or else as those things which men find out by help of that light which God hath given them unto that end. . . . But forasmuch as no Form of Church-Polity is thought by them to be lawful, or to be of God, unless God be so the author of it that it be also set down in Scripture; they should tell us plainly, whether their meaning be that it must be there set down in whole or in part. For if wholly, let them shew what one Form of Polity ever was so. Their own to be so taken out of Scripture they will not affirm; neither deny they that in part, even this which they so much oppugn is also from thence taken. Again, they should tell us, whether only that be taken out of Scripture which is actually and particularly there set down; or else that also which the general principles and rules of Scripture potentially contain. The one way they cannot as much as pretend, that all the parts of their own Discipline are in Scripture; and the other way their mouths are stopped, when they would plead against all other Forms besides their own; seeing the general principles are such as do not particularly prescribe any one, but sundry may equally be consonant unto the general

axioms of the Scripture. But to give them some larger
scope, and not to close them up in these straits: let their
allegations be considered, wherewith they earnestly bend
themselves against all which deny it necessary that any one
complete Form of Church-Polity should be in Scripture.
First, therefore, whereas it hath been told them that matters
of Faith, and, in general, matters necessary unto Salvation,
are of a different nature from Ceremonies, Order, and the
kind of Church-government; that the one are necessary to be
expressly contained in the Word of God, or else manifestly
collected out of the same, the other not so; that it is necessary not to receive the one, unless there be something in
Scripture for them; the other free, if nothing against them
may thence be alleged. Although there do not appear any
just or reasonable cause to reject or dislike of this; nevertheless, as it is not easy to speak to the contentation
of minds exulcerated in themselves, but that somewhat there
will be always which displeaseth; so herein for two things we
are reproved. The first is, misdistinguishing, because matters
of Discipline and Church-government are (as they say) matters necessary to Salvation and of Faith, whereas we put a
difference between the one and the other. Our second fault
is, injurious dealing with the Scripture of God, as if it contained only the principal points of Religion, some rude and
unfashioned matter of building the Church, but had left out
that which belongeth unto the form and fashion of it; as if
there were in the Scripture no more than only to cover the
Church's nakedness, and not chains, bracelets, rings, jewels,
to adorn her; sufficient to quench her thirst, to kill her hunger, but not to minister a more liberal, and (as it were) a
more delicious and dainty diet. In which case our apology
shall not need to be very long.

The mixture of those things by speech which by Nature
are divided, is the mother of all error. To take away therefore that error, which confusion breedeth, distinction is
requisite. Rightly to distinguish, is by conceit of mind to

sever things different in Nature, and to discern wherein they
differ. So that if we imagine a difference where there is
none, because we distinguish where we should not, it may
not be denied that we misdistinguish. The only trial whether
we do so, yea or no, dependeth upon comparison between
our conceit and the nature of things conceived. Touching
matters belonging unto the Church of Christ, this we conceive, that they are not of one suit. Some things are *merely*
of Faith, which things it doth suffice that we know and believe; some things not only to be known but done, because
they concern the actions of men. Articles about the Trinity
are matters of mere Faith, and must be believed. Precepts
concerning the works of charity are matters of action; which
to know unless they be practised, is not enough. This being
so clear to all men's understanding, I somewhat marvel that
they especially should think it absurd to oppose Church-
government, a plain matter of action, unto matters of Faith,
who know that themselves divide the Gospel into Doctrine
and Discipline. For if matters of Discipline be rightly by
them distinguished from matters of Doctrine, why not matters of Government by us as reasonably set against matters
of Faith? Do not they under Doctrine comprehend the same
which we intend by matters of Faith? Do not they under
Discipline comprise the Regiment of the Church? When they
blame that in us which themselves follow, they give men
great cause to doubt that some other thing than judgment
doth guide their speech. What the Church of God standeth
bound to know or do, the same in part Nature teacheth.
And because Nature can teach them but only in part, neither so fully as is requisite for man's Salvation, nor so
easily as to make the way plain and expedite enough that
many may come to the knowledge of it, and so be saved;
therefore in Scripture hath God both collected the most necessary things that the school of Nature teacheth unto that
end, and revealeth also whatsoever we neither could with
safety be ignorant of, nor at all be instructed in but by su-

pernatural Revelation from him. So that Scripture containing all things that are in this kind any way needful for the Church, and the principal of the other sort, this is the next thing wherewith we are charged as with an error: We teach, that whatsoever is unto salvation termed *necessary* by way of excellency; whatsoever it standeth all men upon to know or to do that they may be saved; whatsoever there is whereof it may truly be said, This not to believe, is eternal death and damnation; or, This every soul that will live, must duly observe; of which sort the Articles of Christian Faith, and the Sacraments of the Church of Christ, are; all such things if Scripture did not comprehend, the Church of God should not be able to measure out the length and the breadth of that way wherein for ever she is to walk; Heretics and Schismatics never ceasing, some to abridge, some to enlarge, all to pervert and obscure, the same. But as for those things that are accessory hereunto, those things that so belong to the way of Salvation as to alter them, is no otherwise to change that way, than a path is changed by altering only the uppermost face thereof; which be it laid with gravel, or set with grass, or paved with stone, remaineth still the same path; in such things, because discretion may teach the Church what is convenient, we hold not the Church further tied herein unto Scripture, than that against Scripture nothing be admitted in the Church, lest that path which ought always to be kept even, do thereby come to be overgrown with brambles and thorns. If this be unsound, wherein doth the point of unsoundness lie? It is not that we make some things *necessary*, some things *accessory* and appendent only: for our Lord and Saviour himself doth make that difference, by terming judgment, and mercy, and fidelity, with other things of like nature, "the greater and weightier matters of the Law." Is it then that we account Ceremonies (wherein we do not comprise Sacraments, or any other the like substantial duties in the exercise of Religion, but only of such external Rites as are usually annexed unto Church actions),

is it an oversight that we reckon these things and matters of
Government in the number of things accessory, not things
necessary in such sort as hath been declared? Let them
which therefore think us blameable consider well their own
words. Do they not plainly compare the one unto garments,
which cover the body of the Church; the other unto rings,
bracelets, and jewels, that only adorn it? The one to that
food which the Church doth live by, the other to that
which maketh her diet liberal, dainty, and more delicious?
Is dainty fare a thing necessary to the sustenance; or to
the clothing of the body, rich attire? If not, how can they
urge the necessity of that which themselves resemble by
things not necessary? or by what construction shall any
man living be able to make those comparisons true, holding that distinction untrue, which putteth a difference between things of external Regiment in the Church and
things necessary unto Salvation. . . .

Concerning Rites and Ceremonies there may be fault, either in the kind or in the number and multitude of them.
The first thing blamed about the kind of ours is, that in
many things we have departed from the ancient simplicity of
Christ and his Apostles; we have embraced more outward
stateliness, we have those Orders in the exercise of Religion,
which they who best pleased God, and served him most devoutly, never had. For it is out of doubt that the first state
of things was best, that in the prime of Christian Religion
Faith was soundest, the Scriptures of God were then best
understood by all men, all parts of godliness did then most
abound; and therefore it must needs follow, that Customs,
Laws, and Ordinances devised since are not so good for the
Church of Christ; but the best way is, to cut off later inventions, and to reduce things unto the ancient state wherein at
the first they were. Which Rule or Canon we hold to be
either uncertain, or at leastwise unsufficient, if not both. For
in case it be certain, hard it cannot be for them to shew us
where we shall find it so exactly set down, that we may say,

without all controversy, These were the Orders of the
Apostles' times, these wholly and only, neither fewer nor
moe [more] than these. True it is, that many things of this
nature be alluded unto, yea, many things declared, and
many things necessarily collected out of the Apostles' writings. But is it necessary that all the Orders of the Church
which were then in use should be contained in their books?
Surely no. For if the tenor of their writings be well observed, it shall unto any man easily appear, that no more of
them are there touched than were needful to be spoken of,
sometimes by one occasion, and sometimes by another. Will
they allow then of any other records besides? Well assured
I am they are far enough from acknowledging, that the
Church ought to keep any thing as Apostolical, which is not
found in the Apostles' writings, in what other records soever it be found. And therefore, whereas St. Augustine affirmeth, that those things which the whole Church of Christ
doth hold, may well be thought to be Apostolical, although
they be not found written; this his judgment they utterly
condemn. I will not here stand in defence of St. Augustine's
opinion, which is, that such things are indeed Apostolical;
but yet with this exception, unless the decree of some general Council have happily caused them to be received: for of
positive Laws and Orders received throughout the whole
Christian world, St. Augustine could imagine no other fountain, save these two. But to let pass St. Augustine, they
who condemn him herein must needs confess it a very uncertain thing, what the Orders of the Church were in the
Apostles' times, seeing the Scriptures do not mention them
all, and other records thereof besides they utterly reject. So
that in tying the Church to the Orders of the Apostles'
times, they tie it to a marvellous uncertain rule; unless they
require the observation of no Orders but only those which
are known to be Apostolical by the Apostles' own writings.
But then is not this their rule of such sufficiency, that we
should use it as a touchstone to try the Orders of the Church

by for ever. Our end ought always to be the same; our ways and means thereunto not so. The glory of God and the good of his Church was the thing which the Apostles aimed at, and therefore ought to be the mark whereat we also level. But seeing those Rites and Orders may be at one time more which at another are less available unto that purpose, what reason is there in these things to urge the state of one only age as a pattern for all to follow? It is not, I am right sure, their meaning that we should now assemble our people to serve God in close and secret meetings; or that common brooks or rivers should be used for places of Baptism; or that the Eucharist should be ministered after meat; or that the custom of Church-feasting should be renewed; or that all kind of standing provision for the Ministry should be utterly taken away, and their estate made again dependent upon the voluntary devotion of men. In these things they easily perceive how unfit that were for the present, which was for the first age convenient enough. The faith, zeal, and godliness of former times is worthily had in honour; but doth this prove that the Orders of the Church of Christ must be still the self-same with theirs, that nothing may be which was not then, or that nothing which then was may lawfully since have ceased? They who recall the Church unto that which was at the first, must necessarily set bounds and limits unto their speeches. If any thing have been received repugnant unto that which was first delivered, the first things in this case must stand, the last give place unto them. But where difference is without repugnancy, that which hath been can be no prejudice to that which is. Let the state of the people of God when they were in the house of bondage, and their manner of serving God in a strange land, be compared with that which Canaan and Jerusalem did afford; and who seeth not what huge difference there was between them? In Egypt, it may be, they were right glad to take some corner of a poor cottage, and there to serve God upon their knees, peradventure covered in dust and straw sometimes. Neither were they therefore the less accepted of God: but he was with them in all their afflictions, and at the length, by working their admirable deliverance, did testify that they served him not in vain. Notwithstanding in the very desert they are no sooner possest of some little thing of their own, but a Tabernacle is required at their hands. Being planted in the land of Canaan, and having David to be their King, when the Lord had given him rest from all his enemies, it grieved his religious mind to consider the growth of his own estate and dignity, the affairs of Religion continuing still in the former manner: "Behold now I dwell in an house of cedar-trees, and the Ark of God remaineth still within curtains." What he did purpose, it was the pleasure of God that Solomon, his son, should perform, and perform it in a manner suitable unto their present, not their ancient estate and condition. For which cause Solomon writeth unto the King of Tyrus, "The house which I build is great and wonderful; for great is our God above all gods." Whereby it clearly appeareth, that the Orders of the Church of God may be acceptable unto him, as well being framed suitable to the greatness and dignity of later, as when they keep the reverend simplicity of ancienter times. Such dissimilitude, therefore, between us and the Apostles of Christ, in the order of some outward things, is no argument of default.

Yea, but we have framed ourselves to the customs of the Church of Rome; our Orders and Ceremonies are Papistical. It is espied that our Church-founders were not so careful as in this matter they should have been, but contented themselves with such Discipline as they took from the Church of Rome. Their error we ought to reform by abolishing all Popish Orders. There must be no communion nor fellowship with Papists, "neither in Doctrine, Ceremonies, nor Government." It is not enough that we are divided from the Church of Rome by the single wall of Doctrine, retaining as we do part of their Ceremonies and almost their whole Government; but Government or Ceremonies, or whatsoever it be which is Popish, away with it. This is the thing they require in us, the utter relinquishment of all things Popish. Wherein, to the end we may answer them according unto their plain direct meaning, and not take advantage of doubtful speech, whereby controversies grow always endless; their main position being this, "that nothing should be placed in the Church but what God in his Word hath commanded," they must of necessity hold all for Popish which the Church of Rome hath over and besides this. By Popish Orders, Ceremonies, and Government, they must therefore mean in every of these so much as the Church of Rome hath embraced without commandment of God's Word: so that whatsoever such thing we have, if the Church of Rome have it also, it goeth under the name of those things that are Popish, yea, although it be lawful, although agreeable to the Word of God. For so they plainly affirm, saying, "Although the Forms and Ceremonies which they (the Church of Rome) used were not unlawful, and that they contained nothing which is not agreeable to the Word of God, yet notwithstanding neither the Word of God, nor Reason, nor the examples of the eldest Churches, both Jewish and Christian, do permit us to use the same Forms and Ceremonies, being neither commanded of God, neither such as there may not as good as they, and rather better, be established." The question therefore is, whether we may follow the Church of Rome in those Orders, Rites, and Ceremonies, wherein we do not think them blameable; or else ought to devise others, and to have no conformity with them, no not as much as in these things? In this sense and construction therefore as they affirm, so we deny, that whatsoever is Popish we ought to abrogate. . . .

For the Ceremonies in use amongst us being in no other respect retained, saving only for that to retain them is to our seeming good and profitable; yea, so profitable and so good, that if we had either simply taken them clean away, or else removed them so as to place in their stead others, we had done worse; the plain and direct way against us herein had been only to prove, that all such Ceremonies as they require to be abolished, are retained by us with the hurt of the Church, or with less benefit than the abolishment of them would bring. But forasmuch as they saw how hardly they should be able to perform this, they took a more compendious way, traducing the Ceremonies of our Church under the name of being Popish. The cause why this way seemed better unto them was, for that the name of Popery is more odious than very Paganism amongst divers of the more simple sort; so as whatsoever they hear named Popish, they presently conceive deep hatred against it, imagining there can be nothing contained in that name but needs it must be exceeding detestable. The ears of the people they have therefore filled with strong clamours; "The Church of England is fraught with Popish Ceremonies: they that favour the cause of reformation, maintain nothing but the sincerity of the Gospel of Jesus Christ: all such as withstand them, fight for the Laws of his sworn enemy, uphold the filthy relics of Antichrist, and are defenders of that which is Popish." These are the notes wherewith are drawn from the hearts of the multitude so many sighs; with these tunes their minds are exasperated against the lawful guides and governors of their souls; these are the voices that fill them with general discontentment, as though the bosom of that famous Church wherein they live were more noisome than any dungeon. But when the authors of so scandalous incantations are examined and called to account, how they can justify such their deals; when they are urged directly to answer, whether it be lawful for us to use any such Ceremonies as the Church of Rome useth, although the same be not commanded in the Word of God; being driven to see that the use of some such Ceremonies must of necessity be granted lawful, they go about to make us believe that they are just of the same opinion, and that they only think such

Ceremonies are not to be used when they are unprofitable, or "when as good or better may be established." Which answer is both idle in regard of us, and also repugnant to themselves. It is, in regard of us, very vain to make this answer, because they know that what Ceremonies we retain common unto the Church of Rome, we therefore retain them, for what we judge them to be profitable in their stead, they trifle, and they beat the air about nothing which toucheth us, unless they mean that we ought to abrogate all Romish Ceremonies, which in their judgment have either no use, or less use that some other might have. But then must they shew some commission, whereby they are authorized to sit as Judges, and we required to take their judgment for good in this case. . . .

A thousand five hundred years and upward the Church of Christ hath now continued under the sacred regiment of Bishops. Neither for so long hath Christianity been ever planted in any kingdom throughout the world but with this kind of government alone; which to have been ordained of God, I am for mine own part even as resolutely persuaded, as that any other kind of government in the world whatsoever is of God. In this realm of England, before Normans, yea before Saxons, there being Christians, the chief pastors of their souls were Bishops. This Order from about the first establishment of Christian Religion, which was publicly begun through the virtuous disposition of King Lucie not fully two hundred years after Christ, continued till the coming in of the Saxons, by whom Paganism being everywhere else replanted, only one part of the island, whereinto the ancient natural inhabitants the Britons were driven, retained constantly the Faith of Christ, together with the same form of spiritual regiment, which their fathers had before received. Wherefore in the histories of the Church we find very ancient mention made of our Bishops. At the Council of Ariminum, about the year three hundred and fifty-nine, Britain had three of her Bishops present. At the arrival of Augustine, the monk whom Gregory sent hither to reclaim the Saxons from Gentility about six hundred years after Christ the Britons he found observers still of the selfsame form it remained till the days of the Norman Conquerer. By him and his successors thereunto sworn, it hath from that time till now by the space of five hundred years more been upheld. . . .

For whatsoever we bring from Antiquity, by way of defence in this cause of Bishops, it is cast off as impertinent matter, all is wiped away with an odd kind of shifting answer, "That the Bishops which now are be not like unto them which were." We therefore beseech all indifferent judges to weigh sincerely with themselves how the case doth stand. If it should be at this day a controversy whether kingly regiment were lawful or no, peradventure in defence thereof the long continuance which it hath had sithence the first beginning might be alleged. Mention perhaps might be made what kings there were of old, even in Abraham's time, what sovereign princes both before and after. Suppose that herein some man purposely bending his wit against sovereignty should think to elude all such allegations by making ample discovery through a number of particularities, wherein the kings that are do differ from those that have been, and should therefore in the end conclude that such ancient examples are no convenient proofs of that royalty that is now in use. Surely for decision of truth in this case there were no remedy, but only to show the nature of sovereignty, to sever it from accidental properties, make it clear that ancient and present regality are one and the same in substance, how great odds soever otherwise may seem to be between them. In like manner, whereas a question of late hath grown, whether Ecclesiastical Regiment by Bishops be lawful in the Church of Christ or no; in which question, they that hold the negative, being pressed with that general received order, according whereunto the most renowned

lights of the Christian world have governed the same in
every age of Bishops; seeing their manner is to reply, that
such Bishops as those ancient were, ours are not; there is
no remedy but to show, that to be a Bishop is now the self-
same thing which it hath been; that one definition agreeth
fully and truly as well to those elder, as to these latter
Bishops. Sundry dissimilitudes we grant there are, which
notwithstanding are not such that they cause any equivo-
cation in the name, whereby we should think a Bishop in
those times to have had a clean other definition than doth
rightly agree unto Bishops as they are now. Many things
there are in the state of Bishops which the times have
changed; many a parsonage at this day is larger than some
ancient Bishoprics were; many an ancient Bishop poorer
than at this day sundry under them in degree. The simple,
hereupon lacking judgment and knowledge to discern between the nature of things which changeth not and these
outward variable accidents, are made believe that a Bishop
heretofore and now are things in their very nature so distinct that they cannot be judged the same. Yet to men that
have any part of skill, what more evident and plain in Bishops, than that augmentation or diminution in their precincts,
allowances, privileges, and such like, do make a difference
indeed, but no essential difference between one Bishop and
another? As for those things in regard whereof we use properly to term them Bishops, those things whereby they essentially differ from other pastors, those things which the
natural definition of a Bishop must contain, what one of
them is there more or less appliable unto Bishops now than
of old?

The name "Bishop" hath been borrowed from the Grecians, with whom it signifieth one which hath principal
charge to guide and oversee others. The same word in Ecclesiastical writings being applied unto Church Governors, at
the first unto all and not unto the chiefest only, grew in

short time peculiar and proper to signify such Episcopal authority alone as the chiefest governors exercised over the rest. For with all names this is usual, that inasmuch as they are not given till the things whereunto they are given have been sometime first observed therefore generally things are ancienter than the names whereby they are called. . . .

But to let go the name, and come to the very nature of that thing which is thereby signified. In all kinds of regiment whether ecclesiastical or civil, as there are sundry operations, some being of principal respect, and therefore not fit to be dealt in by everyone to whom public actions, and those of good importance, are notwithstanding well and fitly enough committed. From hence have grown those different degrees of magistrates or public persons even ecclesiastical as well as civil. Amongst ecclesiastical persons therefore Bishops being chief ones, a Bishop's function must be defined by that wherein his chiefty consisteth.

A Bishop is a minister of God, unto whom with permanent continuance there is given not only power of administering the Word and Sacraments, which power other Presbyters have, but also a further power to ordain ecclesiastical persons and a power of chiefty in government over Presbyters as well as Laymen, a power to be by way of jurisdiction a Pastor even to Pastors themselves. So that this office, as he is a Presbyter or Pastor, consisteth in those things which are common unto him with other Pastors, as in ministering the Word and Sacraments: but those things incident unto his office, which do properly make him a Bishop, cannot be common unto him with other Pastors.

Now even as pastors, so likewise Bishops being principal pastors, are either at large or else with restraint: at large, when the subject of their regiment is indefinite, and not tied to any certain place; Bishops with restraint are they whose regiment over the Church is contained within some definite, local compass, beyond which compass their jurisdiction

reacheth not. Such therefore we always mean when we speak
of that regiment by Bishops which we hold a thing most
lawful, divine, and holy in the Church of Christ. . . .

A great part of the cause wherefore religious minds
are so inflamed with the love of public devotion is that virtue, force, and efficacy, which by experience they find that
the very form and reverend solemnity of common prayer
duly ordered hath to help that imbecility and weakness in
us, by means whereof we are otherwise of ourselves the less
apt to perform unto God so heavenly a service, with such
affection of heart and disposition in the powers of our souls
as is requisite. To this end therefore all things hereunto appertaining have been ever thought convenient to be done
with the most solemnity and majesty that the wisest could
devise. It is not with public as with private prayer. In this
rather secrecy is commended than outward show, whereas
that being the public act of a whole society, requireth accordingly more care to be had of external appearance. The
very assembling of men therefore unto this service hath
been ever solemn.

And concerning the place of assembly, although it serve
for other uses as well as this, yet seeing that Our Lord Himself hath to this as to the chiefest of all other plainly sanctified His Own Temple, by entitling it "the House of Prayer,"
what pre-eminence of dignity soever hath been either by the
ordinance or through the special favour and providence of
God annexed unto His Sanctuary, the principal cause thereof
must needs be in regard to Common Prayer. For the honour
and furtherance whereof, if it be as the gravest of the ancient Fathers seriously were persuaded and do oftentimes
plainly teach, affirming that the house of prayer is a Court
beautified with the presence of celestial powers; that there
we stand, we pray, we sound forth hymns unto God, having
His Angels intermingled as our associates; and that with
reference hereunto the Apostle doth require so great care

to be had of decency for the Angels' sake; how can we come to the house of prayer, and not be moved with the very glory of the place itself so to frame our affections praying, as doth best beseem them, whose suits the Almighty doth sit there to hear, and His Angels attend to further? When this was ingrafted in the minds of men, there needed no penal statues to draw them unto public prayer. The warning sound was no sooner heard, but the Churches were presently filled, the pavements covered with bodies prostrate, and washed with their tears of devout joy.

And as the place of public prayer is a circumstance in the outward form thereof, which hath moment to help devotion, so the person much more with whom the people of God do join themselves in this action, as with him that standeth and speaketh in the presence of God for them. The authority of his place, the fervour of his zeal, the piety and gravity of his whole behaviour must needs exceedingly both grace and set forward the service he doth. . . .

But of all helps for due performance of this service the greatest is that very set and standing order itself, which framed with common advice, hath both for matter and form prescribed whatsoever is herein publicly done. No doubt from God it hath proceeded, and by us it must be acknowledged a work of His singular care and providence, that the Church hath evermore held a prescript form of Common Prayer, although not in all things every where the same, yet for the most part retaining still the same analogy. So that if the liturgies of all ancient Churches throughout the world be compared amongst themselves, it may be easily perceived they had all one original mould, and that the public prayers of the people of God in Churches thoroughly settled did never use to be voluntary dictates proceeding from any man's extemporal wit.

To him which considereth the grievous and scandalous inconveniences whereunto they make themselves daily subject, with whom any blind and secret corner is judged a fit house of Common Prayer, the manifold confusions which they fall into where every man's private spirit and gift (as they term it) is the only Bishop that ordaineth him to this ministry, the irksome deformities whereby through endless and senseless effusions of indigested prayers they oftentimes disgrace in most unsufferable manner the worthiest part of Christian duty towards God, who herein are subject to no certain order, but pray both what and how they list; to him I say which weigheth duly all these things the reasons cannot be obscure, why God doth in public prayer so much respect the solemnity of places where, the authority and calling of persons by whom, and the precise appointment even with what words or sentences His name should be called on amongst His people. . . .

Nor doth the solemn dedication of Churches serve only to make them public, but farther also to surrender up that right which otherwise their founders might have in them, and to make God Himself their owner. For which cause at the erection and consecration as well of the Tabernacle as of the Temple, it pleased the Almighty to give a manifest sign that He took possession of both. Finally, it notifieth in solemn manner the holy and religious use whereunto it is intended such houses shall be put. . . .

When therefore we sanctify or hallow Churches, that which we do is only to testify that we make them places of public resort, that we invest God Himself with them, that we sever them from common uses. In which action, other solemnities than such as are decent and fit for that purpose we approve none.

Indeed we condemn not all as unmeet, the like whereunto have been either devised or used haply amongst idolaters. For why should conformity with them in matter of opinion be lawful when they think that which is true, if in action when they do that which is meet it be not lawful to be like unto them? Are we to forsake any true opinion because idolators have maintained it? Nor to shun any requisite action only because we have in the practice thereof been prevented by idolaters. It is no impossible thing but that sometimes they may judge as rightly what is decent about such external affairs of God, as in greater things what is true. Not therefore whatsoever idolaters have either thought or done, but let whatsoever they have either thought or done *idolatrously be so far forth* abhorred. For of that which is good even in evil things God is Author.

Touching the names of Angels and Saints whereby the most of our Churches are called, as the custom of so naming them is very ancient, so neither was the cause thereof at the first, nor is the use and continuance with us at this present, hurtful. That Churches were consecrated unto none but the Lord only, the very general name itself doth sufficiently shew, inasmuch as by plain grammatical construction "Church" doth signify no other thing than "the Lord's House." And because the multitude as of persons so of things particular causeth variety of proper names to be devised for distinction sake, founders of Churches did herein that which best liked their own conceit at the present time, yet each intending that as oft as those buildings came to be mentioned, the name should put men in mind of some memorable thing or person. Thus therefore it cometh to pass that all Churches have had their names, some as memorials of Peace, some of Wisdom, some in memory of the Trinity itself, some of Christ under sundry titles, of the blessed Virgin not a few, many of one Apostle, Saint, or Martyr, many of all. . . .

Again, albeit the true worship of God be to God in itself acceptable, Who respecteth not so much in what place as with what affection He is served, and therefore Moses in the midst of the sea, Job on the dunghill, Ezechias in bed, Jeremy in mire, Jonas in the whale, Daniel in the den, the children in the furnace, the thief on the Cross, Peter and Paul in prison, calling unto God were heard, as St. Basil noteth; manifest notwithstanding it is, that the very majesty and holiness of the place, where God is worshipped, hath *in regard of us* great virtue, force, and efficacy, for that it serveth as a sensible help to stir up devotion, and *in that respect* no doubt *bettereth* even our holiest and best actions in this kind. As therefore we every where exhort all men to worship God, even so for performance of this service by the people of God assembled, we think not any place *so good* as the Church, neither any exhortation so fit as that of David, O *worship the Lord in the beauty of holiness.*

The Ecclesiastical Polity and Other Works of Richard Hooker,
Edited by Benjamin Hanbury.
London: Holdsworth and Ball, 1830.

COTTON
MATHER

1663 – 1728

ON

COTTON MATHER

THE NATURE AND HISTORY OF PROTESTANTISM MADE INEVITA-
able the idea of a theocracy. Revolting from the rule of the
pope, the early Reformers turned to civil government as
their reliance. In Lutheran lands the result was state-
churches, but in Geneva Calvin established a theocracy.
There civil and ecclesiastical rule was so blended that, while
each constitutent had its distinctive functions, both were
regarded as divinely commissioned to sustain and enforce
the true religion. Since, moreover, the definition of true
religion was in the hands of the church, the total government was powerfully influenced by the clergy.

To many who fell under the spell of the Genevan system,
this became the ideal. John Knox called Geneva "the most
godly reformed church and city of the world," and as he
strove to reproduce something like it in Scotland, so too in
England the Puritans set themselves to achieve a "Divine
Commonwealth." In their hoped-for theocracy, the civil government's duty would be, as one of their leaders put it, "to
suppress and root out by their authority all false ministers,
voluntary religions and counterfeit worship of God, and establish and maintain by their laws every part of God's
word."

The Church of England, however, was not so constituted
as to serve the Puritan purpose. Henry VIII had carried over
the pre-Reformation ecclesiastical establishment—saving that
he himself, and not the pope, was head of the English
church—and from his reign on for many years the question
whether papal supremacy should be reintroduced into England was still kept alive. Meanwhile the Puritans were gathering their strength around a far more radical idea of the
Reformation. Under the persecutions of "Bloody Mary,"
many of their leaders had fled to Europe, had visited and
fallen in love with Geneva, and were determined to achieve
in England their ideal of a theocracy. They stood for what
Thomas Cartwright called "semi-congregationalism"—not
separation from the Church of England, as Robert Browne
taught, but a thoroughgoing rebuilding of the church, with
the episcopacy elided, with each congregation sharing authority in the selection of its minister, and with the congregations so co-operating, and the civil state so serving the
church's interests and aims, that the will of God, defined by
the church, should be dominant in the government.

This endeavor to achieve the Puritan theocracy in England
met with continual frustration. The inherited structure of
the episcopacy stood its ground. When, after Queen Elizabeth's reign, James I came down from Scotland to assume
the crown of both nations, Puritan hopes ran high. James I,
however, had become exasperated against the Scotch system
and his dictum was peremptory: "If you aim at a Scottish
Presbytery, it agreeth as well with monarchy as God with
the devil." When Oliver Cromwell came to power, Puritan
hopes were again encouraged. Cromwell stood for a national church without episcopacy; under his regime the
public worship of Anglicans, as well as of Roman Catholics,
was made illegal; clergymen using the English Prayer Book
were deposed; and many stringent measures of reform were
introduced. To be sure, Cromwell wanted no "persecution."
"I had rather," he said, "that Mohammedanism were per-

mitted among us, than that one of God's children should be persecuted." He encouraged tolerance toward Quakers and Jews, and non-episcopal Protestant groups of various sorts had considerable liberty. The total result was far different from the theocracy which the Puritans had dreamed, and even this was short-lived, as Charles II succeeded Cromwell.

Richard Baxter was one of the last outstanding leaders of Puritanism in England. "In a true theocracy, or Divine Commonwealth," he wrote, "the Matter of the Church and Commonwealth should be altogether or much the same, though the forms of them and administrations are different. . . . It is this Theocratical Polity or Divine Commonwealth which is the unquestionable reign of Christ on Earth." By 1659, however, his hopes of achieving any such ideal in England had faded, and he lamented "How impossible it is, that honest plain and faithful dealing, in Ministers or others, should ordinarily find acceptance in the world."

In New England, however, there was a free field, and thither Puritan hopes had turned, especially after the Pilgrims—not Puritans, but Separatists who denied all association with the Church of England—had settled on Cape Cod Bay in 1620. Ten years later the Puritans landed at Salem and began their momentous experiment. What could not be done in England might be done here. Here they would build their "Divine Commonwealth." By this time, the long opposition between the Puritans and the Church of England had driven the reforming movement further and further toward congregationalism. When an English bishop commanded the use of the Book of Common Prayer, or the observance of saints' days, the Puritans had fallen back upon the claim that the individual congregation had the right to decide. By the time the Puritans established themselves in New England, therefore, the pattern was clear—the individual congregations in large measure independent, under the binding power of the covenant; the co-operation of the congregations in the synod, which exercised a delegated authority;

the close integration of church and civil rule so that the government, guided by the church, should advance and, if need be, compel godly belief and life.

When Cotton Mather wrote his *Magnalia Christi Americana*, the third generation of New England Puritans was struggling to keep their theocracy intact. It was obviously weakening, but its basic principles were still in control, and Cotton Mather makes them evident. To be sure, various motives, besides concern about religion, had multiplied the emigrants. Some had fled from persecution. To understand the Puritans one needs to remember such scenes as Richard Baxter before the infamous Judge Jeffries—a saintly, seventy-year-old man, now called by the judge "an old rogue, an old schismatical knave, a hypocritical villain, a conceited, stubborn, fanatical dog, a snivelling Presbyterian." Judge Jeffries threatened him with whipping at the cart's tail through London, but let him off with a fine of 500 marks and eighteen months in jail! Others had come for economic reasons. Cotton Mather tells us that a minister from the Bay visited certain plantations northward of New Plymouth and "urged them to approve themselves a religious people from this consideration, that otherwise they would contradict the main end of planting this wilderness; whereupon a well-known person, then in the assembly, cryed out, Sir, you are mistaken, you think you are preaching to people at the Bay; *our* main end was to catch fish."

Nevertheless, Puritans in New England, as a whole, had come to that "most hideous, boundless and unknown wilderness in the world" for one major purpose—to found a theocracy. In achieving that end they did not propose to be disturbed by heretical opinions. "All Familists, Antinomians, Anabaptists and other enthusiasts shall have free liberty to keep away from us," said Nathaniel Ward. "I look upon an unbounded toleration as the first-born of all abominations," cried Urian Oakes.

Cotton Mather is a fascinating illustration of the tensions

of his time. He felt the exclusion of heretics from the Commonwealth to be as right and reasonable as the protection of families from "contagious, noisome and mortal diseases"; yet, at the end, he began to see that persecution defeats its own purposes. His tragic and superstitious error in backing the Salem witch-trials has blackened his name; yet, when the new astronomy was still being denounced as anti-Biblical, Mather eagerly welcomed it: "The arguments that prove the stability of the sun and the motion of the earth have now rendered it indisputable." He was an incorrigible reactionary in his supernatural interpretation of yellow fever and small-pox as caused by demons, and of thunder and lightning as the specific threatening of God; yet he led the way in introducing inoculation against small-pox and, despite abuse and threats, inoculated his own children.

Such books as the following will introduce the reader to the stirring story of the Puritans in England and America: *The Puritan Oligarchy*, by Thomas Jefferson Wertenbaker; *The New England Mind*, by Perry Miller; *The Rise of the Puritans*, by William Haller; *The Puritans*, by Perry Miller and T. H. Johnson; *Cotton Mather, The Puritan Priest*, by Barrett Wendell. Nothing ever written, however, gives a more vivid picture of Puritan ideas and policies than Cotton Mather's *Magnalia*, from which this anthology presents a few excerpts.

If one is to understand Puritanism, one must look not alone at its theocratic methods and legalistic restraints, but at its vital effect on personal character. It built robust, sturdy personalities, like John Bunyan's Mr. Great-heart: "When he came to the Hill Difficulty he made no stick at that, nor did he much fear the lions." Indeed, John Bunyan himself illustrates the effect of vital Puritan religion on character. It was far from being merely a restraining force; it worked astounding results in the creation of intrepid, productive personalities. A strolling tinker, his whole life spent within walking distance of Bedford, with no literary training except what he gained from the Bible, and with twelve years spent in prison for his faith's sake, produced a masterpiece which Macaulay called the most popular religious writing in the English language. If the reader would understand Puritanism, he should add *The Pilgrim's Progress* to this anthology.

From

MAGNALIA CHRISTI

AMERICANA

THE PURITANS COME TO NEW ENGLAND

IT WAS FOR A MATTER OF TWELVE YEARS TOGETHER, THAT persons of all ranks, well affected unto *Church-reformation*, kept sometimes *dropping*, and sometimes *flocking* into New-England, though some that were coming into New-England were not suffered so to do. The persecutors of those *Puritans*, as they were called, who were now *retiring* into that *cold* country from the *heat* of their persecution, did all that was possible to hinder as many as was possible from enjoying that *retirement*. There were many *countermands* given to the passage of people that were now steering of this *western course*; and there was a sort of uproar made among no small part of the nation, that this people should not be *let go*. Among those bound for New-England, that were so stopt, there were especially three famous persons, whom I suppose their adversaries would not have so studiously detained at home, if they had *foreseen* events; those were Oliver Cromwell, and Mr. Hambden, and Sir Arthur Haselrig; nevertheless, this is not the only instance of *persecuting church-mens* not having the *spirit of prophesy*. But many others were diverted from an intended voyage hither by the pure providence of God, which had provided other improvements for them; and of this take one instance instead of many. Before the woeful wars which broke forth

371

in the three kingdoms, there were divers gentlemen in Scotland, who, being uneasie under the ecclesiastical burdens of the times, wrote unto New-England their enquiries, Whether they might be there suffered freely to exercise their *Presbyterian* church-government? And it was freely answered, "That they might." Hereupon, they sent over an agent, who pitched upon a tract of land near the mouth of the Merrimack River, whither they intended them to transplant themselves: but although they had so far proceeded in their voyage, as to be *half-seas* through; the manifold crosses they met withal, made them give over their intentions; and the providence of God so ordered it, that some of these very gentlemen were afterwards the *revivers* of that well-known *solemn league and covenant* which had so great an influence upon the following circumstances of the nations. However, the number of those who did actually arrive at New-England before the year 1640, have been computed about four thousand; since which time far more have gone out of the country than have come to it; and yet the God of Heaven so smiled upon the Plantation, while, under an *easie* and *equal* government, the designs of Christianity in well-formed churches have been carried on, that no history can *parallel* it. That saying of Eutropius about Rome, which hath been sometimes applied unto the church, is capable of some application to this little part of the church: *Never was anything more mean in inception or more mighty in progress.* Never was any plantation brought unto such a considerableness, in a space of time so inconsiderable! an *howling wilderness* in a few years became a *pleasant land*, accommodated with the *necessaries*—yea, and the *conveniences* of humane life; the *gospel* has carried with it a *fulness of all other blessings*; and (albeit, that mankind generally, as far as we have means of enquiry, have increased in one and the same given proportion, and so no more than *doubled* themselves in about three hundred and sixty years, in all the past ages of the world, since the fixing of the present period

of humane life) the four thousand first planters, in less than
fifty years, notwithstanding all transportations and mortali-
ties, increased into, they say, more than an hundred thousand.

THE PURITAN IDEAL FOR BOSTON

God help the town to manifest all that PIETY, which a
town so helped of him is obliged unto! When the people of
God had been carried by his help through their difficulties,
they set up *stones* to keep in mind how he had helped them;
and something was written on the stones: but what was written? see Josh. viii. 32, "Joshua wrote upon the stones a
copy of the law." Truly upon those Ebenezers we set up,
we should write the law of our God, and recognize the obli-
gations which the help of our God has laid upon us
to keep it.

We are a very unpardonable town, if, after all the help
which our God has given us, we do not ingenuously enquire,
"What shall we render to the Lord for all his benefits?"
Render! Oh! let us ourselves thus answer the enquiry:
"Lord, we will render all possible and filial obedience unto
thee, because hitherto thou hast helped us: only do thou also
help us to render that obedience!" Mark what I say: if there
be so much as one *prayerless house* in such a town as this,
'tis inexcusable! How inexcusable then will be all flagitious
outrages? There was a town ('twas the town of Sodom!)
that had been wonderfully saved out of the hand of their
enemies. But after the help that God sent unto them, the
town went on to sin against God in very prodigious
instances. At last a provoked God sent a fire upon the town
that made it an eternal desolation. Ah, Boston, beware,
beware, lest the sins of Sodom get footing in thee! And
what were the sins of Sodom? We find in Ezek. xvi. 49,
"Behold this was the iniquity of Sodom; pride, fulness of
bread, and abundance of idleness was in her; neither did
she strengthen the hand of the poor and the needy;" there

was much oppression there. If you know of any scandalous disorders in the town, do all you can to suppress them, and redress them; and let not those that send their sons hither from other parts of the world, for to be improved in virtue, have cause to complain, "That after they came to Boston, they lost what little virtue was before budding in them; that in Boston they grew more debauched and more malignant than ever they were before!" It was noted concerning the famous town of Port-Royal in Jamaica, which you know was the other day swallowed up in a stupendous earthquake, that just before the earthquake the people were violently and scandalously set upon going to *Fortune-tellers* upon all occasions: much notice was taken of this *impiety* generally prevailing among the people: but none of those wretched Fortune-tellers could foresee or forestal the direful catastrophe. I have heard that there are Fortune-tellers in this town sometimes consulted by some of the sinful inhabitants. I wish the town could be made too hot for these *dangerous transgressors*. I am sure the preservation of the town from horrendous earthquakes, is one thing that bespeaks our Ebenezers; 'tis from the merciful *help* of our God unto us. But beware, I beseech you, of those provoking evils that may expose us to a plague, exceeding all that are in the catalogue of the twenty-eighth Deuteronomy. Let me go on to say, What! shall there be any bawdy-houses in such a town as this! It may be the neighbours, that could smoke them and rout them, if they would, are loth to stir, for fear of being reputed ill neighbours. But I say unto you, that you are ill neighbours because you do not do it. All the neighbours are like to have their children and servants poisoned, and their dwellings laid in ashes, because you do it not. And, Oh! that the drinking-houses in the town might once come under a laudable *regulation*. The town has an *enormous number* of them; will the *haunters* of those houses hear the counsels of Heaven? For you that are the town-dwellers, to be oft or

long in your visits of the *ordinary*, 'twill certainly expose
you to mischiefs more than ordinary. I have seen certain
taverns, where the pictures of horrible devourers were
hanged out for signs; and, thought I, 'twere well if such
signs were not sometimes too *significant*; alas men have
their estates *devoured*, their names *devoured*, their hours
devoured, and their very souls *devoured*, when they are so
besotted that they are not in their element, except they be
tipling at such houses. . . . But I pray God assist you that
keep ordinaries, to keep the commandments of God in
them. There was an Inn at Bethlehem where the Lord
JESUS CHRIST was to be met withal. Can Boston boast of
many such? Alas, too ordinarily it may be said, "there is
no room for him in the Inn!" My friends, let me beg it of
you, banish the unfruitful works of darkness from your
houses, and then the sun of righteousness will shine upon
them. Don't countenance drunkenness, revelling, and mis-
spending of precious time in your houses; let none have
the snares of death laid for them in your houses. You'll say,
"I shall starve then!" I say, "Better starve than sin:" but
you shall not. It is the word of the Most High, "Trust in the
Lord, and do good, and verily thou shalt be fed." And is
not *peace of conscience* with a *little* better than those riches
that will shortly melt away, and then run like scalding
metal down the very bowels of thy soul?

What shall I say more? There is one article of *piety*
more to be recommended unto us all; and it is an article
which all piety does exceedingly turn upon, that is, THE
SANCTIFICATION OF THE LORD'S DAY. Some very judicious
persons have observed, that as "they sanctify the Lord's day,
remissly or carefully, just so their affairs usually prospered
all the ensuing week." Sirs, you cannot more consult the
prosperity of the town, in all its affairs, than by endeavouring
that the Lord's day may be exemplarily sanctified. When
people about Jerusalem took too much liberty on the Sabbath, the ruler of the town contended with them, and said,

"Ye bring wrath upon Israel, by prophaning the Sabbath."
And what wrath? Ah, Lord, prevent it! But there is an awful
sentence in Jer. xvii. 27, "If ye will not hearken unto me, to
sanctifie the Sabbath day, then will I kindle a fire *on the
town*, and it shall devour, and shall not be quenched."

Finally, Let the piety of the town manifest itself in a
due regard unto the INSTITUTIONS of Him whose *help* has
hitherto been a shield unto us. Let the *ark* be in the town,
and God will bless the town! I believe it may be found, that
in the mortal scourges of heaven, which this town has felt,
there has been a *discernible* distinction of those that have
come up to attend all the ordinances of the Lord Jesus
Christ, in the communion of his churches. Though these
have had, as 'tis fit they should, a share in the common
deaths, yet the destroying angel has not had so great a
proportion of these in his commission, as he has had of others. Whether *this* be so, or no, to uphold, and support, and
attend the ordinances of the Lord Jesus Christ in reforming
churches, this will entitle the town to the *help* of heaven;
for "Upon the glory there shall be a defence!" There were
the victorious forces of Alexander, that in going backward
and forward, passed by Jerusalem without hurting it. Why
so? Said the Lord in Zech. ix. 8, "I will encamp about my
house, because of the army." If our God have an
house here, he'll encamp about it. Nazianzen, a famous minister of the gospel, taking his farewel of Constantinople, an
old man that had sat under his ministry, cried out, "Oh! my
father, don't you dare to go away: you'll carry the whole
Trinity with you!" How much more may it be cried out, "If
we lose or slight the ordinances of the Lord Jesus Christ,
we forego the help of all the Trinity with them!"

TYPICAL TEACHING ON CHURCH DISCIPLINE

It yet more endears unto us the memory of our Eliot that
he was not only an evangelical minister, but also a true
New-English one; he was a Protestant and a Puritan, and

one very full of that spirit which actuated the first planters of this country in their *peaceable secession* from the unwarrantable things elsewhere imposed upon their consciences. The *judgment* and *practice* of one that readily underwent all the misery attending the infancy of this plantation, for the sake of a true church order, is a thing which we young people should count worthy to be enquired after; and since we saw him so well "behaving himself in the house of God," it cannot but be worth while to know what he thought about the frame, and form, and constitution of that blessed house.

He was a modest, humble, but very reasonable nonconformist unto the *ceremonies* which have been such unhappy apples of strife in the Church of England; otherwise the dismal thickets of America had never seen such a person in them.

It afflicted him to see these, and more such as these, things continued in the Church of England, by the artifice of certain persons who were loth to have the reformation carried on unto those further degrees which the most eminent of the *first reformers* had in their holy design.

We see what *was not* his opinion! But let us hear what it was. It was his as well as his master, the great Ramus's principle, "That in the reformation of the churches, to be now endeavoured, things ought to be reduced unto the order wherein we find them at their primitive, original apostolic institution." And in pursuance of this principle, he justly espoused that way of church-government which we call the *congregational*; he was fully perswaded, that the church state which our Lord Jesus Christ hath instituted in the New-Testament, is, "In a congregation or society of professed believers, agreeing and assembling together among themselves, with officers of divine appointment for the celebration of evangelical ordinances, and their own mutual edification;" for he saw it must be a *cruel hardship* used upon the Scriptures, to make them so much as lisp the least intimation of any other church-state prescribed unto us; and he could assert, "That no approved writers, for the space of two hundred years after Christ, make any mention of any other organical, visible, professing church, but that only which is congregational." He looked upon the congregational way as a largess of divine bounty bestowed by the Lord Jesus Christ on his people, that followed him into this wilderness, with a peculiar zeal for communion with him in his pure worship here. He perceived in it a sweet sort of temperament, between *rigid* Presbyterianism and *levelling* Brownism; so that on the one side, the *liberties* of the people are not oppressed and overlaid; on the other side, the authority of the elders is not rendered insignificant, but a due balance is herein kept upon them both, and hence he closed with *our* "platform of church-discipline," as being the nearest of what he had yet seen to the directions of Heaven.

He could not comprehend that this church-state can arise from any other *formal cause*, but the consent, concurrence, confederation of those concerned in it; he looked upon a relation unto a church as not a *natural* or a *violent*, but a *voluntary* thing, and so that it is to be entered no otherwise than by an holy covenant, or, as the Scripture speaks, by "giving our selves first unto the Lord, and then unto one another." He could not think that baptism alone was to be accounted the *cause*, but rather the *effect*, of church membership; inasmuch as, upon the dissolution of the church to which a man belongs, his *baptism* would not become a nullity: nor that meer *profession* would render men members of this or that church; for then it would be impossible to cut off a corrupt member from the body politic: nor that meer *cohabitation* would make church members; for then the vilest infidels would be actually incorporated with us. And a covenant was all that he now saw remaining in the inventory.

But for the *subjects* to be admitted by churches unto all the privileges of this fellowship with them, he thought they ought to be such as *trying charity*, or a *charitable tryal*,

should pronounce *regenerate*. He found the first churches of
the gospel mentioned in the Scriptures to be "churches of
saints": and that the apostles writing to them, still acknowledge them to be a holy brethren, and such as were made
"meet for to be partakers of the inheritance of the saints in
light"; and that a main end of church-fellowship, is to represent unto the world the qualifications of those that shall
"ascend into the hill of the Lord, and stand in his holy
place forever." He would therefore have a *good mind*, a
pure heart, and a *spotless life* required, as Lactantius tells
us they were in his days of all communicants at the table
of the Lord; and, with holy Chrysostom, he would sooner
have given his *heart blood*, than the *cup of the Lord* unto
such as had not the hopeful marks of our Lord's disciples
on them. The churches of New-England still retain a custom which the great Justin Martyr, in the second century,
assures us to have been in the primitive churches of his
time; namely, "To examine those they receive, not only
about their perswasion, but also whether they have attained
unto a work of grace upon their souls." In the prosecution
hereof, besides the enquiries of the elders into the *knowledge*, and *belief*, and *conversation* of them that offer themselves unto church-fellowship, it is expected, though I hope
not with any severity of imposition, that in the addresses
which they make to the churches, they give *written*, if not
oral account, of what impressions the regenerating word of
God has had upon their souls. This was a *custom* which this
holy man had a marvellous esteem and value for. . . .

There were especially two things which he was loth to
see, and yet feared he *saw*, falling in the churches of New-
England. One was, a thorough establishment of ruling
elders in our churches; which he thought sufficiently warranted by the apostles' mention of, "elders that rule well,
who yet labour not in word and doctrine." He was very desirous to have prudent and gracious men set over our
churches, for the assistance of their pastors in the church

acts that concern *admission* and *exclusion* of members, and the *inspection* of the conversation led by the communicant, and the *instruction* of their several families, and the *visitation* of the afflicted in their flock, over which they should preside. Such "helps in governments" had he himself been blessed withal; the last of which was the well-deserving Elder Bowles; and of him did this good man, in a speech to a synod of all the churches in this colony, take occasion to say, "There is my brother Bowles, the godly elder of our church at Roxbury, God helps him to do great things among us!" Had all our pastors been so well accommodated, it is possible there would be more encouragement given to such an office as that of ruling elders.

But the mention of a Synod brings to mind another thing, which he was concerned that we might never want; and that is, a frequent repetition of *needful synods* in our churches. For though he had a deep and a due care to preserve the "rights of particular churches," yet he thought all the churches of the Lord Jesus Christ by their *union* in what they *profess*, in what they *intend*, and in what they *enjoy*, so compacted into one *body mystical*, as that all the several particular churches every where should act with a regard unto the good of the whole, and unto the common *advice* and *council* of the neighbourhood; which cannot be done always by *letters missive* like those that passed between Corinth and Rome in the early days of Christianity; but it requires a convention of the churches in synods, by their delegates and messengers. He did not count churches to be so independent, as that they can always discharge their whole duty, and yet not act in conjunction with neighbour churches; nor would he be of any church that will not acknowledge it self *accountable* to rightly composed synods, which may have occasion to enquire into the circumstances of it; he saw the main interest and business of churches might quickly come to be utterly lost, if synods were not called for the repairing of inconveniences, and he was much in contriving for the regular and repeated meeting of such assemblies.

He wished for *councils* to suppress all damnable heresies or pernicious opinions that might ever arise among us; for councils to extinguish all dangerous divisions and scandalous contentions which might ever begin to flame in our borders; for councils to rectify all mal-administrations in the midst of us, or to recover any particular churches out of any disorders which they may be plunged into: for councils to enquire into the love, the peace, the holiness maintained by the several churches; in fine for councils to send forth fit labourers into those parts of our Lord's harvest which are without the gospel of God. He beheld an apostolical precept and pattern for such councils; and when such councils convened in the name of our Lord Jesus Christ, by the consent of several churches concerned in mutual communion, have declared, explained, recommended the mind of God from his word unto us, he reckoned a truth so delivered, challenged an observation from a great authority.

THE PURITAN THEOCRACY

God, the supreme Lord and King of all the world, hath ordained civil magistrates to be under him, over the people for his own glory and the public good: And to this end has armed them with the power of the sword for the defence and encouragement of them that do good, and for the punishment of evil doers.

It is lawful for Christians to accept and execute the office of a magistrate, when called thereunto: In the management whereof, as they ought especially to maintain piety, justice and peace, according to the wholesome laws of each common-wealth, so for that end, they may lawfully now under the New Testament wage war upon just and necessary occasion.

They who upon pretence of Christian liberty shall oppose any lawful power, or the lawful exercises of it, resist the ordinance of God; and for their publishing of such opinions, or maintaining of such practices, as are contrary to the light of nature, or to the known principles of Christianity, whether concerning faith, worship or conversation, or to the power of godliness, or such erroneous opinions or practices, as either in their own nature, or in the manner of publishing or maintaining them, are destructive to the external peace and order which Christ hath established in the church, they may lawfully be called to account, and proceeded against by the censures of the church, and by the power of the civil magistrate; yet in such differences about the doctrines of the gospel, or ways of the worship of God, as may befal men, exercising a good conscience, manifesting it in their conversation, and holding the foundation, and duly observing the rules of peace and order, there is no warrant for the magistrate to abridge them of their liberty.

It is the duty of people to pray for magistrates, to honour their persons, to pay them tribute and other dues, to obey their lawful commands, and to be subject to their authority for conscience sake. Infidelity or difference in religion does not make void the magistrate's just and legal authority, nor free the people from their due obedience to him: From which ecclesiastical persons are not exempted, much less has the Pope any power or jurisdiction over them in their dominions, or over any of their people, and least of all to deprive them of their dominions or lives, if he shall judge them to be hereticks, or upon any other pretence whatsoever: . . .

It is the duty of the magistrate to take care of matters of religion, and to improve his civil authority for the observing of the duties commanded in the first, as well as for observing of the duties commanded in the second table. They are called *gods*. (Psa. lxxxwiii. 8.) The end of the magistrate's office is not only the quiet and peaceable life of the subject in matters of righteousness and honesty, but also in matters of godliness; yea, of all godliness. (I Tim. ii. 1,

2; I Kings xv. 14, and xii. 43; II Kings xii. 3, and xiv. 4, and xv. 35.) Moses, Joshua, David, Solomon, Asa, Jehosaphat, Hezekiah, Josiah, are much commended by the Holy Ghost, for the putting forth their authority in matters of religion; on the contrary, such kings as have been failing this way, are frequently taxed and reproved of the Lord. (I Kings xx. 42; Job xxix. 25, and xxxi. 26. 28; Neh. xiii.; Jonah iii. 7; Ezra vii.; Dan. iii. 29.) And not only the kings of Juda, but also Job, Nehemiah, the king of Nineveh, Darius, Artaxerxes, Nebuchadnezzar, whom none looked at as types of Christ, (tho' were it so there were no place for any just objection) are commended in the books of God for exercising their authority this way.

The objects of the power of the magistrate are not things meerly inward, and so not subject to his cognizance and views: as unbelief, hardness of heart, erroneous opinions not vented, but only such things as are acted by the outward man: neither their power to be exercised in commanding such acts of the outward man, and punishing neglect thereof, as are but mere inventions and devices of man (I Kings xx. 28. 42.), but about such acts as are commanded and forbidden in the word: yea, such as the word doth clearly determine, tho' not always clearly to the judgment of the magistrate or others, yet clearly in its self. In these he, of right, ought to put forth his authority, tho' oft-times actually he doth it not.

Idolatry, blasphemy, heresie (Deut. xiii.; I Kings xx. 28. 42), venting corrupt and pernicious opinions, that destroy the foundation (Dan. iii. 29), open contempt of the word preached (Zech. xiii. 3), prophanation of the Lord's-Day (Neh. xiii 31), disturbing the peaceable administration and exercise of the worship and holy things of God (I Tim. ii. 2) and the like (Rom. xiii 4), are to be restrained and punished by civil authority.

If any church, one or more, shall grow schismatical, rending itself from the communion of other churches, or shall work incorrigibly and obstinately in any corrupt way of their own, contrary to the rule of the word; in such case, the magistrate (Josh. xxii.) is to put forth his coercive power, as the matter shall require. . . .

QUESTION.—Whether, or how far the Discipline of our Churches upon Offences in them, is to depend upon the Conviction of those Offences in the Courts of Civil Jurica-ture?

1 To bring the discipline of the church into a dependance on the direction of the civil magistrate, is to put it under undue and unsafe disadvantages. The mutual depend-ance of those on each other, as 'tis not founded in the oracles of our Lord Jesus Christ, so it has been the occa-sion of no little confusion in the world.

2 Some things may be censured in the *Court* for trans-gressions of the laws, which may scarce deserve the cen-sures of the *church*.

3 Some things may be censured in the *church* for offenses, against which the *court* has no censures by any law pro-vided.

4 Persons may be so defective in their defence of them-selves by *legal* formalities, as to fall under the censures of the court; and yet the church may see cause, and do well to acquit them.

5 Persons may be acquitted in the court of crimes laid to their charge, for want of *conviction*, and yet the evi-dence may be so convictive, that church may condemn them thereupon.

6 When a church passes a censure on any delinquent, it is convenient and advisable that the circumstances of it be so managed as to expose as little as may be the cen-sured person unto the sentence of the court.

7 A church may do well sometimes to express its faithful-ness unto the Lord Jesus Christ, by censuring some evils which a court may faultily neglect to animadvert upon.

8 Sometimes a case may be so dark, that a church may
hope to be eased of *labour*, and freed from *error*, by a
court first sifting of it, and then *Christian prudence*
would make use of that help, to come at the knowledge
of the truth.

9 When a session of a court is very near, a church may
prudently forbear, for a *little* while, a process, which the
necessity of a soul fallen into sin, and the vindication of
the name of the Lord, makes not proper to be forborn
for a *greater* while.

10 When things are not very *apparent* or very *important*,
it is prudently done of a church to defer the early decision of a matter which will produce between it and the
court a controversie of dangerous consequence.

11 As 'tis the duty of a church to see that the witness of a
crime, to be judged by it, be obliged to speak, as in the
special presence of the great God, so if it be feared that
the witnesses will not be faithful, unless they be upon
oath, it is prudence to defer 'till the civil magistrate have
examined them.

12 Or, if witnesses refuse to come at all unto the church,
which the civil magistrate may and will compel to give in
their testimonies, a church can in prudence do no other
than defer 'till those witnesses can be brought to testi-
fie what is expected from them.

SELF REFORMATION NEEDED IN NEW-ENGLAND

That God hath a controversie with his New-England people
is undeniable, the Lord having written his displeasure in dismal characters against us. Though personal afflictions do
oftentimes come only or chiefly for probation, yet, as to
publick judgments, it is not wont to be so; especially when,
by a continued series of providence, the Lord doth appear
and plead against his people (II Sam. xxi, 1) as with us
it hath been from year to year. Would the Lord
have whetted his glittering sword, and his hand have taken

hold on judgment? Would he have sent such a mortal contagion, like a besom of destruction, in the midst of us? Would he have said, "Sword! go through the land, and cut off man and beast?" Or would he have kindled such devouring fires, and made such fearful desolations in the earth, if he had not been angry? It is not for nothing that the merciful God, who doth not willingly afflict nor grieve the children of men, hath done all those things unto us; yea, and sometimes with a cloud covered himself, that our prayer should not pass through; and although 'tis possible that the Lord may contend with us partly on account of secret unobserved sins (Josh. vii. 12; II Kings xvii. 9; Psalm xc. 8), in which respect, a deep and most serious inquiry into the causes of his controversie ought to be attended; nevertheless, it is sadly evident that there are visible evils manifest, which without doubt the Lord is provoked by. For,

There is a great and visible decay of the power of Godliness amongst many professors in these churches. It may be feared that there is in too many spiritual and heart apostacy from God, whence communion with him in the ways of his worship, especially in secret, is much neglected, and whereby men cease to know, and fear, and love, and trust in him; but take up their contentment and satisfaction in something else. . . .

Church fellowship and other divine institutions are greatly neglected. Many of the rising generation are not mindful of that which their baptism doth engage them unto, viz: to use utmost endeavours that they may be fit for, and so partake in all the holy ordinances of the Lord Jesus (Matt. xxvii. 20). There are too many that with profane Esau slight spiritual priviledges. Nor is there so much discipline extended towards children of the covenant, as we are generally agreed ought to be done. On the other hand, humane inventions and will-worship have been set up even in Jerusalem. Men have set up their thresholds by God's threshold, and their posts by his post. Quakers are false worshippers; and

such Anabaptists as have risen up among us, in opposition
to the churches of the Lord Jesus receiving into their society
those that have been for scandal delivered unto Satan; yes,
and improving those as administrators of holy things who
have been (as doth appear) justly under church-censures, do
no better than set up an altar against the Lord's altar.
Wherefore it must needs be provoking to God if these things
be not duly and fully testified against, by every one in their
several capacities respectively. . . .

There is much Sabbath-breaking; since there are multitudes that do profanely absent themselves or theirs from the
public worship of God on his holy day, especially in the
most populous places of the land; and many, under pretence of differing apprehensions about the beginning of the
Sabbath, do not keep a seventh part of time holy unto
the Lord, as the fourth commandment requireth; walking
abroad, and travelling (not meerly on the account of worshipping God in the solemn assemblies of his people, or to
attend works of necessity or mercy) being a common practice
on the Sabbath day, which is contrary unto that rest enjoyned
by the commandment. Yea, some that attend their particular
servile callings and employments after the Sabbath is begun,
or before it is ended. Worldly, unsuitable discourses are very
common upon the Lord's day, contrary to the Scripture,
which requireth that men should not on holy times find
their own pleasure nor speak their own words (Isa. lviii.
13). Many that do not take care so to dispatch their worldly
businesses, that they may be free and fit for the duties of
the Sabbath, and that do (if not wholly neglect) after a
careless, heartless manner, perform the duties that concern
the sanctification of the Sabbath. This brings wrath, fires
and other judgments upon a professing people (Neh. iii.
17, 18; Jer. xvii. 27).

As to what concerns families and government thereof,
there is much amiss. There are many families that do not
pray to God constantly morning and evening, and many

more wherein the Scriptures are not daily read, that so the word of Christ might dwell richly with them. Some, and too many houses, that are full of ignorance and prophaneness, and these not duly inspected, for which cause wrath may come upon others round about them, as well as upon themselves (Jos. xxii. 20; Jerem. v. 7, and x. 25). And many householders who profess religion, do not cause all that are within their gates to become subjects unto good order, as ought to be (Exod. xx. 10). Nay, children and servants, that are not kept in due subjection, their masters and parents especially being sinfully indulgent towards them. This is a sin which brings great judgments, as we see in Eli's, and David's family. In this respect Christians in this land have become too like unto the Indians, and then we need not wonder if the Lord hath afflicted us by them. Sometimes a sin is discerned by the instrument that Providence doth punish with. Most of the evils that abound amongst us, proceed from defects as to family government. . . .

There is much intemperance. That heathenish and idolatrous practice of health-drinking is too frequent; that shameful iniquity of sinful drinking is become too general a provocation. Days of training, and other publick solemnities, have been abused in this respect; and not only English, but Indians, have been debauched by those that call themselves Christians, who have put their bottles to them, and made them drunk also. This is a crying sin, and the more aggravated, in that the first planters of this colony did (as is the patent expressed) come into this land with a design to convert the heathen unto Christ: but if, instead of that, they be taught wickedness, which before they were never guilty of, the Lord may well punish us by them. Moreover, the sword, sickness, poverty, and almost all the judgments which have been upon New-England, are mentioned in the Scripture, as the woful fruit of *that sin*. (Jer. v. 11,12, and xxviii. 1,2, and lvi. 9. 12; Prov. xxii. 21. 29,30, and xxi. 17; Hos. vii. 5, and xxviii. 9.) There are more temptations and occasions unto *that sin*, publickly allowed of, than any necessity doth require; the proper end of taverns, &c., being for the entertainment of strangers, which, if they were improved to that end only, a far less number would suffice: But it is a common practice for town-dwellers—yea, and church-members—to frequent publick houses, and there to misspend precious time, unto the dishonour of the gospel, and the scandalizing of others, who are by such examples induced to sin against God. In which respect for church-members to be unnecessarily in such houses, is sinful, scandalous, and provoking to God (I Cor. viii. 9,10; Rom. xiv. 21; Matt. xvii. 27, and xviii. 7).

And there are other heinous breaches of the seventh commandment. Temptations thereunto are become too common, viz: such as immodest apparel (Prov. vii. 10), laying out of hair, borders, naked necks and arms, or, which is more abominable, naked breasts, and mixed dancings, with light behaviour and expressions, sinful company-keeping with light and vain persons, unlawful gaming, an abundance of idleness, which brought ruinating judgment upon Sodom, and much more upon Jerusalem (Ezek. xvi. 49), and doth sorely threaten New-England, unless effectual remedies be thoroughly and timously applied.

ROGER WILLIAMS

In the year 1654, a certain Windmill in the Low Countries, whirling round with extraordinary violence, by reason of a violent storm, then blowing; the stone at length by its *rapid motion* became so intensely hot, as to fire the mill, from whence the flames, being dispersed by the high winds, did set a whole town *on fire*. But I can tell my reader that, about twenty years before this, there was a whole country in America like to be set on *fire* by the *rapid motion* of a windmill, in the head of one particular man. Know, then, that about the year 1630, arrived here one Mr. Roger Williams; who being a preacher that had less *light* than *fire* in him, hath by his own sad example, preached unto us the danger of that evil which the apostle mentions in Rom. x. 2: "They have a zeal, but not according to knowledge." . . .

For, first, whereas the king of England had granted a royal charter unto the "governour and company" of this colony; which patent was indeed the very life of the colony, this hotheaded man publickly and furiously preached against the patent, as an "instrument of injustice," and pressed both rulers and people to be humbled for their sin in taking such a patent, and utterly throw it up; on an insignificant pretence of *wrong* thereby done unto the Indians, which were the natives of the country, therein given to the subjects of the English crown. Secondly, an order of the court, upon some just occasion had been made, that an "oath of fidelity" should be, though not *imposed* upon yet *offered* unto the freemen, the better to distinguish those whose fidelity might render them capable of imployment in the government: which order this man vehemently withstood, on a pernisious pretence that it was the prerogative of our Lord Christ alone to have his *office* established with an *oath*; and that an oath being the worship of God, *carnal persons*, whereof he supposed there were many in the land, might not be put upon it. These crimes at last procured a sentence of *banishment* upon him.

The court, about a year before they proceeded unto the *banishment* of this *incendiary*, sent for the pastors of the neighbouring churches, to intimate unto them their design of thus proceeding against him; which yet they were loth to do, before they had advised the *elders* of it, because *he* was himself an elder. Mr. Cotton, with the consent of the other ministers, presented a request unto the magistrates, that they would please to *forbear* prosecuting of him, till they themselves, with their churches, had in a *church-way* endeavoured his conviction and repentance; for they alleged, that they hoped his *violences* proceeded rather from a *misguided conscience*, than from a *seditious principle*. The governour foretold unto them, "You are deceived in the man, if you think he will condescend to learn of any of you:" however, the proposal of the ministers was approved and allowed. But several of the churches having taken the best pains they could, tho' they happily brought the church of Salem to join with them in dealing with the man, yet the effect was, that he renounced them all, as *no churches* of our Lord Jesus Christ. Whereupon the court ordered his removal out of the jurisdiction. . . .

Upon the sentence of the court, Mr. Williams with his party going abroad (as one says) to "seek their providences," removed into the southern parts of New-England, where he, with a few of his own sect, settled a place called Providence. There they proceeded not only unto the *gathering* of a thing like a church, but unto the *renouncing* of their *infant-baptism*; and at this further step of *separation* they stopped not, but Mr. Williams quickly told them, "that being himself misled, he had led them likewise out of the way:" he was now satisfied that there was none upon earth that could administer baptism, and so that their *last* baptism, as well as their *first*, was a *nullity*, for the want of a *called administration*; he advised them therefore to *forego* all, to *dislike* every thing, and wait for the coming of *new* apostles: whereupon they dissolved themselves, and became that sort of sect which we term *Seekers*, keeping to that one principle, "that every one should have the liberty to worship God according to the light of his own conscience;" but owning of no true *churches* or *ordinances* now in the world. It is a memorable reflection made on this occasion by Mr. Cotton, in a book which he published for his own vindication from the printed calumnies of Mr. Williams:

It is a wise proverb, saith he, of a wiser Solomon: the 'backslider in heart [from any truth or way of God] shall be filled with his own ways.' They that separate from their brethren further than they have *just cause*, shall at length find cause, or at least think they have found cause just enough to separate from one another.

I never yet heard of any instance to the contrary, either in England or Holland; and for New-England, there is no such church
of the separation at all that I know of. That separate church (if
it may be called a church) which separated with Mr. Williams,
first broke into a division about a small occasion (as I have
heard) and then broke forth into Anabaptism, and then into
Antibaptism and familism, and now finally into no church at all.

Mr. Williams, after this, was very instrumental in obtaining
a charter for the government of Rhode-Island, which lay
near and with his town of Providence, and was by the people sometimes chosen governour: but for the most part he
led a more private life.

It was more than forty years after his exile that he lived
here, and in many things acquitted himself so laudably, that
many judicious persons judged him to have had the "root
of the matter" in him, during the long winter of this retirement: He used many commendable endeavours to Christian-
ize the Indians in his neighbourhood, of whose language,
tempers and manners he printed a little relation with observations, wherein he *spiritualizes* the *curiosities* with two and
thirty chapters, whereof he entertains his reader. There was
always a good correspondence always held between him and
many worthy and pious people in the colony, from whence
he had been banish'd, tho' his keeping still so many of his
dangerous principles kept the government, unto whose favour some of the English nobility had by letters recommended him, from taking off the sentence of his banishment.
And against the Quakers he afterwards maintained the main
principles of the Protestant religion with much vigour in
some disputations; whereof he afterwards published a large
account, in a book against George Fox and Edward Burrowes, which he entituled, "*George Fox digg'd out of his
burrowes.*" But having reported thus much concerning Mr.
Williams, we shall now supersede further mention of
him. . . .

THE QUAKERS

If the churches of our Lord Jesus Christ must in *every age* be assaulted by HERETICKS, acting under the energy of that old *serpent*, who knowing that as the *first* creation, so the *new* creation begins with *light*, hath used thousands of *blinds* to keep a saving *light* from entring into the souls of men, that being a "people of wrong understanding, he that hath made them shall not have mercy on them;" it must be expected that the churches of New-England should undergo some assaults from the worst of the HERETICKS that *this age* has produced. Now, I know not whether the sect which hath appeared in our days under the name of Quakers, be not upon many accounts the worst of hereticks; for in Quakerism, which has by some been called, the "sink of all heresies," we see the *vomit* cast out in the by-past ages, by whose *kennels* of seducers it has been lick'd up again for a *new digestion*, and once more exposed for the poisoning of mankind; though it pretends unto *light*, yet by the means of that very pretence it leaves the bewildred souls of men "in chains unto darkness," and gives them up to the conduct of an *Ignis Fatuus:* but this I know, they have been the most venomous of all to the churches of America. The beginning of this *upstart sect* has been declared, by one who was a *pillar* of it, in a pamphlet written in the year 1659, where this passage occurs: "It is now about seven years since the Lord raised us up:" And the north of England was reckon'd the place of its nativity. Nevertheless, I can tell the world that the first Quakers that ever were in the world, were certain fanaticks here in our town of Salem, who *held forth* almost all the fancies and whimsies which a few years after were broached by them that were so called in England, with whom yet none of ours had the least communication. . . . Our Salem Quakers indeed of themselves died *childless;* but the numbers of those in England increasing, they did in the year 1657 find a way into New-England, where they first in-

fested Plymouth colony, and were for a while most unhappily successful in seducing the people not only to attend
unto the *mystical dispensations* of the *light within*, as having
the whole of *religion* contained therein, but also to oppose
the good *order*, both *civil* and *sacred*, erected in the colony.
Those persons in Massachusets-colony, whose office it was to
be *watchmen* of it, were much alarmed at the approach of so
great a *plague*, and were at some loss how to prevent it, and
avoid it. Although Quakerism has, by the *new-turn* that such
industrious men as Mr. PENN have given to it, become quite
a *new thing*; yet the old Foxian Quakerism, which then visited New-England, was the grossest collection of *blasphemies*
and *confusions* that ever was heard of. The CHRIST then
witnessed by the Quakers was a "certain heavenly, divine
body, constituted of invisible flesh, blood and bones, in
which Christ came from Heaven; and he put that body into
the other body of our nature, which he took of the Virgin,
and that outermost body he left behind, when he ascended
into heaven, nobody knows where; and this heavenly and
spiritual body" (which the Quakers at length evaporate into
a meet *mystical dispensation*, and at last it is nothing but
that excusing and condemning *principle* in man which we
call *the natural conscience!*) "is the Man Christ, a measure
of which is in the Quakers; upon which accounts the Quakers made themselves to be Christs as truly as ever was Jesus
the Son of Mary." There is in every man a certain excusing
and condemning *principle*, which indeed is nothing but some
remainder of the divine image, left by the compassion of
God upon the conscience of man after his fall; and this
principle the Quakers called, "a measure of the Man Christ
—the *light*, the *seed*, the *word*." The whole history of the
gospel they therefore beheld as acted over again every day
as *literally* as ever it was in Palestine; and what befals this
principle in us, they advanced as the truth of Christ "sacri-
ficed for us, dying, risen, sitting at the right hand of God,
and coming in clouds to judgment."

They set themselves hereupon to extinguish our whole Christian religion, for these airy notions to succeed in the room thereof; they scoffed at "our imagined God beyond the stars:" and said, "your carnal Christ is utterly denied by the light:" the express words in the preachments of these Quaking holders-forth (as 'tis in print attested by some of themselves that had so much Christianity as to leave them upon the *scandal* of it) have been: "it is the work of the devil because people, that have profest the appearance of Christ in the heart, to respect the person without them." And, "it is a delusion to direct the minds of the people to respect Christ, as he is now in heaven above the clouds." They stiled those "blind beasts and liars, who should say that the Scriptures reveal God:" and affirmed it, "the greatest error in the world, and the ground of all errors, to say, the Scriptures are a rule for Christians." They said, "that the Scripture does not tell people of a Trinity, nor three persons in God, but that those three persons are brought in by the Pope." They held "that justification by that righteousness, which Christ fulfilled in his own person without us, is a doctrine of devils." They held, "that they that believe in Christ are not miserable sinners, nor do those things they ought not to do." They said, "if the bodies of men rise again, then there is a pre-eminence in the bodies of men above the bodies of beasts, which is to give Solomon the lie." They said, "they are like to be deceived, who are expecting that Christ's second coming will be personal." They said, "those things called ordinances—as baptism, bread and wine—rose from the Pope's invention." They said, "as for that called the *Lord's day*, people do not understand what they say; every day is the Lord's day." And for *prayer* it self, they said, "all must cease from their own words, and from their own time, and learn to be silent, until the Spirit give them utterance." They said—

But it would be endless to enumerate their heresies; What we have already enumerated is enough to astonish us; in all of which I solemnly protest unto the reader that I have not wronged them at all, but kept close to their *own printed words*. Reader, thou canst not behold these heresies without the exclamation ordinarily used by the blessed Polycarp, when he heard any such matters uttered: "Good God, unto what times hast thou reserved me." The zeal of the Massachuset-colony, to preserve themselves from annoyances of such a blasphemous and confused generation of men, caused them to make *sharp laws* against them, in hopes that the *terror* thereby given to these evil doers would keep them from any invasion upon the colony. But "they must needs go whom the devil drives:" these *devil-driven* creatures did but the more furiously push themselves upon the government, for the *sharp* which had been turned upon them; thereupon the government unhappily proceeded unto the execution of the laws in *scourging*, and then *banishing*, and (upon their mad return) *executing* three or four of the chief offenders: but they considered these wretches, *not as errorists, but as destroyers*, in thus proceeding against them. If the reader enquire with what *spirit* they died, I must sincerely say that, as far as I can learn, they show'd little enough of the spirit of martyrdom. They died not like the true martyrs of Jesus Christ, with the "glorious spirit of God resting" on them. A fierce, a raging, a sullen, and a revengeful spirit, and a degree of *madness* rather inspired them. . . .

A great clamour hath been raised against New-England for their "persecution of the Quakers:" and if any man will appear in the vindication of it, let him do as he please; for my part, I will not. I am verily perswaded these miserable Quakers would in a little while (as we have *now* seen) have come to nothing, if the civil magistrate had not inflicted any civil penalty upon them; nor do I look upon *hæreticide* as an *evangelical* way for the extinguishing of heresies; but rather say, with the judicious Hommius, *Let no magistrate take the life of an offender solely for the crime of heresy;*

but only, when to heresy is added some horrible and insufferable blasphemy against God, or open sedition against the state. 'Tis true, these Quakers did manifest an intolerable contempt of authority, and needlessly pull upon themselves a vengeance, from which the authority would gladly have released them, if they would have accepted of a release; but it is also true, that they were *madmen*—a sort of *lunaticks, dæmoniacks* and *energumens*: He was a wise and good counsellor in Plymouth-Colony who propounded, "that a law might be made for the Quakers to have their heads shaved:" the punishment, I confess, was in some sort capital: but it would have been the best remedy for them; it would have both *sham'd* and *cur'd* them: Or perhaps the punishment which A. Gellius reports the Romans on certain special occasions used upon their soldiers, namely, "to let 'em bleed," had been very agreeable for these Quakers. A *Bethlehem**
seems to have been fitter for them than a *gallows*. Nevertheless, I am not unwilling to transcribe one passage on this occasion, that so my reader, upon the whole, may proceed unto what censure he shall please to bestow upon the matter.

It shall be a few lines of "A Declaration of the General Court of the Massachusets," held at Boston October 18, 1659, published for the satisfaction of the people, a great part of whom were much dissatisfied at what had been done:

About three years since, diverse persons professing themselves Quakers (of whose pernicious opinions and practices we had received intelligence from good hands), both from Barbados and England, arrived at Boston, whose persons were only secured to be sent away by the first opportunity, without censure or punishment, although their professed tenets, turbulent and contemptuous behaviour to authority, would have justified a severer animadversion.—A law was made and published, prohibiting all masters of ships to bring any Quakers into this jurisdiction, and themselves from coming in, on penalty of the house of correction, till they could be sent away. Notwithstanding which, by a *back-door*

* *i.e.* a madhouse

they found entrance; and the penalty inflicted on them proving insufficient to restrain their impudent and insolent obtrusions, was increased—which also being too weak a defence against their impetuous and fanatick fury, necessitated us to endeavour our security; and upon serious consideration, a law was made that such persons should be *banished on pain of death*, according to the example of England, in their provision against Jesuites; which sentence being regularly pronounced, at the last Court of Assistants against these parties, and they either returning, or continuing presumptuously in this jurisdiction after the time limited, were apprehended, and owning themselves to be the persons banished, were sentenced by the Court to *death*—which hath been executed upon two of them. M. D., upon the intercession of a son, had liberty to depart, and accepted of it.—The consideration of our *gradual proceedings*, will vindicate us from the clamorous accusations of *severity*. Our own just and necessary defence calling upon us (other means failing) to offer the *point*, which these persons have violently and wilfully rushed upon, and thereby become *guilty of suicide*—as well as the sparing of *one*, upon an inconsiderable intercession, will manifestly evince we desire their *lives absent*, rather than their *deaths present*.

THE ANABAPTISTS

Now, having done with the Quakers, let it not be misinterpreted if into the *same chapter* we put the inconveniences which the churches of New-England have also suffered from the Anabaptists; albeit they have infinitely more of Christianity among them than the Quakers, and have indeed been useful defenders of Christianity against the assaults of the Quakers; yea, we are willing to acknowledge for our *brethren* as many of them as are willing to be so acknowledged.

It hath been a sore disadvantage unto the reputation of the Anabaptist way, that wherever any *reformation* has been carried on, a sort of people under *that name* have been most unhappy impediments unto the *progress* of it; and thrown it into those confusions that have extremely *scandalized* it, if not utterly *extinguished* it. The histories of the prodigious heresies that have been held, and actions that have been done, by a set of men wearing the Anabaptist name, not only in the low countries in Germany, Switzerland, and Poland, which Melanchton, Luther, Calvin, Bullinger, Zuinglius, Gualteb, Sleidan, Zanchy, who lived in the very time of those extravagances have related, but in England and Ireland also, long since that time, have been improved, *to the perpetual disgrace of false doctrine*. All the world knows, that the most eminent *reformers*, writing against the Anabaptists, have not been able to forbear making their treatises, like what Jerome says of Tertullian's polemical treatises, *every word is a thunderbolt*; and the noble martyr Philpot expressed the mind of them all, when he said, "the Anabaptists are an inordinate kind of men, stirred up by the devil to the destruction of the gospel, having neither Scripture, nor antiquity, nor any thing else for them, but lies and new imaginations, feigning the baptism of children to be the Pope's commandment." Nevertheless, it is well known, that of later times there have been a great many Anti-pedobaptists who have never deserved so hard a character among the churches of God; infant-baptism hath been scrupled by multitudes in our days, who have been in other points most worthy Christians, and as holy, watchful, fruitful, and heavenly people, as perhaps any in the world. Some few of these people have been among the planters of New-England from the beginning, and have been welcome to the communion of our churches, which they have enjoy'd, reserving their *particular opinion* unto themselves. But at length it came to pass that, while *some* of our churches used, it may be, a little too much *cogency* towards the brethren, which would weakly turn their backs when *infants* were brought forth to be baptized in the congregation, there were some of these brethren who, in a day of temptation, broke forth into *schismatical practices* that were justly offensive unto all the churches in this wilderness. . . .

Our Anabaptists, when somewhat of *exasperation* was begun, formed a church at Boston, on May 28, 1665, besides one which they had before at Swanzey, not only with a manifest violation of the *laws* in the Commonwealth, relating to the orderly manner of *gathering* a church, but also with a manifold provocation unto the rest of our churches, by admitting into their own society such as our churches had excommunicated for *moral scandals*; yea, and employing such persons to be administrators of the two sacraments among them. Unto these dissatisfactions of good men at their proceedings, there was added the consideration of their uncharitable disposition to *un-church* all the faithful upon earth besides themselves: 'tis a principle in the confession of their faith, "believers being baptized are visible saints, and the true matter of a visible church." Now, they declared our infant baptism to be a meer nullity, and they arrogate unto themselves the title of Baptists, as if none were baptized but themselves; with *them* therefore our churches were *no churches* of the Lord Jesus Christ, nor are there any "visible saints" among us. Accordingly, when a publick disputation was had with them, it was earnestly and charmingly put unto them in a great assembly, whether they did own the churches of New-England for *true* churches of our Lord Jesus Christ; but they would *not own* it; and when I my self have told some of them, that without putting themselves to so much of travel and expense, as their *separation* cost them, they might enjoy all ordinances in the *fellowship* of our churches, without being treated as offenders for it, if their *conscience tied them up* to withdraw when an infant was baptized; they have replied unto me, "that inasmuch as I was in their judgment an unbaptized man, they could not communicate with me at the table of the Lord." Nor did it at all take off the prejudice of many wise men against them, that they did seem to do what Jereboam was taxed for, in "making priests of the lowest of the people;" or, as the Belgic and others do read it, "of both ends of the people:" and as the learned Zepperus lamented the wrong done to religion in it, that they made *Ministers out of the dregs of*

the rabble—tailors, cobblers, fools; taylors and cobblers,
and other mechanicks, to be ministers, thus these people
chose an honest *shoemaker* to be their pastor; and used
other *mechanicks* in the constant preaching of the gospel:
which caused some other people of a more *liberal education*
to reflect, that if *Goodman* such an one, and *Gaffer* such an
one, were fit for MINISTERS, we had befool'd our selves
in building of Colledges:

> *What need of Muses, since this cobbler stole*
> *Rich inspiration from a leathern sole?*

Yea, some observed, and in print asserted, that this thing
was the real bottom of their combining into a *distinct society* by themselves from divers parts of the colony: These
men having privately exercised their gifts in meetings with
applause, began to think themselves wronged that their light
was put under a bushel: and finding no remedy in our
churches, they threw on a cloak of Anabaptism, and so
gained the thing that they aimed at in a disguise. However it
were, the General Court were so afraid, lest matters might
at last from small beginnings grow into a New "Münster
tragedy," that they enacted some laws for the restraint of
Anabaptistical exorbitances; which laws, though never executed unto the extremity of them, yet were soon laid by,
as to any execution of them at all. There were in this unhappy *schism* several truly godly men, whom it was thought
a very uncomfortable thing to prosecute with severe *impris-
onments* on these controversies; and there came also a letter
from London to the governour of the Massachuset-colony,
(like that which our blessed martyrologist, John Fox, once
wrote unto Queen Elizabeth, to prevent the persecution with
which the Anabaptists were then threatned) subscribed by
no less persons than Dr. Goodwyn, Dr. Owen, Mr. Nye, Mr.
Caryl, and nine other very reverend ministers, wherein were
these among other passages:

We shall not here undertake (in the least) to make any apology
for the persons, opinions and practices of those who are censured
among you. You know our judgment and practice to be contrary
unto theirs, even as yours; wherein (God assisting) we shall continue to the end. Neither shall we return any answer to the
reason of the reverend elders, for the justification of your proceedings, as not being willing to engage in the management of
any the least difference with persons whom we so much love and
honour in the Lord.—But the sum of all which at present we
shall offer to you is, that though the court might apprehend that
they had grounds in general warranting their procedure (in such
cases) in the way wherein they have proceeded, yet that they have
any rule or command rendring their so proceeding indispensably
necessary, under all circumstances of fines or places, we are altogether unsatisfied; and we need not represent unto you how the
case stands with ourselves, and all your brethren and companions
in the services of these latter days in these nations. We are sure
you would be unwilling to put an advantage into the hands of
some who seek pretences and occasions against our liberty, and
to reinforce the former rigour. Now, we cannot deny but this
hath already in some measure been done, in that it hath been
vogued, that persons of our way, principles and spirit, cannot bear
with dissenters from them. And as this greatly reflects on us, so
some of us have observed how already it has turned unto your
own disadvantage.—We leave it to your wisdom to determine
whether, under all these circumstances, and sundry others of the
like nature that might be added, it be not advisable at present to
put an end unto the sufferings and confinements of the persons
censured, and to restore them to their former liberty. You have
the advantage of truth and order; you have the gifts and learning
of an able ministry to manage and defend them; you have the care
and vigilancy of a very worthy magistracy to countenance and
protect them; and to preserve the peace; and (above all) you
have a blessed Lord and Master, who hath the keys of David, who
openeth and no man shutteth, living for ever to take care of his
own concernments among his saints; and assuredly you need not
be disquieted, though some few persons (through their own infirmity and weakness, or through their ignorance, darkness and

prejudices) should to their disadvantage turn out of the way, in some lesser matters, into by-paths of their own.—We only make it our hearty request to you, that you would trust God with his truths and ways so far, as to suspend all rigorous proceedings in corporal restraints or punishments, on persons that dissent from you, and practise the principle of their dissent without danger, or disturbance to the civil peace of the place.

Dated March 25, 1669.

I cannot say that this excellent letter had *immediately* all the effect which it should have had; however, at length it has had its effect; and as Origen pleads against Celsus, that there ever were *differences* among professors of Christianity from the beginning, and it was impossible but that there should be so; nevertheless, these differences hindered not their faith, and love, and obedience: as Justin Martyr pleaded for forbearance, even in the churches, towards Christians that yet thought themselves under obligation to observe the *Mosaic ceremonies*—as Ignatius, before either of them, in his epistle to the Philadelphians, professes, "to persecute men on the account of religion, is to make ourselves conformable to the heathen, who know not God"— the Christians of New-England seem generally to be of such a tolerating disposition towards the Anabaptists; with the synod of Alexandria, condemning all *external force* in religion, of which the Arians were the first among pretended Christians, that were the inventors and promoters: nor hath Anabaptism had one jot the more of growth, I suppose, for it. . . .

THE QUESTIONABLE EFFECT OF PERSECUTION

The great noise that hath been made in the world about the *persecution* made in New-England, I will now stop with only transcribing the words uttered in the sermon to the first "great and general assembly" of the province of Massachuset-Bay, after the two colonies of Massachuset and Plymouth were by a royal charter united:

Things will 'go well,' when magistrates are great promoters of the 'thing that good is,' and of 'what the Lord requireth of them.' I do not mean that it would be well for the civil magistrate, with a civil penalty, to compel men to this or that *way of worship,* which they are *conscientiously* indisposed unto. He is most properly the officer of humane society; and a Christian, by nonconformity to this or that imposed way of worship, does not break the terms on which he is to enjoy the benefits of humane society.

A man has a *right* unto his life, his estate, his liberty, and his family, although he should not come up unto these and those blessed institutions of our Lord. When a man sins in his political capacity, let *political* societies animadvert upon him; but when he sins only in a *religious* capacity, societies more purely *religious* are the fittest then to deal with him. Indeed, in the Old Testament the magistrate was an ecclesiastical officer; and compliance with the Mosaick rites was that which entitled men unto the benefits of Canaan, the typical and renowned land: But now these *figurative* things have more *spiritual* things to answer them. It may be feared that things will not 'go well,' when heresies are not exterminated; but, I pray, when (except once perhaps or so in the case of *Donatism*) did *fines* or *gaols* ever signifie any thing for the cure of hereticks? The primitive church, for the first three hundred years of Christianity, cut off a thousand new Hydra's heads without borrowing such penal laws as have since been used; it was by *sound preaching,* by *discipline,* by *catechizing,* and by *disputation,* that they 'turned to flight the armies of the aliens.' *Then* 'twas that Christians did use to say, *Not by the sword, or dart, or warlike might, is truth promulgated; but by persuasion and conviction.* Afterwards indeed, the *orthodox* engaged the emperors unto severities upon the *hereticks* of those days, but what got they by it? When a wicked Manichee, a sort of Quaker, was put to death, an excellent historian says, ' 'twas a most wretched example, and it made the heresie spread the more.' Such prosecutions do but give a *principle,* which would be but most fatal to the church of God; yea, they do but afford a root for *Cain's club* to grow upon. These *violences* may bring the erroneous to be *hypocrites,* but they will never make them to be believers; no, they naturally prejudice men's minds against the *cause*, which is therein pretended for, as being a weak, a wrong, an evil cause. Wherefore, that things may 'go well,' I would willingly put in a *barr* against the persecution of any that may conscienciously dissent from our way. Possibly the zeal in some famous and worthy disciples of our Lord among our selves has been reported and reckoned as having once had a little too much *fire* on this account; but the churches of God abroad counted that things did not 'go well' among us, until they judged us more fully come up unto the apostolical rule, 'to leave the otherwise minded unto God.' Nor would I desire myself to suffer persecution upon a clearer cause than that of testifying against our persecution of other Christians that are not of my own opinion. I am sure that things will not 'go well' as long as we incur the fulfillment of that aweful word, 'If ye bite and devour one another, take heed that ye be not consumed one of another.' Nevertheless, when things 'go well,' there are magistrates that will set themselves to advance all the *truths* and *ways* of God among their people: Magistrates are not only themselves to *profess* the truths, and *practise* the ways of God but also to *protect* and *favour* all them that shall do the like. There is an aspect of *singular kindness*, defence and support, which magistrates are to bear unto them that *embrace*, and much more to them that *declare* the truths and ways of God. 'Things went well' when it could be said, as in II Chron. xxx. 22, 'Hezekiah spake comfortably unto all that taught the good knowledge of the Lord.' Moreover it belongs unto magistrates to punish all the vices which disturb the good order and repose of humane society; and hence also 'liberty of conscience' is not to be admitted as a cloak for 'liberty of prophaneness.' To live without any *worship* of God, or to *blaspheme* and *revile* his blessed name, is to be chastised as abominably criminal; for there can be no pretence of *conscience* thereunto. Things will 'go well' when we go *thus*, and when there is an accomplishment of that word in Rom. xiii. 3: 'Rulers are not a terror to good works, but unto the evil.'

These things (which were then utter'd with many others, from II Chron. xii. 12, "In Judah things went well") having the thanks of them that represented the province **then** returned for them, I chose in these terms here to represent the *temper* in this matter, which I suppose the considerate part of the province are now come unto: and so long as they continue of it, I durst almost prophesie, that *sectaries* will never be able to make any great impressions upon them.

Magnalia Christi Americana, or The Ecclesiastical History of New-England, Vol. II.,
by the Reverend and Learned Cotton Mather, D. D. F. R. S.
Hartford: Silas Andrus & Son, 1853.

JEREMY
TAYLOR

1 6 1 3 – 1 6 6 7

ROGER
WILLIAMS

c. 1 6 0 4 – 1 6 8 4

JEREMY TAYLOR

ROGER WILLIAMS

FROM THE MODERN POINT OF VIEW ONE OF THE MOST DE-
plorable aspects of historic Christianity is its ruthless persecution of those regarded as heretics. Among the early Christian
Fathers were stout advocates of toleration—Tertullian, Lactantius, Hilary of Poitiers, Ambrose, Martin of Tours. As the
Middle Ages progressed, however, the principle of persecution
for heresy was almost universally accepted. Was not eternal
salvation reserved exclusively for true believers? Were not
heretics by their teachings causing the condemnation of
multitudes to eternal hell? Could any other crime be com-
parable with this in its fearful consequences? Must not heretics, therefore, be stamped out at any cost? This logic seemed
irrefutable, and especially after the institution of the Inquisition, in the thirteenth century, it was acted on with cruel
severity.

To be sure, there were protests from within Roman Catholicism—some from the intellectual point of view, represented by Montaigne's wry remark that "it is setting a high
value on one's opinions to roast men on account of them";
some with more practical motivation, like Erasmus' insistence on the folly and futility of persecution; some from those
who dreamed of toleration as a utopia, like Sir Thomas More

who, approving persecution, admitted that, were it only possible, toleration would be ideal.

If only because they were at first at the receiving end of persecution, the early Reformers disliked it, so that Luther spoke out at the beginning against the death penalty for heresy, and Zwingli with reluctance adopted coercive measures against heretics in Zurich. The pressure of circumstance, however, as well as the old inherited logic which made persecution seem a godly duty, prevented any radical change in the mediaeval idea. Turning from the Roman Church to the civil state for their protection and support, the Reformers conceived kings and magistrates as ordained to defend true religion and to destroy all opposition to it. This sovereign power of the state to determine the religion of the people went so far that in the Peace of Westphalia (1648), which included Roman Catholics, Lutherans, and Swiss Reformers, the princes were granted the privilege of choosing among the three faiths and, if they wished, enforcing their choice upon their people with such penalties for dereliction as they thought needful. Under Protestantism, therefore, the basic principles which supported religious persecution were not at first disturbed; Calvin said, "Liberty of conscience is a devilish doctrine"; and even John Robinson, Pastor of the Pilgrims, gave his hearty approval to the Confession of the Reformed Churches in Belgium, which is typical:

We believe that our gracious God, because of the depravity of mankind, hath apointed kings, princes and magistrates, willing that the world should be governed by certain laws and policies; to the end that the dissoluteness of men might be restrained, and all things carried on among them with good order and decency. For this purpose he hath invested the magistracy with the sword, for the punishment of evil doers, and for the praise of them that do well. And their office is, not only to have regard unto and watch for the welfare of the civil state, but also that they protect the sacred ministry, and thus may prevent and remove all idolatry and false worship; that the kingdom of antichrist may thus be destroyed, and the kingdom of Christ promoted. They must, therefore, countenance the preaching of the gospel everywhere, that God may be honored and worshiped by every one, as he commands in his Word.

From the beginning, however, there were in Protestantism the seeds of revolt against this whole concept of government's function. The Reformers themselves had made one of the most courageous appeals in history for personal religious liberty against authority. The spirit and logic of this appeal were inherent in the Reformation and, although slow in coming to fruition, they never stopped growing. It was to be expected that insight into the iniquity and futility of religious persecution should begin among those who were its victims. The Socinians, for example, anti-trinitarians from whom our modern Unitarians sprang, were driven from Italy to Switzerland and thence to Transylvania and Poland, and in the Socinian Catechism of Rakow (1574) they stoutly asserted the principle of religious liberty.

To be sure, most of these early appeals for freedom in religion were limited in scope. The Socinians thought that the liberty they craved could still be achieved under an established religion in a state-church. Others, pleading for toleration rather than for anything so remote as complete separation of church and state, would have limited freedom of conscience to certain selected Christian sects; or to all Christians but not to Jews and Moslems; or to all religions but not to atheists. John Milton, whose *Areopagitica* was a notable demand for freedom of thought, speech and publication, wrote at the end of his life a tract, entitled *Of True Religion, Heresy, Schism, Toleration*, in which he appealed for tolerance, but within limits. Many sorts of Christians were to be tolerated, even Anabaptists, Arians, Socinians, Arminians, but not "Popery" which, said Milton, "as it extirpates all religious and civil supremacies, so itself should be extirpate; provided first that all charitable and compassionate means be used to win and gain the weak and misled." The movement was afoot, however, by way of toleration, toward the complete deliverance of conscience in matters of religion from the interference of civil government.

It was the Anabaptists, the most persecuted of all the sects, who from the beginning took the most radical stand. At the very beginning of the movement Balthasar Hübmaier wrote a pamphlet, "*Concerning Heretics and Those That Burn Them*," in which he said: "The greatest heretics are the inquisitors themselves, for Christ did not come to butcher and to burn, but to preserve and improve. . . . A Turk or a heretic is not to be overcome by fire or sword, but by patience and instruction. The burning of heretics is an apparent confession but an actual denial of Christ." From then on the stand of the Anabaptists, and of their successors, the Baptists, became ever more clear, more passionate and more radical, until it issued in Roger Williams' demand for complete separation of church and state, and complete liberty of conscience for men and women of all religions or of no religion.

One of the earliest confessions of faith from English Baptists—then in exile in Holland—makes their position clear:

The magistrate, by virtue of his office, is not to meddle with religion or matters of conscience, not to compel men to this or that form of religion or doctrine, but to leave the Christian religion to the free conscience of every one, and to meddle only with political matters (Romans 13:3,4), namely, injustice and wrong of one against another, such as murder, adultery, theft and the like; because Christ alone is the King and Lawgiver of the church and the conscience (James 4:12)."

David Masson, in his *Life of John Milton*, says: "It is believed that this is the first expression of the absolute principle of Liberty of Conscience in the public articles of any body of Christians"; and concerning the little body of Baptists who, returning from Holland, established their congregation in London, he adds: "It was, in short, from their little dingy meeting-house, somewere in Old London that there flashed out, first in England, the absolute doctrine of Religious Liberty."

For the story of the long, hard struggle against the ancient, inveterate ideas which underlay persecution for conscience's sake, one may turn to the article on *Toleration*, in the *Encyclopaedia of Religion and Ethics*, or to such books as *The Contest for Liberty of Conscience in England*, by Wallace St. John; *The Progress of Religious Freedom As Shown in the History of Toleration Acts*, by Philip Schaff; *The Development of Religious Toleration in England*, by W. K. Jordan; *Religion and the State: America*, by E. B. Greene; *The Rise of Religious Liberty in America*, by S. H. Cobb; *The Travail of Religious Liberty*, by Roland H. Bainton; and *Church and State in the United States*, by Anson Phelps Stokes.

For the purposes of this anthology we choose two men, one representing the gradual growth of the spirit of tolerance, the other representing the full claim to complete separation of church and state.

Jeremy Taylor was a distinguished priest of the Church of England, an ardent royalist, who through thick and thin supported Charles I and, after Oliver Cromwell's régime, eagerly welcomed Charles II. As a young man he flourished under the special patronage of Archbishop Laud, a notorious believer in extirpating heretics and, never compromising his staunch devotion to the English church, he was elevated to a bishopric in Ireland under Charles II. While Cromwell was in power, however, Taylor was driven from all his preferments and took refuge in a friendly home in Wales. There he felt the force and saw the meaning of religious intolerance from the victim's point of view, and this experience, illumined by his own genuine piety and by the temperamental gentleness of his disposition and his humane kindliness, issued in one of his most notable books, *The Liberty of Prophesying, Showing the Unreasonableness of Prescribing to Other Men's Faith; and the Iniquity of Persecuting Differing Opinions* (1647). The spirit of this book is radiant with charity, magnanimity, conciliation, made all the more remarkable because it was written in one of the bitterest eras in English history. Taylor is determined no longer to be "hasty in calling every disliked opinion by the name of heresy"; and since we are all so fallible, he is sure that it must be "inconsistent with God's goodness to condemn those who err, when the error hath nothing of the will in it."

To be sure, the scope of the book is limited. Taylor was thinking exclusively of Christians, and his major thesis is that all Christians who accept the Apostle's Creed—as practically all the various sects did—ought to live together with mutual tolerance, understanding and sympathy. Despite this limitation in his objective, however, and despite the further fact that, as a bishop in Ireland years later, he found it so difficult to practise what he preached in dealing with the Presbyterian ministers that, calling them in his exasperation "wild asses of the wilderness," he exiled all of them from his diocese to Scotland, Jeremy Taylor's book is one of the great outstanding appeals in the history of Protestantism for Christian charity toward heretics. The best biography of him which we have is *Jeremy Taylor*, by Edmund Gosse.

Roger Williams, about seven years younger than Taylor, was educated at Cambridge University and was ordained to the priesthood in the English church but, disturbed by scruples concerning the ecclesiastical situation in England, he refused all preferment for conscience's sake and emigrated to New England to find relief. Settled as teacher in the church in Salem, he aroused the hostility of the Puritans. Retreating to the ministry of the church in Plymouth, he returned to Salem after two years, and again met the opposition of his brethren at the Bay. He had early fallen under the influence of the Dutch Anabaptists and his ideas seemed to the Puritans intolerably subversive. He thought that civil government had no jurisdiction over conscience in matters of religion; that the colonists had no right to the Indians' land on the English king's say-so but should pay them for it; that taking an oath in God's name was a religious act and that it should not be required of an unregenerate man. For such opinions he was banished from the colony and, about to be forcibly seized and deported to England, he fled to the wilderness and founded Rhode Island, the first civil state in history where men and women of any religion or of no religion were completely free. He thus brought to its culmination a trend in Protestantism which for long years had been moving toward this climax.

His book, *The Bloudy Tenent of Persecution*, was published during the author's visit to England in 1643-1644. Its style is commonly stilted and often difficult. For the purposes of this anthology his spelling, capitalization and excessive italicizing have been modernized, and his statements of conviction have been lifted from the dialogue between Peace and Truth, which forms the structure of his book. His central message is one of the most important that ever came out of Protestantism. Among many biographies of the author probably no two are better than *Roger Williams, the Pioneer of Religious Liberty*, by Oscar S. Straus, and *Roger Williams, a Study of the Life, Times and Character of a Political Pioneer*, by Edmund J. Carpenter. Two other valuable works are *Roger Williams; New England Firebrand*, by James Ernst, and *The Irrepressible Democrat: Roger Williams*, by S. H. Brockunier.

By the middle of the seventeenth century religious toleration had become a popular cause, with many adherents in one degree or another supporting it. The famous "Act Concerning Religion," drafted in 1649 by Lord Baltimore, a Roman Catholic, for his Maryland colony declared for "liberty of conscience in matters of religion," although as finally passed the Act provided drastic penalties for all who denied Christ's divinity. William Penn's statement is famous: "I abhor two principles in religion, and pity them that own them. The first is obedience to authority without conviction; and the other is destroying them that differ from me for God's sake." As an example of popular revulsion against the persecuting mania, we offer the *Remonstrance*, presented to Governor Stuyvesant of the New Netherlands colony by the citizens of the town of Flushing, Long Island. New Netherlands was competing with New England for emigrants, and the founders of Flushing in 1645, among other benefits, had been granted, in their patent, the right "to have and enjoy liberty of conscience, according to the custom and manner of Holland, without molestation or disturbance from any magistrates, or any other ecclesiastical minister, that may pretend jurisdiction over them." When, therefore, twelve years later Governor Stuyvesant posted proclamations in every town, exiling Quakers and declaring that any person entertaining one of them even for a single night would be fined fifty pounds, Flushing rebelled. Their *Remonstrance* may be taken as an indication of the rising tide of popular resentment against religious persecution.

THE INFINITE VARIETY OF OPINIONS IN MATTERS OF RELIGION,
as they have troubled Christendom with interests, factions,
and partialities, so have they caused great divisions of the
heart, and variety of thoughts and designs amongst pious and
prudent men. For they all, seeing the inconveniences which
the disunion of persuasions and opinions have produced directly or accidentally, have thought themselves obliged to stop
this inundation of mischiefs, and have made attempts accordingly. But it hath happened to most of them as to a mistaken
physician, who gives excellent physic but misapplies it, and so
misses of his cure. So have these men: their attempts have
been ineffectual; for they put their help to a wrong part, or
they have endeavored to cure the symptoms, and have let the
disease alone till it seemed incurable. Some have endeavored
to reunite these fractions, by propounding such a guide which
they were all bound to follow; hoping that the unity of a
guide would have persuaded unity of minds; but who this
guide should be, at last became such a question, that it was
made part of the fire that was to be quenched, so far was it
from extinguishing any part of the flame. Others thought of a
rule, and this must be the means of union, or nothing could
do it. But supposing all the world had been agreed of this

rule, yet the interpretation of it was so full of variety that this also became part of the disease for which the cure was pretended. All men resolved upon this, that though they yet had not hit upon the right, yet some way must be thought upon to reconcile differences in opinion; thinking, so long as this variety should last, Christ's kingdom was not advanced, and the work of the gospel went on but slowly. Few men in the mean time considered, that so long as men had such variety of principles, such several constitutions, educations, tempers, and distempers, hopes, interests, and weaknesses, degrees of light, and degrees of understanding, it was impossible all should be of one mind. And what is impossible to be done is not necessary it should be done; and therefore, although variety of opinions was impossible to be cured (and they who attempted it did like him who claps his shoulder to the ground to stop an earthquake), yet the inconveniences arising from it might possibly be cured, not by uniting their beliefs—that was to be despaired of—but by curing that which caused these mischiefs, and accidental inconveniences of their disagreeings. For although these inconveniences, which every man sees and feels, were consequent to this diversity of persuasions, yet it was but accidentally and by chance; inasmuch as we see that in many things, and they of great concernment, men allow to themselves and to each other a liberty of disagreeing, and no hurt neither. And certainly if diversity of opinions were of itself the cause of mischiefs, it would be so ever, that is, regularly and universally (but that we see it is not), for there are disputes in Christendom concerning matters of greater concernment than most of those opinions that distinguish sects and make factions; and yet because men are permitted to differ in those great matters, such evils are not consequent to such differences as are to the uncharitable managing of smaller and more inconsiderable questions. . . . Since then if men are quiet and charitable in some disagreeings, that then and there the inconvenience ceases, if they were so in all others where lawfully they might (and they may in most), Christendom should be no longer rent in pieces, but would be redintegrated in a new Pentecost; and although the Spirit of God did rest upon us in divided tongues, yet so long as those tongues were of fire not to kindle strife, but to warm our affections and inflame our charities, we should find that this variety of opinions in several persons would be looked upon as an argument only of diversity of operations, while the Spirit is the same; and that another man believes not so well as I, is only an argument that I have a better and a clearer illumination than he, that I have a better gift than he, received a special grace and favor, and excel him in this, and am perhaps excelled by him in many more. And if we all impartially endeavor to find a truth, since this endeavor and search only is in our power, I can see no reason why this pious endeavor to find out truth shall not be of more force to unite us in the bonds of charity, than his misery in missing it shall be to disunite us. So that since a union of persuasion is impossible to be attained, if we would attempt the cure by such remedies as are apt to enkindle and increase charity, I am confident we might see a blessed peace would be the reward and crown of such endeavors. . . .

For if it be evinced that one heaven shall hold men of several opinions, if the unity of faith be not destroyed by that which men call differing religions, and if an unity of charity be the duty of us all even towards persons that are not persuaded of every proposition we believe, then I would fain know to what purpose are all those stirs and great noises in Christendom; those names of faction, the several names of churches not distinguished by the division of kingdoms, the church obeying the government, which was the primitive rule and canon, but distinguished by names of sects and men. These are all become instruments of hatred; thence come schisms and parting of communions, and then persecutions, and then wars and rebellion, and then the dissolutions of all friendships and societies. All these mischiefs proceed not from this, that all men are not of one mind, for that is neither necessary nor possible, but that every opinion is made an article of faith, every article is a ground of a quarrel, every quarrel makes a faction, every faction is zealous, and all zeal pretends for God, and whatsoever is for God cannot be too much. We by this time are come to that pass, we think we love not God except we hate our brother; and we have not the virtue of religion, unless we persecute all religions but our own: for lukewarmness is so odious to God and man, that we, proceeding furiously upon these mistakes, by supposing we preserve the body, we destroy the soul of religion; or by being zealous for faith, we are cold in charity, and so lose the reward of both. . . .

Now, if more were necessary than the articles of the creed (the Apostles' Creed) I demand why was it made the characteristic note of a Christian from a heretic, or a Jew, or an infidel? Or to what purpose was it composed? Or if this was intended as sufficient, did the apostles, or those churches which they founded, know any thing else to be necessary? If they did not, then either nothing more is necessary (I speak of matters of mere belief), or they did not know all the will of the Lord, and so were unfit dispensers of the mysteries of the kingdom; or if they did know more was necessary, and yet would not insert it, they did an act of public notice, and consigned it to all ages of the church, to no purpose, unless to beguile credulous people by making them believe their faith was sufficient, having tried it by that touchstone apostolical, when there was no such matter.

But if this was sufficient to bring men to heaven then, why not now? If the apostles admitted all to their communion that believed this creed, why shall we exclude any that preserve the same entire? Why is not our faith of these articles as of much efficacy for bringing us to heaven, as it was in the churches apostolical?—who had guides more infallible, that might without error have taught them superstructures enough, if they had been necessary. And so they did: but that they did not insert them into the creed, when they might have done it with as much certainty as these articles, makes it clear to my understanding, that other things were not necessary, but these were; that whatever profit and advantages might come from other articles, yet these were sufficient; and however certain persons might accidentally be obliged to believe much more, yet this was the one and only foundation of faith upon which all persons were to build their hopes of heaven; this was therefore necessary to be taught to all, because of necessity to be believed by all. . . .

In the meantime, the church, that is, the governors of the churches, are to judge for themselves, and for all those who cannot judge for themselves. For others, they must know that their governors judge for them, too, so as to keep them in peace and obedience, though not for the determination of their private persuasions. . . . If there be a manifest error, as it often happens, or if the church governors themselves be rent into innumerable sects, as it is this day in Christendom, then we are to be as wise as we can in choosing our guides, and then to follow so long as that reason remains for which we first chose them. And even in that government which was an immediate sanction of God, I mean the ecclesiastical government of the synagogue, where God had consigned the high priest's authority, with a menace of death to them that should disobey . . . it came once to pass, that if the priest had been obeyed in his conciliary degrees, the whole nation had been bound to believe the condemnation of our blessed Savior to have been just; and, at another time, the apostles must no more have preached in the name of Jesus. But here was manifest error: and the case is the same to every man that invincibly, and therefore innocently, believes it so. "Obey God rather than man," is our rule in such cases. For although every man is bound to follow his guide, unless he believes his guide to mislead him, yet when he sees reason against his guide it is best to follow his reason; for though in this he may fall into error, yet he will escape the sin—he may do violence to truth, but never to his own conscience; and an honest error is better than an hypocritical profession of truth, or a violent luxation of the understanding; since, if he retains his honesty and simplicity, he cannot err in a matter of faith or absolute necessity. God's goodness hath secured all honest and careful persons from that—for other things he must follow the best guides he can, and he cannot be obliged to follow better than God hath given him. . . .

He that gives himself up wholly to a guide, is oftentimes (I mean, if he be a discerning person) forced to do violence to his own understanding, and to lose all the benefit of his own discretion, that he may reconcile his reason to his guide. And of this we see infinite inconveniences in the church of Rome; for we find persons of great understanding oftentimes so amused with the authority of their church, that it is pity to see them sweat in answering some objections, which they know not how to do, but yet believe they must, because the church hath said it. So that if they read, study, pray, search records, and use all the means of art and industry in the pursuit of truth, it is not with resolution to follow that which shall seem truth to them, but to confirm what before they did believe; and if any argument shall seem unanswerable against any article of their church, they are to take it for a temptation, not for an illumination, and they are to use it accordingly; which makes them make the devil to be the author of that which God's Spirit hath assisted them to find, in the use of lawful means, and the search of truth; and when the devil of falsehood is like to be cast out by God's

Spirit, they say that it is through Belzebub, which was one of the worst things that ever the Pharisees said or did. . . .

God will have no man pressed with another's inconveniences in matters spiritual and intellectual—no man's salvation to depend upon another; and every tooth that eats sour grapes shall be set on edge for itself, and for none else; and this is remarkable in that saying of God by the prophet: "If the prophet ceases to tell my people of their sins, and leads them into error, the people shall die in their sins, and the blood of them I will require at the hands of that prophet." Meaning, that God hath so set the prophets to guide us; that we also are to follow them by a voluntary assent, by an act of choice and election. For, although accidentally and occasionally the sheep may perish by the shepherd's fault, yet that which hath the chiefest influence upon their final condition, is their own act and election; and therefore God hath so appointed guides to us, that if we perish it may be accounted upon both our scores, upon our own and the guides' too; which says plainly, that although we are intrusted to our guides, yet we are intrusted to ourselves too. Our guides must direct us; and yet, if they fail, God hath not so left us to them, but he hath given us enough to ourselves to discover their failings, and our own duties in all things necessary; and for other things we must do as well as we can. But it is best to follow our guides, if we know nothing better; but if we do, it is better to follow the pillar of fire, than a pillar of cloud, though both possibly may lead to Canaan: but then, also, it is possible that it may be otherwise. But I am sure, if I do my own best; then, if it be best to follow a guide, and if it be also necessary, I shall be sure, by God's grace and my own endeavor, to get to it; but if I, without the particular engagement of my understanding follow a guide, possibly I may be guilty of extreme negligence, or I may extinguish God's Spirit, or do violence to my own reason. And whether intrusting myself wholly with another be not a laying up my talent in a napkin, I am not so well assured: I am certain the other is not. And since another man's answering for me will not hinder, but that I also shall answer for myself; as it concerns him to see he does not willfully misguide me, so it concerns me to see that he shall not, if I can help it; if I cannot, it will not be required at my hands: whether it be his fault or his invincible error, I shall be charged with neither.

This is no other than what is enjoined as a duty. For since God will be justified with a free obedience—and there is an obedience of understanding as well as of will and affection—it is of great concernment, as to be willing to believe whatever God says, so also to inquire diligently whether the will of God be so as it is pretended. Even our acts of understanding are acts of choice; and therefore it is commanded, as a duty, to search the Scriptures, to try the spirits, whether they be of God or no, of ourselves to be able to judge what is right, to prove all things, and to retain that which is best. . . .

No Christian is to be put to death, dismembered, or otherwise directly persecuted for his opinion, which does not teach impiety or blasphemy. If it plainly and apparently brings in a crime, and himself does act it or encourage it, then the matter of fact is punishable according to its proportion or malignity; as, if he preaches treason or sedition, his opinion is not his excuse, because it brings in a crime, and a man is never the less traitor because he believes it lawful to commit treason; and a man is a murderer if he kills his brother unjustly, although he thinks he does God good service in it. Matters of fact are equally judicable, whether the principle of them be from within or from without; and if a man could pretend to innocence in being seditious, blasphemous, or perjured, by persuading himself it is lawful, there were as great a gate opened to all iniquity as will entertain all the pretenses, the designs, the impostures, and disguises of the world. And therefore God hath taken order, that all rules concerning matters of fact and good life shall be so clearly explicated that, without the crime of the man, he cannot be ignorant of all his practical duty. And therefore the apostles and primitive doctors made no scruple of condemning such persons for heretics that did dogmatise a sin. He that teacheth others to sin is worse than he that commits the crime, whether he be tempted by his own interest, or encouraged by the other's doctrine. . . . I deny not, but certain and known idolatry, or any other sort of practical impiety, with its principiant doctrine, may be punished corporally, because it is no other but matter of fact: but no matter of mere opinion, no errors that of themselves are not sins, are to be persecuted, or punished by death, or corporal inflictions. . . .

All the former discourse is sufficient argument how easy it is for us, in such matters, to be deceived. So long as Christian religion was a simple profession of the articles of belief, and a hearty prosecution of the rules of good life, the fewness of the articles and the clearness of the rule was cause of the seldom prevarication. But when divinity is swelled up to so great a body, when the several questions, which the peevishness and wantonness of sixteen ages have commenced, are concentered into one, and from all these questions something is drawn into the body of theology till it hath ascended up to the greatness of a mountain, and the sum of divinity collected by Aquinas makes a volume as great as was that of Livy, mocked at in the epigram,

"A work which shelves like mine can scarce contain—"

it is impossible for any industry to consider so many particulars, in the infinite numbers of questions as are necessary to be considered before we can with certainty determine any. And after all the considerations which we can have in a whole age, we are not sure not to be deceived. The obscurity of some questions, the nicety of some articles, the intricacy of some revelations, the variety of human understandings, the windings of logic, the tricks of adversaries, the subtlety of sophisters, the engagement of education, personal affections, the portentous number of writers, the infinity of authorities, the vastness of some arguments, as consisting in enumeration of many particulars, the uncertainty of others, the several degrees of probability, the difficulties of Scripture, the invalidity of probation of tradition, the opposition of all exterior arguments to each other, and their open contestation, the public violence done to authors and records, the private arts and supplantings, the falsifyings, the indefatigable industry of some men to abuse all understandings and all persuasions into their own opinions—these, and thousands more, even all the difficulty of things, and all the weaknesses of man, and all the arts of the devil, have made it impossible for any man, in so great variety of matter, not to be deceived. No man pretends to it but the pope, and no man is more deceived than he is in that very particular.

From hence proceeds a danger which is consequent to this proceeding; for if we, who are so apt to be deceived and so insecure in our resolution of questions disputable, should persecute a disagreeing person, we are not sure we do not fight against God; for if his proposition be true and persecuted, then, because all truth derives from God, this proceeding is against God; and therefore this is not to be done, upon Gamaliel's ground, lest peradventure we be found to fight against God, of which because we can have no security (at least) in this case, we have all the guilt of a doubtful or an uncertain conscience. For if there be no security in the thing, as I have largely proved, the conscience, in such cases, is as uncertain as the question is: and if it be not doubtful where it is uncertain, it is because the man is not wise, but as confident as ignorant; the first without reason, and the second without excuse. And it is very disproportionable for a man to persecute another certainly, for a proposition, that, if he were wise, he would know is not certain, at least the other person may innocently be uncertain of it. If he be killed he is certainly killed; but if he be called heretic it is not so certain that he is an heretic. It were good, therefore, that proceedings were according to evidence, and the rivers not swell over the banks, nor a certain definitive sentence of death passed upon such persuasions which cannot certainly be defined. And this argument is of so much the more force because we see that the greatest persecutions that ever have been were against truth, even against Christianity itself; and it was a prediction of our blessed Savior that persecution should be the lot of true believers: and if we compute the experience of suffering Christendom, and the prediction, that truth should suffer, with those few instances of suffering heretics, it is odds but persecution is on the wrong side, and that it is error and heresy that is cruel and tyrannical, especially since the truth of Jesus Christ, and of his religion, are so meek, so charitable, and so merciful. And we may, in this case, exactly use the words of St. Paul: "But as then, he that was born after the flesh, persecuted him that was born after the spirit; even so it is now;" and so it ever will be till Christ's second coming.

Whoever persecutes a disagreeing person, arms all the world against himself, and all pious people of his own persuasion, when the scales of authority returns to his adversary and attest his contradictory: and then what can he urge for mercy for himself, or his party, that showeth none to others? If he says, that he is to be spared because he believes true, but the other was justly persecuted because he was in error, he is ridiculous; for he is as confidently believed to be a heretic as he believes his adversary such; and whether he be or no, being the thing in question, of this he is not to be his own judge: but he that hath authority on his side will be sure to judge against him. So that what either side can indifferently make use of, it is good that neither would, because neither side can, with reason sufficient, do it in prejudice of the other. . . .

Either the disagreeing person is in error or not, but a true believer; in either of the cases, to persecute him is extremely imprudent. For if he be a true believer, then it is a clear case that we do open violence to God, and his servants, and his truth. If he be in error, what greater folly and stupidity than to give to error the glory of martyrdom, and the advantages which are accidentally consequent to a persecution? For as it was true of the martyrs, "As often as we die, so often do we begin to live," and the increase of their trouble was the increase of their confidence and the establishment of their persuasions, so it is in all false opinions; for that an opinion is true or false, is extrinsical or accidental to the consequents and advantages it gets by being afflicted. And there is a popular pity that follows all persons in misery, and that compassion breeds likeness of affections, and that very often produces likeness of persuasion; and so much the rather, because there arises a jealousy and pregnant suspicion that they who persecute an opinion are destitute of sufficient arguments to confute it, and that the hangman is the best disputant. For if those arguments which they have for their own doctrine were a sufficient ground of confidence and persuasion, men would be more willing to use those means which are better compliances with human understanding, which more naturally do satisfy it, which are more human and Christian than that way which satisfies none, which destroys many, which provokes more, which makes all men jealous. . . .

It is unnatural and unreasonable to persecute disagreeing opinions. Unnatural; for understanding—being a thing wholly spiritual—cannot be restrained, and therefore neither punished by corporal afflictions. It is in *aliena republica*, a matter of another world: you may as well cure the colic by brushing a man's clothes, or fill a man's belly with a syllogism: these things do not communicate in matter, and therefore neither in action nor passion; and since all punishments, in a prudent government, punish the offender to prevent a future crime, and so it proves more medicinal than vindictive, the punitive act being in order to the cure and prevention; and since no punishment of the body can cure a disease in the soul, it is disproportionable in nature; and in all civil government, to punish where the punishment can do no good, it may be an act of tyranny, but never of justice. For is an opinion ever the more true or false for being persecuted? Some men have believed it the more, as being provoked into a confidence and vexed into a resolution; but the thing itself is not the truer; and though the hangman may confute a man with an inexplicable dilemma, yet not convince his understanding; for such premises can infer no conclusion but that of a man's life; and a wolf may as well give laws to the understanding as he whose dictates are only propounded in violence and writ in blood. And a dog is as capable of a law as a man, if there be no choice in his obedience, nor discourse in his choice, nor reason to satisfy his discourse. And as it is unnatural, so it is unreasonable that Sempronius should force Caius to be of his opinion, because Sempronius is consul this year, and commands the Lictors; as if he that can kill a man cannot but be infallible; and if he be not, why should I do violence to my conscience because he can do violence to my person?

Force in matters of opinion can do no good, but is very apt to do hurt; for no man can change his opinion when he will, or be satisfied in his reason that his opinion is false because discountenanced. If a man could change his opinion when he lists, he might cure many inconveniences of his life: all his fears and his sorrows would soon disband, if he would but alter his opinion, whereby he is persuaded that such an accident that afflicts him is an evil, and such an object formidable; let him but believe himself impregnable, or that he receives a benefit when he is plundered, disgraced, imprisoned, condemned, and afflicted, neither his sleeps need to be disturbed, nor his quietness discomposed. But if a man cannot change his opinion when he lists, nor ever

does heartily or resolutely but when he cannot do otherwise, then to use force may make him an hypocrite but
never to be a right believer; and so, instead of erecting a
trophy to God and true religion, we build a monument for
the devil. . . .

The question, whether the prince may tolerate divers persuasions, is no more than whether he may lawfully persecute
any man for not being of his opinion. Now, in this case, he
is just so to tolerate diversity of persuasions as he is to tolerate public actions; for no opinion is judicable, nor no person punishable, but for a sin; and if his opinion, by reason
of its managing or its effect, be a sin in itself, or becomes a
sin to the person, then, as he is to do towards other sins, so
to that opinion or man so opining. But to believe so, or not
so, when there is no more but mere believing, is not in his
power to enjoin—therefore not to punish. And it is not only
lawful to tolerate disagreeing persuasions, but the authority
of God only is competent to take notice of it, and infallible
to determine it, and fit to judge; and therefore no human
authority is sufficient to do all those things which can justify
the inflicting temporal punishments upon such as do not
conform in their persuasions to a rule or authority which is
not only fallible, but supposed by the disagreeing person to
be actually deceived.

But I consider, that in the toleration of a different opinion, religion is not properly and immediately concerned, so
as in any degree to be endangered. For it may be safe in
diversity of persuasions, and it is also a part of Christian
religion, that the liberty of men's consciences should be preserved in all things where God hath not set a limit and made
a restraint; that the soul of man should be free, and
acknowledge no master but Jesus Christ; that matters spiritual should not be restrained by punishments corporal; that
the same meekness and charity should be preserved in the
promotion of Christianity that gave it foundation, and incre-

ment, and firmness in its first publication; that conclusions should not be more dogmatical than the virtual resolution and efficacy of the premises; and that the persons should not more certainly be condemned than their opinions confuted; and lastly, that the infirmities of men and difficulties of things should be both put in balance, to make abatement in the definitive sentence against men's persons. But then, because toleration of opinions is not properly a question of religion, it may be a question of policy: and although a man may be a good Christian, though he believe an error not fundamental, and not directly or evidently impious, yet his opinion may accidentally disturb the public peace, through the overactiveness of the person, and the confidence of their belief, and the opinion of its appendant necessity; and therefore toleration of differing persuasions, in these cases, is to be considered upon political grounds, and is just so to be admitted or denied as the opinions or toleration of them may consist with the public and necessary ends of government. Only this: as Christian princes must look to the interest of their government, so especially must they consider the interests of Christianity, and not call redargution or modest discovery of an established error, by the name of disturbance of the peace. Let them remember but the gentleness of Christianity, the liberty of consciences which ought to be preserved; and let them do justice to the persons, whoever they are that are peevish, provided no man's person be overborne with prejudice. For if it be necessary for all men to subscribe to the present established religion, by the same reason, at another time, a man may be bound to subscribe to the contradictory, and so to all religions in the world. And they only who by their too much confidence entitle God to all their fancies, and make them to be questions of religion and evidences for heaven, or consignations to hell, they only think this doctrine unreasonable; and they are the men that first disturb the church's peace, and then think there is no appeasing the tumult but by getting the victory. But they that consider things wisely, understand that since salvation and damnation depend not upon impertinencies, and yet that public peace and tranquillity may, the prince is in this case to seek how to secure government, and the issues and intentions of that, while there is in the cases directly no insecurity to religion, unless by the accidental uncharitableness of them that dispute; which uncharitableness is much prevented when the public peace is secured, and no person is on either side engaged upon revenge, or troubled with disgrace, or vexed with punishments by any decretory sentence against him. It was the saying of a wise stateman (I mean Thuanus), "If you persecute heretics or discrepants, they unite themselves as to a common defence: if you permit them, they divide themselves upon private interest." . . .

Let the prince and the secular power have a care the commonwealth be safe. For whether such and such a section of Christians be to be permitted, is a question rather political than religious; for as for the concernments of religion, these instances have furnished us with sufficient to determine us in our duties as to that particular, and by one of these all particulars may be judged.

And now it were a strange inhumanity to permit Jews in a commonwealth, whose interest is served by their inhabitation, and yet, upon equal grounds of state and policy, not to permit differing sects of Christians; for although possibly there is more danger men's persuasions should be altered in a commixture of divers sects of Christians, yet there is not so much danger when they are changed from Christian to Christian, as if they be turned from Christian to Jew, as many are daily in Spain and Portugal.

And this is not to be excused by saying the church hath no power over them *qui foris sunt*, "who are without," as Jews are. For it is true the church in the capacity of spiritual regiments, hath nothing to do with them, when they are subjects of his regiment; they may not be excommunicate any more than a stone may be killed, because they are not of the Christian communion, but they are living persons, parts of the commonwealth, infinitely deceived in their religion, and very dangerous if they offer to persuade men to their opinions, and are the greatest enemies of Christ, whose honor and the interest of whose service a Christian prince is bound with all his power to maintain. And when the question is of punishing disagreeing persons with death, the church hath equally nothing to do with them both, for she hath nothing to do with the temporal sword; but the prince, whose subjects equally Christians and Jews are, hath equal power over their persons; for a Christian is not more a subject than a Jew is; the prince hath upon them both the same power of life and death; so that the Jew by being no Christian is not *foris*, or any more an exempt person for his body or his life than the Christian is. And yet in all churches where the secular power hath temporal reason to tolerate the Jews, they are tolerated without any scruple in religion; which thing is of more consideration, because the Jews are direct blasphemers of the Son of God, and blasphemy by their own law, the law of Moses, is made capital, and might with greater reason, be inflicted upon them who acknowledge its obligation than urged upon Christians as an authority, enabling princes to put them to death who are accused of accidental and consequentive blasphemy and idolatry respectively, which yet they hate and disavow with much zeal and heartiness of persuasion. And I cannot yet learn a reason why we shall not be more complying with them who are of the household of faith: for at least they are children though they be but rebellious children (and if they were not, what hath the mother to do with them any more than with the Jews?)—they are in some relation or habitude of the family, for they are consigned with the same baptism, profess the same faith delivered by the apostles, are erected in the same hope, and look for the same glory to be revealed to them at the coming of their common Lord and

Savior, to whose service, according to their understanding,
they have vowed themselves: and if the disagreeing persons
be to be esteemed as heathens and publicans, yet not worse,
"have no company with them," that is the worst that is to be
done to such a man in St. Paul's judgment: "yet count him
not as an enemy, but admonish him as a brother."

The Liberty of Prophesying, by Jeremy Taylor.
Duff Green, 1834.

From

THE BLOODY TENET
OF PERSECUTION

by

ROGER WILLIAMS

MY EARS HAVE LONG BEEN FILLED WITH A THREEFOLD doleful outcry.

First, of one hundred forty-four thousand virgins (Rev. 14) forced and ravished by emperors, kings and governors to their beds of worship and religion, set up (like Absalom's) on high in their several estates and countries.

Secondly, the cry of those precious souls under the altar (Rev. 6), the souls of such as have been persecuted and slain for the testimony and witness of Jesus, whose blood has been spilt like water, upon the earth, and that because they have held fast the truth and witness of Jesus, against the worship of the states and times, compelling to an uniformity of state religion.

These cries of murdered virgins who can sit still and hear? Who but can run with zeal inflamed to prevent the deflowering of chaste souls, and spilling of the blood of the innocents? Humanity stirs up and prompts the sons of men to draw material swords for a virgin's chastity and life, against a ravishing murderer. And piety and Christianity must needs awaken the sons of God to draw the spiritual sword (the Word of God) to preserve the chastity and life of spiritual virgins, who abhor the spiritual defilements of false worship (Rev. 14).

Thirdly, the cry of the whole earth, made drunk with the blood of its inhabitants, slaughtering each other in their blinded zeal, for conscience, for religion, against the Catholics, against the Lutherans, etc.

What fearful cries within these twenty years of hundred thousands men, women, children, fathers, mothers, husbands, wives, brethren, sisters, old and young, high and low, plundered, ravished, slaughtered, murdered, famished! And hence these cries, because men fling away the spiritual sword and spiritual artillery (in spiritual and religious causes) and rather trust for the suppressing of each other's God, conscience and religion (as they suppose) to an arm of flesh and sword of steel. . . .

I acknowledge that to molest any person, Jew or Gentile, for either professing doctrine, or practising worship merely religious or spiritual, it is to persecute him, and such a person (whether his doctrine or practise be true or false) suffereth persecution for conscience.

But withal I desire it may be well observed, that this distinction is not full and complete: for besides this that a man may be persecuted because he holds or practises what he believes in conscience to be a truth (as Daniel did, for which he was cast into the lions' den, Dan. 6) and many thousands of Christians, because they durst not cease to preach and practise what they believed was by God commanded, as the apostles answered (Acts 4 and 5). I say besides this a man may also be persecuted, because he dares not be constrained to yield obedience to such doctrines and worships as are by men invented and appointed. So the three famous Jews were cast into the fiery furnace for refusing to fall down (in a non-comformity to the whole conforming world) before the golden image (Dan. 3, 21). So thousands of Christ's witnesses (and of late in those bloody Marian days) have rather chosen to yield their bodies to all sorts of torments than to subscribe to doctrines, or practise worships, unto which the states and times (as Nebuchadnezzar to his golden image) have compelled and urged them. . . .

O, how lost are the sons of men in this point! To illustrate this: The church or company of worshippers (whether true or false) is like unto a body or college of physicians in a city; like unto a corporation, or company of East Indian or Turkish merchants, or any other society or company in London: which companies may hold their courts, keep their records, hold disputations; and in matters concerning their society, may dissent, divide, break into schisms and factions, sue and implead each other at the law, yea wholly break up and dissolve into pieces and nothing, and yet the peace of the city not be in the least measure impaired or disturbed; because the essence or being of the city, and so the well-being and peace thereof is essentially distinct from those particular societies; the city courts, city laws, city punishments distinct from theirs. The city was before them, and stands absolute and entire, when such a corporation or society is taken down. For instance further, the city or civil state of Ephesus was essentially distinct from the worship of Diana in the city, or of the whole city. Again, the church of Christ in Ephesus (which were God's people, converted and called out from the worship of that city unto Christianity or worship of God in Christ) was distinct from both.

Now suppose that God remove the Candlestick from Ephesus, yea though the whole worship of the city of Ephesus be altered: yet (if men be true and honestly ingenuous to city covenants, combinations and principles) all this might be without the least impeachment or infringement of peace of the city of Ephesus.

Thus in the city of Smyrna was the city itself or civil state one thing, the spiritual or religious state of Smyrna another; the church of Christ in Smyrna, distinct from them both; and the synagogue of the Jews, whether literally Jews (as some think) or mystically, false Christians, (as others) called the Synagogue of Satan (Rev. 2), distinct from all these. And

notwithstanding these spiritual oppositions in point of worship and religion, yet hear we not the least noise (nor need
we, if men keep but the bond of civility) of any civil breach,
or breach of civil peace amongst them: and to persecute
God's people there for religion, that only was a breach of
civility itself. . . .

Breach of civil peace may arise, when false and idolatrous
practises are held forth, and yet no breach of civil peace
from the doctrine or practise, or the manner of holding
forth, but from that wrong and preposterous way of
suppressing, preventing and extinguishing such doctrines or
practises by weapons of wrath and blood, whips, stocks, imprisonment, death etc. by which men commonly are persuaded to convert heretics, and to cast out unclean spirits,
which only the finger of God can do, that is the mighty
power of the Spirit in the Word.

Hence the town is in an uproar and the country takes the
alarm to expel that fog or mist of error, heresy, blasphemy
(as is supposed) with swords and guns: whereas 'tis light
alone, even light from the bright shining Sun of Righteousness, which is able, in the souls and conscience of men to
dispel and scatter such fogs and darkness.

Hence the sons of men (as David speaks in another case,
Ps. 39) disquiet themselves in vain, and unmercifully disquiet others, as (by the help of the Lord) in the sequel of
this discourse shall more appear. . . .

The worship which a state professeth may be contradicted
and preached against, and yet no breach of civil peace.
And if a breach follow, it is not made by such doctrines, but
by the boisterous and violent opposers of them.

Such persons only break the cities' and kingdoms' peace,
who cry out for prisons and swords against such who cross
their judgment or practise in religion. For as Joseph's mis-
tress accused Joseph of uncleanness, and calls out for civil
violence against him, when Joseph was chaste, and herself

guilty: so commonly the meek and peaceable of the earth are traduced as rebels, factious, peace-breakers, although they deal not with the state or state matters, but matters of divine or spiritual nature, when their traducers are the only unpeaceable, and guilty of breach of civil peace. . . .

It is a truth, the mischief of a blind Pharisee's blind guidance is greater than if he acted treasons, murders etc. and the loss of one soul by his seduction is greater mischief than if he blew up parliaments and cut the throats of kings or emperors, so precious is that invaluable jewel of a soul, above all the present lives and bodies of all men in the world! and therefore a firm justice calling for eye for eye, tooth for tooth, life for life; calls also soul for soul, which the blind-guiding seducing Pharisee shall surely pay in that dreadful Ditch which the Lord Jesus speaks of, but this sentence against him the Lord Jesus only pronounces in his church, his spiritual judicature, and executes this sentence in part at present and hereafter to all eternity: such a sentence no civil judge can pass, such a death no civil sword can inflict. . . .

If it be the magistrate's duty or office [to prevent soul infection from heretics] then is he both a temporal and ecclesiastical officer; contrary to which most men will affirm: and yet we know the policy of our own land and country has established to the kings and queens thereof, the supreme heads or governors of the Church of England.

That doctrine or distinction that a magistrate may punish an heretic civilly will not here avail; for what is Babel if this be not confusedly to punish corporal or civil offense with spiritual or church censures (the offender not being a member of it) or to punish soul or spiritual offenses with corporal or temporal weapons proper to delinquents against the temporal or civil state.

Lastly, woe were it with the civil magistrate (and most intolerable burdens do they lay upon their backs that teach this doctrine) if together with the common care and charge of the commonwealth (the peace and safety of the town, city, state or kingdom) the blood of every soul that perishes should cry against him, unless he could say with Paul, Acts 20 (in spiritual regards) I am clear from the blood of all men, that is the blood of souls, which was his charge to look after, so far as his preaching went, not the blood of bodies which belongs to the civil magistrate.

I acknowledge he ought to cherish (as a foster-father) the Lord Jesus in his truth, in his saints, to cleave unto them himself, and to countenance them even to the death, yea also to break the teeth of the lions, who offer civil violence and injury unto them.

But to see all his subjects Christians, to keep such church or Christians in the purity of worship, and see them do their duty, this belongs to the head of the body, Christ Jesus, and such spiritual officers as he has to this purpose deputed, whose right it is according to the true pattern. . . .

True it is, the sword may make (as once the Lord complained, Isa. 10) a whole nation of hypocrites: but to recover a soul from Satan by repentance, and to bring them from antichristian doctrine or worship, to the doctrine or worship Christian, in the least true internal or external submission, that only works the all-powerful God, by the sword of the Spirit in the hand of his spiritual officers.

What a most woeful proof hereof have the nations of the earth given in all ages! And to seek no further than our native soil, within a few score of years, how many wonderful changes in religion has the whole kingdom made, according to the change of governors thereof, in the several religions which they themselves embraced! Henry VII finds and leaves the kingdom absolutely papish. Henry VIII casts it into a mold half Protestant. Edward VI brings forth an edition all Protestant. Queen Mary within a few years defaces Edward's work, and renders the kingdom (after her grandfather Henry VII his pattern) all papish. Mary's short life and religion end together: and Elizabeth revives her brother Edward's model, all Protestant: and some eminent witnesses of God's truth against antichrist, have inclined to believe, that before the downfall of that beast, England must once again bow down her fair neck to his proud usurping yoke and foot.

It has been England's sinful shame, to fashion and change their garments and religions with wondrous ease and lightness, as a higher power, a stronger sword has prevailed: after the ancient pattern of Nebuchadnezzar's bowing the whole world in one most solemn uniformity of worship to his golden image, Dan. 3. . . .

A carnal weapon or sword of steel may produce a carnal repentance, a show, an outside, an uniformity through a state or kingdom: but it has pleased the Father to exalt the Lord Jesus only, to be a prince (armed with power and means sufficient) to give repentance to Israel, Acts 5. 31.

Accordingly an unbelieving soul being dead in sin (although he be changed from one worship to another, like a dead man shifted into several changes of apparel) cannot please God, Heb. 11, and consequently, whatever such an unregenerate and unbelieving person acts in worship or religion, it is but sin, Rom. 14. *Preaching* sin; *praying* (though without beads or books) sin; *breaking of bread*, or *Lord's Supper*, sin; yea as odious as the oblation of swine's blood, a dog's neck, or killing of a man, Isa. 66.

But faith, it is that gift which proceeds alone from the Father of light, Phil. 1. 29. and till he please to make his light arise and open the eyes of blind sinners, their souls shall be fast asleep (and the faster, in that a sword of steel compels them to a worship in hypocrisy) in the dungeons of spiritual darkness and Satan's slavery.

A civil sword (as woeful experience in all ages has proved) is so far from bringing or helping forward an opposite (that is, a hostile man) in religion to repentance, that magistrates sin grievously against the work of God and blood of souls, by such proceedings. Because as (commonly) the sufferings of false and antichristian teachers harden their followers, who being blind, by this means are occasioned to tumble into the ditch of Hell after their blind leaders, with more inflamed zeal of lying confidence. So secondly, violence and a sword of steel begets such an impression in the sufferers that certainly they conclude (as indeed that religion cannot be true which needs such instruments of violence to uphold it so) that persecutors are far from soft and gentle commiseration of the blindness of others. To this purpose it pleased the Father of spirits, of old, to constrain the emperor of Rome, Antoninus Pius, to write to all the governors of his province to forbear to persecute the Christians, because such dealing must needs be so far from converting the Christians from their way, that it rather begat in their minds an opinion of their cruelty etc. . . .

But oh, what streams of the blood of saints have been and must be shed (until the Lamb has obtained the victory, Rev. 17) by this unmerciful (and in the state of the New Testament, when the church is spread all the world over) most bloody doctrine, viz. The wolves (heretics) are to be driven away, their brains knocked out, the poor sheep to be preserved for whom Christ died, etc.

Is not this to take Christ Jesus, and make him a temporal king by force? John 6. 15. Is not this to make his kingdom of this world, to set up a civil and temporal Israel, to bound out new earthly holy Lands of Canaan, yea and to set up a Spanish Inquisition in all parts of the world, to the speedy destruction of thousands, yea of millions of souls, and to frustrate the sweet end of the coming of the Lord Jesus, to wit, to save men's souls (and to that end not to destroy their bodies) by his own blood? . . .

If this practise be so abominable in his (Mr. Cotton's) eyes from the papists, viz. that they are so partial as to persecute when they sit at helm, and yet cry out against persecution when they are under the hatches, I shall beseech the righteous Judge of the whole world to present as in a water or glass (where face answers to face) the faces of the Papist to the Protestant, answering to each other in the sameness of partiality, both of this doctrine and practise.

When Mr. Cotton and others have formerly been under the hatches, what sad and true complaints have they abundantly poured forth against persecution! How have they opened that heavenly Scripture, Cant. 4. 8. where Christ Jesus calls his tender wife and spouse from the fellowship with persecutors in their dens of lions, and mountains of leopards!

But coming to the helm (as he speaks of the papists) how, both by preaching, writing, printing, practise, do they themselves (I hope in their persons lambs) unnaturally and partially express toward others the cruel nature of such lions and leopards!

O, that the God of heaven might please to tell them how abominable in his eyes are a weight and a weight, a stone and a stone in a bag of weights! one weight for themselves when they are under hatches, and another for others when they come to helm.

Nor shall their confidence of their being in the truth (which they judge the papists and others are not in) no, nor the truth itself privilege them to persecute others and to exempt themselves from persecution. . . .

Laws respecting religion may be such as merely concern the civil state, bodies and goods of such and such persons, professing these and these religions, viz. that such and such persons, notorious for mutinies, treasons, rebellions, massacres, be disarmed; again, that no persons, papists, Jews, Turks, or Indians be disturbed at their worship (a thing which the very Indians abhor to practise toward any). Also that immunity and freedom from tax and toll may be granted unto the people of such or such a religion, as the magistrate pleaseth, Ezra 7.

These and such as are of this nature, concerning only the

bodies and goods of such and such religious persons, I confess are merely civil.

But now on the other hand,

That laws restraining persons from such and such a worship, because the civil state judgeth it to be false;

That laws constraining to such and such a worship because the civil state judgeth this to be the only true way of worshipping God;

That such and such a reformation of worship be submitted unto by all subjects in such a jurisdiction;

That such and such churches, ministers, ministries be pulled down, and such and such churches, ministries and ministrations set up;

That *such* laws properly concerning religion, God, the souls of men, should be civil laws and constitutions, is as far from reason as that the commandments of Paul, which he gave the churches concerning Christ's worship (I Cor. 11 and I Cor. 14), were civil and earthly constitutions; or that the canons and constitutions of either ecumenical or national synods concerning religion should be civil and state conclusions and agreements. . . .

Who can deny but that there may be now many lawful governors, magistrates and kings in the nations of the world, where is no true church of Jesus Christ?

Secondly, we know the many excellent gifts wherewith it has pleased God to furnish many, enabling them for public service to their countries both in peace and war (as all ages and experience testifies) on whose souls he has not yet pleased to shine in the face of Jesus Christ: which gifts and talents must all lie buried in the earth, unless such persons may lawfully be called and chosen to, and improved in public service, notwithstanding their different or contrary conscience and worship.

Thirdly, if none but true Christians, members of Jesus Christ, must be civil magistrates, and publicly entrusted with civil affairs, then none but Christians should be husbands of wives, fathers of children, masters of servants: but against this doctrine the whole creation, the whole world may justly rise up in arms, as not only contrary to true piety, but common humanity itself. For if a commonwealth be lawful amongst men that have not heard of God nor Christ, certainly their officers, ministers and governors must be lawful also.

Fourthly, it is notoriously known to be the dangerous doctrine professed by some papists, that princes degenerating from their religion and turning heretics, are to be deposed, and their subjects actually discharged from their obedience. Which doctrine all such must necessarily hold (however most loathe to own it) that hold the magistrate guardian of both Tables, and consequently such an one as is enabled to judge, yea and to demonstrate to all men the worship of God: yea and being thus governor and head of the church he must necessarily be a part of it himself: which when by heresy he falls from (though it may be by truth, miscalled heresy) he falls from his calling of magistracy, and is utterly disabled from his (pretended) guardianship and government of the church.

Lastly, we may remember the practise of the Lord Jesus and his followers, commanding and practising obedience to the higher powers, though we find not one civil magistrate a Christian in all the first churches. But contrarily the civil magistrate at that time was the bloody beast, made up (as Daniel seems to imply concerning the Roman state, Dan. 7. 7.) of the lion, the bear and the leopard, Rev. 13. 2. . . . .

The dispute lies not concerning the monarchical power of the Lord Jesus, the power of making laws, and making ordinances to his saints and subjects: but concerning a deputed and ministerial power, and this distinction the very pope himself acknowledges.

There are three great competitors for this deputed or ministerial power of the Lord Jesus.

First, the arch-vicar of Satan, the pretended Vicar of Christ on earth, who sits as God over the temple of God, exalting himself not only above all that is called God, but over the souls and consciences of all his vassals, yea over the spirit of Christ, over the Holy Scriptures, yea and God himself (Dan. 8 and 11 Chap. and Rev. 15, together with II Thes. 2).

This pretender, although he professes to claim but the ministerial power of Christ, to declare his ordinances, to preach, baptize, ordain ministers, and yet doth he upon the point challenge the monarchical or absolute power also, being full of self-exalting and blaspheming (Dan. 7. 25 and 11. 36. Rev. 13. 6) speaking blasphemies against the God of heaven, thinking to change times and laws: but he is the son of perdition arising out of the bottomless pit and comes to destruction (Rev. 17) for so has the Lord Jesus decreed to consume him by the breath of his mouth, II Thes. 2.

The second great competitor to this crown of the Lord Jesus is the civil magistrate, whether emperors, kings or other inferior officers of state who are made to believe by the false prophets of the world that they are antitypes of the kings of Israel and Judah, and wear the crown of Christ.

Under the wing of the civil magistrate do three great factions shelter themselves, and mutually oppose each other, striving as for life who shall sit down under the shadow of that arm of flesh.

First, the prelacy, who (though some extravagants of late have inclined to waive the king, and to creep under the wings of the pope, yet) so far depend upon the king, that it is justly said they are the king's bishops.

Secondly, the presbytery, who (though in truth they ascribe not so much to the civil magistrate as some too grossly do, yet they) give so much to the civil magistrate as to make him absolutely the head of the church: for, if they make him the reformer of the church, the suppressor of schismatics and heretics, the protector and defender of the church etc. what is this in true plain English but to make him the judge of the true and false church, judge of what is truth and what error; who is schismatical, who heretical, unless they make him only an executioner, as the pope does in his punishment of heretics.

I doubt not but the aristocratical government of Presbyterians may well subsist in a monarchy (not only regulated but also tyrannical) yet does it more naturally delight in the element of an aristocratical government of state, and so may properly be said to be (as the prelates, the king's, so these) the state's bishops.

The third, though not so great, yet growing faction is that (so called) Independent: I prejudice not the personal worth of any of the three sorts: this latter jumps with the prelates and (though not more fully, yet) more explicitly than the Presbyterians casts down the crown of the Lord Jesus at the feet of the civil magistrate: and although they pretend to receive their ministry from the choice of 2 or 3 private persons in church covenant, yet would they fain persuade the Mother, Old England, to imitate her Daughter, New England's practise, viz. to keep out the Presbyterians, and only to embrace themselves, both as the state's and the people's Bishops.

The third competition for this crown and power of the Lord Jesus is of those that separate both from one and t'other, yet divided also amongst themselves into many several professions. Of these they that go furthest, profess they must yet come nearer to the ways of the Son of God: and doubtless, so far as they have gone, they bid the most and make the fairest plea for the purity and power of Christ Jesus, let the rest of the inhabitants of the world be judges.

Let all the former well be viewed in their external state, pomp, riches, conformity to the world etc. And on the other side, let the latter be considered, in their more thorough departure from sin and sinful worship, their condescending (generally) to the lowest and meanest contentments of this life, their exposing of themselves for Christ to greater sufferings, and their desiring no civil sword or arm of flesh, but the two-edged sword of God's Spirit to try out the matter by: and then let the inhabitants of the world judge, which come nearest to the doctrine, holiness, poverty, patience and practise of the Lord Jesus Christ: and whether or no these latter deserve not so much of humanity, and the subject's liberty, as (not offending the civil state) in the freedom of their souls, to enjoy the common air to breathe in. . . .

A pagan or antichristian pilot may be as skilful to carry the ship to its desired port, as any Christian mariner or pilot in the world, and may perform that work with as much safety and speed: yet have they not command over the souls and consciences of their passengers or mariners under them, although they may justly see to the labor of the one, and the civil behavior of all in the ship. A Christian pilot he performs the same work (as likewise doth the metaphorical pilot in the ship of the commonweal) from a principle of knowledge and experience: but more than this, he acts from a root of the fear of God and love to mankind in his whole course. Secondly, his aim is more to glorify God than to gain his pay, or make his voyage. Thirdly, he walks heavenly with men, and God, in a constant observation of God's hand in storms, calms, etc. So that the thread of navigation being equally spun by a believing or unbelieving pilot, yet it is drawn over with the gold of Godliness and Christianity by a Christian pilot, while he is holy in all manner of Christianity, I Pet. 1. 15. But lastly, the Christian pilot's power over the souls and consciences of his sailors and passengers is not greater than that of the antichristian, otherwise than he can subdue the souls of any by the two-edged sword of the Spirit, the word of God, and by his holy demeanor in his place, etc. . . .

PEACE.   If English ground must yet be drunk with English blood, O where shall Peace repose her wearied head and heavy heart?

TRUTH. Dear Peace, if those find welcome, and the God of peace miraculously please to quench these all-devouring flames, yet where shall Truth find rest from cruel persecutions?

PEACE. Oh, will not the authority of Holy Scripture, the commands and declarations of the Son of God, therein produced by thee, together with all the lamentable experiences of former and present slaughters prevail with the sons of men (especially with the sons of peace) to depart from the dens of lions, and mountains of leopards, and to put on the bowels (if not of Christianity, yet) of humanity to each other!

TRUTH. Dear Peace, Habakkuk's fishes (1. 13,14) keep their constant bloody game of persecutions in the world's mighty ocean; the greater taking, plundering, swallowing up the lesser: O, happy he whose portion is the God of Jacob! who has nothing to lose under the sun, but hath a state, a house, an inheritance, a name, a crown, a life, past all the plunderers', ravishers', murderers' reach and fury!

PEACE. But lo! Who's here?

TRUTH. Our sister, Patience, whose desired company is as needful as delightful. . . . The God of peace, the God of truth will shortly reach this truth, and confirm this witness, and make it evident to the whole world—
That the doctrine of persecution for cause of conscience is most evidently and lamentably contrary to the doctrine of Christ Jesus, the prince of peace. Amen.

The Bloody Tenet of Persecution, by Roger Williams.
Providence, R. I.: The Narragansett Club, 1867.
(Modernized by Harry Emerson Fosdick)

REMONSTRANCE

OF THE INHABITANTS OF THE TOWN OF FLUSHING
TO GOVERNOR STUYVESANT, DECEMBER 27, 1657

OF THE INHABITANTS OF THE TOWN OF FLUSHING
TO GOVERNOR STUYVESANT, DECEMBER 27, 1657

Right Honorable,

You have been pleased to send up unto us a certain prohibition or command that we should not receive or entertain any of those people called Quakers because they are supposed to be, by some, seducers of the people. For our part we cannot condemn them in this case, neither can we stretch out our hands against them, to punish, banish or persecute them, for out of Christ God is a consuming fire, and it is a fearful thing to fall into the hands of the living God.

Wee desire therefore in this case not to judge least we be judged, neither to condemn least we be condemned, but rather let every man stand and fall to his own Master. Wee are bounde by the Law to doe good unto all men, especially to those of the household of faith. And though for the present we seem to be unsensible of the law and the Law giver, yet when death and the Law assault us, if wee have our advocate to seeke, who shall plead for us in this case of conscience betwixt God and our own souls; the powers of this world can neither attack us, neither excuse us, for if God justifye who can condemn and if God condemn there is none can justifye.

And for those jealousies and suspicions which some have of them, that they are destructive unto Magistracy and Ministerye, that can not bee, for the magistrate hath the sword in his hand and the minister hath the sword in his hand, as witnesse those two great examples which all magistrates and ministers are to follow, Moses and Christ, whom God raised up maintained and defended against all the enemies both of flesh and spirit; and therefore that which is of God will stand, and that which is of man will come to nothing. And as the Lord hath taught Moses or the civil power to give an outward liberty in the state by the law written in his heart designed for the good of all, and can truly judge who is good, who is evil, who is true and who is false, and can pass definitive sentence of life or death against that man which rises up against the fundamental law of the States General; soe he hath made his ministers a savor of life unto life, and a savor of death unto death.

The law of love, peace and liberty in the states extending to Jews, Turks, and Egyptians, as they are considered the sonnes of Adam, which is the glory of the outward state of Holland, soe love, peace and liberty, extending to all in Christ Jesus, condemns hatred, war and bondage. And because our Saviour saith it is impossible but that offenses will come, but woe unto him by whom they cometh, our desire is not to offend one of his little ones, in whatsoever form, name or title hee appears in, whether Presbyterian, Independent, Baptist or Quaker, but shall be glad to see anything of God in any of them, desiring to doe unto all men as wee desire all men should doe unto us, which is the true law both of Church and State; for our Saviour saith this is the law and the prophets.

Therefore if any of these said persons come in love unto us, we cannot in conscience lay violent hands upon them, but give them free egresse and regresse unto our Town, and houses, as God shall persuade our consciences. And in this we are true subjects both of Church and State, for we are bounde by the law of God and man to doe good unto all men and evil to noe man. And this is according to the patent and charter of our Towne, given unto us in the name of the States General, which we are not willing to infringe, and violate, but shall houlde to our patent and shall remaine, your humble subjects, the inhabitants of Vlishing.

Written this 27th of December, in the year 1657, by mee

EDWARD HART, *Clericus*

GEORGE FOX

1624 – 1691

JOHN WOOLMAN

1720 – 1772

GEORGE FOX
AND
JOHN WOOLMAN

QUAKERS TODAY ARE THOUGHT OF AS THE MOST QUIET, gentle and peaceable of Christian people, but at the first their contemporaries considered them anything but that. They began their ministry when the Puritans were in power, and against the hardness and fixity of Puritan doctrine and practice they aggressively rebelled. As they saw it, Puritanism taught that God in ancient times had spoken in the Holy Scriptures and in the finished work of Christ, and would speak again at the last judgment, but presently he was not revealing himself by immediate communication to men's souls. Against that assumption George Fox and his followers took their stand. God was speaking to men now as truly as he ever did; his dwelling place was immanently in the human spirit; there he could and did unveil his light, reveal his truth, declare his will, so that the ultimate authority in religion was neither pope nor book, but the inner illumination in each man's soul.

Said Edward Burroughs, who became a Quaker in 1652:

"In all things we found the Light, which we were inlightened withall and all mankind (which is Christ), to be alone and onelie sufficient to bring to life and eternal salvation . . . And so we ceased from the teachings of all men, and their words, and

455

their worships, and their temples, and all their baptismes and Churches . . . and we met together often, and waited upon the Lord in pure silence, from our own words and all men's words, and hearkened to the voice of the Lord, and felt his word in our hearts to burn up and beat down all that was contrary to God, and we obeyed the Light of Christ in us."

This reliance upon mystical experience and inner illumination did not at first make the Quakers mild and pacific. In the current thinking of the time natural and supernatural, human and divine, were sharply distinguished; what was one was altogether *not* the other. If, therefore, the "inner light" which illumined them was divine, it was authoritative, infallible, and, so believing, they were as dogmatic and denunciatory in their way as the Puritans were in theirs. George Fox was infuriated by the sound of church bells, calling worshippers to their "steeple-houses." He interrupted the sermons of the ministers, whom he called "priests"; he rose in his pew and preached to them and to their disturbed and astonished auditors; he enraged the rabble, who beat him and rolled him in the mud; he admonished and lectured the magistrates when he was arrested; he walked barefoot through a cathedral town, crying, "Woe to the bloody city of Litchfield!" From the Puritan standpoint, one of his worst offenses in doctrine was his treatment of the Bible:

"The Scriptures, what are they but the words of prophets, of Christ and His apostles, uttered by men who enjoyed and possessed this Light which they received from the Lord? What have you to do with the words of the Scriptures, unless you come to the same Spirit which gave them forth? You open the Bible, and say, 'Christ saith this', and 'the apostles say that', but what do you say yourselves? Art thou a child of the Light? Hast thou walked in the Light? What thou sayest concerning God, does it come to thee inwardly from Him?"

Altogether the Quakers seemed to the Puritans the most intractable and cantankerous of the sects. Said Richard Baxter: "There is scarce a scold heard among us in seven years' time, that useth so many railing words . . . as these people will use familiarly in their religious exercises against the faithful servants of Christ."

The Quakers, however, had laid hold on a truth which went far back in the Christian tradition and which had a long future ahead of it. Despite the external overlay of institutions, ceremonies and sacraments, mysticism had never died out, and at the very heart of the Reformation, from the early days of Luther, lay the appeal to inward, personal experience of God's saving presence, grace and power. As to George Fox's indebtedness to other mystics—Jacob Boehme, for example—the evidence is uncertain, but clearly he came to his profound conviction concerning the "inner light" by an intense experience of his own:

"When all my hopes in men were gone, so that I had nothing outwardly to help me, nor could tell what to do, then, O then, I heard a voice which said, 'There is one, even Christ Jesus, that can speak to thy condition'; and when I heard it my heart did leap for joy. . . . I *knew experimentally* that Jesus Christ enlightens, gives grace and faith and power. *I now knew God by revelation,* as he who hath the key did open. . . . This I saw in the pure Openings of the Light, without any help of any Man, neither did I then know where to find it in the Scriptures, though afterwards, searching the Scriptures, I found it."

Out of this kind of experience, shared with a rapidly expanding group of ardent followers in Fox's day, came one of the most notable and influential movements in Protestant history. From the first the Quakers stepped out into some positions far ahead of their time. "All bloody principles and practices," said Fox, "we (as to our own particular) do utterly deny, with all outward wars and strife and fightings with outward weapons, for any end or under any pretence whatsoever." They attacked the wretched conditions in the prisons; called for reform in the penal system; denounced the servile and fawning bowings and leg-scrapings and hair pullings of the "lower classes," doing obsequious homage to their "superiors"; were among the first to campaign for the rights and privileges of women; in America were leaders in denouncing Negro slavery as sin and in demanding fair treatment of the Indians; and, in general, believing every human person to be a potential focus of divine self-revelation, they were foes of anything that degraded them.

They had their faults. Their confidence in their own private illuminations begat egotistical self-assurance and dogmatism. Their reliance on immediate divine guidance blinded them to the values in tradition and in human means of self-improvement, such as education. Their "inner light," ignorantly understood, led to hysterical extremes, to trances and ecstacies, as among the Holy Rollers today. But, at their best, their experience of the divine presence and power within made them outstanding characters and valiant champions of the Christian way of life, independent, intrepid, fearless. George Fox was one of the outstanding religious geniuses in English history, and William Penn's tribute to him is not to be gainsaid: "I write by knowledge and not report. . . . having been with him for weeks and months together on diverse occasions, and those of the nearest and most exercising nature, and that by night and by day, by sea and by land, in this and in foreign countries: and I can say I never saw him out of his place, or not a match for every service or occasion."

The Beginnings of Quakerism, by William C. Braithwaite, and *The Story of Quakerism*, by Elizabeth Braithwaite Emmott, are valuable treatises, and *George Fox*, by Thomas Hodgkin, is a good biography. *The Journal of George Fox* itself, however, is the indispensable book for one who would understand the origins of the Society of Friends, and Robert Barclay's *Apology* is an excellent complement to it. As for John Woolman, American born and the major pioneer of Quakerism on the new continent, his *Journal* is a classic, and his biography by Janet Whitney lights up his venture-some career.

The Quakers were far from welcome in America. Roger Williams granted them full protection and civil liberty in Rhode Island, but he did not like them: "Amongst Jews and Turks, Papists, Protestants and Pagans (with all of which I have conversed) I never met with such a judging, censuring, reviling spirit as is the spirit of the Quakers." As for the New England Puritans, when they heard that a colony of Quakers was to be founded by William Penn, they were furious, as a letter by Cotton Mather, dated September 15, 1682, shockingly reveals:

"There bee now at sea a shippee (for our friend Mr. Esasias Halcraft of Lond., did advise me by the last packet that it would sail sometime in August) called ye *Welcome*, R. Greenway master, which has aboard an hundred or more of ye heretics and malignants called Quakers, with Wm Penne who is ye chief scamp at the hedde of them. Ye General Court has accordingly given secret orders to Master Malachi Huxett of ye brig *Porpoise* to way lay ye said *Welcome* as near the coast of caddee as may be, and make captive of ye said Penn and his ungodly crew so that ye Lord may be glorified & not mocked on ye soil of this new countre with ye heathen worship of these people. Much spoil can be made by selling ye lotte to Barbadoes, these slaves fetch good prices in rum & sugar, & we shall not only do thye Lord great service by punishing thye wicked but shall make great gayne for his ministres & people. Master Huxett feels hopeful and I will set down the news he brings when his shippee comes back.

Yours in ye bowels of Christ
COTTON MATHER."

Nevertheless, the Quakers made their way, although Cotton Mather never could have dreamed that one day the American Friends' Service Committee would receive the Nobel Peace Prize. Their concept of religion was deep and vital—

an inward, immediate, reciprocal relationship between the soul and God. Their idea of the Divine was essentially that of the New Testament—God an indwelling Spirit whose focal point of revelation was the human soul. Their idea of man lifted him to superhuman dignity—a being in whom the eternal Light could be made manifest. Their idea of the Christian way of life was an uncompromising acceptance of the Sermon on the Mount.

In point of numbers the Quakers have always been a small minority. All the picturesque, dramatic, flamboyant elements in worship they surrendered. Their silent meetings, their self-contained societies, with marriage outside the Quaker circle long forbidden, their protests against current social customs, their rigorous manner of life, the nearest to monasticism in the Protestant movement, no oaths, no display in dress, no lifted hats, no "your obedient servant" even in correspondence—all this, along with their pacifism, was not popular. In point of vitality, however, they have been one of the most influential factors in Protestantism. The meaning and value of their silent worship—see *The Quaker Meeting*, by H. E. Collier—gradually gained recognition. Their devotional literature has been called "the best Protestantism has produced." Their protest against obsequious and fawning gestures, manners and phrases, which at first seemed outrageous, has been accepted in common practice. Even their habit of quietly getting "the sense of the meeting," rather than merely counting votes, is now familiar in many groups. Their humanitarian service has girdled the globe, and their valiant stand against war and their insistence that no Christian experience is genuine without the "inner light" have won many adherents outside their Society.

Concerning such matters Rufus Jones' *Faith and Practice of the Quakers and* W. W. Comfort's *Just Among Friends* bear informing testimony.

THE JOURNAL OF
GEORGE FOX

ONE MORNING, AS I WAS SITTING BY THE FIRE, A GREAT cloud came over me, and a temptation beset me; but I sate still. And it was said, "All things come by nature"; and the elements and stars came over me, so that I was in a manner quite clouded with it. But inasmuch as I sate still and silent the people of the house perceived nothing. And as I sate still under it, and let it alone, a living hope arose in me, and a true voice, which said, "There is a living God who made all things." And immediately the cloud and temptation vanished away, and life rose over it all; my heart was glad and I praised the living God. After some time, I met with some people who had such a notion that there was no God, but that all things came by nature. I had a great dispute with them and overturned them and made some of them confess that there is a living God. Then I saw that it was good that I had gone through that exercise. . . .

Now I was come up in spirit through the flaming sword, into the paradise of God. All things were new; and all creation gave another smell unto me than before, beyond what words can utter. I knew nothing but pureness, and innocency, and righteousness, being renewed up into the image of God by Christ Jesus, to the state of Adam, which he was in before he fell. The creation was opened to me; and it was shewed me how all things had their names given them according to their nature and virtue. I was at a stand in my mind whether I should practise physic for the good of mankind, seeing the nature and virtues of the creatures were so opened to me by the Lord. But I was immediately taken up in spirit, to see into another and more steadfast state than Adam's in innocency, even into the state in Christ Jesus that should never fall. And the Lord showed me that such as were faithful to Him, in the power and light of Christ, should come up into that state in which Adam was before he fell; in which the admirable works of the creation and the virtues thereof, may be known through the openings of that divine Word of wisdom and power by which they were made. Great things did the Lord lead me into, and wonderful depths were opened unto me beyond what can by words be declared; but as people come into subjection to the Spirit of God, and grow up in the image and power of the Almighty, they may receive the word of wisdom, that opens all things, and come to know the hidden unity in the Eternal Being. . . .

Now as I went towards Nottingham on a First-day in the morning with Friends to a meeting there, when I came on top of a hill in sight of the town, I espied the great steeple-house; and the Lord said unto me, "Thou must go cry against yonder great idol, and against the worshippers therein." I said nothing of this to the Friends that were with me, but went on with them to the meeting, where the mighty power of the Lord was amongst us; in which I left Friends sitting in the meeting, and I went away to the steeple-house. When I came there all the people looked like fallow-ground, and the priest, like a great lump of earth, stood in his pulpit above. He took for his text these words of Peter, "We have also a more sure Word of prophecy, whereunto ye do well that ye take heed, as unto a light that shineth in a dark place, until the day dawn, and the day-star arise in your hearts." And he told the people that this was the Scriptures, by which they were to try all doctrines, religions, and opinions. Now the Lord's power was so mighty upon me, and so strong in me, that I could not hold, but was made to cry out and say, "Oh, no, it is not the Scriptures." But I told them what it was, namely, the Holy Spirit, by which the holy men of God gave forth the Scriptures, whereby opinions, religions, and judgments were to be tried; for it led into all Truth, and so gave the knowledge of all Truth. The Jews had the Scriptures, and yet resisted the Holy Ghost and rejected Christ the bright morning-star. They persecuted Christ and His apostles, and took upon them to try their doctrines by the Scriptures, but erred in judgment, and did not try them aright, because they tried without the Holy Ghost. Now as I spake thus amongst them, the officers came and took me away, and put me into a nasty, stinking prison, where the wind brought all the stench of the house of office into the place, the stench whereof got so into my nose and throat that it very much annoyed me.

But that day the Lord's power sounded so in their ears, that they were amazed at the voice; and could not get it out of their ears for some time after, they were so reached by the Lord's power in the steeple-house. At night they took me before the mayor, the aldermen, and sheriffs of the town; and when I was brought before them, the mayor was in a peevish, fretful temper, but the Lord's power allayed him. They examined me at large; and I told them how the Lord had moved me to come. After some discourse between them and me, they sent me back to prison again; but some time after the head sheriff, whose name was John Reckless, sent for me to his house. When I came in, his wife met me in the hall and said, "Salvation is come to our house." She took me by the hand, and was much wrought upon by the power of the Lord God; and her husband, and children, and servants were much changed, for the power of the Lord wrought upon them. I lodged at the sheriff's, and great meetings we had in his house. Some persons of considerable condition in the world came to them, and the Lord's power appeared eminently amongst them. This sheriff sent for the other sheriff, and for a woman they had had dealings with in the way of trade; and he told her before the other sheriff that they had wronged her in their dealings with her (for the other sheriff and he were partners), and that they ought to make her restitution. This he spake cheerfully; but the other sheriff denied it; and the woman said she knew nothing of it. But the friendly sheriff said it was so, and that the other knew it well enough; and having discovered the matter, and acknowledged the wrong done by them, he made restitution to the woman, and exhorted the other sheriff to do the like. . . .

Now the time of my commitment to the House of Correction (in Derby) being nearly out, and there being many new soldiers raised, the commissioners would have made me captain over them; and the soldiers cried they would have none but me. So the keeper of the House of Correction was commanded to bring me before the commissioners and soldiers in the market-place; and there they offered me that preferment (as they called it), asking me if I would not take up arms for the Commonwealth against Charles Stuart? I told them I knew from whence all wars arose, even from the lust, according to James's doctrine; and that I lived in the virtue of that life and power that took away the occasion of all wars. But they courted me to accept their offer, and thought I did but compliment with them. But I told them I was come into the covenant of peace which was before wars and strife were. They said they offered it in love and kindness to me because of my virtue; and such like flattering words they used. But I told them if that was their love and kindness, I trampled it under my feet. Then their rage got up, and they said, "Take him away, jailer, and put him into the dungeon amongst the rogues and felons." So I was had away and put into a lousy, stinking place, low in the ground, without any bed; amongst thirty felons, where I was kept almost half a year, unless it were at times; for they would sometimes let me walk in the garden, having a belief that I would not go away. Now when they had got me into the Derby dungeon, it was the belief and saying of people that I should never come out; but I had faith in God, and believed I should be delivered in His time; for the Lord had said to me before that I was not to be removed from that place yet, being set there for a service which He had for me to do. . . .

Moreover I laid before the judges what a sore thing it was that prisoners should lie so long in jail; shewing how that they learned badness one of another in talking of their bad deeds: and therefore speedy justice should be done. For I was a tender youth, and dwelt in the fear of God, and being grieved to hear their bad language, I was often made to reprove them for their wicked words and evil conduct towards each other. People admired that I was so preserved and kept; for they could never catch a word or action from me, to make anything of against me, all the time I was there; for the Lord's infinite power upheld and preserved me all that time; to Him be praises and glory forever!

While I was here in prison, there was a young woman in the jail for robbing her master of some money. When she was to be tried for her life, I wrote to the judge and to the jury about her, shewing them how contrary it was to the law of God in old time to put people to death for stealing, and moving them to shew mercy. Yet she was condemned to die, and a grave was made for her; and at the time appointed she was carried forth to execution. Then I wrote a few words, warning all people to beware of greediness or covetousness, for it leads from God, but that all should fear the Lord and avoid all earthly lusts, and prize their time while they have it: this I gave to be read at the gallows. And though they had her upon the ladder, with a cloth bound over her face, ready to be turned off, yet they did not put her to death, but brought her back again to prison: and in the prison she afterwards came to be convinced of God's everlasting truth. . . .

The judges (in Carlisle) were resolved not to suffer me to be brought before them; but reviling and scoffing at me behind my back, left me to the magistrates of the town, giving them what encouragement they could to exercise their cruelty upon me. Whereupon (though I had been kept up so close in the jailer's house that Friends were not suffered to visit me, and Colonel Benson and Justice Pearson were denied to see me) the next day after the judges were gone out of town, an order was sent to the jailer to put me down in the dungeon among the moss-troopers, thieves and murderers, which accordingly he did. A filthy, nasty place it was, where men and women were put together in a very uncivil manner, and not even a house of office to it; and the prisoners so lousy that one woman was almost eaten to death with lice. Yet, as bad as the place was, the prisoners were all made very loving and subject to me; and some of them were convinced of the truth, as the publicans and harlots were of old; so that they were able to confound any priest that might come to the grates to dispute. But the jailer was very cruel, and the under-jailer very abusive to me and to Friends that came to see me; for he would beat Friends with a great cudgel that did but come to the window to look in upon me, as if he had been beating a pack of wool. I could get up to the grate, where sometimes I took in meat; at which the jailer was greatly offended. One time he came in a great rage, and beat me with a great cudgel, though I was not at the grate at that time; and as he beat me, he cried, "Come out of the window," though I was then far enough from it. While he struck me, I was made to sing in the Lord's power; and that made him rage the more. Then he fetched a fiddler, and brought him in where I was, and set him to play, thinking to vex me thereby; but while he played I was moved in the everlasting power of the Lord God to sing; and my voice drowned the noise of the fiddle, and made the fiddler sigh and give over fiddling and pass away with shame.

Justice Benson's wife was moved of the Lord to come to visit me, and to eat no meat but what she ate with me at the bars of the dungeon window. She was afterwards herself imprisoned at York, when she was great with child, for speaking to a priest; and was kept in prison, and not suffered to go out when the time of her travail was come; so she was delivered of her child in prison. She was an honest, tender woman, and continued faithful to the truth until she died. . . .

Now when I saw that I was not like to be brought to a public hearing and trial (although I had answered before, in writing, the particular matters charged against me, at the time of my first examination and commitment), I was moved to send the following paper as a public challenge to all those that belied the truth and me behind my back, to come forth and make good their charge:

If any in Westmoreland, or Cumberland, or elsewhere, that profess Christianity, and pretend to love God and Christ, are not satisfied concerning the things of God, which I, George Fox, have spoken and declared, let them publish their dissatisfaction in writing, and not back-bite, nor lie, nor persecute, in secret; this I demand of you all in the presence of the living God, as ye will answer it to Him. For the exaltation of the truth, and the counfounding of deceit, is this given forth. To that of God in your consciences I speak; declare or write your dissatisfactions to any of them whom you call Quakers, that Truth may be exalted, and all may come to the light, with which Christ has enlightened every one that cometh into the world: that nothing may be hid in darkness, in prisons, holes, or corners, but that all things may be brought to the light of Christ, and by it may be tried.

This am I moved of the Lord to write, and send forth to be set upon the market-crosses in Westmoreland, and elsewhere. To the light of Christ in you I speak, that none of you may speak evil of the things of God, which you know not; nor act contrary to the light, that gave forth the Scriptures; lest you be found fighters against God, and the hand of the Lord be turned against you.

G. F.

While I thus lay in the dungeon at Carlisle, the report raised at the time of the Assize that I should be put to death was gone far and near; insomuch that the Little Parliament then sitting, hearing that a young man at Carlisle was to die for religion, caused a letter to be sent to the sheriff and magistrates concerning me. . . .

Not long after this, the Lord's power came over the justices, and they were made to set me at liberty. But some time previous, the governor, and Anthony Pearson, came down into the dungeon to see the place where I was kept, and understand what usage I had. They found the place so bad, and the savour so ill, that they cried shame on the magistrates for suffering the jailer to do such things. They called for the jailers into the dungeon, and required them to find sureties for their good behavior, and the under-jailer, who had been such a cruel fellow, they put into the dungeon with me amongst the moss-troopers. . . .

About this time the priests and professors* fell to prophesying against us afresh. They had said long before, that we should be all knocked down within a month; and after that, they prolonged the time to half a year; but that time being long expired, and we mightily increased in number, they now

* He means the clergymen and those professing to be Christians.

gave forth that we would eat out one another. For often after meetings, many tender people, having a great way to go, tarried at Friends' houses by the way, and sometimes more than there were beds to lie in; so that some have lain on the hay-mows. Hereupon Cain's fear possessed the professors and world's people, for they were afraid that when we had eaten one another out, we would all come to be maintained by the parishes, and be chargeable to them. But after awhile, when they saw that the Lord blessed and increased Friends, as He did Abraham, both in the field and in the basket, at their goings forth and comings in, at their risings up and lyings down, and that all things prospered with them, then they saw the falseness of all their prophecies against us; and that it was in vain to curse where God had blessed.

At the first convincement, when Friends could not put off their hats to people, or say You to a single person, but Thou and Thee; when they could not bow, or use flattering words in salutations, or adopt the fashions and customs of the world, many Friends, that were tradesmen of several sorts, lost their custom at first; for the people were shy of them, and would not trade with them; so that for a time some Friends could hardly get money enough to buy bread. But afterwards, when people came to have experience of Friends' honesty and truthfulness, and found that their Yea was yea, and their Nay was nay; that they kept to a word in their dealings, and that they would not cozen and cheat them; but that if they sent a child to their shops for anything, they were as well used as if they had come themselves; the lives and conversations of Friends did preach, and reached to the witness of God in the people. Then things altered so, that all the inquiry was, "Where is there a draper, or shopkeeper, or tailor, or shoemaker, or any other tradesman, that is a Quaker?" Insomuch that Friends had more trade than many of their neighbors, and if there was any trading, they had a great part of it. Then the envious professors altered their note, and began to cry out, "If we let these Quakers alone, they will take the trade of the nation out of our hands." . . .

After Captain Drury had lodged me at the Mermaid, he left me there, and went to give the Protector* an account of me. When he came to me again, he told me the Protector required that I should promise not to take up a carnal sword or weapon against him or the Government. And I should write it in what words I saw good, and set my hand to it. I said little in reply to Captain Drury. But the next morning I was moved of the Lord to write a paper, "To the Protector by the name of Oliver Cromwell," wherein I did in the presence of the Lord God declare that I did deny the wearing or drawing of a carnal sword, or any other outward weapon, against him or any man: and that I was sent of God to stand a witness against all violence, and against the works of darkness; and to turn people from darkness to light; and to bring them from the occasion of war and fighting to the peaceable gospel, and from being evil-doers which the magistrates' swords should be a terror to. When I had written what the Lord had given me to write, I set my name to it, and gave it to Captain Drury to hand to Oliver Cromwell, which he did.

Then after some time Captain Drury brought me before the Protector himself at Whitehall. It was in a morning, before he was dressed, and one Harvey, who had come a little among Friends, but was disobedient, waited upon him. When I came in, I was moved to say, "Peace be in this house"; and I bid him to keep in the fear of God, that he might receive wisdom from Him, that by it he might be directed, and order all things under his hand to God's glory. I spake much to him of truth, and much discourse I had with him about religion; wherein he carried himself very moderately. But he said we quarreled with priests, whom he called

* Oliver Cromwell

ministers. I told him I did not quarrel with them, but they quarreled with me and my friends. "But," said I, "if we own the prophets, Christ, and the apostles, we cannot hold up such teachers, prophets, and shepherds as the prophets, Christ, and the apostles declared against; but we must declare against them by the same power and Spirit." Then I shewed him that the prophets, Christ, and the apostles declared freely, and against them that did not declare freely, such as preached for filthy lucre, and divined for money, and preached for hire, and were covetous and greedy, like the dumb dogs that can never have enough; and that they that have the same Spirit that Christ and the apostles and the prophets had, could not but declare against all such now, as they did then. As I spake, he several times said it was very good and it was truth. I told him that all Christendom (so called) possessed the Scriptures, but wanted the power and Spirit that they had who gave forth the Scriptures, and that was the reason they were not in fellowship with the Son or with the Father, or with the Scriptures, or one with another.

Many more words I had with him, but people coming in, I drew a little back; and as I was turning, he caught me by the hand, and with tears in his eyes, said, "Come again to my house, for if thou and I were but an hour a day together, we should be nearer one to the other"; adding that he wished me no more ill than he did his own soul. I told him if he did he wronged his own soul; and I bid him hearken to God's voice, that he might stand in His counsel and obey it; and if he did so, that would keep him from hardness of heart; but if he did not hear God's voice, his heart would be hardened. He said it was true. Then I went out; and when Captain Drury came out after me, he told me his Lord Protector said I was at liberty, and might go whither I would. "And my Lord says," he says, "you are not a fool and said he never saw such a paper in his life" as I had sent him. Then I was brought into a great hall where the Protector's gentlemen were to dine; and I asked them what they brought me thither for. They said it was by the Protector's order that I might dine with them. I bid them let the Protector know I would not eat a bit of his bread, nor drink a sup of his drink. When he heard this he said, "Now I see there is a people risen and come up that I cannot win either with gifts, honours, offices or places; but all other sects and people I can." It was told him again that we had forsaken our own, and were not likely to look for such things from him. . . .

And in the old Parliament's days many people that used to wear ribands, and lace, and costly apparel, and followed junketing and feasting with priests and professors, came to leave it and to walk and serve God in spirit as the Apostle did. They left off their curious apparel and ribands and lace, and their sporting and feasting with priests and professors, and would not go to wakes or plays or shows, as they formerly had used to do, and would not wear gold or silver or lace or ribands, nor make them.

Then the priests and professors raged exceedingly against us and printed books against us; and said that our religion lay in not wearing fine clothes, and lace, and ribands, and in not eating good cheer, when we could not make feasts for the priests or professors as we used to do, nor feasts for companies in the cities; but if they would join with us, when they made feasts, to feast such as could not feast them again, we would make a feast for all the poor of the Parish that could not feast us and them again. And this was according to Christ's command, but in this their selfish principle would never join with us.

We told them that when they went to their sports, and games, and plays, and the like, they had better serve God than spend their time so vainly. And that costly apparel, with the lace that we had formerly hung upon our backs that kept us not warm, with that we could maintain a company of poor people that had no clothes.

And so our religion lay not in meats, nor drinks, nor clothes, nor Thee nor Thou, nor putting off hats for making curtseys (at which they were greatly offended because we Thee'd and Thou'd them and could not put off our hats nor bow to them), and therefore they said our religion lay in such things. But our answer was, "Nay; for though the spirit of God led into that which was comely and decent, and from chambering and wantonness, and from sporting and pastimes and feasting as in the day of slaughter, and from wearing costly apparel, as the Apostle commands, and from the world's honour, fashions and customs—our religion lies in that which brings to visit the poor, and fatherless, and widows, and keeps from the spots of the world (which religion is pure and undefiled before God). This is our religion which we own, which the apostles were in above 1600 years since; and we do deny all vain religions got up since, which are not only spotted with the world, but plead for a body of sin and death to the grave; and their widows and fatherless lie begging up and down the streets and countries." . . .

Before this time we received an account from New England that the Government there had made a law to banish Quakers out of their colonies upon pain of death in case they returned; and that several Friends, having been so banished, and returning, were taken, and actually hanged, and that many more were in prison, in danger of the like sentence being executed upon them. When those were put to death, I was in prison at Lancaster, and had a perfect sense of their sufferings, as though it had been myself, and as though the halter had been put about my own neck; though we had not at that time heard of it.

But as soon as we heard of it, Edward Burrough went to the King and told him there was a vein of innocent blood opened in his dominions, which, if it were not stopped, would overrun all. To which the King replied, "But I will stop that vein." Edward Burrough said, "Then do it speedily, for we do not know how many may soon be put to death." The King answered, "As speedily as ye will. Call," said he to some present, "the secretary and I will do it presently." The secretary being called, a mandamus was forthwith granted. A day or two after, Edward Burrough going again to the King to desire the matter might be expedited, the King said he had no occasion at present to send a ship thither, but if we would send one, we might do it as soon as we chose. Edward Burrough then asked the King if it would please him to grant his deputation to one called a Quaker, to carry the mandamus to New England. He said, "Yes, to whom you will." Whereupon E. B. named Samuel Shattock, as I remember, who being an inhabitant of New England, was banished by their law, to be hanged if he came again; and to him the deputation was granted. Then we sent for Ralph Goldsmith, an honest Friend, who was master of a good ship, and agreed with him for three hundred pounds, goods or no goods, to sail in ten days. He forthwith prepared to set sail, and, with a prosperous gale, in about six weeks arrived before the town of Boston, in New England, upon a First-day morning, called Sunday. Many passengers went with him, both of New and Old England, Friends, whom the Lord moved to go to bear testimony against those bloody persecutors, who had exceeded all the world in that age in their persecutions.

The townsmen at Boston seeing a ship come into the bay with English colours, soon came on board, and asked for the captain. Ralph Goldsmith told them he was the commander. They asked him if he had any letters. He said, "Yes." They asked if he would deliver them. He said, "No, not to-day." So they went on shore, and reported there was a ship full of Quakers, and that Samuel Shattock was among them, who, they knew, was, by their law, to be put to death, for coming again after banishment; but they knew not his errand nor his authority.

So all being kept close that day, and none of the ship's company suffered to land, next morning Samuel Shattock, the King's deputy, and Ralph Goldsmith, the commander of the vessel, went on shore; and sending back to the ship the men that landed them, they two went through the town to the door of the governor, John Endicott, and knocked. He sent out a man to know their business. They sent him word their business was from the King of England, and they would deliver their message to none but the governor himself. They were then admitted, and the governor came to them; and having received the deputation and the mandamus, he laid off his hat, and looked upon them. Then going out, he bid the Friends follow him. He went to the deputy-governor, and after a short consultation, came out to the Friends, and said, "We shall obey His Majesty's commands." After this the master gave liberty to the passengers to come on shore; and presently the noise of the business flew about the town, and the Friends of the town and the passengers of the ship met together to offer up their praises and thanksgivings to God, who had so wonderfully delivered them from the teeth of the devourer. While they were thus met, in came a poor Friend who, being sentenced by their bloody law to die, had lain some time in irons, expecting execution. This added to their joy, and caused them to lift up their hearts in high praises to God, who is worthy for ever to have the praise, the glory and the honour; for He only is able to deliver and to save, and to support all that sincerely put their trust in Him. . . .

Now he (the judge) had caused the jury to be called, and they stood by; for after they had brought in their former verdict, he would not dismiss them, though they desired it; but told them he could not dismiss them yet, for he should have business for them, and therefore they must attend and be ready when they were called. When he said so, I felt his intent that if I was freed he would come on again. So I looked him in the face, and the witness of God started up in him and made him blush when he looked at me again, for he saw that I saw him. Nevertheless, hardening himself, he caused the oath to be read to me, the jury standing by; and when it was read, he asked me whether I would take the oath or not. Then said I, "Ye have given me a book here to kiss, and to swear on, and this book which ye have given me to kiss, says, 'Kiss the Son'; and the Son says in this book, 'Swear not at all'; and so also say the apostle James. Now, I say as the book says, and yet ye imprison me; how chance ye do not imprison the book for saying so? How comes it that the book is at liberty amongst you, which bids me not swear, and yet ye imprison me for doing as the book bids me? Why don't ye imprison the book?" Now as I was speaking this to them, and held up the Bible open in my hand, to shew them the place in the book where Christ forbids swearing, they plucked the book out of my hand again; and the judge said, "Nay, but we will imprison George Fox." Yet this got abroad all over the country as a by-word that they gave me a book to swear on that commanded me not to swear at all; and that the Bible was at liberty, and I in prison for doing as the Bible said. . . .

Being returned to London, I stayed some time there visiting Friends' meetings in and about the City. While I was in London, I went one day to visit Esquire Marsh, who had shewed much kindness both to me and to Friends; I happened to go when he was at dinner. He no sooner heard my name than he sent for me up and would have had me sit down with him to dinner; but I had not freedom to do so. Several great persons were at dinner with him; and he said to one of them who was a great Papist, "Here is a Quaker, whom you have not seen before." The Papist asked me whether I owned the christening of children. I told him there was no Scripture for any such practice. "What!" said he, "not for christening children?" I said, "Nay." I told him the one baptism by the one Spirit into one body we owned; but to throw a little water on a child's face, and say that was baptising and christening it, there was no Scripture for that. Then he asked me whether I did own the Catholic faith. I said yes, but added that neither the Pope nor the Papists were in that Catholic faith; for the true faith works by love and purifies the heart, and if they were in that faith that gives victory, by which they might have access to God, they would not tell the people of a purgatory after they were dead. So I undertook to prove that neither Pope nor Papists that held a purgatory hereafter were in the true faith; for the true, precious, divine faith, which Christ is the author of, gives victory over the Devil and sin, that had separated man and woman from God. And if they (the Papists) were in the true faith, they would never use racks, prisons and fines to persecute and force others to their religion that were not of their faith. This was not the practice of the apostles and primitive Christians, who witnessed and enjoyed the true faith of Christ; but it was the practice of the faithless Jews and Heathens so to do.

"But," said I, "seeing thou art a great and leading man among the Papists, and hast been taught and bred up under the Pope, and seeing thou sayest there is no salvation but in our Church, I desire to know of thee, what it is that doth bring salvation in your Church." He answered, "A good life." "And nothing else?" said I. "Yes," said he. "Good works." "And is this it that brings salvation in your Church, a good life and good works? Is this your doctrine and your principle?" said I. "Yes," said he. "Then," said I, "neither thou, nor the pope, nor any of the Papists know what it is that brings salvation." Then he asked me what brought salvation in our Church. I told him, "That which brought salvation to the Church in the apostles' days, the same brings salvation to us, and not another; namely, 'the grace of God, which,' the Scripture says, 'brings salvation, and hath appeared to all men,' which taught the saints then, and teaches us now. This grace which brings salvation teaches to deny ungodliness and worldly lusts, and to live godly, soberly and righteously. So it is not the good works nor the good life that brings salvation, but the grace." "What!" said the Papist, "doth this grace that brings salvation appear unto all men?" "Yes," said I. "Then," said he, "I deny that." But I said, "All that deny that are sect-makers, and are not in the universal faith, grace and truth which the apostles were in."

The Journal of George Fox,
Edited by Norman Penny.
J. M. Dent and Sons, Ltd.; New York: E. P. Dutton & Co., 1924.

From

THE JOURNAL OF
JOHN WOOLMAN

I WENT TO MEETINGS IN AN AWFUL FRAME OF MIND AND EN-
deavoured to keep to my exercise till one day feeling the
word of the Lord in my heart I stood up and said some
words in a Meeting, but not keeping close to the true
Opener I said more than He directed me to say. I was soon
sensible of my error and afflicted in mind some weeks without any light or comfort, to that degree that I could take satisfaction in nothing. I remembered God and was troubled,
and in the depths of my distress I cried to Him, who in this
time of my humiliation sent the Comforter, for which I was
truly thankful.

And after this, my mind being calm and quiet, and feeling the spring of Divine Love opened and the concern to
speak, I said a few words in a Meeting, in which I found
peace. This I believe was about six or seven weeks from the
first time. And as I was thus humbled and disciplined under
the cross my understanding became more strengthened to
know the language of the pure Spirit which moves upon the
intellectual deep, and to wait in silence sometimes many
weeks together, until I felt that rise which prepares the creature to stand like a trumpet through which the Lord speaks
to His people.

From an inward purifying and steadfast abiding in it,
springs a lively operative desire for the good of others. All

479

faithful people are not called to the public ministry; but whoever are called to it are called to minister of that which they have tasted and handled spiritually. The outward modes of worship are various, but wherever men are true ministers of Jesus Christ it is from the operation of His spirit upon their hearts, first purifying them and then giving them a feeling sense of the conditions of the people.

This truth was early fixed on my mind, and I was taught carefully to watch the opening lest while I was standing to speak, my own will should get uppermost, uttering words from worldly wisdom, and so depart from the true channel of the gospel ministry. . . .

As my mind was often inward, meditating on God's Providence manifested in the visible world, I was more and more confirmed in my judgment that to place my whole trust in Him was best for me, and laboured from one month to another to come into that condition of trusting in God with all my heart and not to lean to my own understanding. I found renewed engagements that in all things I might act on an inward principle of virtue, and pursue worldly business no further than as truth opened my way. . . .

Within a year after my coming to Mt. Holly, my master, having a Negro, sold her, and told me to write a bill of sale. The thoughts of writing an instrument of slavery for one of my fellow creatures gave me trouble, and I was distressed in my mind about it. At length I considered that I was hired by the year, it was my master bid me do it, and that it was an elderly man, a member of our Society, who bought her, so I wrote the bill of sale. But at the executing of it I was depressed in my mind and said before my master and the Friend that I believed slave-keeping to be a practise inconsistent with the Christian religion; saying so abated my uneasiness; yet as often as I reflected seriously upon it I thought I should have been clearer if, leaving all consequences, I had craved to be excused from it, as a thing against my conscience; for such it was.

Some time after a young man of our Society spoke to me to write an instrument of slavery, he having lately taken a Negro into his house. After a short prayer I told him I was not easy to write it, for though many people kept slaves in our Society as well as others, and seemed easy in it, I however could not see it to be right, and craved to be excused from it. I spoke to him in goodwill and he told me that keeping slaves was not clearly agreeable to his mind, but that the slave was a gift to his wife from some of her friends, and so we parted. . . .

We took the Meetings in course through Virginia; were in some degree baptized into a feeling sense of the conditions of the people. The pure lamblike nature of Jesus Christ being too much departed from by many of them, our exercise in general was somewhat painful. Yet through the goodness of our Heavenly Father the well of living waters was at times opened to our encouragement and the refreshment of the sincere-hearted. We went on to Perquimans, in North Carolina; had several large Meetings and found some openness in those parts, and a hopeful appearance among the young people. Afterwards we turned again to Virginia, and attended most of the Meetings which we had not been at before, labouring amongst Friends in the love of Jesus Christ as ability was given. Thence went to the mountains, up James River to a new settlement, and had several Meetings amongst the people, some of whom had lately joined in membership with our Society. In our journeying to and fro we found some honest-hearted Friends who appeared to be concerned for the cause of truth among a back-sliding people.

From Virginia we crossed over the river Potomac at Hoe's Ferry, and made a general visit to the Meetings of Friends on the western shore of Maryland, were also at their Quarterly Meeting at Herring Creek. We had some hard labour amongst them, endeavouring to discharge our duty honestly as way opened in the love of truth. . . .

Two things were remarkable to me in this journey; first, in regard to my entertainment. When I ate, drunk and lodged free-cost with people that lived in ease on the toil of their slaves I felt uneasy, and as my mind was inward I found from place to place this uneasiness to return upon me through the whole visit. Where the masters bore a considerable share of the burden, and living on moderate expenses made their servants labour moderately and live pretty well, I felt some easier; but where they lived in a costly way, a'quitted labour and laid the whole on their slaves, my exercise was sore, and I frequently had conversation with them in private concerning it. Secondly, this trade of importing slaves from Guinea being so much encouraged among them; and the white people living so much without labour, the nature of this trade to Guinea and the tendency of it in these southern colonies was frequently the subject of my serious thoughts. And I saw so many vices and corruptions spreading, in a great measure occasioned by this trade and way of life, that it appeared to me as a dark gloominess hanging over the land; and though now many do willingly run into it, yet in future the consequences will be grievous to posterity. I express it as it appeared to me not once nor twice but as a matter fixed in my mind. . . .

On the way, happening in company with a Colonel of the Militia, who appeared to be a thoughtful man, I took occasion to remark on the difference in general betwixt a people used to labour moderately for their living, training up their children in frugality and business, and those who live on the labour of slaves; the former, in my view, being the most happy life. He concurred in the remark, and mentioned the trouble arising from the untoward, slothful disposition of the Negroes, adding that one of our labourers would do as much in a day as two of their slaves. I replied that free men whose minds were properly on their business, found a satisfaction in the improving, cultivating, and providing for their families; but Negroes, labouring to support those who claim them as their property, and expecting nothing but slavery during life, had not the like inducement to be industrious.

After some further conversation I said that men having power too often misapplied it; that though we made slaves of the Negroes, and the Turks made slaves of the Christians, I believed that liberty was the natural right of all men equally. This he did not deny, but said the lives of the Negroes were so wretched in their own country that many of them lived better here than there. I only said, "There's great odds in regard to us on what principle we act"; and so the conversation on that head ended. I may here add that another person some time afterwards mentioned the wretchedness of the Negroes occasioned by their intestine wars as an argument in favor of our fetching them away for slaves. To which I replied, if compassion for the Africans, on account of their domestic troubles, was the real motive of our purchasing them, that spirit of tenderness being attended to would incite us to use them kindly, that as strangers brought out of affliction their lives might be happy among us. And as they are human creatures, whose souls are as precious as ours, and who may receive the same help and comfort from the Holy Scriptures as we do, we could not omit suitable endeavours to instruct them therein; but while we manifest by our conduct that our views in purchasing them are to advance ourselves, and while our buying captives taken in war animates those parties to push on that war and increase desolation amongst them, to say they live unhappy in Africa is far from being an argument in our favour. I further said, the present circumstances of these provinces to me appear difficult; the slaves look like a burdensome stone to such as burden themselves with them; and that if the white people retain a resolution to prefer their own outward prospect of gain to all other considerations, and do not act conscientiously toward them as fellow creatures, I believe that burden will grow heavier and heavier until times change in a way disagreeable to us. At which the person appeared very serious and acknowledged that in considering their condition and the manner of their treatment in these provinces he had sometimes thought it might be just in the Almighty to so order it. . . .

The prospect of a road lying open to the same degeneracy in some parts of this newly settled land of America in respect to our conduct towards the Negroes hath deeply bowed my mind in this journey, and though to briefly relate how these people are treated is no agreeable work, yet, after reading over the notes I made as I travelled, I find my mind engaged to preserve them. Many of the white people in those provinces take little or no care of Negro marriages; and when Negroes marry after their own way, some make so little account of those marriages that with views of outward interest they often part men from their wives by selling them far asunder, which is common when estates are sold by executors at vendue. Many whose labour is heavy being followed in the field by a man with a whip, hired for that purpose, have in common little else to eat but one peck of Indian corn and some salt, for one week, with a few potatoes; and the latter they commonly raise by their labour on the first day of the week. The correction ensuing on their disobedience to overseers, or slothfulness in business, is often very severe, and sometimes desperate.

Men and women have many times scarce clothes sufficient to hide their nakedness, and boys and girls ten and twelve years old are often stark naked amongst their master's children. Some of our Society, and some of the society called Newlights, use some endeavours to instruct those they have in reading; but in common this is not only neglected, but disapproved. These are a people by whose labour the other inhabitants are in a great measure supported, and many of them in the luxuries of life. These are a people who have made no agreement to serve us, and who have not forfeited their liberty that we know of. These are the souls for whom Christ died, and for our conduct towards them we must answer before that Almighty Being who is no respector of persons. They who know the only true God, and Jesus Christ whom He hath sent, and are thus acquainted with the merciful, benevolent, Gospel Spirit, will therein perceive that the indignation of God is kindled against oppression and cruelty, and in beholding the great distress of so numerous a people will find cause for mourning. . . .

In this Yearly Meeting [1758] several weighty matters were considered, and toward the last that in relation to dealing with persons who purchase slaves. During the several sittings of the said meeting, my mind was frequently covered with inward prayer, and I could say with David, "that tears were my meat day and night." The case of slave-keeping lay heavy upon me, nor did I find any engagement to speak directly to any other matter before the meeting. Now when this case was opened several faithful Friends spake weightily thereto, with which I was comforted; and feeling a concern to cast in my mite, I said in substance as follows:

"In the difficulties attending us in this life nothing is more precious than the mind of Truth inwardly manifested; and it is my earnest desire that in this weighty matter we may be so truly humbled as to be favoured with a clear understanding of the mind of Truth, and follow it; this would be of more advantage to the Society than any mediums which are not in the clearness of Divine wisdom. The case is difficult to some who have slaves, but if such set aside all self-interest, and come to be weaned from the desire of getting estates, or even from holding them together, when truth requires the contrary, I believe way will open that they will know how to steer through those difficulties."

Many Friends appeared to be deeply bowed under the weight of the work, and manifested much firmness in their love to the cause of truth and universal righteousness on the earth. And though none did openly justify the practice of slave-keeping in general, yet some appeared concerned lest the meeting should go into such measures as might give uneasiness to many brethren, alleging that if Friends patiently continued under the exercise the Lord in time to come might open a way for the deliverance of these people. Finding an engagement to speak, I said, "My mind is often led to consider the purity of the Divine Being, and the justice of His judgments; and herein my soul is covered with awfulness. I cannot omit to hint of some cases where people have not been treated with the purity of justice, and the event hath been lamentable. Many slaves on this continent are oppressed, and their cries have reached the ears of the Most High. Such are the purity and certainty of His judgments, that He cannot be partial in our favour. In infinite love and goodness He hath opened our understanding from time to time respecting our duty toward this people, and it is not a time for delay. Should we now be sensible of what He requires of us, and through a respect to the private interest of some persons, or through a regard to some friendships which do not stand on the immutable foundation, neglect to do our duty in firmness and constancy, still waiting for some extraordinary means to bring about their freedom, God may by terrible things in righteousness answer us in this matter." . . . .

I have been informed that Thomas à Kempis lived and died in the profession of the Roman Catholic religion; and, in reading his writings, I have believed him to be a man of a true Christian spirit, as fully so as many who died martyrs because they could not join with some superstitions in that church. All true Christians are of the same spirit, but their gifts are diverse, Jesus Christ appointing to each one his peculiar office, agreeably to His infinite wisdom.

John Huss contended against the errors which had crept into the church, in opposition to the Council of Constance, which the historian reports to have consisted of some thousand persons. He modestly vindicated the cause which he believed was right; and though his language and conduct towards his judges appear to have been respectful, yet he never could be moved from the principles settled in his mind. To use his own words: "This I most humbly require you all, even for His sake who is the God of us all, that I be not compelled to the thing which my conscience doth repugn or strive against." And again, in his answer to the Emperor: "I refuse nothing, most noble Emperor, whatsoever the Council shall decree or determine upon me, only this one thing I except, that I do not offend God and my conscience." At length, rather than conform to a thing reverse to that which he believed the Lord required of him, he chose to suffer death by fire. Thomas à Kempis, without disputing against the articles then generally agreed to, appears to have laboured, by a pious example as well as by preaching and writing, to promote virtue and the inward spiritual religion; and I believe they were both sincere-hearted followers of Christ. True charity is an excellent virtue; and to sincerely labour for their good whose belief in all points doth not agree with ours is a happy case.

The Journal of John Woolman,
Edited by Janet Whitney.
Chicago: Henry Regnery Company, 1950.

JOHN WESLEY

1 7 0 3 - 1 7 9 1

BY THE BEGINNING OF THE EIGHTEENTH CENTURY THE REF-
ormation in England needed to be reformed. A familiar
saying has it that, in those days, the two texts most commonly preached upon were "Be not righteous overmuch" and
"Let all things be done decently and in order." Formality and
decorum had so displaced vitality, and the general tone of
religious life was so decadent that R. H. Tawney can describe current religion as "morality tempered by prudence,
and softened on occasion by a rather sentimental compassion for inferiors." Moreover, the popular morality of
high and low alike was commonly not even "tempered by
prudence." The brutality of popular pastimes in England—
bull-baiting, bear-baiting, cock-fighting and the like—was notorious in Europe, so that Sir Richard Steele, faced with the
excuse that such cruel sports were only the amusements of
the common people, retorted: "It is true, but they are the
amusements of no other common people." Drunkenness was
both rampant and respectable; gambling became a mania;
reckless criminals became public heroes, and thousands gathered to see them hanged; highway robbery was so common
that Horace Walpole wrote, "People are almost afraid of
stirring after dark"; the slave-trade, which John Wesley

described as "that execrable sum of all the villainies," was in full swing; legal penalties were increased in vain, although some two hundred and fifty-three offenses were punishable by death, and one could be hanged for shooting a rabbit, for picking a man's pocket of more than twelve pence or for stealing linen from a bleaching ground; and, as for popular speech and manners, Wesley's charge that "senseless, shameless, stupid profaneness is the true characteristic of the English nation" has ample support from contemporary observers.

Centuries, like individuals, can be slandered, and the eighteenth century in England had noble elements in it, good men and women, lovely homes, upright public servants and devoted Christians, so that Carlyle's acrid phrase about it, "Soul extinct; stomach well alive," does not tell the whole truth. Nevertheless, it was a degenerate time, with religion and morals alike sunk to a dismaying level. J. R. Green was writing as an objective historian when he said: "There was open revolt against religion and against Churches in both extremes of English society. The poor were ignorant and brutal to a degree impossible now to realize; the rich, to an almost utter disbelief in religion, linked a foulness of life now happily almost inconceivable."

At Oxford University, in the early thirties of the century, a group of young men met habitually for prayer and Bible reading. Their intently serious search for a vital religion, issuing in a disciplined life, aroused the ridicule of their fellows, and they were nicknamed "the Holy Club," "the Godly Club," "Bible Moths," "Bible Bigots," and "Methodists." John Wesley, his brother Charles, and George Whitefield were among the moving spirits in that Oxford circle. They were not in rebellion against the Church of England. They frequented its services, partook of its Communion at least once a week, and became its ordained ministers. They were not concerned about a new theology, a new liturgy or any change in the ecclesiastical structure. They were simply in earnest about their personal religion. So far as their group represented revolt, it was revolt against the moral laxity of their times, against the substitution of churchly decorum for spiritual vitality, against the drab, half-hearted, inconsequential recitation of great beliefs without taking them in earnest. They set out to discipline themselves, often with ascetic rigor, in a way of daily living consonant with their profession of Christian faith. They sternly examined themselves, made rules for themselves, set tasks for themselves such as visiting prisoners in the jails, and they prayed, spontaneously when they could, by schedule when they couldn't.

John Wesley, son of a Church of England rector and of one of the most remarkable mothers in English history, was at the heart of this group. He was doing his best to be a genuine Christian, devoted, disciplined, endlessly examining his motives and searching his soul, but that he was not satisfied is made evident when, at the age of thirty-two, he accepted appointment as a missionary to Georgia. "My chief motive is the hope of saving my own soul," he wrote. "I hope to learn the true sense of the Gospel of Christ by preaching it to the heathen." His experience in Georgia, however, only brought him deeper self-disdain. In the Atlantic storms he found himself afraid of death, while Moravians with whom he traveled were not afraid. He was inept and clumsy in handling his parish relationships—even absurd in his indecision as to whether or not to marry a Georgia girl. He returned to England under a cloud of hostility from many of his parishioners, and under a still darker cloud of self-reproach and spiritual dissatisfaction. His experience was much like Luther's. He was trying to save his soul by "works," by self-discipline, by legalistic righteousness. Decent outward behavior he could thereby manage, but there was no joy in his religion, no inward liberation of the soul; the drive and power and exultation which were later his he lacked.

Then, renewing his relationships with the Moravians, he

fell under the influence of Peter Böhler, and one night at a meeting in London came the crucial turning point in Wesley's life and ministry:

"In the evening I went very unwillingly to a society in Aldersgate Street, where one was reading Luther's preface to the *Epistle to the Romans*. About a quarter before nine, while he was describing the change which God works in the heart through faith in Christ, I felt my heart strangely warmed. I felt I did trust in Christ, Christ alone for my salvation; and an assurance was given me that He had taken away *my* sins, even *mine*, and saved *me* from the law of sin and of death."

From that hour Wesley dated his rebirth. He had returned from Georgia crying, "I went to America to convert the Indians, but oh! who shall convert me?" Now he had his answer. The basic Reformation doctrine of justification by faith was made real in his experience. He had thrown himself on Christ, accepted his redemption, gained inner assurance so that he need fear no more. He was a released soul, jubilant, exultant, indefatigable, going out to be "the man who brought Christianity back to life in England."

The evangelical revival which John Wesley launched and captained was a major event in English history, affecting every area of the nation's life—personal character, public morals, social ideals and practices, education and religion. "It is no exaggeration to say," writes W. E. H. Lecky, "that Wesley had a wider constructive influence in the sphere of practical religion than any other man who has appeared since the sixteenth century".

The primary emphasis of his movement was on individual evangelism. Wesley's appeal was intensely personal:

"Who art Thou that now seest and feelest both Thine inward and outward ungodliness? Thou art the man! I want Thee for my Lord! I challenge Thee for a child of God by faith. The Lord hath need of Thee. Thou who feelest Thou art just fit for hell, art just fit to advance His glory—the glory of His free grace, justifying the ungodly and him that worketh not. O come quickly! Believe in the Lord Jesus Christ and Thou, even Thou, art reconciled to God."

Such preaching was out of order in the Church of England; it violated the proprieties; it encouraged unseemly emotionalism and enthusiasm. The pulpits of the established Church were speedily closed to these "Methodist" irregulars. Thereupon George Whitefield turned to preaching in the fields. His first audience out-of-doors numbered two hundred, his second three thousand, his third five thousand, and from then on he commonly preached all over England and America to crowds of twenty thousand and more. John Wesley, reluctantly persuaded to follow him in field preaching, met with similar results. He went after the plain people. "I love the poor," he said, "in many of them I find pure genuine grace unmixed with paint, folly and affectations." Wesley was no such orator as Whitefield was; he argued and reasoned as well as appealed; but the crowds responded, and Wesley responded to the crowds. "My heart was so enlarged I knew not how to give over," he wrote of one sermon, "so we continued three hours." On one typical occasion, standing on a chair amid a partly hostile mob, he conquered them: "The winds were hushed and all was calm and still; my heart was filled with love, my eyes with tears and my mouth with arguments. They were amazed. They were ashamed. They were melted down. They devoured every word."

Between his thirty-sixth year and the time he "first began to feel old at eighty-five," Wesley traveled some two hundred and twenty-five thousand miles, preaching over forty thousand sermons, many of them to audiences of over twenty thousand people. Throughout these fifty years his central message was clear and constant: Christ has paid the price of our redemption; we can experience complete assurance of pardon and of restored fellowship with God; divine power can be released in and through us with transforming and victorious effect; God's ideal for us can be not a vague hope but a present and actual attainment.

This intensely personal message, however, had social effects which transformed England. "The Gospel of Christ knows of no religion but social," said Wesley, "no holiness but social holiness." Without the evangelical revival there is no explaining John Howard's prison reforms or William Wilberforce's anti-slavery campaign. "O be not weary of well-doing!" wrote Wesley to Wilberforce, "Go on, in the name of God and in the power of His might, till even American slavery (the vilest that ever saw the sun) shall vanish away before it." A new social conscience was created in England, with results so far-reaching that Lecky attributes England's escape from a French Revolution largely to the evangelical movement, and J. R. Green says that "a religious revival burst forth which changed in a few years the whole temper of English society."

All this inevitably involved controversy. "Lord, if I must dispute, let it be with the children of the devil! Let me be at peace with thy children!" cried Wesley, but it was an unanswered prayer. Whitefield, for example, was a convinced Calvinist, believing in God's absolute predestination, while Wesley was a convinced Arminian, believing in man's free will, and while their friendship remained unbroken until Wesley preached Whitefield's funeral sermon, the tension was often difficult. Repeatedly John and his brother, Charles, were at loggerheads, and endless problems within the Wesleyan societies tried the souls of the evangelicals.

No problem, however, was so important or so oppressive as their relationship with the Church of England. John Wesley himself never left the Church and fought a lifelong battle to save his societies from leaving it. He intended his societies to be an Order within the English establishment, and at one stage he went so far as to say, "When the Methodists leave the Church of England, God will leave them." Nevertheless, for the English church's sake they would not cease trying to save souls, nor surrender the effective means which they were creating to serve the spiritual welfare of their followers, nor hold back men, like Francis Asbury, who were covering the American continent with a network of Methodist circuits and conferences. Gradually an independent organization developed, closely articulated and carefully disciplined, until at last it was ordaining its own ministers, and administering its own sacraments. So, in the end, without intending it, Wesley died, "leaving behind him nothing but a good library of books, a well-worn clergyman's gown, a much-abused reputation, and—the Methodist Church."

In many of his ideas Wesley was, of course, a child of his time. He believed in the reality of witchcraft. He understood the violent emotional reactions which sometimes convulsed his hearers, throwing them into spasms and causing wild outcries, as the work of demons fighting against the gospel. He undertook to supply the lack in medical service by publishing prescriptions for his people's use—many of them excellent, but some no better than magical charms. He had no use for democracy and was arbitrary and dictatorial in handling the affairs of his societies. He had his faults—nowhere more absurdly evident than in his lack of common sense in dealing with his uniformly unfortunate love affairs. But along with one of the noblest life-stories of achievement in history, he left the memory of an untarnished character, and of a wise and gracious spirit for the like of which all churches may well pray.

Wesley himself never ceased being a High Church Episcopalian, placing strong emphasis on the importance of the sacraments, but with this he blended an evangelical fervor which set his hearers and followers on fire. The early societies which he directed combined two elements usually dissonant and incongruous—on one side, legalistic rules, strictly disciplining the members, and forbidding to them practically all the most popular pastimes of the day; and, on the other, a jubilant elation voicing itself, for example, in rousing hymns, one of Methodism's major contributions, and in the most contagious group singing England had ever known.

A man of rigorous and powerful personal convictions, Wesley nevertheless had so vital an idea of what a genuine Christian really is that his private opinions did not prevent an extraordinary openmindedness and inclusiveness. Even more than his theological and ecclesiastical ideas, a passage such as the following reveals the man:

"I will not quarrel with you about my opinion; only see that your heart is right toward God, that you know and love the Lord Jesus Christ; that you love your neighbor, and walk as your Master walked, and I desire no more. I am sick of opinions; am weary to bear them; my soul loathes this frothy food. Give me solid and substantial religion; give me a humble, gentle lover of God and man; a man full of mercy and good faith, without partiality and without hypocrisy; a man laying himself out in the work of faith, the patience of hope, the labour of love. Let my soul be with these Christians wheresoever they are, and whatsoever opinion they are of!"

The Heart of John Wesley's Journal, edited by Percy Livingston Parker, is of primary importance to the student. A *New History of Methodism*, by W. J. Townsend and H. B. Workman, *Wesley and His Century*, by William Henry Fitchett, *England Before and After Wesley*, by J. W. Bready, are valuable treatises. *John Wesley*, by Francis J. McConnell, and *Son to Susanah*, by E. G. Harrison, are good biographies; *John Wesley, a Portrait*, by Abram Lipsky, is well worth reading; *The Theology of John Wesley*, by W. R. Cannon is excellent; and an interesting picture of Wesley and his work from a Roman Catholic point of view is given in *Enthusiasm*, by R. A. Knox, chapters XVIII through XXI.

A PLAIN ACCOUNT OF THE
PEOPLE CALLED METHODISTS

ABOUT TEN YEARS AGO MY BROTHER AND I WERE DESIRED
to preach in many parts of London. We had no view therein
but, so far as we were able (and we knew God could work
by whomsoever it pleased him), to convince those who
would hear what true Christianity was and to persuade them
to embrace it.

The points we chiefly insisted upon were four: First, that
orthodoxy or right opinions is, at best, but a very slender
part of religion, if it can be allowed to be any part of it at
all; that neither does religion consist in negatives, in bare
harmlessness of any kind; nor merely in externals, in doing
good, or using the means of grace, in works of piety (so-
called) or of charity; that it is nothing short of or different
from "the mind that was in Christ;" the image of God
stamped upon the heart; inward righteousness, attended
with the peace of God; and "joy in the Holy Ghost." Secondly, that the only way under heaven to this religion is to
"repent and believe the Gospel;" or (as the apostle words
it), "repentance toward God, and faith in our Lord Jesus
Christ." Thirdly, that by this faith "he that worketh not,
but believeth on him that justifieth the ungodly, is justified
freely by his grace, through the redemption which is in Jesus
Christ." And, lastly, that "being justified by faith" we taste
of the heaven to which we are going; we are holy and happy;

we tread down sin and fear, and "sit in heavenly places with Jesus Christ."

Many of those who heard this began to cry out that we brought "strange things to their ears"; that this was doctrine which they never heard before, or at least never regarded. They "searched the Scriptures whether these things were so," and acknowledged "the truth as it is in Jesus." Their hearts also were influenced as well as their understandings, and they determined to follow "Jesus Christ, and him crucified."

Immediately they were surrounded with difficulties; all the world rose up against them; neighbors, strangers, acquaintances, relations, friends, began to cry out amain, "Be not righteous overmuch; why shouldst thou destroy thyself?" Let not "much religion make thee mad."

One and another and another came to us, asking what they should do, being distressed on every side; as every one strove to weaken, and none to strengthen, their hands in God. We advised them, "Strengthen you one another. Talk together as often as you can. And pray earnestly with and for one another, that you may 'endure to the end and be saved.'" Against this advice we presumed there could be no objection; as being grounded on the plainest reason, and on so many Scriptures, both of the Old Testament and New, that it would be tedious to recite them.

They said, "But we want you likewise to talk with us often, to direct and quicken us in our way, to give us the advices which you well know we need, and to pray with us, as well as for us." I asked, Which of you desire this? Let me know your names and places of abode. They did so. But I soon found they were too many for me to talk with severally so often as they wanted it. So I told them, "If you will all of you come together every Thursday, in the evening, I will gladly spend some time with you in prayer and give you the best advice I can."

Thus arose, without any previous design on either side, what was afterward called *a Society*; a very innocent name, and very common in London, for any number of people associating themselves together. The thing proposed in their associating themselves together was obvious to every one. They wanted to "flee from the wrath to come," and to assist each other in so doing. They therefore united themselves "in order to pray together, to receive the word of exhortation, and to watch over one another in love, that they might help each other to work out their salvation."

There is one only condition previously required in those who desire admission into this society—"a desire to flee from the wrath to come, to be saved from their sins." (See the Rules of the United Societies.) They now likewise agreed that as many of them as had an opportunity would meet together every Friday, and spend the dinner-hour in crying to God, both for each other and for all mankind.

It quickly appeared that their thus uniting together answered the end proposed therein. In a few months the far greater part of those who had begun to "fear God, and work righteousness," but were not united together, grew faint in their minds and fell back into what they were before. Meanwhile the far greater part of those who were thus united together continued "striving to enter in at the strait gate," and to "lay hold on eternal life."

Upon reflection I could not but observe, This is the very thing which was from the beginning of Christianity. In the earliest times, those whom God had sent forth "preached the Gospel to every creature." And, "the body of hearers," were mostly either Jews or heathens. But as soon as any of these were so convinced of the truth as to forsake sin and seek the gospel salvation they immediately joined them together, took an account of their names, advised them to watch over each other, and met these "catechumens" (as they were then called), apart from the great congregation, that they might instruct, rebuke, exhort, and pray with them, and for them, according to their several necessities.

But it was not long before an objection was made to this

which had not once entered into my thought: "Is not this making a schism? Is not the joining these people together, gathering churches out of churches?"

It was easily answered, "If you mean only gathering people out of buildings called churches, it is. But if you mean dividing Christians from Christians, and so destroying Christian fellowship, it is not. For, (1) These were not Christians before they were thus joined. Most of them were barefaced heathens. (2) Neither are they Christians from whom you suppose them to be divided. You will not look me in the face and say they are. What! drunken Christians! cursing and swearing Christians! lying Christians! cheating Christians! If these are Christians at all, they are devil Christians, as the poor Malabarians term them. (3) Neither are they divided any more than they were before, even from these wretched devil Christians. They are as ready as ever to assist them, and to perform every office of real kindness toward them. (4) If it be said, "But there are some true Christians in the parish, and you destroy the Christian fellowship between these and them," I answer, That which never existed cannot be destroyed. But the fellowship you speak of never existed. Therefore it cannot be destroyed. Which of those true Christians had any such fellowship with these? Who watched over them in love? Who marked their growth in grace? Who advised and exhorted them from time to time? Who prayed with them and for them, as they had need? This and this alone, is Christian fellowship; But, alas! where is it to be found? Look east or west, north or south; name what parish you please; is this Christian fellowship there? Rather, are not the bulk of the parishioners a mere rope of sand? What Christian connection is there between them? What intercourse in spiritual things? What watching over each other's souls? What bearing of one another's burdens? What a mere jest is it, then, to talk so gravely of destroying what never was! The real truth is just the reverse of this: we introduce Christian fellowship where it was utterly destroyed.

And the fruits of it have been peace, love, joy, and zeal for every good word and work.

But as much as we endeavored to watch over each other, we soon found some who did not live the Gospel. I do not know that any hypocrites were crept in; for, indeed, there was no temptation; but several grew cold, and gave way to the sins which had long easily beset them. We quickly perceived there were many ill consequences of suffering these to remain among us. It was dangerous to others, inasmuch as all sin is of an infectious nature. It brought such a scandal on their brethren as exposed them to what was not properly the reproach of Christ. It laid a stumbling-block in the way of others, and caused the truth to be evil spoken of.

We groaned under these inconveniences long before a remedy could be found. The people were scattered so wide in all parts of the town, from Wapping to Westminster, that I could not easily see what the behavior of each person in his own neighborhood was, so that several disorderly walkers did much hurt before I was apprised of it.

At length, while we were thinking of quite another thing, we struck upon a method for which we have cause to bless God ever since. I was talking with several of the society in Bristol concerning the means of paying the debts there, when one stood up and said, "Let every member of the society give a penny a week till all are paid." Another answered, "But many of them are poor, and cannot afford to do it." "Then," said he, "put eleven of the poorest with me, and if they can give anything, well: I will call on them weekly, and if they can give nothing, I will give for them as well as for myself. And each of you call on eleven of your neighbors weekly, receive what they give, and make up what is wanting." It was done. In a while some of these informed me they found such and such an one did not live as he ought. It struck me immediately, "This is the thing, the very thing we have wanted so long." I called together all the leaders of the classes (so we used to term them and their companies), and desired that each would make a particular inquiry into the behavior of those whom he saw weekly. They did so. Many disorderly walkers were detected. Some turned from the evil of their ways. Some were put away from us. Many saw it with fear, and rejoiced unto God with reverence.

As soon as possible the same method was used in London and all other places. Evil men were detected and reproved. They were borne with, for a season. If they forsook their sins, we received them gladly; if they obstinately persisted therein, it was openly declared that they were not of us. The rest mourned and prayed for them, and yet rejoiced that, in as far as in us lay, the scandal was rolled away from the society.

From

THE CHARACTER OF
A METHODIST

THE DISTINGUISHING MARKS OF A METHODIST ARE NOT HIS opinions of any sort. His assenting to this or that scheme of religion, his embracing any particular set of notions, his espousing the judgment of one man or of another are all quite wide of the point. Whosoever, therefore, imagines that a Methodist is a man of such or such an opinion is grossly ignorant of the whole affair; he mistakes the truth totally. We believe, indeed, that "all Scripture is given by the inspiration of God;" and herein we are distinguished from Jews, Turks, and infidels. We believe the written word of God to be the only and sufficient rule both of Christian faith and practice; and herein we are fundamentally distinguished from those of the Roman Church. We believe Christ to be the eternal supreme God; and herein we are distinguished from the Socinians and Arians. But as to all opinions which do not strike at the root of Christianity, we think and let think. So that, whatsoever they are, whether right or wrong, they are no distinguishing marks of a Methodist.

Neither are words or phrases of any sort. We do not place our religion, or any part of it, in being attached to any peculiar mode of speaking, any quaint or uncommon set of expressions. The most obvious, easy, common words wherein our meaning can be conveyed we prefer before others,

505

both on ordinary occasions and when we speak of the things of God. We never, therefore, willingly or designedly, deviate from the most usual way of speaking; unless when we express Scripture truths in Scripture words, which, we presume, no Christian will condemn. Neither do we affect to use any particular expressions of Scripture more frequently than others, unless they are such as are more frequently used by the inspired writers themselves. So that it is as gross an error to place the marks of a Methodist in his words as in opinions of any sort.

Nor do we desire to be distinguished by actions, customs, or usages of an indifferent nature. Our religion does not lie in doing what God has not enjoined, or abstaining from what he hath not forbidden. It does not lie in the form of our apparel, in the posture of our body, or the covering of our heads, nor yet in abstaining from marriage, or from meats and drinks, which are all good if received with thanksgiving. Therefore, neither will any man who knows whereof he affirms fix the mark of a Methodist here, in any actions or customs purely indifferent, undetermined by the word of God.

Nor, lastly, is he distinguished by laying the whole stress of religion on any single part of it. If you say, "Yes, he is; for he thinks 'we are saved by faith alone,'" I answer, You do not understand the terms. By salvation he means holiness of heart and life. And this he affirms to spring from true faith alone. Can even a nominal Christian deny it? Is this placing a part of religion for the whole? "Do we then make void the law through faith? God forbid! Yea, we establish the law." We do not place the whole of religion (as too many do, God knoweth) either in not doing harm or in doing good, or in using the ordinances of God. No, not in all of them together; wherein we know by experience a man may labor many years and at the end have no religion at all, no more than he had at the beginning. Much less in any one of these; or, it may be, in a scrap of one of them; like her who fancies herself a virtuous woman only because she is not a prostitute or him who dreams he is an honest man merely because he does not rob or steal. May the Lord God of my fathers preserve me from such a poor, starved religion as this! Were this the mark of a Methodist, I would sooner choose to be a sincere Jew, Turk or Pagan.

"What, then, is the mark? Who is a Methodist according to your own account?" I answer, "A Methodist is one who has the love of God shed abroad in his heart by the Holy Ghost given unto him"; one who "loves the Lord his God with all his heart, and with all his soul, and with all his mind, and with all his strength." God is the joy of his heart and the desire of his soul, which is constantly crying out, "Whom have I in heaven but thee? and there is none upon earth that I desire beside thee! My God and my all! Thou art the strength of my heart, and my portion forever!"

He is therefore happy in God, yea, always happy, as having in him "a well of water springing up into everlasting life," and overflowing his soul with peace and joy. "Perfect love" having now "cast out fear," he "rejoices evermore." He "rejoices in the Lord always," even "in God his Saviour," and in the Father, "through our Lord Jesus Christ, by whom he hath now received the atonement." "Having" found "redemption through his blood, the forgiveness of his sins," he cannot but rejoice whenever he looks back on the horrible pit out of which he is delivered, when he sees "all his transgressions blotted out as a cloud, and his iniquities as a thick cloud." He cannot but rejoice whenever he looks on the state wherein he now is, "being justified freely, and having peace with God through our Lord Jesus Christ." For "he that believeth hath the witness" of this "in himself," being now the son of God by faith. "Because he is a son, God hath sent forth the Spirit of his son into his heart, crying, Abba, Father!" And "the spirit itself beareth witness with his spirit, that he is a child of God." He rejoiceth also, whenever he looks forward, "in hope of the glory that shall be revealed;" yes, this his joy is full, and all his bones cry out, "Blessed be the God and Father of our Lord Jesus Christ, who, according to his abundant mercy, hath begotten me again to a living hope—of an inheritance incorruptible, undefiled, and that fadeth not away, reserved in heaven for me!"

And he who hath this hope, thus "full of immortality, in everything giveth thanks;" as knowing that this (whatsoever it is) "is the will of God in Christ Jesus concerning him." From him, therefore, he cheerfully receives all, saying, "Good is the will of the Lord;" and whether the Lord giveth or taketh away, equally "blessing the name of the Lord." For he hath "learned in whatsoever state he is, therewith to be content." He knoweth "both how to be abased, and how to abound. Everywhere and in all things he is instructed both to be full and to be hungry, both to abound and to suffer need." Whether in ease or pain, whether in sickness or in health, whether in life or death, he giveth thanks from the ground of his heart to Him who orders it for good; knowing that as "every good gift cometh from above," so none but good can come from the Father of lights, into whose hand he has wholly committed his body and soul, as into the hands of a faithful Creator. He is therefore "careful" (anxiously or uneasily) "for nothing;" as having "cast all his care on Him that careth for him," and "in all things" resting on him, after "making his request known to him with thanksgiving."

For indeed he "prays without ceasing." It is given him "always to pray, and not to faint." Not that he is always in the house of prayer, though he neglects no opportunity of being there. Neither is he always on his knees, although he often is, or on his face before the Lord his God. Nor yet is he always crying aloud to God or calling upon him in words; for many times "the Spirit maketh intercession for him with groans that cannot be uttered." But at all times the language of his heart is this: "Thou brightness of the eternal glory, unto thee is my heart, though without a voice, and my silence speaketh unto thee." And this is true prayer, and this alone. But his heart is ever lifted up to God at all times and in all places. In this he is never hindered, much less interrupted, by any person or thing. In retirement or company, in leisure, business, or conversation, his heart is ever with the Lord. Whether he lie down or rise up, God is in all his thoughts; he walks with God continually, having the loving eye of his mind still fixed upon him, and every-where "seeing him that is invisible."

And while he thus always exercises his love to God by praying without ceasing, rejoicing evermore and in every thing giving thanks, this commandment is written in his heart, "That he who loveth God, love his brother also." And he accordingly loves his neighbor as himself; he loves every man as his own soul. His heart is full of love to all mankind, to every child of the "Father of the spirits of all flesh." That a man is not personally known to him is no bar to his love; no, nor that he is known to be such as he approves not, that he repays hatred for good will. For he "loves his enemies;" yea, and the enemies of God, "the evil and the unthankful." And if it be not in his power to "do good to them that hate him," yet he ceases not to pray for them, though they continue to spurn his love, and still "despitefully use him and persecute him."

For he is "pure in heart." The love of God has purified his heart from all revengeful passions, from envy, malice, and wrath, from every unkind temper or malign affectation. It hath cleansed him from pride and haughtiness of spirit, whereof alone cometh contention. And he hath now "put on bowels of mercies, kindness, humbleness of mind, meekness, long suffering" So that he "forbears and forgives if he had a quarrel against any, even as God in Christ hath forgiven him." And, indeed, all possible ground for contention on his part is utterly cut off. For none can take from him what he desires, seeing he "loves not the world, nor" any of "the things of the world;" being now "crucified to the world, and the world crucified to him;" being dead to all that is in the world, both to "the lust of the flesh, the lust of the eye, and the pride of life." For "all his desire is unto God, and to the remembrance of his name."

Agreeable to this his one desire is the one design of his life, namely, "not to do his own will, but the will of Him that sent him." His one intention at all times and in all things is, not to please himself, but him whom his soul loveth. He has a single eye. And because "his eye is single his whole body is full of light." Indeed, where the loving eye of the soul is continually fixed upon God there can be no darkness at all, "but the whole is light, as when the bright shining of a candle doth enlighten the house." God then reigns alone. All that is in the soul is holiness to the Lord. There is not a motion in his heart but is according to his will. Every thought that arises points to him and is in obedience to the law of Christ.

And the tree is known by its fruits. For as he loves God, so he keeps his commandments, not only some or most of them, but all, from the least to the greatest. He is not content to "keep the whole law and offend in one point," but has in all points "a conscience void of offense toward God and toward man." Whatever God has forbidden, he avoids; whatever God hath enjoined, he doeth; and that whether it be little or great, hard or easy, joyous or grievous to the flesh. He "runs the way of God's commandments," now he hath set his heart at liberty. It is his glory so to do, it is his daily crown of rejoicing, "to do the will of God on earth, as it is done in heaven;" knowing it is the highest privilege of "the angels of God, of those that excel in strength, to fulfill his commandments and harken to the voice of his word."

All the commandments of God he accordingly keeps, and that with all his might. For his obedience is in proportion to his love, the source from whence it flows. And therefore, loving God with all his heart, he serves him with all his strength. He continually presents his soul and body a living sacrifice, holy, acceptable to God; entirely and without reserve devoting himself, all he has, and all he is, to his glory. All the talents he has received he constantly employs according to his Master's will, every power and faculty of his soul, every member of his body. Once he "yielded" them "unto sin" and the devil, "as instruments of unrighteousness," but now, "being alive from the dead, he yields" them all "as instruments of righteousness unto God."

By consequence, whatsoever he doeth, it is all to the glory of God. In all his employments of every kind he not only aims at this (which is implied in having a single eye), but actually attains it. His business and refreshments, as well as his prayers, all serve this great end. Whether he sit in his house or walk by the way, whether he lie down or rise up, he is promoting in all he speaks or does the one business of his life; whether he put on his apparel, or labor, or eat and drink, or divert himself from too wasting labor, it all tends to advance the glory of God by peace and good-will among men. His one invariable rule is this: "Whatsoever ye do, in word or deed, do it all in the name of the Lord Jesus, giving thanks to God and the Father by him."

Nor do the customs of the world at all hinder his "running the race that is set before him." He knows that vice does not lose its nature though it becomes ever so fashionable, and remembers that "every man is to give an account of himself to God." He cannot, therefore, "follow" even "a multitude to do evil." He cannot "fare sumptuously every day," or "make provision for the flesh to fulfill the lusts thereof." He cannot "lay up treasures upon earth," any more than he can take fire into his bosom. He cannot "adorn himself," on any pretense, "with gold or costly apparel." He cannot join in or countenance any diversion which has the least tendency to vice of any kind. He cannot "speak evil" of his neighbor any more than he can lie either for God or man. He cannot utter an unkind word of anyone, for love keeps the door of his lips. He cannot speak "idle words," "no corrupt communication" ever "comes out of his mouth," as is all that "which is" not "good to the use of edifying," not "fit to minister grace to the hearers." But "whatsoever things" are justly "of good report," he thinks and speaks and acts, "adorning the Gospel of our Lord Jesus Christ in all things."

Lastly. As he has time he "does good unto all men," unto neighbors and strangers, friends and enemies; and that in every possible kind, not only to their bodies by "feeding the hungry, clothing the naked, visiting those that are sick or in prison;" but much more does he labor to do good to their souls as of the ability which God giveth, to awaken those that sleep in death; to bring those who are awakened to the atoning blood that, "being justified by faith, they may have peace with God," and to provoke those who have peace with God to abound more in love and in good works. And he is willing to "spend and be spent herein," even "to be offered up on the sacrifice and service of their faith," so that they may "all come unto the measure of the stature of the fullness of Christ."

These are the principles and practises of our sect; these are the true marks of a true Methodist. By these alone do those who are in derision so called desire to be distinguished from other men. If any man say, "Why, these are only the common, fundamental principles of Christianity!" Thou hast said: so I mean; this is the very truth. I know they are no other, and I would to God both thou and all men knew that I and all who follow my judgment do vehemently refuse to be distinguished from other men by any but the common principles of Christianity—the plain old Christianity that I teach, renouncing and detesting all other marks of distinction. And whosoever is what I preach (let him be called what he will, for names change not the nature of things), he is a Christian, not in name only, but in heart and in life. He is inwardly and outwardly conformed to the will of God, as revealed in the written word. He thinks, speaks, and lives according to the method laid down in the revelation of Jesus Christ. His soul is renewed after the image of God, in righteousness and in all true holiness. And having the mind that was in Christ, he so walks as Christ also walked.

By these marks, by these fruits of a living faith, do we labor to distinguish ourselves from the unbelieving world, from all those whose minds or lives are not according to the Gospel of Christ. But from early Christians, of whatsoever denomination they be, we earnestly desire not to be distinguished at all; not from any who sincerely follow after what they know they have not yet attained. No. "Whosoever doeth the will of my father which is in heaven, the same is my brother, and sister, and mother." And I beseech you, brethren, by the mercies of God, that we be in no wise divided among ourselves. Is thy heart right, as my heart is with thine? I ask no further question. If it be, give me thy hand. For opinions or terms let us not destroy the work of God. Dost thou love and serve God? It is enough. I give thee the right hand of fellowship. If there be any consolation in Christ, in any comfort of love, if any fellowship of the Spirit, if any bowels and mercies, let us strive together for the faith of the Gospel, walking worthy of the vocation wherewith we are called; with all lowliness and meekness, with long suffering, forbearing one another in love, endeavoring to keep the unity of the Spirit in the bonds of peace, remembering there is one body and one Spirit, even as we are called with one hope of our calling, "one Lord, one faith, one baptism, one God and Father of all, who is above all, and through all, and in you all."

From

WHAT IS AN ARMINIAN?

TO SAY, "THIS MAN IS AN ARMINIAN," HAS THE SAME EF-fect on many hearers as to say, "This is a mad dog." It puts them into a fright at once: they run away from him with all speed and diligence; and will hardly stop, unless it be to throw a stone at the dreadful and mischievous animal.

The more unintelligible the word is, the better it answers the purpose. Those on whom it is fixed know not what to do; not understanding what it means, they cannot tell what defense to make, or how to clear themselves from the charge. And it is not easy to remove the prejudice which others have imbibed, who know no more of it than that it is "something *very* bad," if not "*all* that is bad!"

To clear the meaning, therefore, of this ambiguous term, may be of use to many: to those who so freely pin this name upon others, that they may not say what they do not understand; to those that hear them, that they may no longer be abused by men's saying they know not what; and to those upon whom the name is fixed, that they may know how to answer for themselves.

It may be necessary to observe, first, that many confound Arminians with Arians. But this is entirely a different thing; the one has no resemblance to the other. An Arian is one who denies the Godhead of Christ; we scarce need say, the supreme, eternal Godhead, because there can be no God but the supreme, eternal God, unless we will make two Gods, a great God and a little one. Now, none have ever more firmly believed or more strongly asserted the Godhead of Christ than many of the (so called) Arminians have done, yes, and do at this day. Arminianism, therefore (whatever it be), is totally different from Arianism.

The rise of the word was this: JAMES HARMENS—in Latin *Jacobus Arminius*—was first one of the ministers of Amsterdam, and afterward Professor of Divinity at Leyden. He was educated at Geneva; but in the year 1591 began to doubt of the principles which he had till then received. And being more and more convinced that they were wrong, when he was vested with the professorship he publicly taught what he believed the truth, till, in the year 1609, he died in peace. But a few years after his death some zealous men, with the Prince of Orange at their head, furiously assaulted all that held what were his opinions; and, having procured them to be solemnly condemned in the famous Synod of Dort (not so numerous or learned, but full as impartial as the Council or the Synod of Trent), some were put to death, some banished, some imprisoned for life, all turned out of their employments, and made incapable of holding any office, either in Church or State.

The errors charged upon these (usually termed *Arminians*) by their opponents are five: (1) That they deny original sin; (2) That they deny justification by faith; (3) That they deny absolute predestination; (4) That they deny the Grace of God to be irresistible; and (5) That they affirm a believer may fall from grace.

With regard to the first two of these charges, they plead, Not Guilty. They are entirely false. No man that ever lived, not John Calvin himself, ever asserted either original sin or justification by faith in more strong, more clear and express terms, than Arminius has done. These two points, therefore, are to be set out of the question; in these both parties agree. In this respect, there is not a hair's breadth difference between Mr. Wesley and Mr. Whitefield.

But there is undeniable difference between the Calvinists

and Arminians with regard to the three other questions. Here they divide; the former believe absolute, the latter only conditional, predestination. The Calvinists hold (1) God has absolutely decreed, from all eternity, to save such and such persons, and no others; and that Christ died for these and none else. The Arminians hold that God has decreed from all eternity, touching all that have the written word, "He that believeth shall be saved; he that believeth not, shall be condemned;" and in order to this, "Christ died for all, all that were dead in trespasses and sins;" that is, for every child of Adam, since "in Adam all died."

The Calvinists hold, secondly, that the saving grace of God is abolutely irresistible; that no man is any more able to resist it than to resist the stroke of lightning. The Arminians hold that, although there may be some moments wherein the grace of God acts irresistibly, yet, in general, any man may resist, and that to his eternal ruin, the grace whereby it was the will of God he should have been eternally saved.

The Calvinists hold, thirdly, that a true believer in Christ, cannot possibly fall from grace. The Arminians hold that a true believer may "make shipwreck of faith and a good conscience;" that he may fall, not only foully, but finally, so as to perish forever.

Indeed, the two latter points, irresistible grace and infallible perseverance, are the natural consequence of the former, of the unconditional decree. For, if God has eternally and absolutely decreed to save such and such persons it follows, both that they cannot resist his saving grace (else they might miss of salvation), and that they cannot finally fall from that grace which they cannot resist. So that in effect the three questions come into one, "Is predestination absolute or conditional?" The Arminians believe it is conditional; the Calvinists, that it is absolute.

Away, then with all ambiguity! Away with all expressions which only puzzle the cause! Let honest men speak out, and not play with hard words which they do not understand.

And how can any man know what Arminius held who has never read one page of his writings. Let no man bawl against Arminians till he knows what the term means; and then he will know that Arminians and Calvinists are just upon a level. And Arminians have as much right to be angry at Calvinists as Calvinists have to be angry at Arminians. John Calvin was a pious, learned, sensible man; and so was James Harmens. Many Calvinists are pious, learned, sensible men; and so are many Arminians. Only the former hold absolute predestination; the latter, conditional.

One word more: Is it not the duty of every Arminian preacher, first, never, in public or private, to use the word *Calvinist*, as a term of reproach; seeing it is neither better nor worse than calling names?—a practice no more consistent with good sense or good manners than it is with Christianity. Secondly, to do all that in him lies to prevent his hearers from doing it, by showing them the sin and folly of it? And is it not equally the duty of every Calvinist preacher, first, never in public or in private, in preaching or in conversation, to use the word *Arminian* as a term of reproach? Secondly, to do all that in him lies to prevent his hearers from doing it, by showing them the sin and folly thereof; and that the more earnestly and diligently if they have been accustomed so to do? perhaps encouraged therein by his own example!

GOD'S SOVEREIGNTY

GOD REVEALS HIMSELF UNDER A TWOFOLD CHARACTER; AS A Creator, and as a Governor. These are no way inconsistent with each other, but they are totally different.

As a Creator, he has acted in all things according to his own sovereign will. Justice has not, cannot have, any place here; for nothing is due to what has no being. Here, therefore, he may, in the most absolute sense, do what he will with his own. Accordingly, he created the heavens and the earth, and all things that are therein, in every conceivable respect, "according to his own good pleasure." 1. He began his creation at what time, or rather at what part of eternity it seemed him good. Had it pleased him, it might have been millions of years sooner, or millions of ages later. 2. He determined, by his sovereign will, the duration of the universe; whether it should last seven thousand, or seven hundred thousand, or numberless millions of years. 3. By the same, he appointed the place of the universe in the immensity of space. 4. Of his sovereign will he determined the number of stars, of all the component parts of the universe, and the magnitude of every atom, of every fixed star, every planet and every comet. 5. As Sovereign, he created the earth, with all the furniture of it, whether animate or inanimate; and gave to each such a nature, with such properties. 6. Of his own good pleasure he made such a creature as man, an embodied spirit, and, in consequence of his spiritual nature, endued with understanding, will, and liberty. 7. He has determined the times for every nation to come into being, with the bounds of their habitations. 8. He has allotted the time, the place, the circumstances, for the birth of each individual:

> If of parents I came that honor'd Thy name
> 'Twas thy goodness appointed it so.

9. He has given to each a body, as it pleased him, weak or strong, healthy or sickly. This implies, 10. That he gives them various degrees of understanding, and of knowledge, diversified by numberless circumstances. It is hard to say how far this extends; what an amazing difference there is, as to the means of improvement, between one born and brought up in a pious English family and one born and bred among the Hottentots. Only we are sure the difference cannot be so great as to necessitate one to be good, or the other to be evil; to force one into everlasting glory, or the other into everlasting burnings. This cannot be, because it would suppose the character of God as a Creator to interfere with God as a Governor; wherein he does not, cannot possibly, act according to his own mere sovereign will; but, as he has expressly told us, according to the invariable rules both of justice and mercy.

Whether, therefore, we can account for it or no (which indeed we cannot in a thousand cases), we must absolutely maintain that God is a rewarder of them that diligently seek him. But he cannot reward the sun for shining, because the sun is not a free agent. Neither could he reward us for letting our light shine before men, if we acted as necessarily as the sun. All reward, as well as all punishment, presupposes free agency; and whatever creature is incapable of choice is incapable of either one or the other.

Whenever, therefore, God acts as a Governor, as a rewarder, or punisher, he no longer acts as a mere Sovereign, by his own sole will and pleasure; but as an impartial Judge, guided in all things by invariable justice.

Yet it is true, that, in some cases, mercy rejoices over justice; although severity never does. God may reward more, but he will never punish more, than strict justice requires. It may be allowed that God acts as Sovereign in convincing some souls of sin; arresting them in mid-career, by his resistless power. It seems also that, at the moment of our conversion, he acts irresistibly. There may likewise be many irresistible touches during the course of our Christian warfare; with regard to which every believer may say:

> "In the time of my distress
> Thou hast my succor been,
> In my utter helplessness
> Restraining me from sin."

But still, as St. Paul might have been either obedient or "disobedient to the heavenly vision," so every individual may, after all that God has done, either improve his grace or make it of none effect.

Whatever, therefore, it has pleased God to do of his sovereign pleasure as Creator of heaven and earth, and whatever his mercy may do on particular occasions, over and above what justice requires, the general rule stands firm as the pillars of heaven: "The Judge of all the earth will do right. He will judge the world in righteousness," and every man therein, according to the strictest justice. He will punish no man for doing any thing which he could not possibly avoid; neither for omitting any thing which he could not possibly do. Every punishment supposes the offender might have avoided the offense for which he is punished; otherwise, to punish him would be palpably unjust, and inconsistent with the character of God our Governor.

Let, then, these two ideas of God and the Creator, the

sovereign Creator, and God the Governor, the just Governor, be always kept apart. Let us distinguish them from each other with the utmost care. So shall we give God the full glory of his sovereign grace without impeaching his inviolable justice.

From

A LETTER TO A ROMAN

CATHOLIC

You have heard ten thousand stories of us who are commonly called Protestants, of which, if you believe only one in a thousand, you must think very hardly of us. But this is quite contrary to our Lord's rule, "Judge not, that ye be not judged," and has many ill-consequences, particularly this—it inclines us to think hardly of you. Hence, we are on both sides less willing to help one another, and more ready to hurt each other. Hence, brotherly love is utterly destroyed, and each side, looking on the other as monsters, gives way to anger, hatred, malice, to every unkind affection; which have frequently broke out in such inhuman barbarities as are scarce named among the heathen.

Now, can nothing be done, even allowing us on both sides to retain our own opinions, for the softening of our hearts toward each other, the giving a check to this flood of unkindness, and restoring at least some small degree of love among our neighbors and countrymen? Do not you wish for this? Are you not fully convinced that malice, hatred, revenge, bitterness, whether in us or in you, in our hearts or yours, are an abomination to the Lord? Be our opinions right or be they wrong, these tempers are undeniably wrong. They are the broad road that leads to destruction, to the nethermost hell.

I do not suppose all the bitterness is on your side. I know

there is too much on our side also; so much that I fear many Protestants (so called) will be angry at me, too, for writing to you in this manner and will say, "It is showing you too much favor; you deserve no such treatment at our hands."

But I think you do. I think you deserve the tenderest regard I can show, were it only because the same God hath raised you and me from the dust of the earth, and has made us both capable of loving and enjoying him to eternity; were it only because the Son of God has bought you and me with his own blood. How much more if you are a person fearing God (as without question many of you are), and studying to have a conscience void of offense toward God and toward man?

I shall, therefore, as mildly and inoffensively as I can, endeavor to remove in some measure the ground of your unkindness by plainly declaring what our belief and what our practice is, that you may see we are not altogether such monsters as, perhaps, you imagined us to be.

A true Protestant may express his belief in these or like words:

As I am assured that there is an infinite and independent Being, and that it is impossible that there should be more than one, so I believe that this One God is the Father of all things, especially of angels and men; that he is in a peculiar manner the Father of those whom he regenerates by his Spirit, whom he adopts in his Son, as co-heirs with him, and crowns with an eternal inheritance; but in a still higher sense, the Father of his only Son, whom he hath begotten from eternity.

I believe this Father of all not only to be able to do whatsoever pleaseth him, but also to have an eternal right of making what and when and how he pleaseth, and of possessing and disposing of all that he has made; and that he of his own goodness created heaven and earth, and all that is therein.

I believe that Jesus of Nazareth was the Saviour of the world, the Messiah so long foretold; that, being anointed with the Holy Ghost, he was a Prophet, revealing to us the whole will of God; that he was a Priest, who gave himself a sacrifice for sin, and still makes intercession for transgressors; that he is a King, who has all power in heaven and in earth, and will reign till he has subdued all things to himself.

I believe he is the proper, natural Son of God, God of God, very God of very God; and that he is the Lord of all, having absolute, supreme, universal dominion over all things; but more peculiarly our Lord, who believe in him both by conquest, purchase, and voluntary obligation.

I believe that he was made man, joining the human nature with the divine in one person; being conceived by the singular operation of the Holy Ghost, and born of the blessed Virgin Mary, who, as well after as before she brought him forth, continued a pure and unspotted virgin.

I believe he suffered inexpressible pains both of body and soul and at last death, even the death of the cross, at the time that Pontius Pilate governed Judea under the Roman emperor; that his body was then laid in the grave, and his soul went to the place of separate spirits; that the third day he rose again from the dead; that he ascended into heaven; where he remains in the midst of the throne of God, in the highest power and glory, as Mediator till the end of the world, as God to all eternity; that, in the end, he will come down from heaven to judge every man according to his works, both those who shall then be alive and all who have died before that day.

I believe the infinite and eternal Spirit of God, equal with the Father and the Son, to be not only perfectly holy in himself, but the immediate cause of all holiness in us; enlightening our understandings, rectifying our wills and affections, renewing our natures, uniting our persons to Christ, assuring us of the adoption of sons, leading us in our actions—purifying and sanctifying our souls and bodies to a full and eternal enjoyment of God.

I believe that Christ by his apostles gathered unto himself a Church, to which he has continually added such as shall be saved; that this Catholic—that is, universal—Church, extending to all nations and all ages, is holy in all its members who have fellowship with God the Father, Son, and Holy Ghost; that they have fellowship with the holy angels, who constantly minister to these heirs of salvation, and with all the living members of Christ on earth, as well as all who are departed in his faith and fear.

I believe God forgives all the sins of them that truly repent and unfeignedly believe his holy Gospel; and that at the last day all men shall rise again, every one with his own body.

I believe that as the unjust shall, after their resurrection, be tormented in hell forever, so the just shall enjoy inconceivable happiness in the presence of God to all eternity.

Now, is there any thing wrong in this? Is there any one point which you do not believe as well as we?

But you think we ought to believe more. We will not now enter into the dispute. Only let me ask, if a man sincerely believes thus much, and practices accordingly, can any one possibly persuade you to think that such a man shall perish everlastingly?

"But does he practice accordingly?" If he does not, we grant all his faith will not save him. And this leads me to show you, in few and plain words, what the practice of a true Protestant is.

I say, *a true Protestant*; for I disclaim all common swearers, Sabbath-breakers, drunkards; all whoremongers, liars, cheats, extortioners; in a word, all that live in open sin. These are no Protestants; they are no Christians at all. Give them their own names; they are open heathens. They are the curse of the nation, the bane of society, the shame of mankind, the scum of the earth.

A true Protestant believes in God, has a full confidence in his mercy, fears him with a filial fear, and loves him with all his soul. He worships God in spirit and in truth, in every thing gives him thanks; calls upon him with his heart as well as his lips, at all times and in all places; honors his holy name and his word, and serves him truly all the days of his life.

Now, do not you yourself approve of this? Is there any one point you can condemn? Do not you practice as well as approve of it? Can you ever be happy if you do not? Can you ever expect true peace in this or glory in the world to come if you do not believe in God through Christ? If you do not thus fear and love God? My dear friend, consider: I am not persuading you to leave or change your religion, but to follow after that fear and love of God without which all religion is vain. I say not a word to you about your opinions or outward manner of worship. But I say all worship is an abomination to the Lord, unless you worship him in spirit and in truth; with your heart as well as your lips; with your spirit and with your understanding also. Be your form of worship what it will, but in every thing give him thanks; else it is all but lost labor. Use whatever outward observances you please, but put your whole trust in him; but honor his holy name and his word, and serve him truly all the days of your life.

Again: A true Protestant loves his neighbor—that is, every man, friend or enemy, good or bad, as himself, as he loves his own soul, as Christ loved us. And as Christ laid down his life for us, so is he ready to lay down his life for his brethren. He shows this love by doing to all men, in all points, as he would they should do unto him. He loves, honors, and obeys his father and mother, and helps them to the uttermost of his power. He honors and obeys the king, and all that are put in authority under him. He cheerfully submits to all his governors, teachers, spiritual pastors, and masters. He behaves lowly and reverently to all his betters. He hurts nobody by word or deed. He is true and just in all his dealings. He bears no malice or hatred in his heart. He abstains from all evil speaking, lying, and slandering; neither is guile found in his mouth. Knowing his body to be the temple of the Holy Ghost, he keeps it in sobriety, temperance and chastity. He does not desire other men's goods, but is content with that he hath; labors to get his own living, and to do the whole will of God in that state of life unto which it has pleased God to call him.

Have you anything to reprove in this? Are you not herein even as he? If not (tell the truth), are you not condemned both by God and your own conscience? Can you fall short of any one point hereof without falling short of being a Christian?

Come, my brother, and let us reason together. Are you right if you only love your friend and hate your enemy? Do not even the heathens and publicans so? You are called to love your enemies, to bless them that curse you, and to pray for them that despitefully use you and persecute you. But are you not disobedient to the heavenly calling? Does your tender love to all men, not only the good, but also the evil and unthankful, approve you the child of your Father which is in heaven? Otherwise, whatever you believe and whatever you practice, you are of your father the devil. Are you ready to lay down your life for your brethren? And do you do unto all as you would they should do unto you? If not, do not deceive your own soul. You are but a heathen still. Do you love, honor, and obey your father and mother? and help them to the utmost of your power? Do you honor and obey all in authority? all your governors, spiritual pastors, and masters? Do you behave lowly and reverently to all your betters? Do you hurt nobody by word or deed? Are you true and just in all your dealings? Do you take care to pay whatever you owe? Do you feel no malice or envy or revenge, no hatred or bitterness to any man? If you do it is plain you are not of God; for all these are tempers of the devil. Do you speak the truth from your heart to all men, and that in tenderness and love? Are you "an Israelite, indeed, in whom is no guile?" Do you keep your body in sobriety, temperance, and chastity, as knowing it is the temple of the Holy Ghost, and, that if any man defile the temple of God, him will God destroy? Have you learned in every state wherein you are herewith to be content? Do you labor to get your own living, abhoring idleness as you abhor hell-fire? The devil tempts other men, but an idle man tempts the devil. An idle man's brain is the devil's shop, where he is continually working mischief. Are you not slothful in business? Whatever your hand finds to do, do you do it with your might? And do you do all as unto the Lord, as a sacrifice unto God, acceptable in Christ Jesus?

This, and this alone, is the old religion. This is true primitive Christianity. O, when shall it spread over all the earth! When shall it be found both in us and you? Without waiting for others, let each of us, by the grace of God, amend one.

Are we not thus far agreed? Let us thank God for this, and receive it as a fresh token of his love. But if God still loveth us, we ought also to love one another. We ought, without this endless jangling about opinions, to provoke one another to love and to good works. Let the points wherein we differ stand aside; here are enough wherein we agree, enough to be the ground of every Christian temper, and of every Christian action.

O brethren, let us not still fall out by the way! I hope to see you in heaven. And if I practice the religion above described you dare not say I shall go to hell. You cannot think so. None can persuade you to it. Your own conscience tells you the contrary. Then if we cannot as yet think alike in all things, at least we may love alike. Herein we cannot possibly do amiss. For one point none can doubt a moment —"God is love; and he that dwelleth in love, dwelleth in God, and God in him."

In the name, then, and in the strength of God, let us resolve, first, not to hurt one another; to do nothing unkind or unfriendly to each other, nothing which we would not have done to ourselves. Rather let us endeavor after every instance of a kind, friendly, and Christian behavior toward each other.

Let us resolve, secondly, God being our helper, to speak nothing harsh or unkind of each other. The sure way to avoid this is to say all the good we can both of and to one another. In all our conversation, either with or concerning each other, to use only the language of love; to speak with all softness and tenderness; with the most endearing expression which is consistent with truth and sincerity.

Let us, thirdly, resolve to harbor no unkind thought, no unfriendly temper toward each other. Let us lay the ax to the root of the tree; let us examine all that rises in our heart, and suffer no disposition there which is contrary to tender affection. Then shall we easily refrain from unkind actions and words when the very root of bitterness is cut up.

Let us, fourthly, endeavor to help each other on in whatever we are agreed leads to the kingdom. So far as we can, let us always rejoice to strengthen each other's hands in God. Above all, let us each take heed to himself (since each must give an account of himself to God) that he fall not short of the religion of love; that he be not condemned in that he himself approveth. O, let you and me (whatever others do) press on to the prize of our high calling! that, being justified by faith, we may have peace with God through our Lord Jesus Christ, by whom we have received the atonement; that the love of God may be shed abroad in our hearts by the Holy Ghost which is given unto us. Let us count all things but loss for the excellency of the knowledge of Jesus Christ our Lord; being ready for him to suffer the loss of all things, and counting them but dung, that we may win Christ.

I am your affectionate servant, for Christ's sake.

Dublin, July 18, 1749.

A WORD TO A PROTESTANT

1. Do not you call yourself a Protestant? Why so? Do you know what the word means? What is a Protestant? I suppose you mean one that is not a papist. But what is a papist? If you do not know, say so; acknowledge you cannot tell. Is this not the case? You call yourself a Protestant; but you do not know what a Protestant is. You talk against papists; and yet neither do you know what a papist is. Why do you pretend, then, to the knowledge which you have not? Why do you use words which you do not understand?

2. Are you desirous to know what these words, *papist* and *Protestant*, mean? A papist is one who holds the Pope or Bishop of Rome (the name *papa*—that is, *father*—was formerly given to all bishops) to be head of the whole Christian Church; and the Church of Rome, or that which owns the pope as their head, to be the only Christian Church.

3. In a course of years many errors crept into this Church, of which good men complained from time to time. At last, about two hundred years ago, the pope appointed many bishops and others to meet at a town in Germany called Trent. But these, instead of amending those errors, established them all by a law, and so delivered them down to all succeeding generations.

4. Among these errors may be numbered their doctrine of seven sacraments; of transubstantiation; of communion

in one kind only; of purgatory, and praying for the dead therein; of veneration of relics; and of indulgences, or pardons granted by the pope, and to be bought for money.

It is thought by some that these errors, great as they are, do only defile the purity of Christianity; but it is sure the following strike at its very root, and tend to banish true religion out of the world:

5. First. The doctrine of merit. The very foundation of Christianity is that a man can merit nothing of God; that we are "justified freely by his grace, through the redemption that is in Jesus Christ;" not for any of our works or of our deservings, but by faith in the blood of the covenant.

But the papists hold that a man may by his works merit or deserve eternal life; and that we are justified not by faith in Christ alone, but by faith and works together. This doctrine strikes at the root of Christian faith, the only foundation of true religion.

6. Secondly. The doctrine of praying to saints and worshiping of images. To the Virgin Mary they pray in these words: "O Mother of God, O Queen of Heaven, command thy Son to have mercy upon us!" And, "The right use of images," says the Council of Trent, "is to honor them by bowing down before them."

This doctrine strikes at the root of that great commandment (which the papists call part of the first), "Thou shalt not bow down to them nor worship them"—that is, not any image whatsoever. It is gross, open, palpable idolatry, such as can neither be denied nor excused; and tends directly to destroy the love of God, which is, indeed, the first and great commandant.

7. Thirdly. The doctrine of persecution. This has been for many ages a favorite doctrine of the Church of Rome. And the papists in general still maintain that all heretics (that is, all that differ from them) ought to be com-

pelled to receive what they call the true faith; to be forced into the Church or out of the world.

Now, this strikes at the root of, and utterly tears up, the second great commandment. It directly tends to bring in blind, bitter zeal; anger, hatred, malice, variance; every temper, word, and work that is just contrary to the loving our neighbor as ourselves.

So plain it is that these grand popish doctrines of merit, idolatry, and persecution, by destroying both faith and the love of God and of our neighbor, tend to banish true Christianity out of the world.

8. Well might our forefathers protest against these. And hence it was that they were called Protestants; even because they publicly protested, as against all the errors of the papists, so against these three in particular: The making void Christian faith, by holding that man may merit heaven by his own works; the overthrowing the love of God by idolatry, and the love of our neighbor by persecution.

Are you then a Protestant, truly so-called? Do you protest, as against all the rest, so in particular against these three grand fundamental errors of popery? Do you publicly protest against all merit in man? all salvation by your own works? against all idolatry of every sort? and against every kind and degree of persecution?

I question not but you do. You publicly protest against all these horrible errors of popery. But does your heart agree with your lips? Do you not inwardly cherish what you outwardly renounce? It is well if you who cry out so much against papists are not one yourself. It is well if you are not yourself (as little as you may think of it) a rank papist in your heart.

9. For, first, how do you hope to be saved? by doing thus and thus? by doing no harm and paying every man his own and saying your prayers and going to church and sacrament? Alas! Alas! Now you have thrown off the

mask. This is popery barefaced. You may just as well
speak and say, "I trust to be saved by the merits of my
own works." But where is Christ all this time? Why, he
is not to come in till you get to the end of your prayer;
and then you will say, "for Jesus Christ's sake," because
so it stands in your book. O, my friend, your very foundation is popish. You seek salvation by your works. You
trample upon the "blood of the covenant." And what
can a poor papist do more?

10. But let us go on: Are you clear of idolatry any more
than the papists are? It may be, indeed, yours is in a
different way. But how little does that signify! They set
up their idols in their churches; you set up yours in
your heart. Their idols are only covered with gold or
silver; but yours is solid gold. They worship the picture
of the Queen of Heaven; you, the picture of the Queen
or King of England. In another way they idolize a dead
man or woman; whereas your idol is still alive. O, how
little is the difference before God! How small pre-
eminence has the money-worshipper at London over the
image-worshipper at Rome; or the idolizer of a living
sinner over him that prays to a dead saint!

11. Take one step farther: Does the papist abroad persecute? Does he force another man's conscience? So does
the papist at home as far as he can, for all he calls himself a Protestant. Will the man in Italy tolerate no opinion but his own? No more, if he could help it, would the
man in England. Would you? Do not you think the
government much overseen, in bearing with any but
those of the Church? Do not you wish they would put
down such and such people? You know what you would
do if you were in their place. And by the very same
spirit you would continue the Inquisition at Rome and
rekindle the fires at Smithfield.

12. It is because our nation is overrun with such Protestants,
who are full of their own good deservings as well as of

abominable idolatry, and of blind, fiery zeal of the whole spirit of persecution, that the sword of God, the great, the just, the jealous God, is even now drawn in our land; that the armies of the aliens are hovering over it as a vulture over his prey; and that the open papists are on the point of swallowing up the pretended Protestants. (This was wrote during the late rebellion.)

13. Do you desire to escape the scourge of God? Then I entreat you, first, be a real Protestant. By the Spirit of God assisting you (for without him you know you can do nothing) cast away all that trust in your own righteousness, all hope of being saved by your own works. Own your merit is everlasting damnation; that you deserve the damnation of hell. Humble yourself under the mighty hand of God. Lie in the dust. Let your mouth be stopped, and let all your confidence be in the "blood of sprinkling," all your hope in Jesus Christ "the righteous," all your faith in "Him that justifieth the ungodly, through the redemption that is in Jesus."

O put away your idols out of your heart. "Love not the world, neither the things of the world." "Having food to eat and raiment to put on, be content;" desire nothing more but God. Today hear his voice who continually cries, "My son, give me thy heart." Give yourself to him who gave himself for you. May you love God as he has loved us! Let him be your desire, your delight, your joy, your portion, in time and in eternity.

And if you love God you will love your brother also; you will be ready to lay down your life for his sake; so far from any desire to take away his life or hurt a hair of his head. You will then leave his conscience uncontrolled; you will no more think of forcing him into your own opinions, as neither can he force you to judge by his conscience. But each shall "give an account of himself to God."

14. It is true if his conscience be misinformed you should

endeavor to inform him better. But whatever you do let it be done in charity, in love, and meekness of wisdom. Be zealous for God, but remember that "the wrath of man worketh not the righteousness of God;" that angry zeal, though opposing sin, is the servant of sin; that true zeal is only the flame of love. Let this be your truly Protestant zeal. While you abhor every kind and degree of persecution, let your heart burn with love to all mankind, to friends and enemies, neighbors and strangers; to Christians, heathens, Jews, Turks, papists, heretics; to every soul which God hath made. "Let" this "your light so shine before men, that they may glorify your Father which is in heaven."

Living Thoughts of John Wesley,
by James H. Potts.
Hunt & Eaton: New York; Cranston & Stowe: Philadelphia, 1891.

1739. *March* 15.—During my stay (in London) I was fully employed; between our own society in Fetter Lane, and many others, where I was continually desired to expound; so that I had no thought of leaving London, when I received, after several others, a letter from Mr. Whitefield, and another from Mr. Seward, entreating me, in the most pressing manner, to come to Bristol without delay. This I was not at all forward to do.

Wed. 28.—My journey was proposed to our society in Fetter Lane. But my brother Charles would scarce bear mention of it; till appealing to the oracles of God, he received those words as spoken to himself, and answered not again: "Son of man, behold, I take from thee the desire of thine eyes with a stroke: yet shalt thou not mourn or weep, neither shall thy tears run down." Our other brethren, however, continuing the dispute, without any probability of their coming to one conclusion, we at length all agreed to decide it by lot. And by this it was determined I should go.

Thur. 29.—I left London, and in the evening expounded to a small company at Basingstoke. Saturday, 31. In the evening I reached Bristol, and met Mr. Whitefield there. I could scarce reconcile myself at first to this strange way of preaching in the fields, of which he set me an example on Sunday; having been all my life (till very lately) so tenacious of every point relating to decency and order, that I should have thought the saving of souls almost a sin, if it had not been done in a church.

April 1.—In the evening (Mr. Whitefield being gone) I begun expounding our Lord's sermon on the mount (one pretty remarkable precedent of field-preaching, though I suppose there were churches at that time also), to a little society which was accustomed to meet once or twice a week in Nicholas Street.

Mon. 2.—At four in the aftnoon, I submitted to be more vile, and proclaimed in the highways the glad tidings of salvation, speaking from a little eminence in a ground adjoining to the city, to about three thousand people. The Scripture on which I spoke was this (is it possible anyone should be ignorant, that it is fulfilled in every true minister of Christ?) "The Spirit of the Lord is upon me, because he hath anointed me to preach the Gospel to the poor; he hath sent me to heal the broken-hearted; to preach deliverance to the captives; and recovery of sight to the blind; to set at liberty them that are bruised, to proclaim the acceptable year of the Lord."

Sun. 8.—At seven in the morning I preached to about a thousand persons at Bristol, and afterwards to about fifteen hundred on the top of Hannam-mount in Kingswood. I called to them, in the words of the evangelical Prophet, "Ho! every one that thirsteth, come ye to the waters; come, and buy wine and milk without money and without price." About five thousand were in the afternoon at Rosegreen (on the other side of Kingswood); among whom I stood and cried, in the name of the Lord, "If any man thirst, let him come unto me and drink. He that believeth on me, as the Scripture hath said, out of his belly shall flow rivers of living water."

Tues. 17.—At five in the afternoon I was at a little society in the Back Lane. The room in which we were was propped beneath, but the weight of people made the floor give way; so that in the beginning of the expounding, the post which propped it fell down with a great noise. But the floor sunk no further; so that, after a little surprise at first, they quietly attended to the things that were spoken.

Mon. May 7.—I was preparing to set out for Pensford, having now had leave to preach in the church, when I received the following note:

"Sir—Our minister, having been informed you are beside yourself, does not care you should preach in any of his churches."—I went, however; and on Priestdown, about half a mile from Pensford, preached Christ our "wisdom, righteousness, sanctification, and redemption."

Tues. 8.—I went to Bath, but was not suffered to be in the meadow where I was before, which occasioned the offer of a much more convenient place, where I preached Christ to about a thousand souls. . . .

Sun. 20.—Seeing many of the rich at Clifton church, my heart was much pained for them, and I was ernestly desirous that some even of them might "enter into the kingdom of heaven." But full as I was, I knew not where to begin in warning them to flee from the wrath to come till my Testament opened on these words: "I came not to call the righteous, but sinners to repentance"; in applying which my soul was so enlarged that methought I could have cried out (in another sense than the poor vain Archimedes), "Give me where to stand, and I will shake the earth." God's sending forth lightning with the rain did not hinder about fifteen hundred from staying at Rosegreen. Our Scripture was, "It is the glorious God that maketh the thunder. The voice of the Lord is mighty in operation; the voice of the Lord is a glorious voice." In the evening he spoke to three whose souls were all storm and tempest, and immediately there was a great calm.

During this whole time I was almost continually asked, either by those who purposely came to Bristol to inquire concerning this strange work, or by my old or new correspondents, "How can these things be?" And innumerable cautions were given me (generally grounded on gross misrepresentations of things), not to regard visions or dreams, or to fancy people had remission of sins because of their cries, or tears, or bare outward professions. To one who had many times wrote to me on this head, the sum of my answer was as follows:

"The question between us turns chiefly, if not wholly, on matter of fact. You deny that God does now work these effects; at least, that he works them in this manner. I affirm both, because I have heard these things with my own ears, and. have seen with my eyes. I have seen (as far as a thing of this kind can be seen) very many persons changed in a moment from the spirit of fear, horror, despair, to the spirit of love, joy, and peace; and from sinful desire, till then reigning over them, to a pure desire of doing the will of God. These are matters of fact, whereof I have been, and almost daily am, an eye or ear witness.

"What I have to say touching dreams or visions, is this: I know several persons in whom this great change was wrought in a dream, or during a strong representation to the eye of their mind, of Christ either on the cross or in the glory. This is the fact; let any judge of it as they please. And that such a change was then wrought appears (not from their shedding tears only, or falling into fit, or crying out; these are not the fruits, as you seem to suppose, whereby I judge, but) from the whole tenor of their life, till then many ways wicked; from that time holy, just, and good.

"I will show you him that was a lion till then, and is now a lamb; him that was a drunkard, and is now exemplarily sober; the whoremonger that was, who now abhors the very 'garment spotted by the flesh.' These are my living arguments for what I assert, viz., 'that God does now, as aforetime, give remission of sins and the gift of the Holy Ghost even to us and to our children; yea, and that always suddenly as far as I have known, and often in dreams or in the visions of God.' If it be not so, I am found a false witness before God. For these things I do, and by his grace, will testify."

EPILOGUE

"PROTESTANTISM," IN ITS GENERALLY UNDERSTOOD USAGE, IS NO adequate word with which to describe the movement this anthology has presented. At the first diet of Speyer, in 1526, each state within the Empire was authorized to decide for itself whether the Edict of Worms (putting Luther under the imperial ban) should be enforced or not. The second diet of Speyer, however, three years later withdrew this limited degree of toleration, and nineteen states protested against this and other reactionary decrees. These original "protestants" based their action on strongly affirmative principles—that the Bible's authority is supreme above that of councils and popes; that the Bible is to be interpreted by its own mutually compared statements, rather than by the church's tradition; and that the reformed churches are independent of Rome and no longer under Roman jurisdiction.

While, however, the word "protestant" thus had early origin in the Reformation, its general use to describe churches outside the Roman communion was long postponed, and even now such terms as "reformed" or "evangelical" are commonly employed in Europe and Latin America. It was in Elizabethan days in England, when to protest meant not to object but to affirm, to bear witness, to make a positive avowal, that the word came into general currency. The English church protested its principles in the Thirty-nine Articles, but Quakers, Anabaptists and such like, while non-papist, would not have shared such protestation. Then gradually "protest" lost its affirmative significance, and, in common parlance, meant objection and disapproval, until "protestant" was applied in general to dissenters from Roman Catholicism.

This negative connotation of the word is obviously incompetent to express what the Reformation stood for. The Reformers certainly did dissent from and strenuously object to evils in current Romanism, but many leading Catholics, including popes, did the same. As Pope Adrian VI declared in 1523 about Luther's revolt: "We freely acknowledge that God has allowed this chastisement to come upon His Church because of the sins of men, and especially because of the sins of priests and prelates. . . . We know well that for many years much that must be regarded with horror has come to pass in this Holy See." At the heart of the Reformation, however, was much more than negative dissent. From the beginning there was positive affirmation of basic principles, of which the following are typical.

The sole Head of the church is Jesus Christ himself. Far from delegating his authority to any succession of infallible vicars on earth, he remains the one final court of appeal. From the day when John Huss, in his disillusionment, appealed from the Vatican to Christ, determined to live and speak in the light of Christ's standards and criteria only, this principle was dominant in the Reformation. As Schleiermacher put it, Roman Catholicism sees the relation of the believer to Christ as depending on his relation to the church, while Protestantism sees the relation of the believer to the church as depending on his relation to Christ.

The will of Christ for the church and its members is revealed in the Bible. The sufficiency of the Scriptures as the rule of faith and practice for all Christians is one of the most consistently maintained principles of the Reformation. To

be sure, Protestants, like Roman Catholics (and like all religions with sacred writings) not only discovered in the
Holy Scriptures what veritably is there, but read into them
what they desired to find there. Nevertheless, this affirmation of the Bible's authority was a revolutionary doctrine,
with far-reaching positive effects. As time went on, old methods of Biblical interpretation, such as allegory, were abandoned; the dogma of Biblical inerrancy, especially in the
realms of history and science, was commonly denied; the
Biblical message was interpreted as a developing revelation,
its central and essential meanings unveiled in the New
Testament's good news; and the Quaker teaching that the
Scriptures could be understood only by those who themselves shared the spirit which produced the Scriptures was
increasingly accepted. The affirmation, however, that the
norm of Christian faith and practice is to be found in the
Bible, while it has been held in varied forms and meanings,
is basic in Protestantism.

Man's only security and hope are to be found in the acceptance of God's grace by faith. "Justification by faith" is
the official name of this affirmation and, like all doctrines, it
can be and has been stated in stereotyped, legalistic forms.
At its experiential source, however, it was and still is profoundly real and vital. Faith, to quote Luther, means not so
much "a believing about God" as "a lively, reckless confidence in the grace of God." It is not so much believing in
something as trusting in Someone. It achieves a saving, personal relationship between the soul and God, as revealed in
Christ. This is the door to salvation, Protestantism has asserted; good character and right living are its outcome;
and without it no sacraments or rituals or creedal subscrip-
tions have any efficacy or substantial meaning.

Every soul can have immediate access to God. Christ having opened the way, no human or ecclesiastical mediator is
required to grant the soul its right of direct approach to

God. His grace, pardon and power are individually available. By some interpreted in specifically mystical terms, by most understood in terms of such transforming experiences as spiritual rebirth, forgiveness, guidance, inward strength and sustaining prayer, this principle has been central in Protestantism. The individual soul and God confront each other; they are made for each other; neither Mary nor any saint stands between them; the road from one to the other is direct and open.

Nevertheless, the church is essential. It is the community of believers, and its fellowship, its ordinances, its shared experiences and convictions, are indispensable. Calvin endorsed, with his own interpretation, the ancient saying that "No man can have God for his father who has not the church for his mother," and Luther, thinking in terms not of dogma but of practical experience, said that "anyone who is to find Christ must first find the church." To be sure, there is no priestly overlordship in the church's ministers; the "priesthood of all believers" is fundamental to the Protestant position; but Christians, while individually redeemed, are also socially bound together in a transcendently important brotherhood of the saved.

Every Christian, in every vocation, is under obligation to obey the whole law of Christ. All distinction between priests and laymen, between monks and nuns on one side and common folk on the other, is abolished, so far as the basic Christian way of life is concerned. All honorable vocations are of God; the secular is sacred if handled in Christ's spirit; there are no gradations of responsibility in meeting the requirements of Christ and in living as he commands. In the depths of our souls, in the quality of our living, in our obligation to be Christlike in every relationship, we all alike face the same standards, and are called to be "saints."

Such, briefly and inadequately stated, are certain basic

Protestant principles, and they are obviously affirmative avowals of conviction, not merely negative objections to evils in the Roman church.

At least two consequences are involved in such a group of principles, and Protestantism has illustrated both—disharmony and progressive change. With such fundamental ideas as Protestantism started with, it could not possibly have been either unanimous or static.

Lack of unanimity was manifest from the first, because freedom of individual judgment was inherent in the principles of the Reformation. Some of the early Reformers tried to limit or even deny this freedom, insisting, for example, that the Scriptures are infallibly authoritative and that their meaning is indubitably clear. Honest men differed among themselves about Biblical interpretation, however, and it soon became evident that the monolithic totalitarianism of the Roman church was impossible in the churches of the Reformation. Within Roman Catholicism, too, there were and are divisions and rivalries, even wide varieties of theological opinion, and certainly sharp differences as to practical policy, but always the central, dictatorial, supposedly infallible authority in Rome can compel obedience and outward uniformity. Protestantism threw this over, and, making the individual soul immediately responsible to God, encouraged, even when it did not wish to do so, the expression and organization of diverse theologies and polities, conscientiously believed in and honestly upheld.

The partition of Protestantism began early. Two groups of churches emerged out of the Reformation: one clinging to the ideal of a uniform national church dominating the people of a given state; the other supporting congregational autonomy and the rights of individual insight and faith. The first group comprised the Anglican church, the Lutheran churches of Germany and the Scandinavian countries, the Reformed churches of Switzerland, France, the Netherlands, Scotland and Puritan New England. The second group comprised a growing number of sectarian movements, such as the Anabaptists, the Quakers, the Baptists and English Independents.

Denominational fission in Protestantism has produced in the United States over two hundred and fifty sects, and presents the movement launched by the Reformation with one of its most importunate problems. The ecumenical reaction has now set strongly in, and the Protestant churches, having moved out long since from mutual persecution to toleration, and from toleration to co-operation, now are headed from co-operation toward unity. As a matter of fact about ninety percent of all Protestant church members in the United States are included within twenty denominations, so that the inefficiency and scandal of trivial division are not incurable, and intelligent leadership in all the churches is stressing ecumenical communion and unity as against partition.

The quality in Protestantism which produced rampant denominationalism has not by any means been a total loss. The right of private judgment, freedom to differ, liberty to experiment and pioneer in new directions, independence in discovering new truths in the gospel and in rediscovering neglected and forgotten truths, have enriched and enlarged the Christian movement. Protestantism, so long as it is faithful to its basic positions, can never become rigid, cast into a permanent mould, static and stationary. It is not bound by its own past infallible decrees. It can face new truth, accept new light, adjust itself to new knowledge and new situations. The Protestant Reformation is still young, and an anthology, recapturing the spirit of its early history, reveals at the same time a forward-reaching, independent, adventurous spirit, prophetic of a progressive future.

The founders of Protestantism, whom we have quoted, while they are profoundly admired, are far from sacrosanct. No inerrancy attaches to them. They were trail-blazers, and gratitude to them does not prevent criticism of them. They started a movement whose principles, if faithfully adhered to, imply adventure and progress. The basic ideas of the Reformation have indeed made Protestant unity difficult, but they have produced another result which John Robinson, addressing the Pilgrims in Leyden, in 1620, expressly stated, as one hearer, Edward Winslow, reports him:

"He charged us before God and his blessed Angels, to follow him no further than he followed Christ. And if God should reveal anything to us by any other instrument of his, to be as ready to receive it, as ever we were to receive any truth by his Ministry: For he was very confident the Lord had more truth and light yet to breake forth out of his holy Word. He took occasion also miserably to bewaile the state and condition of the Reformed churches, who were come to a period in Religion, and would goe no further than the instruments of their Reformation: As for example, the *Lutherans* they could not be drawne to goe beyond what *Luther* saw, for whatever part of God's will he had further imparted and revealed to Calvin, they will rather die than embrace it. And so also, saith he, you see the Calvinists, they stick where he left them: A misery much to bee lamented; For though they were precious shining lights in their times, yet God had not revealed his whole will to them: And were they now living, saith hee, they would bee as ready and willing to embrace further light, as that they had received. Here also he put us in mind of our Church-Covenant (at least that part of it) whereby wee promise and covenant with God and one with another, to receive whatsoever light or truth shall be made known to us from his written Word: but withall exhorted us to take heed what we received for truth, and well to examine and compare, and weigh it with our Scriptures of truth, before we received it; For, saith he, *It is not possible the Christian world should come so lately out of such thick Antichristian darknesse, and that full perfection of knowledge should breake forth at once.*"